TIME® LIFE BOOKS COMPLETE GUIDE TO HOME IMPROVEMENT

BY THE EDITORS OF TIME-LIFE BOOKS, ALEXANDRIA, VIRGINIA

ABOUT THIS BOOK

The information in this book will help you maintain, improve, and protect what is probably the biggest investment of your life—your house. No matter how substantial its original construction, over the years weather, constant use, and the normal aging of materials result in problems that need attention. Some of these are primarily matters of maintenance; others may call for making repairs or replacements. The advantage of home maintenance and repair is that you can do a great deal yourself, at great savings.

In these pages, the editors of Time-Life Books and consulting experts have identified the most common problems and concerns in home maintenance and improvement. They show you how to inspect and evaluate all aspects of the interior and exterior of your home; how to correct or repair any problems you find; and how to keep items in condition to minimize the need for future repairs. Each of the hundreds of projects is explained step by step, so you can do the work yourself or talk knowledgeably with any workers you hire.

Altogether, this book gives you a wealth of useful instruction and information to make it both easy and profitable to perform the maintenance and make the repairs that will keep your house in excellent condition.

CONTENTS

CHAPTER 1

KITCHENS

A kitchen's daily exposure to heavy traffic and hard use frequently leads to scratched countertops and marred floors. But you can often restore worn items to virtually new condition. Simple repairs to countertops are shown on the following pages; easy fixes for the resilient flooring frequently found in kitchens are provided on pages 154 to 157.

You can also bring an old-fashioned kitchen up to date by building on what you already have. Easy-to-add modern amenities such as a countertop in a fresh color will give a face-lift to a timeworn kitchen.

This chapter also presents simple fixes for kitchen appliances. Major appliances are built to give many years of reliable service, but when a problem arises, it can often appear more serious than it really is. In many instances, you can make repairs easily and safely without specialized knowledge of the machines. Doing the work yourself not only spares you the cost of a service call but may well save money on parts.

Since the mid-1970s, the National Electrical Code has required that any electrical appliance that is installed within six feet of a sink must be protected by a ground-fault circuit interrupter, or GFCI. This device detects the smallest leakage of electrical current and turns off power in the receptacle. Replacing an old receptacle with a new GFCI, as shown on page 192, is economical insurance.

Available in a wide range of colors, patterns, and styles, prelaminated countertops are easy to install. The job can usually be completed in a single day. Fixing countertop scratches and gouges is even simpler.

Problems with an electric range are often easy to pinpoint with a careful visual inspection. Burns, pits, or cracks can direct you to the source of trouble. ▶

Although diagnosis and repair of a microwave's electronic components are best left to a qualified service technician, there are a surprising number of mechanical parts that an average homeowner can repair.

Keeping a dishwasher working effectively is relatively easy to do. You can often restore a machine to peak performance by clearing a blockage or adjusting the door latch.

Many cooks consider gas ranges the best source of stovetop heat. Routine maintenance is the best way to avoid problems with these appliances.

Fixing Damaged Countertops

Although countertop surfaces—plastic laminate, ceramic tile, or hardwood butcher block—are strong and durable, daily use and accidents eventually take their toll. But minor surface damage can often be repaired.

Quick Repairs for Minor Damage: Scratches and gouges in laminate can be hidden with a matching plastic seam filler, available from countertop fabricators. Broken or lifted edges can be reglued. Stains on butcher block can usually be scraped or sanded away.

With care, a cracked ceramic tile can be removed and replaced without marring the surrounding tiles. Scrape away old grout around the edges of the tile with a grout saw. For a damaged tile at the edge of the sink, remove the sink *(page 16)* and cut the new tile to fit .

Replacing a Section of Countertop: An extensively damaged laminate countertop can be cut out and replaced with an inset of heat-proof glass *(page 13)*, which is available as a kit from home-supply centers. Since the metal-rimmed glass inset requires that the countertop be cut through, check for braces or crosspieces under the countertop before proceeding. Another option for patching the damaged section is to inlay ceramic tiles *(page 14)*.

To install a tile inset, remove the damaged area using a router fitted with a $\frac{3}{8}$-inch double-fluted bit. To determine the required depth of the cut, add $\frac{1}{4}$ inch for a plywood underlayment to the thickness of your tiles, then subtract $\frac{1}{32}$ inch so that the tiles will sit slightly higher than the surface of the countertop.

 **TOOLS**

 **MATERIALS**

  **SAFETY TIPS**

Putty knife	Electric drill with $\frac{1}{4}$-inch bit	Plastic seam filler	Ceramic tiles	
Steel scraper	$\frac{1}{4}$-inch plywood	Carpenter's glue	
Orbital sander	$\frac{1}{4}$-inch masonry bit	Silicone caulk	Epoxy-based or	
Saber saw with laminate blade	Utility knife with laminate blade	Grout	acrylic tile adhesive	
Router	Grout saw	Silicone sealer		
$\frac{3}{8}$-inch double-fluted bit	Pry bar			
C-clamp	Cold chisel			
	Notched trowel			

Protect your eyes with goggles when using a hammer and chisel, power saw, sander, or router. Never start the router with the bit touching the surface to be routed. Wear rubber gloves when handling tile adhesive.

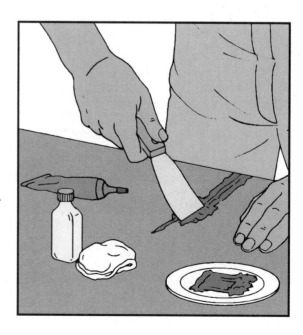

A quick fix for countertop scratches.
◆ Squeeze a small quantity of plastic seam filler onto a plastic plate, and work it with a clean putty knife until it begins to thicken.
◆ Wipe the scratch with a cloth dipped in the solvent that comes with the filler, then press the paste into the scratch with the putty knife *(right)*. Immediately wipe away excess filler with the cloth. If the filler shrinks as it hardens, wait an hour and repeat the process.

Restoring a blemished butcher block.

◆ Set the edge of a steel scraper against the butcher block at a 60° angle, beveled edge up *(left)*, and pull it across the blemished area.

◆ If scraping fails, run an orbital electric sander with medium-grit sandpaper over an area slightly larger than the stain. Keep the sander moving to avoid grinding a depression into the surface.

◆ Smooth the surface with fine-grit sandpaper, and apply vegetable oil or a nontoxic finish.

REGLUING PLASTIC LAMINATE

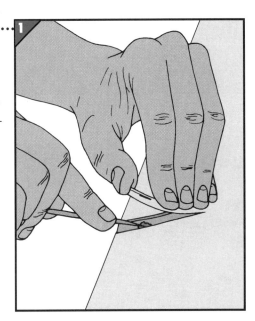

1. Applying the adhesive.

◆ First try reviving the old adhesive by placing a cloth over the area and heating it with a cool iron, then press the loose piece down with a roller.

◆ Alternatively, lift the loose edge gently and scrape out dried glue with a utility knife. Blow out any loose debris with a straw.

◆ Using a toothpick, spread carpenter's glue sparingly on the exposed countertop core *(right)*.

◆ Press the laminate back into place and wipe off excess glue.

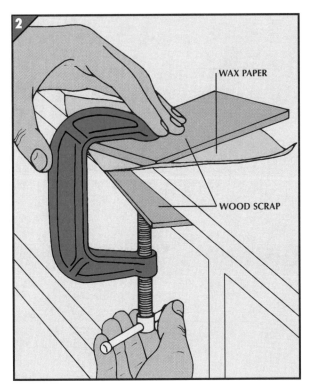

WAX PAPER

WOOD SCRAP

2. Clamping down the repair.

◆ Lay a piece of wax paper over the repair, then cover it with a scrap of wood. With another scrap protecting the underside of the countertop, clamp the repair tightly *(left)*.

◆ Wait 24 hours for the glue to set, then release the clamp.

REPLACING A CRACKED CERAMIC TILE

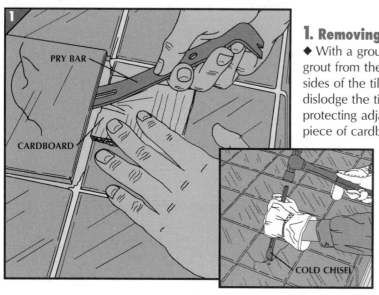

1. Removing the tile.

◆ With a grout saw, scratch the grout from the joints on all four sides of the tile, then attempt to dislodge the tile with a pry bar, protecting adjacent tiles with a piece of cardboard *(left)*.

◆ If the tile resists prying, drill four holes near the center with a masonry bit, then chip out the tile with a cold chisel and hammer *(inset)*.

◆ Scrape any old adhesive or grout from the opening in the countertop with a putty knife or a cold chisel, making the surface as even as possible. Wipe away dust with a damp cloth.

2. Applying the adhesive.

Use the flat edge of a notched trowel to coat the back of the replacement tile with adhesive, then comb the adhesive with the notched edge, leaving visible ridges *(above)*.

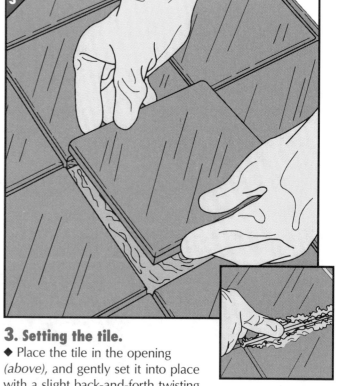

3. Setting the tile.

◆ Place the tile in the opening *(above)*, and gently set it into place with a slight back-and-forth twisting motion.

◆ Remove any adhesive from the tile surface with a damp cloth.

◆ Lay an 18-inch length of 2-by-4 on the replacement tile. Tap the board with a hammer to bring the surface of the replacement tile even with the surfaces of the other tiles.

◆ Allow the adhesive to cure, then grout the surrounding joints with your fingertip *(inset)*.

A GLASS INSET FOR A SCARRED COUNTERTOP

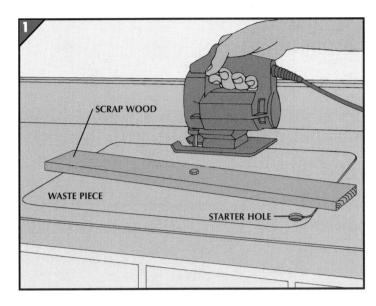

1. Cutting the hole.

◆ Set the rim of the inset or the template provided by its manufacturer over the damaged area, and mark a cut line on the countertop.
◆ Loosely bolt a piece of scrap lumber to the countertop to support the cutout as you saw *(left)*.
◆ Just inside a corner of the marked area, drill a starter hole for a saber saw. Cut out the opening, rotating the board ahead of the saw as you go.
◆ Lift out the waste piece with the board, and test-fit the metal rim in the opening. If necessary, enlarge the opening slightly with a coarse file.

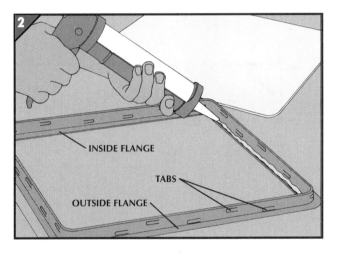

2. Preparing the inset.

◆ Set the rim of the inset upside down and squeeze a thin bead of silicone caulk around the inside flange *(left)*.
◆ Turn the glass piece upside down and press it into the rim of the inset. With a screwdriver, bend the metal tabs along the rim outward to hold the glass in place.
◆ Apply a heavier bead of caulk to the outside flange of the rim, then set the assembly into the countertop.

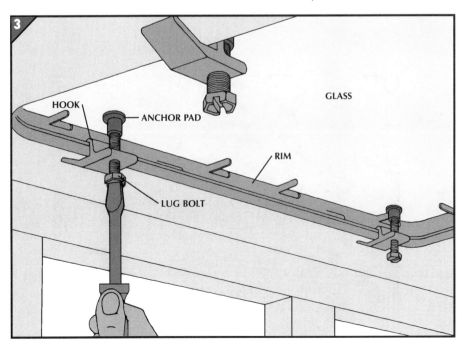

3. Fastening the inset.

◆ Underneath the countertop, hook one of the lugs provided by the manufacturer over the edge of the metal rim, insert the lug bolt and thread it into an anchor pad, then screw the pad against the underside of the inset piece *(left)*.
◆ Repeat this procedure on the lug and bolt diagonally opposite, then on the remaining bolts.
◆ On the countertop, use a putty knife to scrape off excess caulk around the edge of the rim.

AN INLAY OF CERAMIC TILES

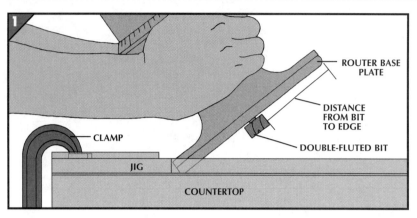

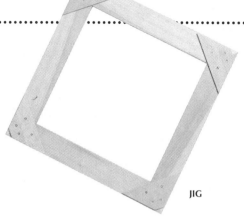

JIG

1. Measuring the area.

◆ Draw a rectangle on the countertop $\frac{1}{4}$ inch larger in each dimension than the area to be tiled.

◆ In each corner of the rectangle—and touching its edges—drill a $\frac{1}{4}$-inch hole to the depth of the router cut you plan.

◆ Measure between the router bit and the base plate edge. Double the measurement, and add the result to the dimensions of the rectangle. Make a jig for the router *(photograph)*, using these figures as inside dimensions.

◆ Clamp the jig in place. After adjusting the router to cut half the planned depth, place the router base against the jig *(above)*.

2. Routing the inset area.

◆ Turn on the router, lower it into the countertop, and move it to the center.

◆ To ensure support for the router, cut a clockwise spiral *(right)* to the edge of the jig, then rout along the perimeter. Set the bit to the full depth and retrace the spiral.

◆ Beginning in the center, finish routing the remaining countertop inside the jig.

◆ To remove small countertop remnants in corners around the drill holes, score the laminate with a laminate blade in a utility knife, then chisel away the underlying wood.

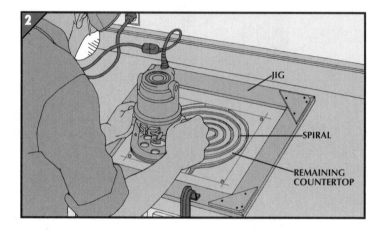

3. Laying the tiles.

◆ Cut a piece of plywood to fit the routed area, and glue it in place.

◆ With a notched trowel, spread adhesive over the plywood. Then set the tiles in the inset *(right)*, and let the adhesive cure according to the manufacturer's recommendations.

◆ Grout and seal the joints between tiles.

◆ After the grout has cured, caulk the $\frac{1}{4}$-inch space between the tiles and the countertop with silicone caulk.

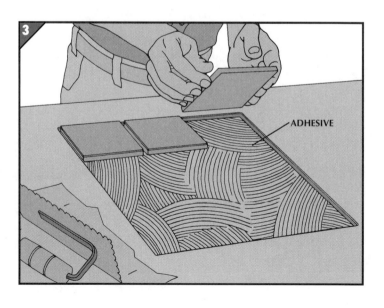

Replacing a Prelaminated Countertop

Replacing an old laminated countertop with a new one can make a quick and dramatic change in the appearance of your kitchen. Aside from the cutting of an opening for the sink, the job consists mostly of simple steps—drilling holes, driving screws, hooking up the sink—and can usually be completed in a single day.

Critical Measurements: The most important element in a smooth installation is the precise measurement of the existing countertop *(below)*. Check your results carefully, and take them, along with a sketch of the counter layout, to the supplier, who will provide the replacement.

Choosing a Style: Available in a wide variety of laminate colors and patterns, countertops also come in

two styles: custom self-edge and postform. The difference lies in the treatment of the front edge and of the joint between the work surface and the backsplash, the short vertical surface that catches overflows and spills at the counter's rear.

In a custom self-edge countertop, the work surface and the backsplash meet in a sharp 90° angle. The front edge is also perpendicular to the work surface. Custom self-edge is the style to choose if you wish to finish the edge with wood trim called bullnose.

A postform counter has a gently rounded front edge and backsplash joint, with the laminate curving smoothly over them. Whichever style you choose, specify that the countertop ends be covered with laminate, even those that abut a wall or appliance. This will help ensure a neat job.

TOOLS

Tape measure
Basin wrench
Open-end
  wrenches
Screwdriver

Utility knife
Flashlight
Drill
Saber saw

MATERIALS

Prelaminated countertop segments
Corner fasteners
2-by-2s
Roll of paper
  (25" wide)

Masking tape
  (2")
Utility handle
Silicone caulk
Denatured alcohol

Taking the measurements.

◆ First, measure the length of the countertop. For an L-shaped counter *(left)*, hook the end of a tape measure over the backsplash and measure the length of each leg of the old countertop.

◆ Check the distance from the back of the backsplash to the front edge. If the distance differs from the standard 25 inches, specify the actual measurement when ordering the replacement.

1. Removing the sink.
◆ Turn off the water supply to the faucet. Open the faucet to drain the supply lines, then disconnect them from the faucet with a basin wrench. Use the same tool to remove the dishwasher air gap *(page 22)*.
◆ Cut power to the dishwasher and garbage disposer at the service panel. Disconnect drain and dishwasher plumbing from the disposer, then detach it from the sink *(left)*, either by turning it to unlock it or by loosening mounting screws under the sink. Set the disposer on the cabinet floor.
◆ Unscrew the anchors under the countertop that hold the sink. Separate the countertop and the edge of the sink with a utility knife, then lift out the sink and set it aside.

2. Making a sink template.
◆ Cut a sheet of paper long enough to extend from one end of the countertop past the sink cutout. Tape the paper even with the end of the countertop and with one edge against the backsplash. Mark these edges of the paper with Xs.
◆ Using the corners of the sink cutout as guides, cut through the paper with a utility knife to make an opening at each corner *(right)*.

CORNER OPENING

3. Removing the old countertop.
◆ Using a flashlight to illuminate the dark corners, examine cabinet corner braces for screws in the underside of the countertop *(right)*. Remove any screws you find and save them for securing the new countertop.
◆ Remove the screws that secure the dishwasher to the underside of the countertop.
◆ If the space between the backsplash and the wall is filled with caulk, cut the caulk away with a utility knife.
◆ With a helper, lift the old countertop from the cabinets.

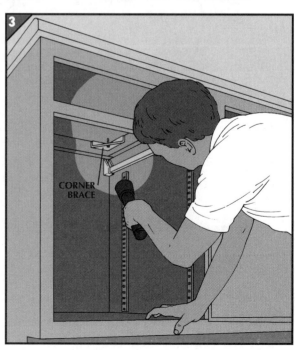

CORNER BRACE

INSTALLING THE NEW COUNTERTOP

1. Marking a sink cutout.
◆ Cut 2-by-2s to support the new countertop when marking and cutting the sink opening. With a helper, set the countertop on the supports.
◆ Tape the template to the countertop using the marks that were made earlier to position it.
◆ With a marker, transfer the corners cut into the template to the countertop *(left)*. Remove the template and join the corners with the marker and a straightedge.
◆ Cover the resulting outline of the sink cutout with strips of 2-inch-wide masking tape to protect the laminate when you saw it. If the cutting line is not visible through the tape, remove the tape and darken the line, then replace the tape.

2. Cutting the sink opening.
◆ Screw a handle to the countertop in the center of the cutout, then drill a 1-inch-diameter hole inside the cutout area, near a corner.
◆ Fit a blade suitable for cutting laminate into a saber saw. Start the saw with the blade in the hole and cut toward the line, then along it *(left)*.
◆ As you approach the end of the cut, grasp the handle to prevent the waste piece from sagging, which might split the laminate.

3. Positioning the countertop.

◆ While you lift the countertop slightly at the sink cutout, have a helper slide out the front 2-by-2 support, followed by the rear support *(above)*.

◆ For an L-shaped cabinet, lift the other countertop section onto the cabinet to help align both pieces while you finish installing the first one.

◆ Set the sink in the cutout, adjusting sink and countertop so that the sink drain aligns with the drainpipe in the wall and the backsplash fits against the wall.

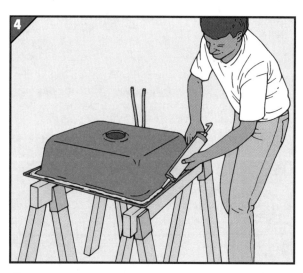

4. Caulking the sink.

◆ Pencil a line perpendicular to the front edge of the sink and continue it onto the countertop to mark the sink position. Draw a similar line at one edge of the sink, then remove the sink and support it upside down above the floor.

◆ Clean any old caulk from the underside of the sink, then apply a thin bead of caulk around the outer edge of the sink lip *(above)*.

◆ Apply a $\frac{1}{4}$-inch-thick bead of caulk to the countertop around the edge of the sink cutout.

5. Installing the sink.

◆ To avoid disturbing the fresh caulk, lift the sink by the base of the faucet and the drain hole.

◆ Set the sink into the cutout, aligning the pencil marks on the sink edges with those on the countertop *(right)*.

◆ Reconnect all plumbing detached during removal of the sink.

◆ Screw in the anchors that hold the sink in place, drilling pilot holes for the screws if necessary.

◆ Wipe excess caulk from around the sink edge with a rag dampened with denatured alcohol.

6. Securing the countertop.

◆ To bore pilot holes for the anchoring screws from the old countertop, use a drill bit slightly narrower than the screws. Prevent the bit from going all the way through the countertop by wrapping the bit with tape. Place the tape at a distance from the drill tip equal to the screw length less $\frac{1}{8}$ inch.

◆ Drill pilot holes through the existing holes in the cabinet corner braces *(left)*—the pilot holes need not be vertical. Screw the countertop in place.

◆ Screw the dishwasher to the underside of the countertop.

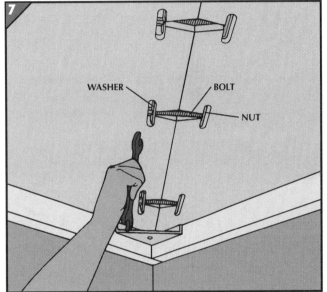

7. Completing an L-shaped countertop.

◆ Slide the unfastened section along the cabinet and apply a thin bead of caulk to the mitered edge. Then slip the sections together again.

◆ Insert a corner fastener—a bolt with a rectangular nut and washer—in each of the channels precut at the joint. With a helper to hold the countertop sections flush with each other, tighten the fasteners with a wrench, back to front *(right)*. Wipe excess caulk from the joint.

◆ Screw the countertop to the cabinet.

8. Caulking the backsplash.

To prevent water seepage between the countertop and the wall, fill the gap between the top of the backsplash and the wall with a bead of caulk *(left)*. It is not necessary to seal the ends of the backsplash.

Dishwasher Repairs

The most common complaints about dishwashers—they leak, don't drain, or don't clean well—often arise from clogs or mechanical breakdowns that are easily fixed, and in some cases the dishwasher may not be at fault.

Hot Water Helps to Clean: Dirty or spotted dishes, for example, may simply be the result of insufficiently hot water. To check your water supply, place a candy thermometer or meat thermometer in a coffee mug,

then turn the kitchen tap to its hottest setting and run water into the mug for 2 minutes. If the temperature is below 120°, raise the setting on your water heater to 120°.

Fixing Leaks: Inspect the gaskets around the door, and check hose connections at the water inlet valve, pump, and drain valve. Reseat a slipped gasket in its track, and tighten or replace any loose hose clamps. Replace hoses that look as if they are cracked or brittle.

More serious are problems involving the pump, motor, or timer, as these three parts are the hardest to fix. Only disassembling and cleaning the pump is shown (*page 24*)—in all other cases you should call for service.

 Before attempting any repair of a dishwasher, turn off **CAUTION** *the power to the machine at the house service panel.*

T TOOLS

Multitester
Slip-joint pliers
Screwdriver
Adjustable wrench

Candy thermometer or
   meat thermometer
Tweezers

Anatomy of a dishwasher.

To begin a cycle, the timer signals the water inlet valve to open, allowing water into the tub. The water mixes with detergent, is heated to about 140° by the heating element, and is pumped through the small apertures of the spray arm against the dishes to clean them. Then the dishes are rinsed and the tub drained, and the heating element turns on again to dry the dishes.

To drain the tub at the end of the wash cycle, a dishwasher will have either a drain valve or a reversible motor to pump out the water. Most models have a spray tower—a pipe that carries water to the upper spray arm (*right*).

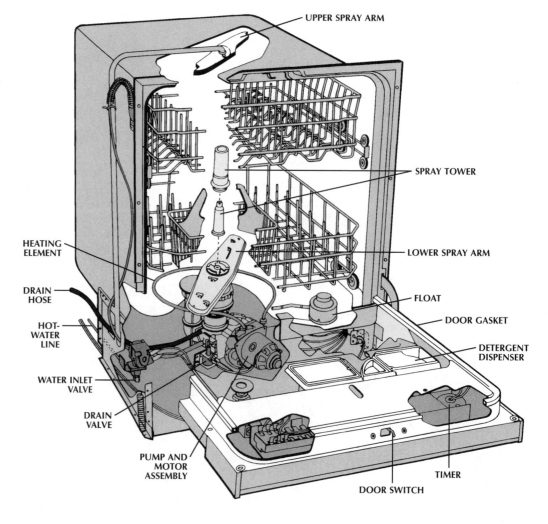

UPPER SPRAY ARM

SPRAY TOWER

LOWER SPRAY ARM

FLOAT

DOOR GASKET

DETERGENT DISPENSER

TIMER

DOOR SWITCH

PUMP AND MOTOR ASSEMBLY

DRAIN VALVE

WATER INLET VALVE

HOT-WATER LINE

DRAIN HOSE

HEATING ELEMENT

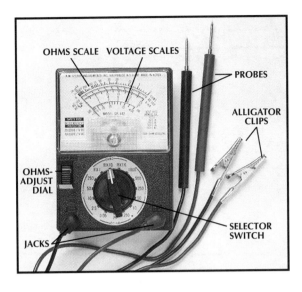

OHMS SCALE VOLTAGE SCALES

PROBES

ALLIGATOR CLIPS

OHMS-ADJUST DIAL

SELECTOR SWITCH

JACKS

The versatile multitester.

A multitester can measure the voltage and current (amperes) reaching an electrical component, as well as its resistance in ohms.

◆ Turn the selector switch to the correct value of amperes, AC volts, DC volts, or ohms you want to measure, and read the scale on the meter. Always use a setting higher than the value expected. The ohms scale is particularly useful in appliance repairs for identifying which part of the machine has failed.

◆ To calibrate the multitester for resistance measurements, select the RX1 (resistance times 1) scale and touch the probes together. Turn the ohms-adjust dial until the meter reads 0 ohms. For other tests, follow the directions in the owner's manual.

Troubleshooting Guide

PROBLEM	REMEDY
Dishes dirty or spotted.	Test water temperature. Check for binding or broken parts in detergent dispenser. Look for obstructions, such as utensils, that fall and block spray arm. Check and clean spray arm *(page 22)*. Check and clean pump *(page 24)*; replace impellers if corroded or chipped. Check and clean filter screen, if there is one *(page 22)*.
Dishwasher doesn't fill with water.	Test water inlet valve solenoid and inspect filter screen *(page 23)*. Check for obstruction propping up float; test float switch *(page 23)*. Check door latch; test door switch *(page 22)*. Check and clean filter screen, if there is one *(page 22)*.
Dishwasher drains during fill.	Inspect drain valve; test valve solenoid and replace it if necessary *(page 24)*.
Water doesn't shut off.	Remove any debris on underside of float; test float switch *(page 23)*. Test water inlet valve *(page 23)*.
Motor doesn't run.	Check for blown fuse or tripped circuit breaker. Adjust door latch if necessary; test door switch *(page 22)*.
Motor hums but doesn't run.	Check and clean pump *(page 24)*; if it still doesn't work, call for service.
Poor water drainage.	Check for clogged air gap *(page 22)*. Check the drain hose for kinks and clogs; remove any that you find. Check and clean filter screen, if there is one *(page 22)*. Check for clogged drain valve and test drain valve solenoid *(page 24)*. Check and clean pump *(page 24)*; replace impellers if corroded or chipped.
Dishwasher leaks around door.	Adjust door latch so door closes tightly *(page 22)*. Replace door gasket if the rubber is hardened or damaged.
Dishwasher leaks from bottom or below door.	Seal any cracks in tub with silicone rubber sealant or epoxy glue. Tighten water inlet valve connection. Look for loose pump seals or heating element nuts. Check spray arm, especially bottom of arm, for holes.
Door is difficult to close.	Adjust or oil door catch *(page 22)*. Replace catch if broken.

Opening a clogged air gap.

◆ Find the air gap on the back rim of the sink between the dishwasher and the sink faucet. Pull off the chrome cover, and unscrew the plastic cap.

◆ With tweezers, remove any debris from the small tube in the center of the air gap *(right)*.

◆ Clean the cover and cap if necessary; screw on the cap and snap the cover in place.

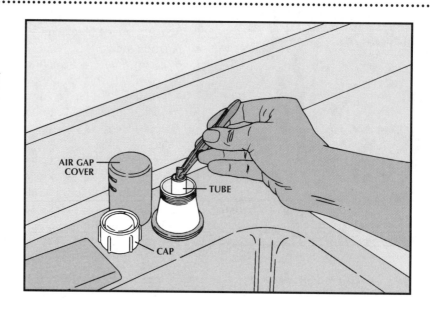

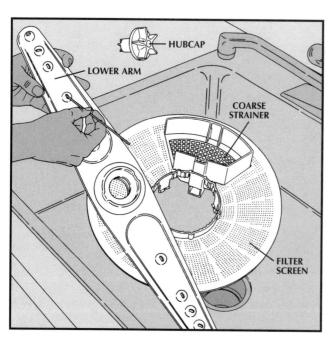

Cleaning the spray arm and filter screen.

◆ After sliding out the lower dish rack, twist off the plastic hubcap, if there is one, that holds the lower spray arm in place, and lift off the arm.

◆ If your machine has a removable coarse strainer and filter screen, unsnap and remove them; otherwise, clean them in place.

◆ Clean out the slotted holes in the spray arm with a wire *(above)*. Scrub the strainer and filter screen with a stiff brush, and then rinse all three before reinstalling them.

◆ Unclog the holes in the upper spray arm without removing the arm from its holder.

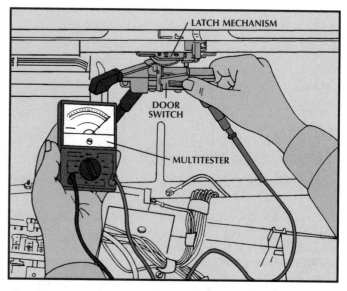

Checking the door latch and switch.

◆ If the latch is difficult to close, lubricate the mechanism with light machine oil. On many models, the latch can be adjusted for a better fit by loosening the mounting screws, sliding the latch in or out, then retightening the screws.

◆ To test the door switch *(above)*, remove the screws on the inside of the door that secure the control panel. Close and lock the door. Gently pull off the panel and disconnect the wires from the door switch terminals, behind the latch. Attach multitester clips to the terminals, and check switch resistance *(page 21)*; any reading other than 0 ohms indicates a faulty switch.

◆ Replace the switch by removing its retaining screws, installing a new switch, and reconnecting the wires.

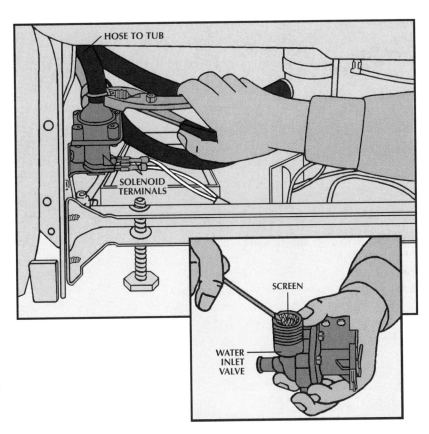

Servicing the water inlet valve.

◆ Turn off the power and water supply to the dishwasher.

◆ With a shallow pan handy, use slip-joint pliers to remove the hose that connects the inlet valve to the tub *(right)*. Then disconnect the flexible copper hot-water line with an adjustable wrench.

◆ Unscrew the valve from its mounting bracket. Without removing the filter screen, scrape it clean *(inset)* and rinse. If the valve appears cracked or otherwise damaged, replace it.

◆ With the multitester, check the solenoid. You should get a reading of between 60 and 500 ohms. Replace the valve assembly if the solenoid is faulty.

◆ Reinstall the valve, then reattach the hot-water line and hose, and tighten all connections.

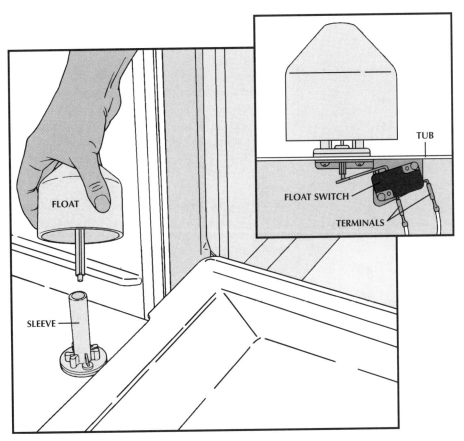

Cleaning and testing the float and its switch.

◆ Lift the float out of its sleeve, and remove any debris from the bottom of the float. Clean out the sleeve as well.

◆ Slide the float into the sleeve *(left)* and run the dishwasher. If no water enters the machine or if it overflows, turn off the power to the dishwasher at the main service panel, bail out any water in the tub, and remove the access panel below the door.

◆ Test the float switch *(inset)* located under the tub by touching the multitester probes to the terminals. You should get 0 ohms with the switch on *(float down)* and infinity with the switch off *(float up)*.

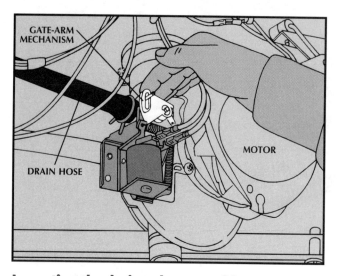

Inspecting the drain valve assembly.

Remove the panel below the door and count the number of wires attached to the motor. Two or three wires indicates a nonreversible motor; four or more is reversible. Only nonreversible motors have drain valves. Locate the valve and its gate-arm mechanism. Move the arm by hand *(above)*; if it doesn't move freely up and down on its two springs, replace them.

Testing the drain valve solenoid.

Disconnect the wires from the drain valve solenoid terminals and check resistance *(below)*. If the reading is not between 60 and 500 ohms, replace the solenoid.

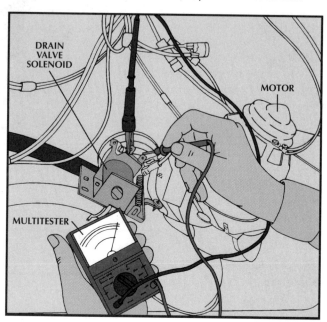

CLEANING THE PUMP

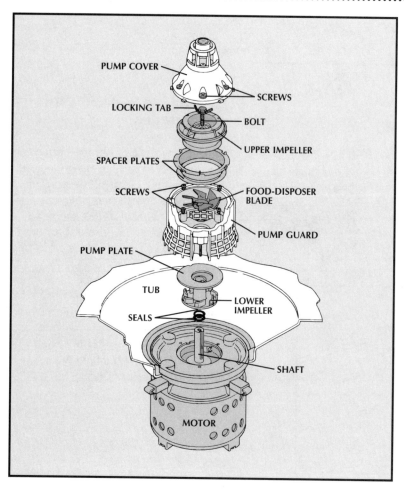

Getting to the impellers.

◆ Take off the lower spray arm *(page 22)*, then remove all screws from the pump cover, exposing the upper impeller.

◆ If there is a bolt-locking tab, bend it up to clear the bolt, then unscrew the bolt, freeing the upper impeller. Check the impeller for debris and for worn or broken blades; clean or replace it as necessary.

◆ Lift out the spacer plates and the food-disposer blade under the impeller; clean the blade.

◆ To reach the lower impeller, unfasten the screws holding the pump guard and remove it. Pull off the pump plate and clean the impeller.

◆ If the lower impeller is damaged, pry it off the motor shaft with a screwdriver or remove it with a pair of locking pliers. When installing a new impeller, replace the underlying seals before pushing the impeller onto the shaft. If the impeller will not slide on easily, sand any rust off the shaft to make it smoother.

◆ To reassemble the pump, first replace the pump plate and screw on the pump guard. Attach the food-disposer blade and spacer plates, then the upper impeller. Secure with the bolt, and put the locking tab, if there is one, on top of the bolt. Screw on the pump cover, and replace the spray arm.

Dealing with a Stuck Garbage Disposer

When a disposer stops working, it is usually because the grinding mechanism has jammed. Bits of food, glass, metal, plastic, or rubber can get caught between the spinning flywheel and the stationary grind ring, causing the motor to overheat and cut off. This may also happen if you pack the unit too tightly. Before starting to work on the disposer, check for a blown fuse or for a tripped circuit breaker at the main service panel.

If the suggestions below don't fix the problem, the disposer should be replaced because repairs will probably cost as much as a new unit. Check your warranty; most run from 3 to 7 years and cover repairs or replacement.

⚠️ **CAUTION** *Always turn off the power at the main panel or unplug the disposer—if it is an outlet unit— before reaching into it.*

Resetting the motor.

If the motor doesn't hum at all, reach into the disposer and feel around for any objects that may be jamming it. Let the motor cool down for 15 minutes, then switch on the power at the main panel and gently push the reset button on the bottom of the unit until you hear it click *(below)*.

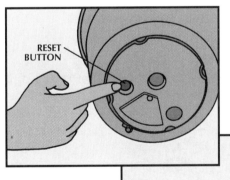

RESET BUTTON

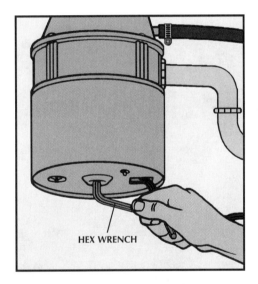

HEX WRENCH

Freeing the grind ring.

If the motor hums but the disposer does not grind, take a $\frac{1}{4}$-inch hex wrench (or the wrench that came with the disposer) and insert one end into the hole on the bottom of the disposer *(left)*. Turn the wrench back and forth to rotate the motor shaft until it moves freely.

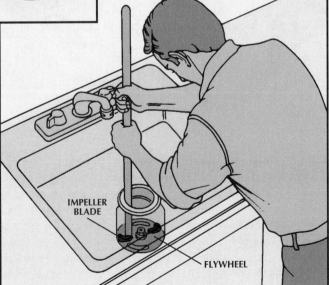

IMPELLER BLADE

FLYWHEEL

Unjamming the disposer with a broom handle.

If you are unable to clear the jam by using a hex wrench, stick a broom handle into the disposer and wedge it against one of the impeller blades on the flywheel *(left)*. Apply force until the wheel begins to turn freely, then work the wheel back and forth until it moves easily in both directions.

Servicing a Microwave Oven

When a microwave oven begins to cook erratically, the fault may lie with one of several easy-to-service components within the machine. If it stops working altogether, first check that the cord has not become unplugged and that the circuit breaker has not tripped.

Defective Door Switches: The parts that fail most often are door-interlock switches. A faulty one can keep the oven from turning on and cause it to turn off unexpectedly. As many as five switches may be present, one behind each door latch and others positioned around the door perimeter. Test each one in turn as shown on page 28.

Other Culprits: If a door switch is not to blame—and the oven light stays off when the door is open—check for a blown fuse inside the appliance. Next test the diode; diagnosis of electronic control panels is best left to a professional. However, if your oven has a dial timer and a mechanical start button, you can test two additional switches where problems originate *(page 29)*.

⚠️ **CAUTION** *An interior component called a capacitor stores an electric charge that can deliver a strong shock. Discharge the capacitor before any test or repair. The procedure* (right) *can produce a large spark.*

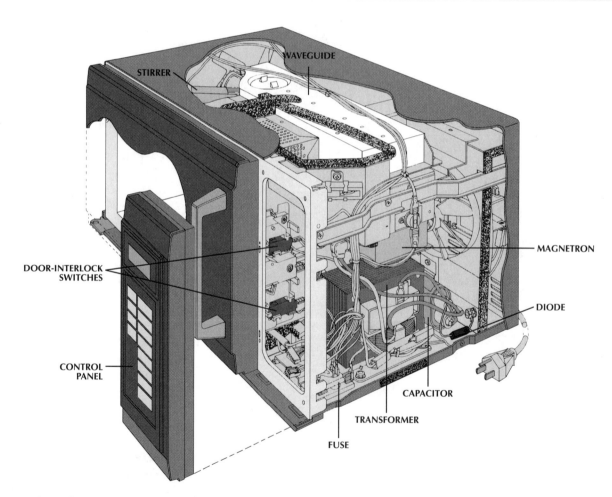

Anatomy of a microwave oven. The heart of a microwave oven is a magnetron, which produces microwaves that travel through a waveguide into the oven. A stirrer bounces the waves around the cooking chamber, where they heat the food. Supplying the magnetron with power are a transformer, a capacitor, and a diode. These components boost 120-volt alternating-current household service to direct current (the kind provided by a battery) at 4,000 volts. A control panel on the front of the oven provides for the selection of cooking times and cycles. Safety devices include door-interlock switches, which prevent the unit from starting with the door ajar, thus prohibiting harmful microwaves from escaping, and a fuse that protects the unit from power surges.

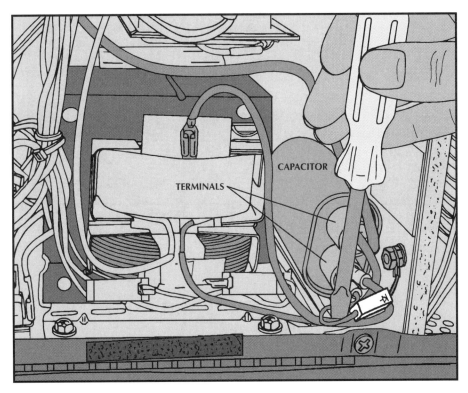

Removing the cover and discharging the capacitor.

◆ Unplug the oven, then remove the screws that secure the cover. Set the cover aside.

◆ Hold an insulated screwdriver by its handle, and lay the shaft across the metal sleeves on the capacitor's two terminals *(left)*.

◆ If this produces a spark, touch the screwdriver to the terminals again to completely discharge the capacitor. If this procedure produces no spark, the capacitor has already discharged.

UNIVERSAL MICROWAVE REPAIRS

Checking the fuse.

◆ With the oven unplugged and the cover off, locate the fuse, usually a cartridge fuse.

◆ Pull the fuse from its holder with your fingers or with a fuse puller if your fingers can't dislodge it *(right)*.

◆ To test the fuse for resistance *(page 31)*, touch a probe of a multitester to each end of the fuse.

◆ If the tester reads infinite ohms, the fuse is blown; replace it with a fuse of equal amperage.

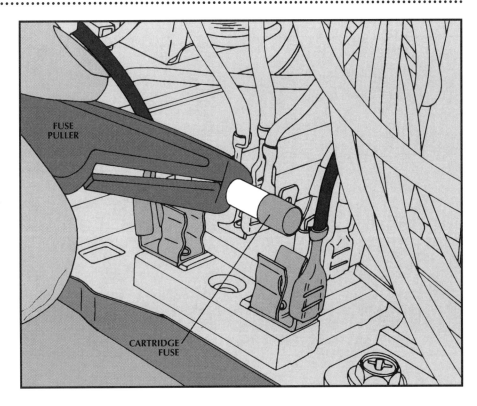

Replacing a diode.

◆ Locate the diode, which is connected to the capacitor and to the frame of the cabinet.

◆ Disconnect the diode from the capacitor and the cabinet *(right)* and examine it. Replace a diode that is cracked or burned.

◆ If there is no visible damage, set a multitester to RX1K and calibrate it *(page 21)*. Touch a probe to the end of each wire *(inset),* and note the multitester reading. Then reverse the probes and check the reading again. One reading should indicate a resistance of several thousand ohms, the other infinite ohms. If the diode fails the test, replace it.

◆ Connect the new diode as the old one was connected. If the wires end in identical fittings, attach the one nearer the diode symbol to the cabinet.

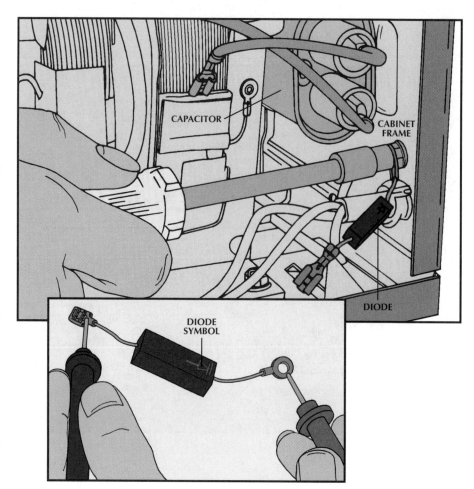

Testing a door switch.

◆ With a two-terminal switch, remove the wire from one of the terminals and check the switch for resistance *(left),* first with the door open (infinite ohms), then with it closed (0 ohms). Replace the switch if it fails either test.

◆ If a door switch has three terminals *(inset),* detach all three wires, then touch one probe to the COMMON terminal and one to the OPEN or NO terminal. A working switch will register 0 ohms with the door closed, infinite ohms with it open.

◆ Check for resistance between the COMMON terminal and the CLOSED or NO terminal with the door both open (0 ohms) and closed (infinite ohms). If the switch fails either test, replace it.

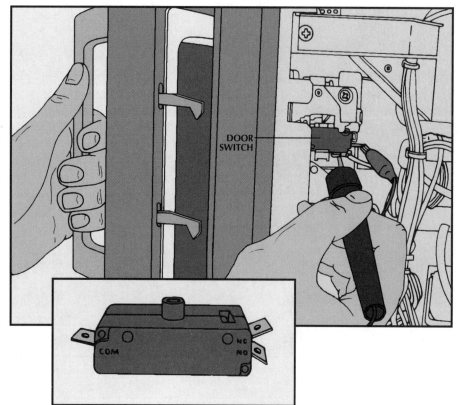

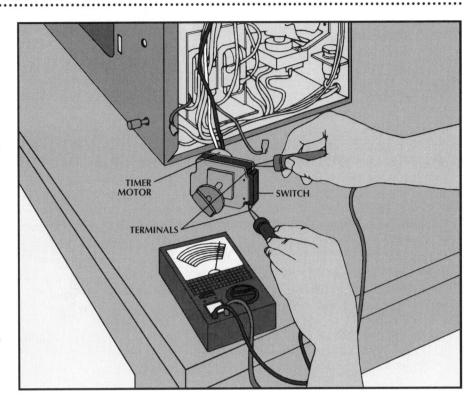

Identifying a faulty timer switch.

◆ Unscrew the timer assembly from the inside front panel and detach the wires from the two switch terminals, located on the back of the timer next to its motor.

◆ Set a multitester to RX1, set the timer for at least 1 minute, then touch the tester probes to the switch terminals *(right)*. Replace the switch if the meter registers more than 0 ohms.

On some ovens, the timer switch is integrated with the timer and cannot be bought separately. Replace the entire timer assembly.

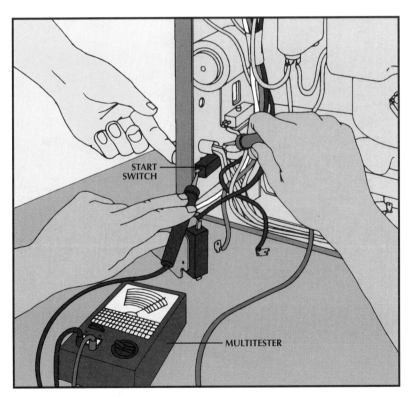

Testing the start switch.

◆ Disconnect the wires from the terminals on the switch behind the start button.

◆ Touch multitester probes to the switch terminals. There should be resistance of infinite ohms.

◆ Have a helper push the button; the meter should read 0 ohms while the button is depressed *(left)*.

◆ If the switch fails either test, replace it by unscrewing or unclipping it from the timer assembly. Install a new one, and connect the wires to its terminals.

When an Electric Range Fails to Heat

You can often locate the source of trouble on an electric range just by looking. Visible burns, pits, or cracks make it easy to identify faulty parts. If no damage is noticeable, continue your diagnosis with a multitester as shown on the following pages.

Checking the Voltage: The heating elements on an electric range run on a 240-volt circuit. High-rise buildings, however, often have three-phase 208-volt current, in which case normal readings on the multitester will be in the range of 197 to 210 volts.

Holding the Right Temperature: A common complaint about electric ranges is that the oven temperature does not match the reading on the control. A frayed or torn door gasket could be the cause; the thermostat is also a likely culprit. To test the thermostat, place an oven thermometer in the center of the oven and set the thermostat to 350°. Let the oven heat up, then check the thermometer every 10 to 15 minutes for the next half-hour. If the temperature is within 50° of 350°, calibrate the thermostat *(page 34);* for digital ranges, adjust the temperature at the control panel. If the temperature is more than 50° off, replace the thermostat *(page 35).*

⚠️ **CAUTION** *Before starting repairs, unplug the range or cut the power at the main service panel, then test the terminal block for incoming voltage (page 31).*

Anatomy of an electric range.

When you turn on a surface unit or the oven, current flows through a calibrated control to a heating element. The element provides resistance to the current, and the energy created radiates outward as heat.

In the oven, a rodlike capillary tube attached to the wall senses the temperature and relays the information to the thermostat, which cycles the current on or off to keep the temperature even. Digital ranges have an electronic temperature sensor.

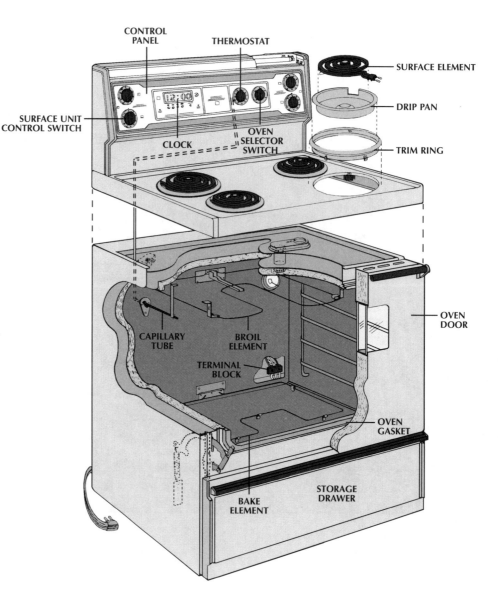

CONTROL PANEL — THERMOSTAT — SURFACE ELEMENT — DRIP PAN — TRIM RING — SURFACE UNIT CONTROL SWITCH — CLOCK — OVEN SELECTOR SWITCH — OVEN DOOR — CAPILLARY TUBE — BROIL ELEMENT — TERMINAL BLOCK — OVEN GASKET — BAKE ELEMENT — STORAGE DRAWER

Troubleshooting Guide

PROBLEM	REMEDY
Nothing works; the elements do not heat, or heat only partially.	Check fuses and circuit breakers at the main service panel. Test terminal block and replace if necessary *(page 31)*.
Surface element doesn't heat.	Test element for resistance and for short; replace if necessary *(page 32)*. Check connection at receptacle, and visually inspect the receptacle *(page 32)*. Test the voltage at the receptacle and, if necessary, at the control switch *(page 33)*. Replace the receptacle if it is faulty.
Oven doesn't heat.	Check the oven element and power to the element *(page 34)*. Test thermostat for resistance; replace if necessary *(page 35)*.
Oven temperature is not the same as temperature setting on control.	Test oven temperature and calibrate thermostat *(page 34)*. On digital ranges, calibrate at control pad, then test the temperature sensor *(page 34)*. Inspect the door gasket and replace if it is frayed or torn. Adjust oven door by loosening screws that secure inner door panel to outer door. Twist door to fit snugly, and tighten screws.
Self-cleaning oven doesn't clean.	Test the bake and broil elements *(page 34)*. Test thermostat for resistance; replace if necessary *(page 35)*.
Oven door doesn't close properly.	Adjust oven door *(see above)*. Adjust or replace door springs.

RESTORING THE INCOMING POWER

Testing the terminal block.
◆ With the power off, pull the range out and remove the back panel.
◆ Set a multitester *(page 21)* for 250 volts and clip the leads to the block's line terminals—marked L_1 and L_2 *(right)*. Restore power. If the meter doesn't show 230 to 240 volts, check for a blown fuse or tripped circuit breaker at the main service panel.
◆ Shut off the power and move a probe to the ground-wire terminal on the lower center screw. Restore power; the meter should now read 120 volts. If it does not, there may be something wrong with the house wiring; call an electrician.
◆ If the block appears burned, replace it by removing the wires and unscrewing it from the range.

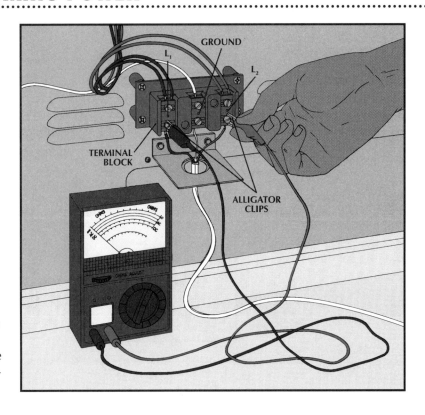

REPLACING A FAULTY BURNER

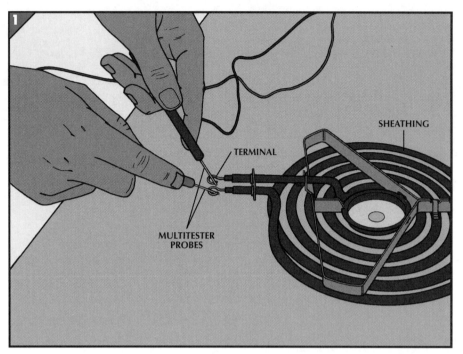

TERMINAL

SHEATHING

MULTITESTER
PROBES

1. Testing the element.

◆ Detach the faulty element from its receptacle and inspect the coil terminals. If they are burned or pitted, replace the element and the receptacle.

◆ To test the element for resistance *(page 21),* set a multitester to RX1 and touch the probes to the terminals *(left).* The meter should read below 60 ohms. If it doesn't, the element should be replaced.

◆ If the element shows the correct resistance, check for a short circuit by leaving one probe on a terminal and placing the other probe on the sheathing. A reading of 0 ohms indicates a short; replace the element.

2. Inspecting the receptacle.

◆ Unscrew the receptacle and pull it out. Check for visible damage to the terminal blades inside the slots and for loose or damaged wires leading into the receptacle. If you find any of these, replace the receptacle.

◆ To do so, cut the wire leading into the old receptacle as close as possible to the back of the receptacle. Strip $\frac{1}{2}$ inch of bare lead with wire strippers and splice it to the short length of wire attached to the new receptacle. Twist a wire cap over the bare ends.

RECEPTACLE

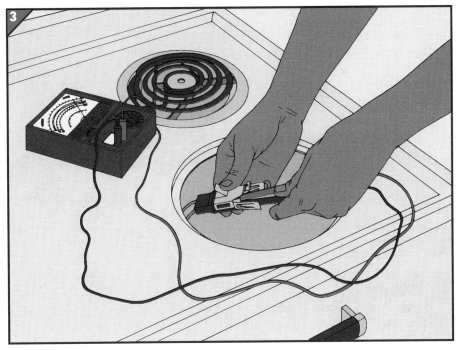

3. Checking the voltage at the receptacle.

◆ With the power off, insert a multitester probe into each receptacle slot so that the probe touches the terminal blade *(left)*.

◆ Set the multitester for 250 volts, restore power to the range, and turn the control knob to HIGH. If the meter does not read 230 to 240 volts, check the control switch *(Step 4)*. If the control switch is fine, replace the receptacle *(Step 2)*.

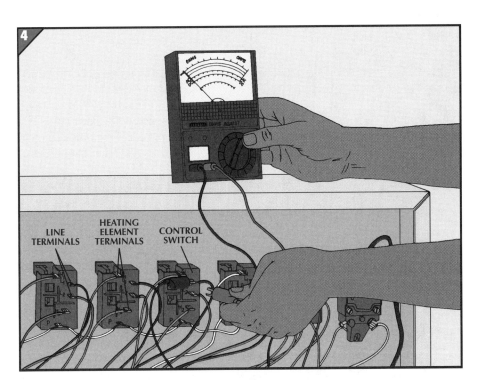

LINE TERMINALS
HEATING ELEMENT TERMINALS
CONTROL SWITCH

4. Testing the control switch.

◆ Locate the switch behind the rear top panel. Cut the power and put multitester clips on the switch's line terminals, marked L_1 and L_2 *(above)*. Set the multitester for 250 volts and restore power; you should get 230 to 240 volts. Turn off the power and move the clips to the heating element terminals, marked H_1 and H_2. Restore power and turn the knob to HIGH. The meter should again read 230 to 240 volts.

◆ If you only get power at L_1 and L_2, or any terminals appear burned, replace the switch. No power at L_1 and L_2 indicates loose or burned terminal block connections; tighten the wires, or replace the block *(page 31)*. If H_1 and H_2 have power but the receptacle does not, splice new range wire—available at appliance-repair shops or electronics stores—between them.

ADJUSTING AN OVEN TEMPERATURE CONTROL

Calibrating the thermostat.

◆ Pull off the thermostat knob and loosen the setscrews on the back *(near right)*. Turn the disk slightly to recalibrate the thermostat—here, moving the disk pointer one notch for each 25°. Retighten the setscrews.

◆ Some ranges have a calibration screw instead. Pull off the thermostat knob and locate the screw inside or beside the shaft *(far right)*. Adjustments vary; consult your owner's manual for which way and how far to turn the screw.

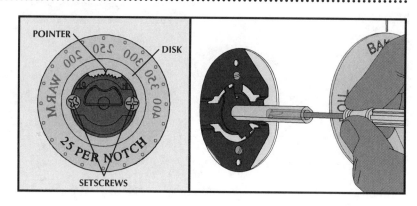

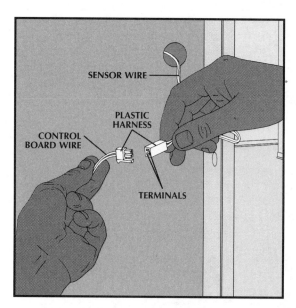

Testing digital oven controls.

◆ To test the temperature sensor—a rod inside the oven on the rear wall—for resistance, pull out the range and remove the back panel. Unclip the plastic harness *(left)*, and touch multitester probes to the terminals inside the harness. Check the owner's manual for the proper resistance reading.

◆ To replace a faulty sensor, unscrew the retaining plate, and pull out the sensor; then insert the new one and reattach the plate. Connect the harness and replace the back panel.

◆ If you get the proper reading, the electronic control board is defective; call for service.

GETTING HEAT FROM A BALKY OVEN

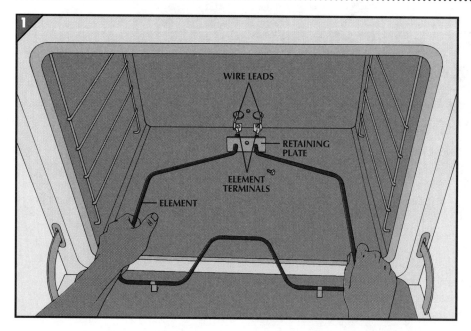

1. Examining the oven elements.

◆ Unscrew the element's retaining plate from the rear wall. Pull the element out and unplug the leads from their terminals or loosen the screws and disconnect the wires.

◆ Replace the element if it has burns and cracks. Cut off a burned or pitted terminal, strip about $\frac{1}{2}$ inch of its wire lead, and attach a new one.

◆ Touch multitester probes to the element terminals to check resistance. You should get 10 to 60 ohms; if you do not, replace the element.

◆ Leave one probe on a terminal and touch one to the element. A 0-ohms reading means the element is shorted; replace it.

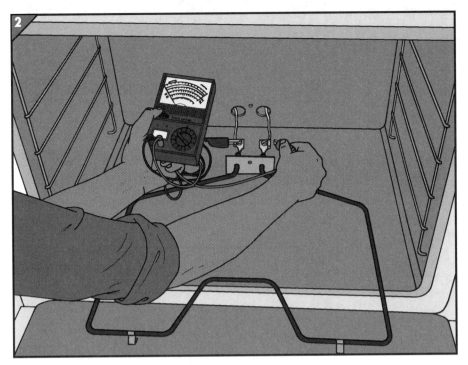

2. Testing the element for power.

◆ Reconnect the leads and attach the multitester clips to the terminals or, if your range has them, to the screws in the element terminals *(above)*.

◆ Set the multitester for 250 volts, then restore power to the range and turn the oven to 300°. If the meter registers 230 to 240 volts after about a minute, power is reaching the element, so the element must be faulty. Turn off the power and replace the element.

◆ If the multitester does not show the proper voltage, turn off the power and check for loose wires at the oven selector switch and thermostat behind the back panel of the range.

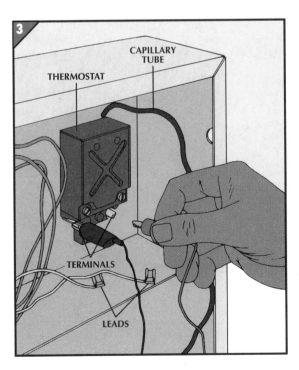

3. Checking the thermostat.

◆ Turn off the power, remove the leads from the back of the thermostat, and attach multitester clips to the terminals *(left)* to test for resistance. With the knob turned to 300° and the power off, the meter should read 0 ohms; if it does not, replace the thermostat.

◆ Examine the capillary tube; if it is damaged, replace the whole thermostat.

◆ To replace a thermostat, shut off the power, remove the leads, and unscrew the thermostat from the back panel. Unclip the capillary tube from the oven wall and pull it out from the back. Push a new tube into the oven, clip it on, and screw on the new thermostat. Reattach the leads.

Safe Repairs for a Gas Range

A gas range is, in essence, a network of pipes that carry gas to burners on the cooktop and in the oven, where it is mixed with air and ignited to produce a controlled flame.

Lighting the Gas: Some ranges have a high-voltage ignition module on the back panel of the range that sends current to an electric igniter when the burner is turned on. Other types use pilots that pro-

duce small, constantly burning flames that ignite the gas. Most problems with either system are caused by accumulated dirt and grease, which can foul the electrodes of electric igniters or clog the small apertures of the pilots.

Routine Maintenance: Keeping the cooking surfaces clean is the best way to avoid problems, and modern ranges are designed with

this in mind. Burner grates and drip pans lift off, and the hinged cooktop can be propped open. Oven doors slide off, and both the oven bottom and the oven burner baffle are removable for easy cleaning and access to the oven burner.

⚠️ **CAUTION** *If the pilot has been out for some time or if you detect an odor of gas, ventilate the room before relighting.*

Anatomy of a gas range.

Natural gas enters the range through the supply pipe in the back. Inside, the pipe branches to carry gas to the oven burner and the manifold, which runs across the front of the range beneath the cooktop and distributes gas to the four surface burner units. An air shutter on each burner's pipe mixes air with the natural gas.

Turning the burner-control knob on the front of the range opens a valve that lets the air/gas mixture flow into the burner tube and the flash tube—where it is ignited—and then through the small holes in the burner head. The oven burner is governed by a thermostat, which senses the temperature inside the oven by means of a capillary tube.

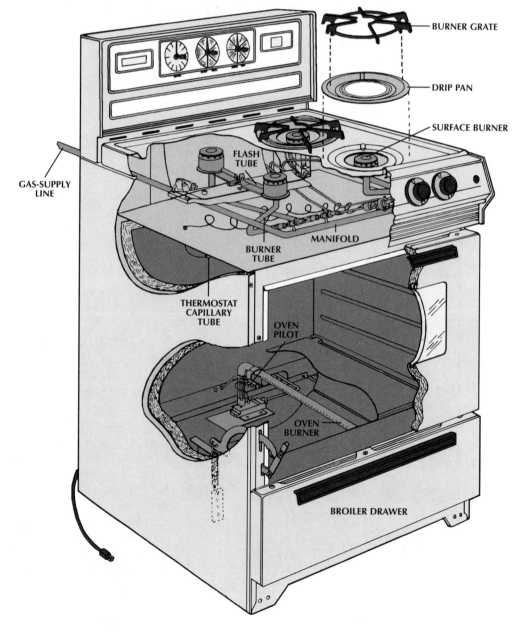

Troubleshooting Guide

PROBLEM	REMEDY
Gas odor.	Ventilate the room. Turn burner controls to OFF. Check burner and oven pilots. Relight them with a match if necessary. If the gas odor persists, turn off gas to the range and call the gas company.
Burner won't light.	Relight extinguished pilot flames *(page 38)* or clean igniter electrodes. Clear the burner portholes with a thin needle *(page 38)*. Close the air shutter slightly *(page 38)*. Reposition a surface burner to align its flash tube with the pilot flame or igniter *(page 38)*. For ovens, check the flame switch *(page 39)*.
Pilot flame won't stay lit.	Clear the pilot opening with a thin needle *(page 38)*. Adjust the pilot flame *(page 38)*.
Electric igniter won't spark.	Check incoming power to the range. Clean igniter electrodes with a cotton swab or cloth. If the igniter still doesn't spark, the igniter, the wiring, or the ignition module is faulty; call for service.

The ideal flame.

In the upper photograph at right, a properly adjusted burner shows a steady, quiet flame with sharply defined blue cones about $\frac{1}{2}$ to $\frac{3}{4}$ inch high. Insufficient air reaching the burner produces a weak red or yellow flame *(below)* that may leave soot deposits on pots and pans. In the lower photograph at right, the burner is getting too much air, resulting in an uneven, noisy flame.

SIMPLE FIXES FOR STOVETOP BURNERS

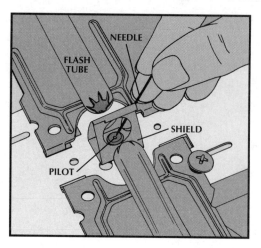

Cleaning the pilot opening.
◆ Insert a needle into the hole in the center of the pilot and move it up and down *(left)*, taking care not to enlarge or deform the opening. If the metal shield over the pilot presents an obstacle, gently lift it out of the way.
◆ With all burner controls turned to the off position, relight the pilot flame with a match held at the opening.

Clearing the portholes.
◆ With the range top propped open, lift out the burner assembly. It is usually unanchored, held in place by its own weight.
◆ Push a needle through each porthole (some burners have a vertical slot instead of portholes), then wash the burner head in warm, soapy water.
◆ To reinstall the burner, slip the burner tube onto the gas manifold *(right)* and align the flash tube with the pilot.

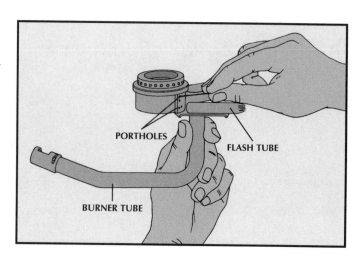

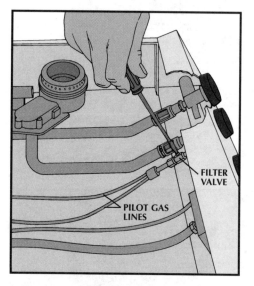

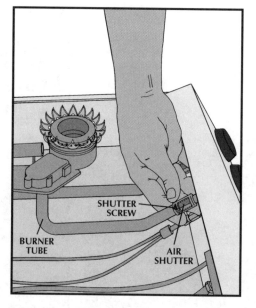

Regulating the burner flame.
◆ To adjust the airflow to a burner, first turn off all the burner controls. Locate the air shutter on the burner tube near the front of the stove.
◆ Loosen the shutter screw until the shutter either twists or slides freely, then turn the burner on high.
◆ Adjust the shutter by hand *(left)* until the burner has the correct airflow *(page 37)* and retighten the shutter screw.

Adjusting the pilot flame.
◆ Follow the thin pilot gas lines to the filter valve at the front of the stove.
◆ Find the screw on the side of the valve, and turn it with a screwdriver until the pilot flame is a compact blue cone with little or no yellow at the tip.

Exposing the pilot and burner.

Loosen any tabs or screws holding the oven floor in place, and lift it from the oven *(below)*. Below the floor is the burner baffle *(inset)*, often held in place by wing nuts. Remove them and the baffle, then pull the broiler drawer out of its opening and set it aside.

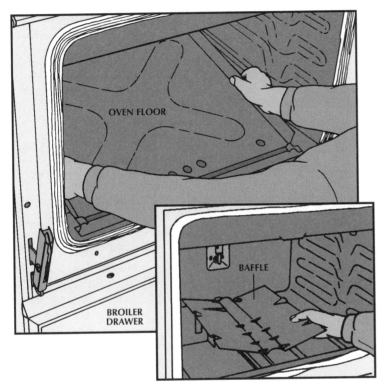

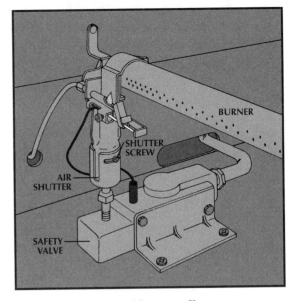

Adjusting pilot and burner flames.

◆ Relight the pilot if it has gone out. If not, increase its height. Pull the oven thermostat knob from its shaft to reveal an adjustment screw labeled "constant pilot," and turn it clockwise.

◆ Replace the knob and turn on the oven. If the burner still does not light, the thermostat or safety valve must be replaced. Call a repair service.

◆ To adjust the burner flame, turn off the oven and loosen the air-shutter screw. Change the shutter opening, then remove your hand from the oven and turn on the oven to observe the flame *(page 37)*.

◆ Make additional adjustments as needed, each time turning off the burner before reaching into the oven.

◆ When the flame is satisfactory, turn off the oven, tighten the shutter screw, and replace the baffle and oven floor.

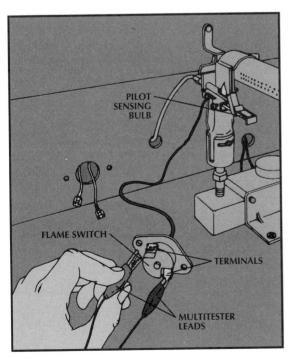

Testing the oven flame switch.

◆ Turn off electrical power to the range, check that the pilot flame is burning, then unscrew the switch from the rear oven wall.

◆ Detach the wires from the two terminals on the back of the flame switch. Check for resistance between the flame switch terminals *(left)* with a multitester set at RX1 *(page 21)*. A reading of 0 ohms indicates a properly work-

ing switch; call a repair service, and expect to have the oven thermostat replaced.

◆ If the multitester shows high resistance, replace the flame switch. Remove it by gently working the pilot sensing bulb from its bracket. To install a new switch, attach the wires to its terminals, screw it to the oven wall, and slip the sensing bulb into the bracket.

Refrigerator Maintenance

Refrigerators usually provide years of trouble-free service. When a problem does arise, you can often make the diagnosis and repairs without any special tools.

Common Problems: A refrigerator usually signals a malfunction by not cooling or by making too much noise. There are many possible causes for a cooling failure, some of them quite simple *(Troubleshooting Guide, opposite)*. Before taking things apart, make sure that the door closes all the way and that the interior light (which produces heat) switches off properly. You should

see the light go off just as the door of the refrigerator closes.

A refrigerator that makes a screeching or rattling sound probably has a faulty evaporator or condenser fan motor. Replace a motor rather than trying to lubricate or repair it. Repairs to the compressor, evaporator, or condenser, which require special skills and tools, should be left to professionals.

Side-by-Sides and Icemakers: The parts of a side-by-side refrigerator may be located in places other than those shown on these pages, but the methods for testing and re-

pairing them remain the same. Many refrigerators include an icemaker or fittings for installing one. Problems that commonly occur with these devices are leaks and loose shutoff arms; for repair instructions, see page 48.

> ⚠ **CAUTION** *Before starting any repair, always unplug the refrigerator or shut off the power at the house service panel. After the repair, wait 15 minutes before plugging in the refrigerator. This delay allows pressures in the cooling system to equalize, lessening the start-up strain on the compressor.*

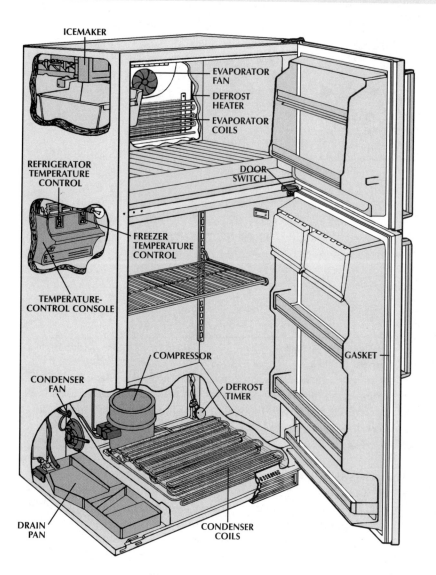

Anatomy of a refrigerator.

The cooling process begins when liquid refrigerant passes through the evaporator coils in the freezer, where it absorbs heat and becomes a gas. The refrigerant then flows to the compressor, which pumps it into the condenser coils. Cooled by air from the condenser fan, it releases its heat, returns to a liquid state, and begins the cycle again.

An evaporator fan circulates cold air within the freezer and, through vents, to the refrigerator area. A temperature control in the freezer regulates the airflow. Another in the refrigerator sets a thermostat that switches the compressor on and off to maintain the proper temperature in both compartments. Gaskets on the doors seal cold air inside. A door switch controls the light in the refrigerator compartment that comes on when the door is opened.

To prevent ice buildup, a defrost heater activated by a timer melts frost from the evaporator coils. A defrost-limit switch turns off the heater before the freezer gets too warm. Meltwater flows down a tube in the back wall and into a drain pan underneath.

Troubleshooting Guide

PROBLEM	REMEDY
Refrigerator not cold enough.	Test thermostat *(page 45)*. Clean condenser coils *(page 42)*. Replace the gasket *(page 43)* if door seal is not tight. Remove and test the door switch *(page 44)*. Replace evaporator fan *(page 45)*. Test defroster components; replace faulty ones *(page 47)*.
Refrigerator too cold.	Test thermostat *(page 45)*
Refrigerator doesn't run, but light works.	Test thermostat *(page 45)*. Clean condenser coils *(page 42)*. Check condenser fan and motor *(page 46)*. Test defrost timer *(page 47)*.
Refrigerator starts and stops frequently.	Clean condenser coils *(page 42)*. Check condenser fan and motor *(page 46)*.
Refrigerator runs constantly. See "Freezer doesn't defrost automatically" (below).	Replace the gasket *(page 43)* if door seal is not tight. Clean condenser coils *(page 42)*. Remove and test the door switch *(page 44)*. Check condenser fan and motor *(page 46)*.
Moisture around refrigerator door or frame.	Reset energy-saver switch. Replace the gasket *(page 43)* if door seal is not tight.
Ice in drain pan or water in bottom of refrigerator.	Clean drain hole *(page 42)*.
Water on floor around refrigerator.	Reposition drain pan. Clean drain hole *(page 42)*.
Interior light doesn't work.	Replace bulb, or test the door switch *(page 44)*.
Refrigerator noisy.	Reposition drain pan. Check condenser fan and motor *(page 46)*. Replace evaporator fan *(page 45)*.
Freezer doesn't defrost automatically.	Test defroster components; replace faulty ones *(page 47)*.
Icemaker doesn't make ice.	Open cold-water-supply valve fully or check water inlet valve *(page 48)*. Set freezer to colder temperature. Test icemaker's thermostat *(page 49)*. Test water inlet valve solenoid *(page 48)*.
Icemaker doesn't stop making ice.	Reseat a loose shutoff arm; test on/off switch *(page 49)*.
Water on the floor behind the refrigerator.	Tighten water inlet valve connections behind refrigerator.
Water overflows from icemaker.	Test water inlet valve and switch *(page 48)*; replace if necessary.
Icemaker doesn't eject ice cubes.	Test holding switch *(page 49)* and icemaker's thermostat *(page 49)*.

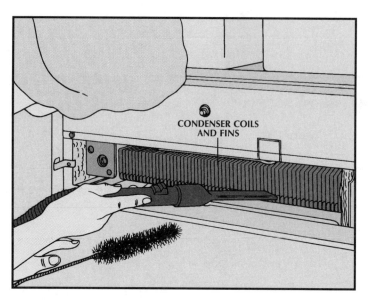

Dusting the cooling system.

Condenser coils and metal cooling fins, which are best cleaned twice a year, are located either at the bottom front *(left)* or on the back of the appliance. To dust bottom-mounted coils, remove the floor-level grille. Use a long-handled brush to dust the coils and fins, taking care not to bend them. Vacuum up debris.

To expose the coils and fins on the back of a refrigerator, roll or walk the appliance away from the wall. Brush dust from the coils and fins, or use a vacuum cleaner with an upholstery-brush attachment.

BASIC REPAIRS FOR DOORS AND DRAINS

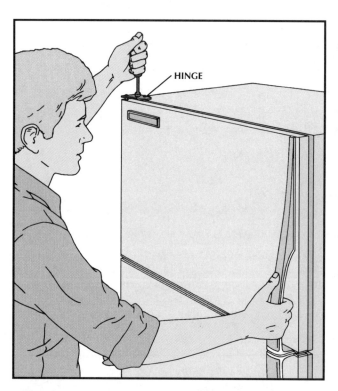

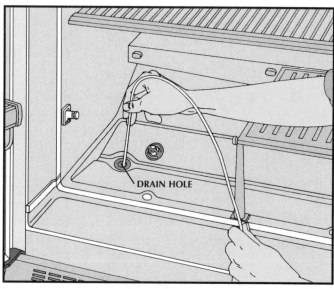

Adjusting a sagging freezer door.

◆ Using a nut driver or a socket wrench, loosen the two hex-headed bolts in the hinge at the top of the freezer door *(above)*.

◆ Reposition the door squarely over the opening of the freezer compartment by pulling upward on the door handle. Hold the door firmly in place and tighten the hinge bolts.

◆ Check the new position by opening and closing the door several times. It should clear the refrigerator door and align with the top of the unit.

Unclogging the drain hole.

◆ Remove the storage bins at the bottom of the refrigerator compartment to expose the drain hole, if there is one. Pry out the stopper plug with a screwdriver.

◆ Clear the drain by inserting a length of flexible $\frac{1}{4}$-inch plastic tubing or a pipe cleaner into the hole and pushing it through the drain canal into the drain pan *(above)*.

◆ Flush the drain with a solution of soapy water and ammonia, forcing it through the canal with a baster.

◆ Empty and wash the drain pan.

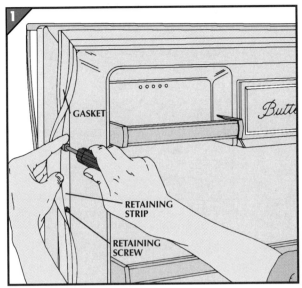

1. Loosening the retaining screws.

◆ Starting at the top outer corner of the door, roll back the rubber gasket with one hand, exposing the metal retaining strip beneath *(left)*.

◆ Use a nut driver to loosen the retaining screws two turns. Working across the top of the door and one-third of the way down each side of it, loosen each of the screws an equal amount.

TRICKS OF THE TRADE

Getting the Wrinkles Out

New gaskets come folded in boxes and are usually kinked and wrinkled. Before installing one, you must straighten it. There are two effective ways to do so: Spread the gasket out in the sun on the hood of a car on a warm day, or soak it a little at a time in a skillet or pan of boiling water *(left)*. Allow a few hours for the first approach. Boiling water should unkink the gasket immediately.

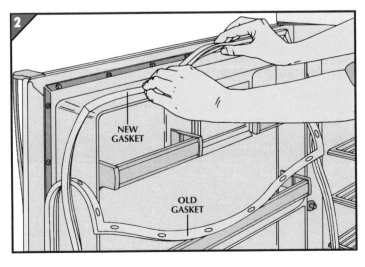

2. Installing a new gasket.

◆ Pull the old gasket straight up to free it from behind the retaining strip at the top of the door.

◆ Let the old gasket hang out of the way, and slide the new gasket behind the retaining strip *(left)*, beginning along the top of the door and working down the sides. Partially tighten the screws.

◆ Working down each side, loosen the screws and strip off the old gasket; then insert the new gasket and partially tighten the screws.

◆ At the bottom of the door, slip out the old gasket at one corner, and replace it with the new gasket before loosening the retaining screws at the other corner. Then complete the last few inches of the installation.

3. Squaring the door.

◆ Close the door and look for gaps between the gasket and the body of the refrigerator. Usually found on the handle side of the door, a gap indicates a slight twist in the door, introduced during gasket installation.

◆ If the door is twisted, open it and have a helper push on the top or bottom of the doorframe to counter the twist. If you don't have any help, support the door with your foot *(left)* while pushing on the frame. Tighten the screws once the door looks straight.

◆ If a gap still shows when you close the door, open it again, loosen the screws a half-turn, and repeat the squaring process.

A NEW DOOR SWITCH

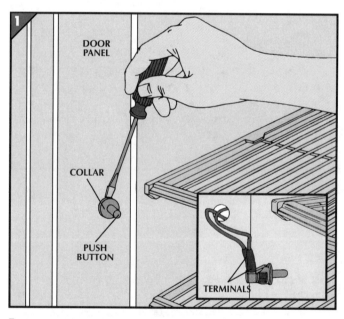

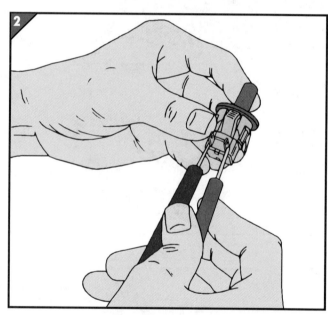

1. Removing the push-button switch.
◆ Unplug the refrigerator, cover a screwdriver tip with masking tape, then gently pry the collar encircling the push button from the door panel.

◆ Tilt the push button so you can get the right-angle terminals through the hole *(inset)*, then pull the switch out of the door panel along with its wires.

2. Checking the switch.
◆ Pull the wires off the terminals and, using a multi-tester, test the switch for resistance *(page 21)*. The switch should show 0 ohms when the push button is up *(above)* and infinite ohms when it is depressed.

◆ Replace a faulty switch by attaching the wires to the new switch and inserting it into the hole in the door panel.

REGAINING CONTROL OF THE TEMPERATURE

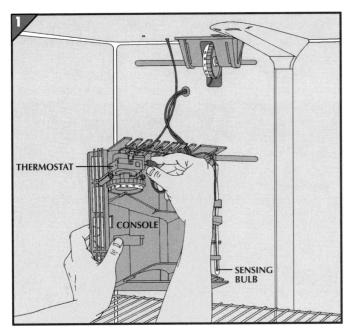

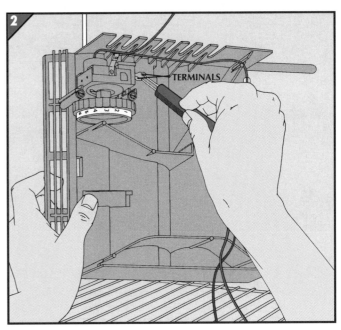

1. Getting at the thermostat.

◆ Unplug the refrigerator and unscrew the temperature-control console. For a control recessed into the top of the compartment, unscrew the breaker strips securing the console and remove it.

◆ Disconnect the wires that are attached to the thermostat terminals *(above)*.

◆ Rest the console on a shelf, taking care not to bend the tube of the sensing bulb.

2. Checking thermostat operation.

◆ Test the thermostat for resistance *(page 21)* by turning the control dial to OFF and touching a multitester's probes to the two terminals *(above)*; the meter should show infinite resistance.

◆ With the probes still touching the terminals, turn the dial to ON and gradually rotate it toward the coldest setting. The meter should show 0 ohms at some point. If it does not, replace the thermostat.

A MOTOR FOR THE EVAPORATOR FAN

1. Gaining access to the fan.

◆ Unplug the refrigerator and remove the icemaker and any shelves from the freezer.

◆ On some models, you must unscrew and remove a fan grille to get at the rear panel. If the grille is also secured by plastic tabs at the freezer floor, bend the grille gently inward to free it from one tab at a time.

◆ Unscrew the freezer's rear panel to reveal the evaporator coils and fan. Lift out the panel *(left)* with its insulation, if any. Cover the exposed evaporator fins with a towel before beginning work on the fan.

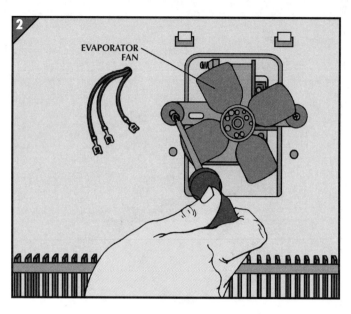

EVAPORATOR FAN

2. Replacing the fan.

◆ If the fan's plastic grille is located behind the rear panel, unscrew it and remove it.
◆ Disconnect the wires from the fan motor, remove the screws that secure the fan to the cabinet *(left)*, and pull out the fan assembly.
◆ Before discarding the old fan, unscrew the blades from the motor shaft. Examine the blades for cracks and replace them if they are damaged; otherwise reuse them.

◆ Secure the fan blades on the shaft of the new motor, then insert the fan in the opening located at the back of the freezer, positioned so that the terminals face the loose wires.
◆ Screw the fan to the cabinet, reattach the wires, and replace the fan grille. Reinstall the rear panel, as well as any equipment removed earlier.

RENEWING AIRFLOW TO THE CONDENSER

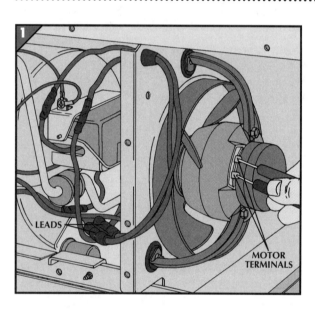

LEADS

MOTOR TERMINALS

1. Testing the motor.

◆ Unplug the refrigerator, move it away from the wall, and remove the rear access panel.
◆ Spin the condenser fan to see if it turns freely. If it does not, the motor bearings are worn; replace the motor *(Step 2)*.
◆ If the fan turns without binding, disconnect the wire leads from the motor and test it for resistance at the terminals *(left)*. With a multitester set at RX1, the meter should read between 200 and 500 ohms; a reading other than that means that the motor should be replaced.

2. Replacing a faulty motor.

◆ With the refrigerator unplugged, remove the screws that secure the condenser fan's mounting brackets to the divider panel *(right)* and lift out the fan assembly.
◆ Unfasten the mounting bracket from the motor and remove the hub nut that holds the fan blades in place.
◆ Wash the blades if they are dirty.
◆ Attach both the blades and the bracket to a new motor, then align the fan assembly in the refrigerator and screw the bracket to the divider panel.
◆ Reconnect the leads to the terminals.

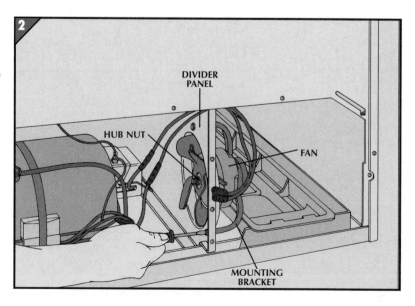

DIVIDER PANEL

HUB NUT

FAN

MOUNTING BRACKET

REPAIRING AN AUTOMATIC DEFROSTER

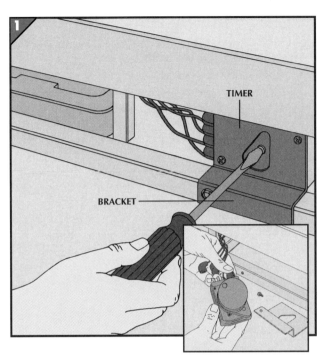

1. Trying the timer.

◆ Locate the defrost timer, which may be behind the bottom front grille or rear access panel, or in the temperature-control console.

◆ With the compressor running, insert a screwdriver blade in the timer slot *(left)* and turn it clockwise until it clicks. If the compressor stops and the freezer begins defrosting, you have a faulty timer.

◆ To replace a timer, unplug the refrigerator and unscrew the timer's mounting bracket. Unscrew the timer from the bracket. If a ground wire is attached to the cabinet, disconnect it. Pull the wires from the timer terminals one by one *(inset)*, transferring each to the corresponding terminal on the new timer.

◆ Screw the new timer to the mounting bracket and reconnect the ground wire. Reinstall the timer on the refrigerator frame.

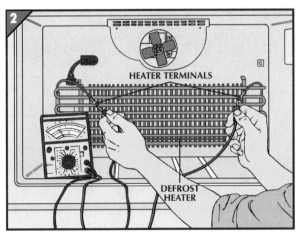

2. Checking the defrost heater.

◆ With the power off, remove the rear panel to reveal the defrost heater—a glass or steel tube that runs behind the evaporator coils and often along the sides. (If the heater is embedded in the coils, leave servicing to a trained technician.) Tighten loose wires to the heater and replace burned ones.

◆ Test resistance *(page 22)* by removing the wires and touching multitester probes to the terminals *(left)*. A reading between 5 and 100 ohms indicates a functional heater.

◆ To replace a defective heater, put on gloves for protection against sharp evaporator fins. Twist the tabs holding the heater in its brackets, remove it, and clip in the new one.

3. Replacing the defrost-limit switch.

◆ If the other defrost components are working, replace the defrost-limit switch; it is usually above or attached to the coils.

◆ Unscrew or unclip the switch and pull off the wire connectors if they are detachable; otherwise cut the wires to the switch and connect a new switch with wire caps *(right)*.

◆ Squeeze silicone caulk into the wire caps' base to protect the connections from moisture.

◆ Clip or screw the switch in place, then replace the insulation and the rear panel.

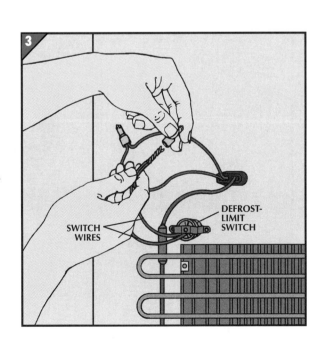

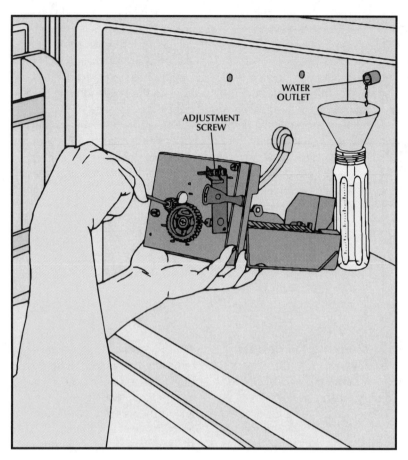

Adjusting the water fill.

◆ Remove the icemaker cover, and if your ice-maker has no label warning against rotating the drive gear on the front of the device, unscrew the unit from the freezer. Do not unplug it. If there is a warning label, try turning the water-adjustment screw as needed.

◆ Put a small funnel in the mouth of a baby bottle or other container marked in ounces and place it under the water outlet.

◆ Insert a screwdriver in the gear slot *(left)* and gently turn the gear counterclockwise about a half-turn, until you hear the motor start.

◆ Allow the unit to complete a cycle, then check the level of the water in the bottle; it should be about 5 ounces.

◆ Increase or reduce the water flow by turning the water-adjustment screw a small amount toward the + or - sign. Run another test cycle to check your adjustment.

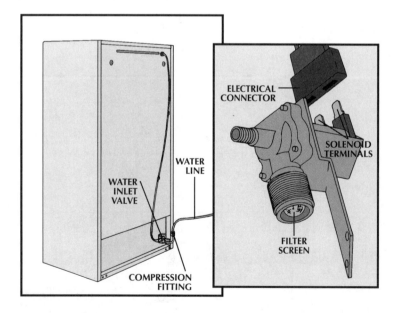

Correcting the water flow.

◆ Close the valve in the water line to the refrigerator and remove the rear access panel to expose the water inlet valve. Place a shallow pan under the line to catch drips, and unscrew the compression fitting at the valve. Discard the used brass ring from the fitting, and obtain a new one for the reinstallation.

◆ Unplug the refrigerator, pull the electrical connector from the water inlet valve *(inset)*, and test the resistance between the solenoid terminals *(page 22)*. If the reading is less than 60 ohms or more than 500 ohms, replace the valve.

◆ If the resistance falls within these limits, try cleaning the filter screen. Remove any screws on the valve and take it apart; scrape the screen, rinse it well, and reassemble the valve.

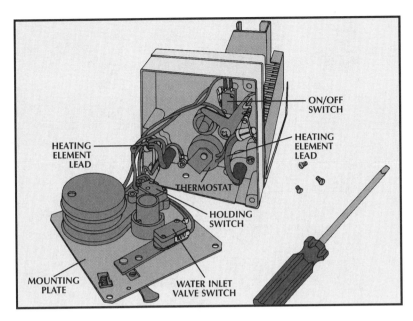

Testing the electrical components.

◆ Unplug the icemaker and remove its cover and mounting plate. To check the thermostat for resistance *(page 21)*, leave the icemaker in the freezer. Remove the heating element leads and touch a probe to each terminal; at temperatures below 15° F., you should get 0 ohms. Retest the icemaker at room temperature. It should read more than 0; if not, replace the thermostat.

◆ Unscrew a clamp to remove the thermostat. Put metallic putty on the back of the new thermostat and stick it down. Screw in the clamp.

◆ To test a switch, disconnect its leads and unscrew the switch. Test each terminal against its common contact (marked "C"); when the switch button is down, one terminal should show 0 ohms, the other more than 0. Readings should be opposite when the button is up.

REPLACING AN ICEMAKER SHUTOFF ARM

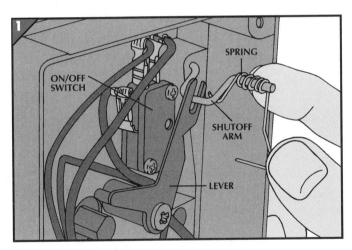

1. Reseating the spring and arm.

◆ Unplug the refrigerator, take out the icemaker, and remove the mounting plate.

◆ Check that the spring is engaged on the shutoff arm *(left)* and that the arm is in the slot in the end of the lever that links it to the on/off switch. If necessary, seat the spring as shown and put the arm back in the slot.

◆ If the shutoff mechanism still does not work, replace the shutoff arm *(below)*.

2. Replacing the shutoff arm.

◆ Carefully disengage the spring and separate the old arm from the lever. Push the arm forward, turning it as required to work it out through the hole in the housing *(right)*.

◆ Slide the new shutoff arm through the front of the housing. Engage the arm in the lever slot and replace the spring *(above)*.

◆ Replace the mounting plate and cover, and reinstall the icemaker.

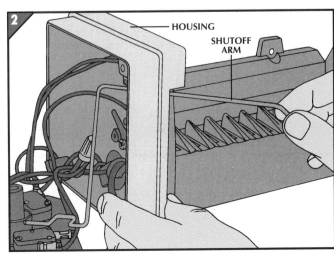

CHAPTER 2

BATHROOMS

With surprisingly little time and effort, you can apply the methods described in this chapter to put an end to drips, clogs, and other bathroom annoyances. It is also easy to replace worn-out fittings with attractive new ones. Keeping up with repairs not only makes your bathroom more comfortable, it may also prevent small problems from turning into big ones, as when an uncorrected leak damages the floor or walls.

The following pages show how to set a soap dish into a tile wall as well as how to install a surface-mounted towel bar. You'll find simple techniques for stopping drips and leaks in four different kinds of faucets, time-tested methods for unclogging drains, and a number of simple toilet repairs.

You can noticeably improve almost any bathroom with a variety of basic amenities. From mounting grab bars for the shower and tub to shockproofing electrical outlets, the modifications explained in this chapter modernize a bathroom and make it safer, more accessible, and generally more agreeable to family members and guests alike.

For easy repairs to tile flooring—whether ceramic, marble, or slate—turn to page 158.

▲
Bathroom accessories such as
soap dishes or towel bars can be
unsightly if they break or become
damaged. By working carefully,
you can often replace a damaged
item without harming the wall.

Stem, or compression, faucets range ▶
from antique brass to modern stainless steel. A leaking faucet handle
can often be fixed by tightening
the packing nut or replacing the
packing washer.

▲

A clogged sink can often be cleared by a hose-mounted drain flusher. The device relies on water pressure to cut through obstructions. In tubs or showers, an ordinary force-cup plunger will handle most clogs.

▲

Whatever its style, any bathroom can be made safer by mounting grab bars as handholds on walls surrounding the bathing area and toilet.

◄ *Adding insulation pads inside the tank can help prevent condensation from forming on this newly installed toilet and the surrounding wall.*

Replacing a Broken Accessory

Towel bars or a soap dish can be a handy addition to a tiled bathroom wall, but an accessory can be an eyesore if it breaks or is damaged. As shown below and opposite, you can often replace the damaged item with no harm to the wall. Work carefully to avoid cracking nearby tiles, and keep them from loosening by laying strips of masking tape from one tile to the next.

A Variety of Accessories: Flush-set accessories, such as the soap dish below, are attached directly to the same backing that the tiles are mounted on. To avoid exposing the backing, replace a flush-set accessory with one of the same dimensions or slightly larger. Other accessories, such as the towel bar opposite, are mounted to the tile surface. Replace a surface-mounted accessory with another that will attach to the same tiles; in the case of a towel bar, the new bar should be the same length as the one it replaces, so that its brackets rest on the same pair of tiles.

Some older bathrooms have recessed accessories, which are sunk into the tiled wall. You can often unscrew a recessed toilet-paper holder from its mounting bracket and install a new one, but a recessed soap dish or other sort of shelf cannot be replaced without extensive retiling.

TOOLS

Cold chisel	Electric drill with
Ball-peen hammer	carbide-tipped
Putty knife	masonry bit
Grout saw	Screwdriver
Punch	Hex wrench

SAFETY TIPS

Wear goggles as you free the accessory with hammer and chisel and whenever you drill into tile.

SETTING A SOAP DISH INTO A TILE WALL

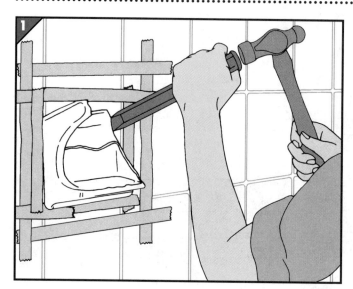

1. Removing the old soap dish.
◆ Protect the tile at the edge of the soap dish with masking tape. Hold down the nearby tiles with more tape.
◆ Remove any caulk or grout around the soap dish, then position a cold chisel at its edge. Tap with a ball-peen hammer *(above)* until the dish comes free.

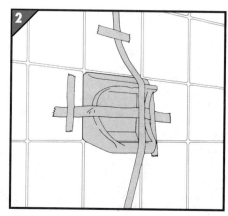

2. Positioning the new dish.
◆ Remove the tape and clean the exposed area with a putty knife.
◆ Apply silicone tile adhesive to the new soap dish, press it into place, and secure it with masking tape *(above)*.
◆ After 24 hours, take off the tape and grout the joints around the soap dish.

ATTACHING A SURFACE-MOUNTED TOWEL BAR

1. Preparing the surface.
◆ With a grout saw, cut out the grout around each tile to which the towel bar is attached *(above)*; this will help minimize any movement of the adjacent tiles as you work.
◆ Lay strips of masking tape around the edges of the towel bar's mounting brackets. For each bracket, add a square of masking tape over the nearby tiles.

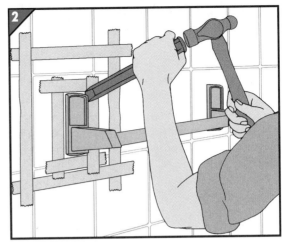

2. Removing the old towel bar.
If you can, remove the old towel bar from its mounting brackets and unscrew the brackets. For brackets secured with adhesive rather than screws, place a cold chisel against each bracket and tap with a ball-peen hammer *(above)* to free it. Clean the exposed area and make sure any marred surface will be covered by the mounting brackets of the new towel bar you select.

3. Preparing the wall for drilling.
For screw-mounted brackets, check whether you can reuse the old screw holes; otherwise, drill new holes large enough for hollow-wall anchors.
◆ Hold a bracket in place; if it has tapered edges, position them at top and bottom. Mark the screw hole. Position the second bracket with a level and mark that hole as well. With a punch, make an indentation on each mark *(left)*.
◆ Fit an electric drill with a carbide-tipped masonry bit; keeping the drill speed as low as possible, make a hole at each indentation.

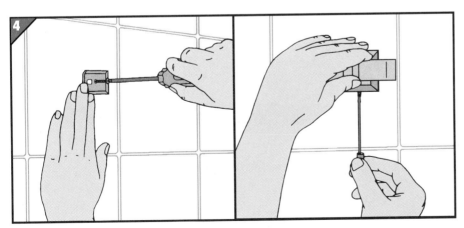

4. Installing the towel bar.
◆ For brackets without screw holes, apply tile adhesive, press the brackets into place, and allow to dry. For screw-mounted brackets, seat hollow-wall anchors in the drilled holes, then screw the brackets into place *(far left)*.
◆ Slip the towel bar onto the mounting brackets; secure a metal towel bar by tightening setscrews with a hex wrench or screwdriver *(near left)*.
◆ Regrout the tile joints that you cut out in Step 1.

Drips and Leaks in Four Kinds of Faucets

Often a bathroom faucet with a dripping spout or leaking handles can be fixed with a small investment of time and some spare parts. Although they come in many sizes and shapes, for repair purposes most faucets are grouped into four types: stem, cartridge, disk, and ball.

Stem, or compression, faucets, depicted below and on pages 58 and 59, employ hard-rubber seat washers to provide a tight seal. When stem faucets drip, check for worn washers. You may also need to replace the stem and the seat, metal parts that come in contact with the washers. For a leaking handle, tighten the packing nut *(below)* or replace the packing washer.

Cartridge, disk, and ball faucets, all of which usually have single handles, develop drips and leaks less often. When they do, repair methods differ from one type to another, as shown on pages 60 to 63. In each case, the trick is to know how to disassemble the faucet.

Before You Begin: As with any plumbing job, locate the main shut-off valve in your house ahead of time in case of emergency. Turn off the shutoff valves below the basin and drain the faucet. If the valves will not close, turn off the main valve; drain the system by opening the faucets at the highest point in the house and working down to the lowest point. This prevents a vacuum from forming.

Plug the drain so parts cannot fall in, and protect the sink with a towel. As you work, set parts aside in the exact order you remove them to allow for easier reassembly.

TOOLS

Utility knife
Screwdriver
Adjustable wrench
Long-nose pliers
Vise
Flashlight
Seat wrench
Hex wrench

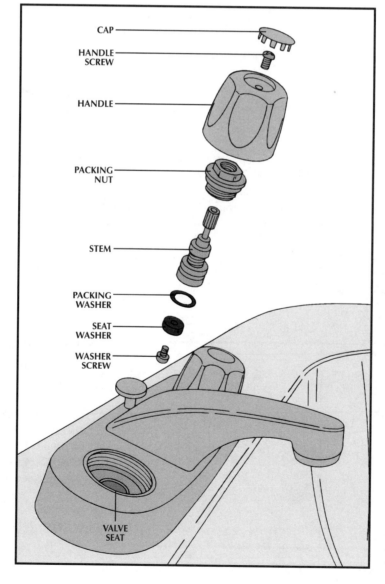

CAP
HANDLE SCREW
HANDLE
PACKING NUT
STEM
PACKING WASHER
SEAT WASHER
WASHER SCREW
VALVE SEAT

The inner anatomy of a stem faucet.

Although they vary in design, most stem faucets include the basic components shown at left. Each of the two handles is secured by a screw, often concealed under a decorative cap. The screw attaches the handle to the packing nut located at the top of the stem. Under the stem and packing washer, the seat washer closes against the valve seat to cut off the flow of water to the spout.

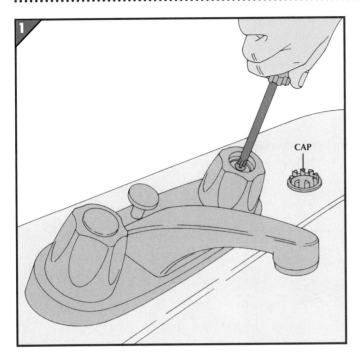

1. Removing a stem-faucet handle.

When a stem faucet drips, repair both hot and cold faucet assemblies. Do one at a time.

◆ Pry out the cap on one handle with a utility knife.

◆ Remove the screw and pull the handle straight up. If it is wedged on tight, protect the basin or base plate underneath with a towel and pry the handle off with a screwdriver. If it is very resistant, use a faucet-handle puller *(below)*.

TRICKS OF THE TRADE

Freeing a Handle

A stubborn handle can be freed with a faucet-handle puller without marring the finish. Insert the center shaft into the hole on the handle, and fit the puller arms under it. Turn the puller handle clockwise to lift the faucet handle off.

CENTER SHAFT

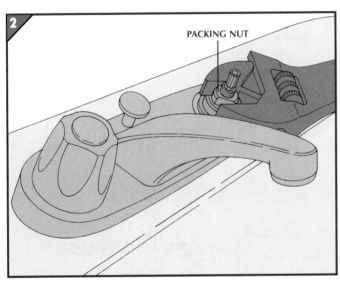

PACKING NUT

2. Removing the packing nut.

Unscrew the packing nut with an adjustable wrench *(above)*. The stem below may come out with the nut; to separate them, protect the stem with electrician's tape, clamp it in a vise, and remove the nut with the wrench.

3. Taking out the stem.

◆ Try to unscrew the stem by hand *(right)*.

◆ Should that fail, set the handle on the stem and turn it in the same direction that you would to turn on the water; this will remove most stems.

◆ If the stem does not unscrew, the faucet may be a diaphragm or a cartridge type; remove the stem as described on page 58.

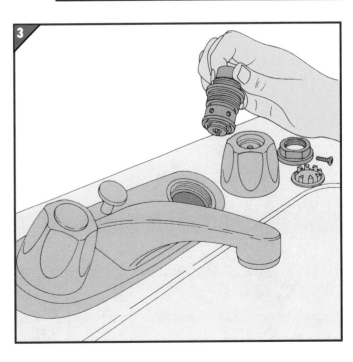

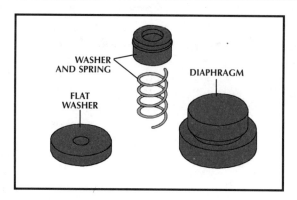

A variety of seat washers.

Different stem faucets require their own type of seat washer. Standard stem faucets use flat washers with holes for washer screws; cartridge-type stem faucets may have washers and springs. In a diaphragm stem faucet, caps called diaphragms do the work of washers, covering the bottom end of each stem. If you are not certain which washers fit your faucet, remove a valve seat *(opposite, below)* and take it to a plumbing-supply store.

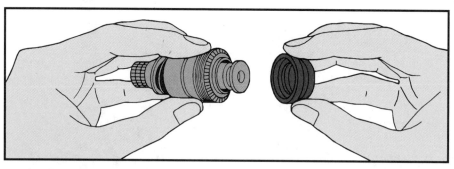

Making repairs to a diaphragm stem faucet.

Suction between the diaphragm and the valve seat may make the stem difficult to remove.

◆ Wrap the top of the stem with cloth and pull out the stem with pliers.

◆ If the old diaphragm sticks, pry it out with the tip of a screwdriver.

◆ Using a flashlight, make sure that there are no pieces of the old diaphragm remaining inside; otherwise, the new one will not seat properly.

◆ Fit the new diaphragm over the bottom of the stem *(above)*, making sure the diaphragm is snug all around.

◆ Replace the stem, the packing nut, and the handle.

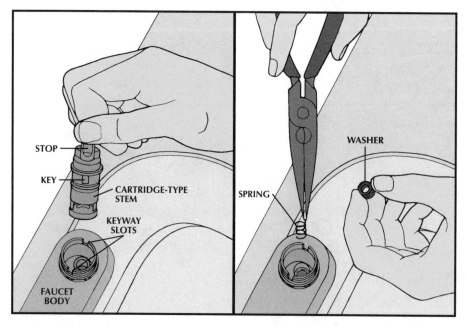

Servicing a cartridge-type stem faucet.

◆ Lift the cartridge out of the faucet *(far left)*, making sure to observe the alignment of the stop on the top of the cartridge and the keys on its side. The latter fit into two keyway slots on the faucet body.

◆ With long-nose pliers, pull the washer and spring out of the faucet body *(near left)*.

◆ Push the new spring and washer firmly into place with a finger. Insert the cartridge in the same orientation as before and attach the handle. If the spout still drips, replace the cartridge.

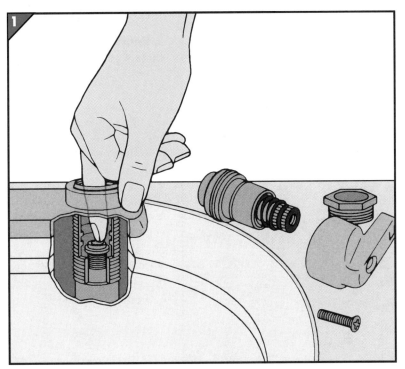

1. Inspecting the valve seat.

If the spout of a stem faucet continues to drip after you have replaced the washers, check the valve seats for signs of wear—scratches, pits, or an uneven surface. Use a flashlight to look inside the faucet body, then run a fingertip around the edge of the valve seat *(left)*. If necessary, install a new seat as shown below.

2. Installing a new seat.

◆ With a seat wrench, turn the valve seat counterclockwise and lift it out *(near right)*. Take it to a plumbing-supply store to get an exact duplicate.

◆ Lubricate the outside of the replacement with a pipe-joint compound, push it onto the wrench, and screw it into the faucet body *(far right)*.

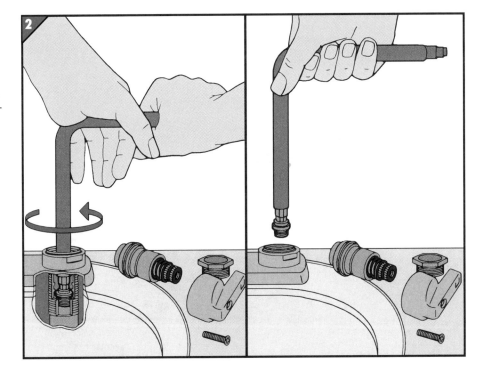

SINGLE-LEVER CARTRIDGE FAUCETS

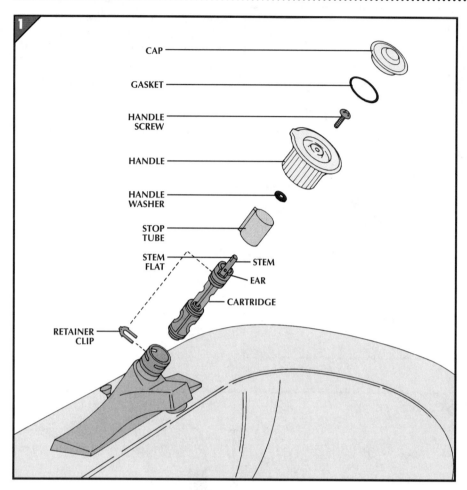

1. Repairing a single-lever cartridge faucet.

Fixing a cartridge faucet usually requires replacing the cartridge. When taking the faucet apart, carefully note the orientation of the cartridge ears and the stem flats, flat areas at the top of the stem *(left)*; position the replacement the same way.

◆ Remove the cap with a utility knife or a very small screwdriver.

◆ Unscrew the handle and remove it.

◆ Remove the stop tube, if there is one present.

◆ Complete the disassembly by removing the retainer clip and cartridge, as shown below.

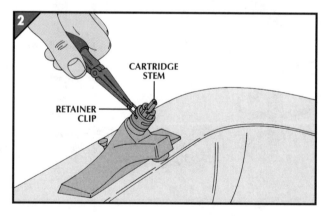

2. Removing the retainer clip.

◆ With long-nose pliers, pull out the retainer clip that holds the cartridge in the faucet body *(left)*.

◆ Lift out the cartridge, using pliers to grip the top of the stem if necessary.

3. Replacing the cartridge.

◆ Position the new cartridge to match the orientation of the old one. With the stem at its highest position, push the cartridge by its ears down into the faucet body *(right)*.

◆ Align the cartridge ears with the faucet body slots; slide the retainer clip through the slots.

◆ Turn the stem to place the stem flats in the same position as in the old cartridge, then reassemble the faucet and turn on the water. If hot water comes out when you try to turn on the cold, and vice versa, remove the handle and stop tube and rotate the stem 180 degrees.

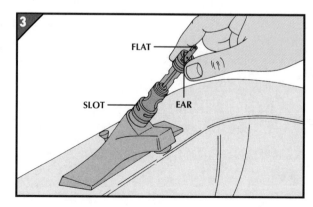

SINGLE-LEVER CERAMIC DISK FAUCETS

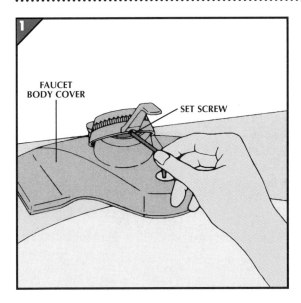

FAUCET BODY COVER

SET SCREW

1. Getting access to a disk cartridge.
In ceramic disk faucets, leaks show up around the body of the faucet or as a puddle under the basin.
◆ Turn the faucet on full and move the handle side to side to dislodge dirt that may be lodged between the disks. If the leak persists, replace the disk cartridge.
◆ After turning off the water and draining the faucet, raise the lever as high as it can go. Unscrew the setscrew under the lever *(left)* and remove the handle.
◆ With older models, remove the pop-up lift rod, remove the screws on the underside of the faucet, and take off the body cover. Newer ceramic disk faucets have a screw in the handle and a metal ring that twists off.

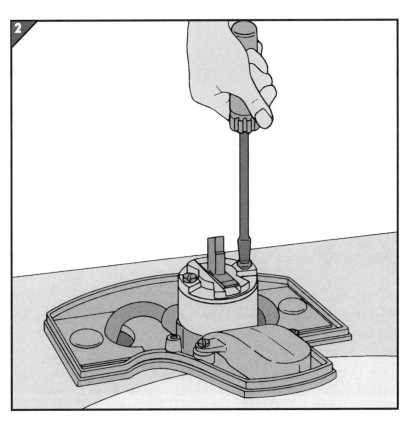

2. Removing the disk cartridge.
◆ Unscrew the bolts that hold the disk cartridge in place *(left)*.
◆ Remove the cartridge and purchase an identical replacement.

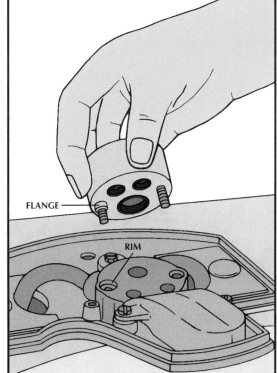

FLANGE

RIM

3. Installing a new cartridge.
◆ Align the three ports on the bottom of the disk cartridge with the three holes in the base of the faucet body *(right)*. One of the bolt holes on the cartridge will have a flange; make sure it fits into the rim around the corresponding bolt hole in the faucet body.
◆ Replace the disk cartridge bolts, the body cover, and the handle.

SINGLE-LEVER BALL FAUCETS

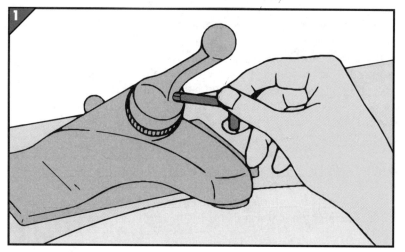

1. Loosening the setscrew.

If the spout of a ball faucet drips when the water is off, replace the two rubber valve seats and metal springs in the bottom of the faucet body.

◆ With a hex wrench, loosen the setscrew under the shank of the handle *(left)*. Do not take the screw all the way out; it is easily lost.

◆ Remove the handle.

2. Removing the cap and ball.

◆ Unscrew the cap assembly and lift out the ball by its stem *(right)*; the plastic-and-rubber cam assembly will come with it.

◆ Inspect the ball; if it is rough or corroded, replace it.

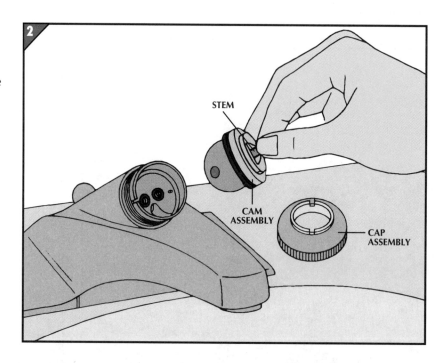

STEM

CAM ASSEMBLY

CAP ASSEMBLY

3. Installing new valve seats and springs.

With long-nose pliers, remove the valve seats and springs (left). Use a fingertip to push replacements firmly into place.

VALVE SEAT

SPRING

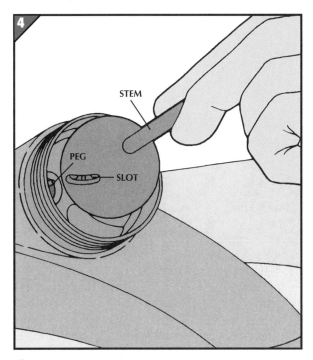

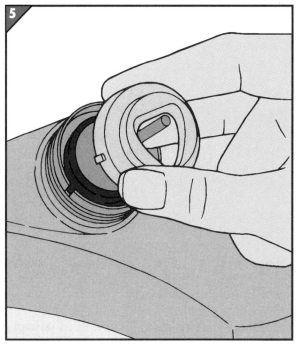

4. Replacing the ball.

A tiny metal peg projects from one side of the cavity into which the ball fits. As you replace the ball, make sure that the peg fits into an oblong slot on it.

5. Replacing the cam assembly.

◆ Replace the cam assembly so that its tab fits into the slot on the faucet body.

◆ Screw on the cap assembly.

6. Setting the adjusting ring.

◆ Turn on the water to the faucet.

◆ Move the ball's stem to the on position. If water leaks out around the stem, tighten the adjusting ring with a tool provided by the manufacturer or with the tip of a small screwdriver *(right)*.

◆ If you must tighten the ring so much that the handle is difficult to work, turn off the water, drain the faucet, and replace the entire cam assembly, including the rubber ring.

◆ Put the cap assembly back in place. Position the handle so that the setscrew is over the flat on the stem and tighten the setscrew.

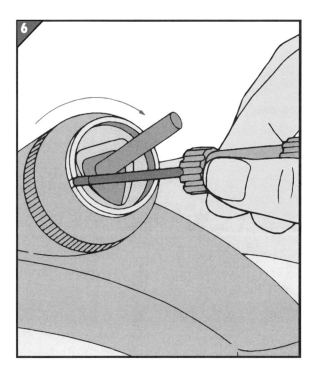

Three Methods for Unclogging Drains

When a bathroom drain stops or slows, see if other drains are affected. If so, the problem may lie elsewhere in the house's plumbing.

A Hierarchy of Solutions: If only one drain is blocked, try a plunger *(right)*. Prepare the drain by removing the strainer, pop-up plug, and overflow plate, if present; take apart a tub's drain hardware as shown in Step 1 on page 65. Stuff any overflow opening with rags.

If the plunger fails, you can sometimes clear a tub or shower drain with water *(below)*. A third method is to use an auger—a trap-and-drain auger for a tub, sink, or shower, and a closet auger for a toilet. Avoid compressed-air devices, which often compact the blockage and may cause old pipe joints to break apart.

Chemical Drain Cleaners: Do not pour chemical cleaning agents into a blocked drain. Many contain lye, and you could be exposed to the caustic substance as you continue work on the stoppage. Cleaners can be helpful once a tub, sink, or shower drain is open; applied regularly, they prevent buildup of debris. Never put such cleaners in a toilet, however. They do no good and can stain the porcelain.

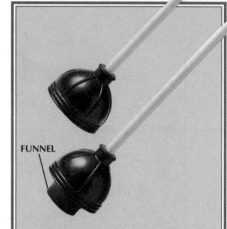

FUNNEL

A Multi-Role Plunger

An ordinary force-cup plunger is suited to many drains, but it will not fit a toilet. For the bathroom, purchase a foldout plunger instead. As shown above, its cup can take on two different shapes.

With a tub, sink, or shower drain, keep the funnel portion tucked inside *(upper photo)*. Coat the rim of the cup with petroleum jelly and center it over the drain. Make sure that standing water covers the cup completely; if it does not, add more water. Without breaking the seal between drain and cup, pump the plunger down and up several times, then jerk it away. When the drain opens, run hot water through it to flush it clean.

For a toilet, extend the plunger's funnel lip *(lower photo)*. If a clogged toilet is too full, bail out some of the contents. If the bowl is empty, add water by hand, not by flushing. Fit the plunger over the opening near the bottom of the bowl and pump vigorously, then jerk it away. If the bowl empties, pour in water to confirm that the drain is fully opened.

 TOOLS

Foldout plunger
Garden hose
Drain flusher

Trap-and-drain
  auger
Closet auger

 SAFETY TIPS

If human waste is present when you are unclogging a toilet, wear goggles and rubber gloves.

CLEARING A STOPPAGE WITH WATER

Flushing a drain with a hose.
A hose-mounted drain flusher, available at most hardware stores, will work in a shower or tub drain.

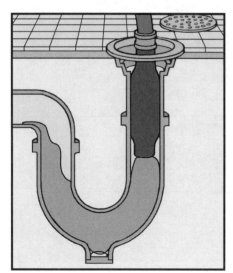

◆ Attach the drain flusher to a garden hose and push it into a shower drain; in a tub, insert it through the overflow opening past the level of the drain. Connect the other end of the hose to a faucet; for an indoor faucet, you will need a threaded adapter.
◆ Have a helper slowly turn on the hose water. The flusher will expand to fill the pipe so that the full force of water is directed at the clog.

⚠ **CAUTION** *Do not flush a clogged drain that contains caustic cleaners, and never leave a hose in any drain. The cleaner could splash into your face, and the hose could draw wastewater into the supply system if the pressure should drop.*

BREAKING UP A CLOG WITH A TRAP-AND-DRAIN AUGER

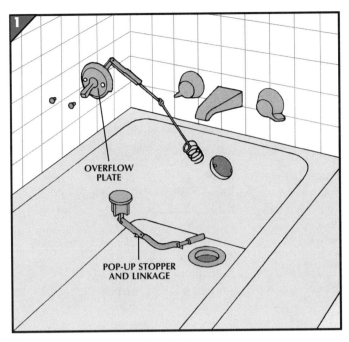

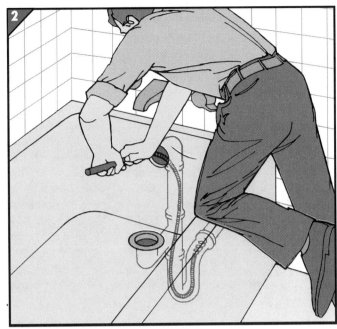

1. Gaining access to the drain.

To unclog a bathtub, unscrew the overflow plate and lift it up and out. Draw out the pop-up stopper and its linkage. Note how the parts line up so that you can put them back in the same way.

OVERFLOW PLATE

POP-UP STOPPER AND LINKAGE

2. Inserting the auger.

◆ Cranking the auger handle clockwise, feed the auger tip through the tub overflow opening.

◆ When the auger wire reaches the blockage, move the auger slowly backward and forward while cranking. Continue to crank clockwise as you withdraw the auger wire; doing so helps to prevent you from dropping the material that caused the blockage.

◆ After clearing the drain, run hot water through it for 2 to 3 minutes.

OPENING A TOILET DRAIN WITH A CLOSET AUGER

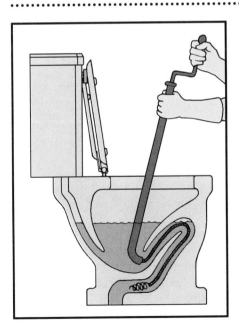

Unclogging a toilet.

The cranking handle of a closet auger attaches to a long sleeve shaped to help guide the tip of the auger into the trap. Closet augers work equally well in toilets with a front drain opening, as shown at left, or with the opening at the back.

◆ Hold the sleeve near the top and position the other end against the drain opening. Crank the auger tip slowly clockwise into the trap until you hook the obstruction or break through it.

◆ Withdraw the auger while cranking the handle clockwise. If the drain remains clogged, repeat the process.

◆ When the drain seems clear, test it with a pail of water before attempting to flush the toilet.

Simple Toilet Repairs

Understanding how the mechanisms inside a toilet tank work can make their repair fairly simple. Certain parts vary, but most operate according to the same scheme. When you press the handle, a lift wire or a chain pulls a stopper off the opening to the bowl. Water rushes into the bowl. The falling water level in the tank causes a float to drop. This, in turn, opens the ball cock—the device that starts and stops the refill cycle. When the tank is nearly empty, the stopper drops into place. Rising water then lifts the float high enough to shut off the ball cock.

Diagnosing the Problem: One way to spot a mechanical breakdown is to lift the tank lid and watch a flush cycle. Also be alert to noises and leaks. The sound of water running constantly may indicate that the tank ball is not properly seated *(opposite)*. A high whine or whistle during flushing means that the ball cock needs attention *(pages 68-69)*. Visible leaks near the tank may be caused by loose bolts, worn washers, or condensation *(page 70)*.

Working Near Porcelain: Most toilets are made of vitreous china, which is easily cracked or broken. Set the lid on padding in an out-of-the-way place while working in the tank, and use gentle pressure when removing or tightening bolts. As shown on page 71, it may be safer to cut corroded seat-cover bolts than to strain to remove them with a wrench near fragile porcelain.

 TOOLS

Adjustable wrench
Plastic cleansing pad or steel wool
Locking-grip pliers
Long-nose pliers

Socket wrench with deep sockets
Screwdriver
Hacksaw

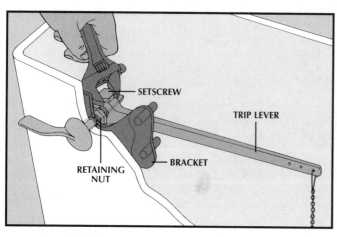

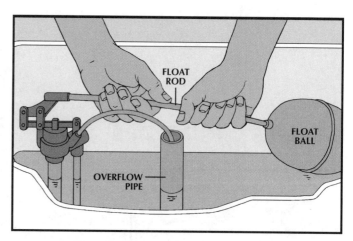

Tightening the handle.

If a toilet handle must be held down until the flush cycle is complete, the linkage between the handle and the trip lever needs to be secured.

◆ For a toilet with a bracket arrangement like the one above, tighten the retaining nut with an adjustable wrench so the bracket does not wobble but still moves freely when the handle is turned. Turn the nut counterclockwise—the opposite direction from that used to tighten most nuts. With a wrench or pliers, turn the trip-lever setscrew against the handle shaft.

◆ In models that have a one-piece handle and trip lever, tighten the nut that holds the handle on its shaft. This nut also must be tightened counterclockwise.

Adjusting the water level.

If water is cascading through the overflow pipe into the bowl, lower the water level by replacing the float ball or adjusting the float rod.

◆ Unscrew the float ball and examine it; if it is worn or there is water in it, replace it.

◆ If the ball is sound, bend the float rod $\frac{1}{2}$ inch downward with both hands *(above)*. Alternatively, unscrew the rod with pliers and bend it over a rounded surface, then put it back. The rod may break when bent; if that happens, replace it with a new one. Reattach the ball.

◆ Flush the toilet. The water should stop rising about $\frac{1}{2}$ inch below the top of the overflow pipe. If it does not, the rod must be readjusted.

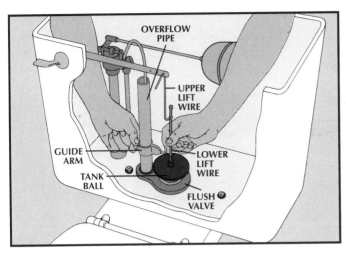

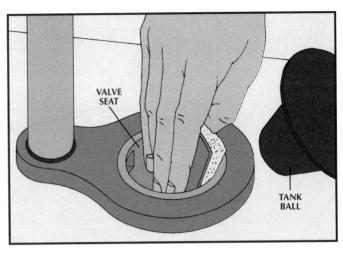

Adjusting the tank ball.

If water runs constantly into the bowl from the tank, sometimes making the toilet flush, first try reseating the tank ball.

◆ Turn off the water at the shutoff valve and remove the lid.

◆ Flush the toilet. If the tank ball does not fall straight into the flush valve opening, loosen the thumbscrew fastening the guide arm to the overflow pipe *(above)*.

◆ Reposition the arm and the lower lift wire so the tank ball is centered over the flush valve. If necessary, straighten the lift wires.

◆ Turn the water on. If the leak persists, clean mineral deposits off the ball and valve seat *(right)*.

Cleaning the tank ball and valve seat.

◆ Turn off the water and empty the tank.

◆ Unscrew the tank ball and wash it with warm water and detergent. If the ball is worn, replace it with a modern flapper ball hinged to prevent misalignment *(below)*.

◆ Gently scour the seat of the flush valve with fine steel wool or a plastic cleansing pad *(above)*.

◆ Replace the ball and turn on the water. If the valve still leaks, a special replacement flush valve seat can be placed over the old one. To replace the old valve seat completely, remove the tank as shown on page 70.

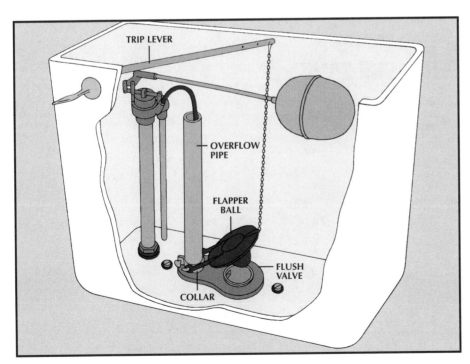

Installing a hinged flapper ball.

◆ Turn off the water, drain the tank, and remove the old guide arm, lift wires, and tank ball.

◆ Slide the collar of the flapper ball to the bottom of the overflow pipe and align the ball over the flush valve. If there is a thumbscrew on the collar, tighten it.

◆ Hook the chain from the ball through a hole in the trip lever directly above, leaving about $\frac{1}{2}$ inch of slack.

◆ Turn the water on, flush the toilet, and check whether the tank drains completely. If it does not, lessen the slack or move the chain one or two holes toward the rear of the lift arm.

REPAIRING THE TANK'S FILL MECHANISM

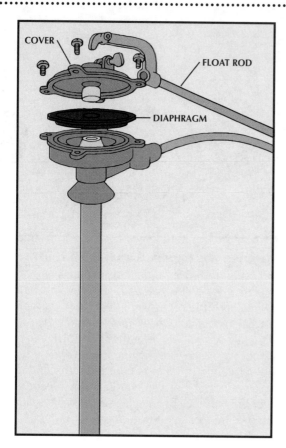

Servicing a ball cock.
When a diaphragm ball cock or a float-cup ball cock develops a minor leak, repair it with parts available at plumbing-supply stores. Replace other, older types of ball cocks *(below)* rather than attempting repairs.

◆ Shut off the water and flush the toilet.

◆ Remove the top screws and lift off the cover and float rod assembly.

◆ In a diaphragm ball cock *(left),* take out and replace the diaphragm, rubber gaskets, and washers. For a float-cup ball cock like the one shown opposite, replace the rubber valve seal and washers.

◆ Attach the ball cock cover and turn the water on. If the ball cock still leaks, or appears worn-out, replace it.

A DEVICE FOR REPLENISHING THE TANK

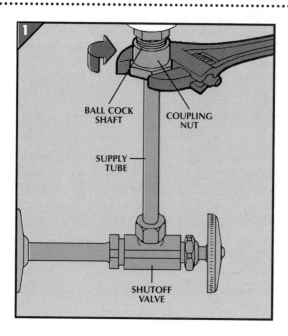

1. Disconnecting the supply tube.

◆ Turn off the water at the shutoff valve, flush the toilet, and sponge out the remaining water from the tank.

◆ With an adjustable wrench, unscrew the coupling nut on the underside of the tank that attaches the supply tube to the ball cock shaft *(left).*

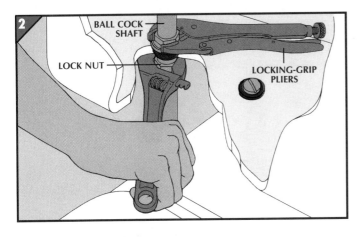

2. Removing the ball cock.

◆ Inside the tank, attach locking-grip pliers to the base of the ball cock shaft. The pliers will wedge against the side of the tank and free your hands.

◆ With an adjustable wrench, unscrew the lock nut that secures the ball cock shaft on the underside of the tank *(left)*. Use firm but gentle pressure to avoid cracking the tank.

◆ If the nut resists, soak it with penetrating oil for 10 or 15 minutes and try again. Once the nut is removed, lift the ball cock out of the tank.

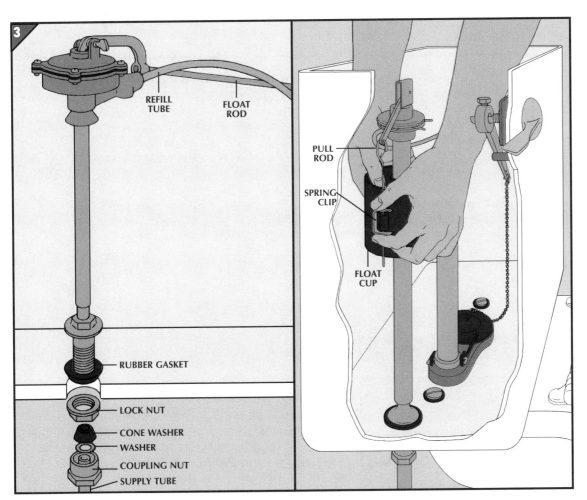

3. Installing a modern ball cock.

Diaphragm ball cocks and float-cup ball cocks are secured in place in the same way. Float-cup ball cocks require a simple adjustment as well. Float-cup ball cocks come in several heights; measure your tank depth before buying one.

◆ Put the new ball cock shank through the rubber gasket supplied with it and through the hole in the tank. Then screw a lock nut onto the ball cock shaft underneath the tank.

◆ Inside the tank, hold the base of the ball cock with locking-grip pliers. Tighten the lock nut.

◆ Insert a new washer in the coupling nut on the supply tube; some supply tubes come with built-in washers. If the tube extends through the nut and washer, place a cone washer over the tube *(above, left)*. Screw the coupling nut to the bottom of the ball cock shaft.

◆ Attach the float rod assembly and refill tube, and turn the water back on at the shutoff valve.

For a float-cup ball cock, adjust the ball cock to change the water level in the tank. To raise the level, pinch the spring clip on the ball cock's pull rod and slide the float cup higher *(above, right)*. To lower the water, move the cup down.

SEALING LEAKS AT BOLTS AND GASKETS

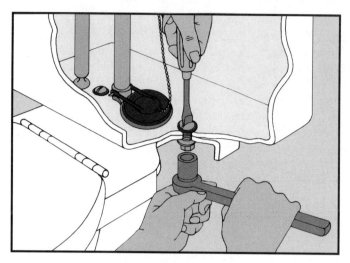

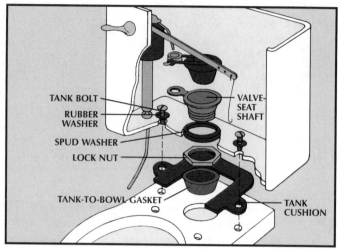

Tightening the tank bolts.

Drips at the tank bolts may be caused by condensation on the tank's exterior, or by seepage from the inside. To check, pour a few drops of food coloring into the tank and hold white tissue over the bolts. If the tissue turns that color, tighten the bolts to stop the leaks.

◆ Turn off the water and drain the tank. Hold the slotted head of the bolt with a screwdriver or have a helper do it.
◆ Tighten the nut below the tank with a socket wrench and a deep socket *(above)*, or use an adjustable wrench.
◆ Turn the water back on.
◆ If the leak persists, drain the tank, remove the bolts, and replace their washers.

Replacing flush-valve washers.

If water leaks outside the toilet at the connection between tank and bowl, you must remove the tank.

◆ Turn off the water, drain the tank, disconnect the supply tube *(page 68)*, and unscrew the tank bolts.
◆ Lift the tank off the bowl and set it on its back on a padded work surface.
◆ The components that connect the tank and bowl appear above in diagrammatic form. Remove the lock nut on the valve-seat shaft protruding from the tank bottom, then pull the shaft into the tank and replace the spud washer and tank-to-bowl gasket. Reattach the lock nut.
◆ Place the tank on the tank cushion, reconnect the tank bolts, and attach the supply tube. Turn on the water.

PREVENTING TOILET TANK CONDENSATION

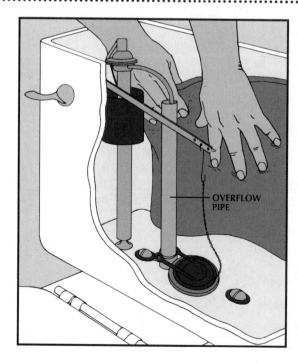

Installing insulation pads.

Condensation on the outside of a toilet tank may signal other problems, such as a constant leak from tank to bowl. If temperature or humidity is the cause, line the tank with a waterproof insulating material such as foam rubber.

◆ Turn off the water, drain the tank, and sponge it dry.
◆ Measure the inside width and depth of the tank and the height from the bottom of the tank to a point 1 inch above the overflow pipe.
◆ Cut four pieces of $\frac{1}{2}$-inch-thick foam rubber to fit the front, the back, and each side.
◆ Trim 1 inch from the width of the front and back pieces so they will abut the side pieces.
◆ Make a cutout for the toilet handle, and be sure the pads do not interfere with other moving parts.
◆ Apply a liberal coating of silicone glue or rubber cement to the inside tank surfaces; press the pads in place *(left)*.
◆ Let the glue dry 24 hours before refilling the tank.

REPLACING A TOILET SEAT

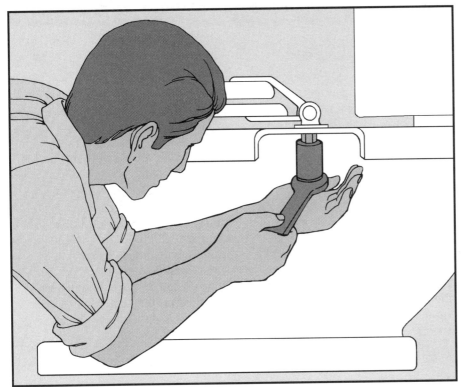

Removing the seat bolts.
To take off an old toilet seat, unscrew the nuts underneath the bowl. First try to turn the nuts with long-nose pliers. Should that fail, twist gently using a socket wrench with a deep socket *(left)*. If the seat bolts are too corroded to loosen, apply the methods below.

Many toilet seats have nylon fasteners that do not require a wrench; turn these with a coin.

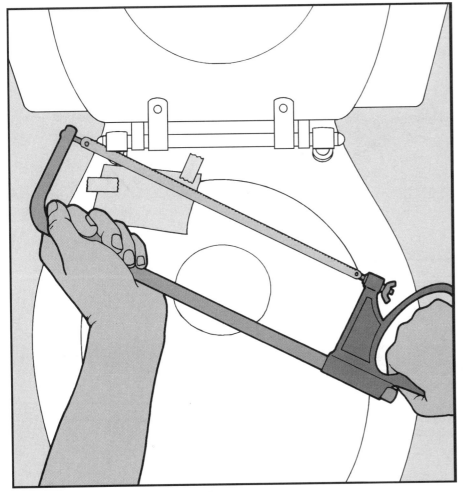

Freeing corroded bolts.
◆ Soak the bolts with penetrating oil for at least 30 minutes—overnight is better still. Then try loosening the nuts once more.
◆ If penetrating oil does not free the nuts, tape thin cardboard on top of the bowl next to the heads of the bolts to protect the china. Then, with a hacksaw, cut off the boltheads, sawing through the attached washers *(left)*.

Making the Bathroom Safe and Accessible

Most bathrooms combine at least three potentially dangerous elements: electricity, water, and slick surfaces. You can improve the safety of your bathroom and the ease with which you can use it by undertaking some or all of the modest projects described here and on pages 73-75.

Measures against Falls: A water-slicked shower floor or tub can be dangerous. To reduce the likelihood of accident, add texture to either surface with grip strips *(below)*.

Also consider installing grab bars *(page 73)* as handholds on walls surrounding the bathing area. Towel

bars are too weak to rely on. Choose grab bars made from metal tubing without sharp corners. And avoid hanging towels on them; someone could accidentally grasp the towel instead and fall.

Preventing Electric Shock: To minimize the hazards of operating electrical appliances near water, the National Electrical Code requires that new bathroom electrical circuits be equipped with a device that is called a ground-fault circuit interrupter, or GFCI. If your bathroom does not have this protection, you can add it by installing a GFCI

outlet in place of the receptacle that already exists *(page 192)*.

Adaptations for Disabilities: For someone with a disability, the typical bathroom can be difficult, or even impossible, to use. Ideally, a bathroom for a family member who needs a wheelchair, a walker, or simply some assistance with standing up or sitting down is designed from the outset for their comfort and capabilities. As described on pages 74 and 75, you can also make an old bathroom somewhat more accessible with a variety of products and modifications.

APPLYING GRIP STRIPS

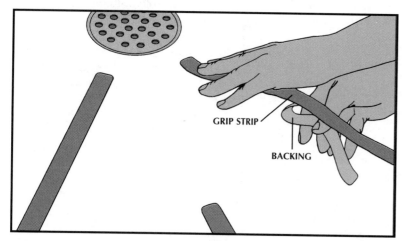

GRIP STRIP

BACKING

Laying a safe pattern of strips.
◆ Wash the shower or tub floor, clean it with rubbing alcohol, and let it dry.
◆ For a shower, plan a star pattern of strips *(below, far left)*; for a tub, arrange strips both in a chevron pointed at the drain and in parallel lines *(below, near left)*.
◆ To apply each strip, peel the backing from one end and press it firmly in place, then continue peeling as you work *(left)*. If you must cut a strip, round the corners so they will not curl later.

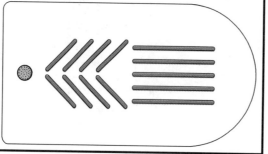

GRAB BARS FOR SHOWER AND TUB

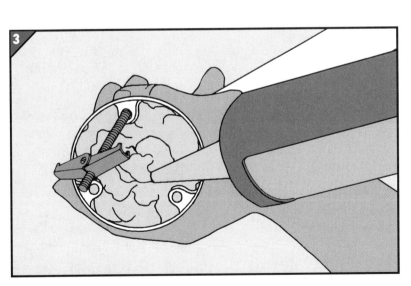

1. Positioning the bar.

The grab bar shown here is designed so each flange is anchored in a stud by a screw and toggle bolt. (To support someone weighing more than 250 pounds, double the studs from the other side of the wall and use three screws.)

◆ Locate studs above the tile with an electronic stud finder.

◆ Drop a plumb line at the center of each stud and mark the width of the stud with masking tape at the height you intend to anchor the flanges.

◆ Place the grab bar so that two mounting holes in each flange lie on the tape. Mark all six hole locations with a pencil (above).

2. Drilling holes.

◆ At each hole location, tap a punch with a hammer to break through the slick tile glaze.

◆ Wearing safety goggles, use a carbide-tipped bit to drill a $\frac{1}{2}$-inch hole through the wall for each toggle bolt. For the screws, drill a hole through the tile slightly larger than the screw diameter, then use an ordinary bit to drill a smaller hole into the wooden stud.

◆ Remove the tape from the wall.

3. Mounting the bar.

◆ Insert a $\frac{3}{16}$-inch toggle bolt into its hole on a flange and fill the inside of the flange with silicone caulk (above). Prepare the other flange the same way.

◆ Position the bar on the wall, pushing the toggle bolts into place. Insert 3-inch-long screws into the remaining holes and tighten screws and toggle bolts with a screwdriver.

◆ Caulk around each flange and let dry for 24 hours.

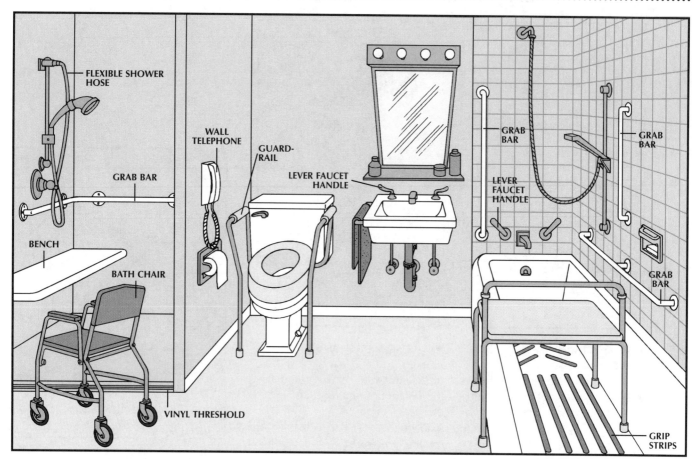

Helpful modifications.

Few bathrooms offer all the features in the composite illustration above, but a person with a disability may find several of them beneficial.

A roll-in shower. For a family member who uses a wheelchair or bath chair, consider a shower with a low flexible-vinyl threshold; either vehicle can easily roll across, and the vinyl keeps water from flowing out. Once inside, a bather may transfer to a bench seat.

An accessible telephone. A wall phone with the dial or keypad in the handset provides a link to help.

Washbasin access. A wall-hung basin lets someone in a wheelchair roll up to the sink; insulate the hot-water pipe to prevent burns.

Lever handles. Equip faucets with long handles, rather than knobs that must be grasped.

An easier-to-use toilet. A thicker-than-usual toilet seat and adjustable guardrails may help someone who has difficulty sitting down or standing up. Alternatively, install a grab bar beside the toilet.

A nonslip floor. Floor tiles in a bathroom are a poor choice for someone who may slip and fall. Carpet or vinyl sheet flooring are among the alternatives.

A convenient mirror. Tilt mirrors downward a bit to make them useful for a person in a wheelchair.

Grab bars and grip strips. As in any bathroom, grab bars and grip strips in tubs and showers help to prevent falls while bathing.

Seating in the bath. Place a bench or bath chair in a tub or shower; install a showerhead with a flexible hose, and mount it on a sliding bar or within easy reach.

Easing the Way for a Wheelchair

✔ A door opening 32 inches wide is usable if the bathroom opens onto a wide hallway, but an opening of 36 inches is better.

✔ Inside the bathroom, the clear floor space should be at least 60 inches square to allow a wheelchair to turn around completely.

✔ Sinks must be no more than 34 inches high, and they must not rest on a vanity.

✔ Buy an add-on toilet seat from a medical-supply store to raise the seat 4 inches—the same height as most wheelchair seats.

✔ Mount such items as the telephone at 33 to 36 inches.

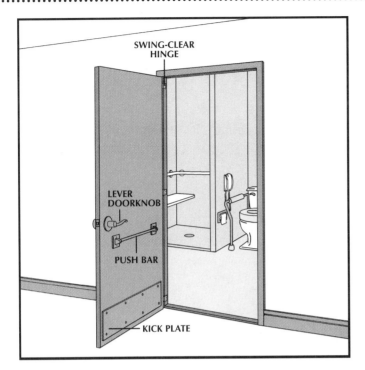

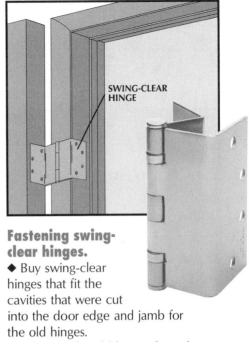

A doorway that provides easier access.

To maximize the width of a door opening, install a pocket door or a sliding door. Rehang a hinged door to open outward *(above)*; you can increase its effective width with swing-clear hinges *(right)*, which add $1\frac{1}{2}$ to 2 inches to the opening. Other useful door hardware includes a kick plate, a lever doorknob *(below)*, and a push bar to help open and close the door.

Fastening swing-clear hinges.

◆ Buy swing-clear hinges that fit the cavities that were cut into the door edge and jamb for the old hinges.

◆ Unscrew the old hinges from the door and the jamb; set the door aside.

◆ If new screw holes are required, pack lengths of dowel, coated with glue, into the existing holes. Let the glue dry overnight, then drill pilot holes for the new screws.

◆ Attach the swing-clear hinges and rehang the door.

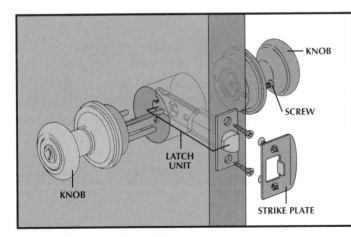

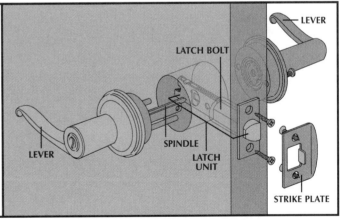

Installing a lever-knob assembly.

◆ Unfasten the two screws that secure the knob plate and pull it off with the knob *(above, left)*. If no screws are visible, depress the metal tab that holds one knob on its shaft. Then remove the knob and the underlying cover plate to reveal the screws.

◆ Pull off the other knob.

◆ Remove the two screws holding the latch unit in place and slide it out of the door.

◆ With a half-round rasp, enlarge the lock and latch holes as needed to accommodate the new mechanism.

◆ Set the latch unit of the lever knob in the door. Screw it to the door edge.

◆ Insert the spindle attached to one of the two lever handles so that it engages the latch unit; then install the other lever. Secure the assembly with screws *(above, right)*.

◆ Check to make sure the strike plate aligns with the latch bolt.

3 CHAPTER

PAINT AND WALLPAPER

Fresh paint is an inexpensive and largely fool-proof way to refurbish a home, and wallpaper makes an attractive alternative or complement to paint. Individually or in combination, paint and wallpaper can transform a room, altering the sense of space, disguising faults, and dramatizing virtues.

Every trade has its tricks, and painting is no exception. This chapter includes helpful techniques and procedures for preparing surfaces, such as stripping old paint, retaping wallboard joints, and repairing cracks and holes in plaster. You'll also find tips on choosing the right tools for applying paint and step-by-step information on painting your home.

Wallpaper is easier to install than ever. New paper, vinyl, and fabric wall coverings, more durable than their predecessors, are often pretrimmed and prepasted. They are tear- and crease-resistant, washable, and more easily removed. The following pages explain how to prepare walls for new paper, describe where to start and where to end, and present a mess-free method for hanging paper. Take the time to plan ahead: An appropriate wall covering, adhesive, and choice of pattern will afford the most pleasing results.

Contrasting tones of yellow and purple combine well in this infant's room, creating a bright and soothing atmosphere. A border featuring peach-colored stenciling completes the effect. ▶

Textured wallpaper above the lintel lends a rich and inviting warmth to this sitting room. A contrasting pattern below adds old-world charm. Wall coverings are available in many different materials, offering a wide variety of textural effects. ▼

Water, acrylic polyure-
thane, and latex paint
were blended together in
equal amounts and then
applied with a sea sponge
to create the subtle, mot-
tled effect on this living-
room wall.

A simple paint scheme of pale yellow
captures the light in this corner.

This opulent room owes its dignified appearance to dark blue wallpaper and a comple-
mentary border. White paint on the trim
keeps the blue from being overwhelming.

Tool Kit for Interior Work

Like most jobs, painting requires a variety of tools and materials. General-purpose items—such as a hammer, a screwdriver, a sturdy knife, a can opener, and masking tape—you probably already have on hand. For cleaning up, you'll need rags and metal containers such as coffee cans or loaf pans.

You may, however, need to purchase many of the tools that are shown here, as well as other items. Buy drop cloths to protect both furniture and floors from paint drips and spatters. You'll also need a sanding block and several grades of sandpaper to smooth repairs to walls and woodwork, and a sponge to clean up dust and dirt and to wash down previously painted walls. As an auxiliary container for paint, a medium-size rustproof pail is ideal.

Appropriate protective gear includes rubber gloves, goggles, and a dust mask. A respirator may be necessary with a few toxic paint removers.

CAULKING GUN

Tools for repairing surfaces.
For patching wallboard, plaster, and trim before painting, you will need both stiff- and flexible-blade putty knives, and a wide-blade putty knife for taping wallboard. Extensive filling of joints around trim and baseboards requires a caulking gun.

6" PUTTY KNIFE

3" PUTTY KNIFE

$1\frac{1}{4}$" PUTTY KNIFE

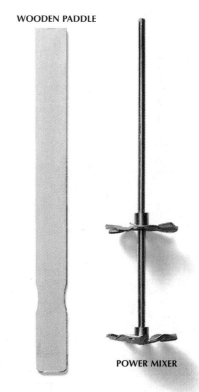

WOODEN PADDLE

POWER MIXER

Mixing tools.
Paint must be stirred thoroughly to cover surfaces evenly. For small quantities, wooden paddles are satisfactory, but a power mixer driven by an electric drill works faster, especially when blending large quantities.

PAINT SHIELD

ROLLER TRAY AND GRATING

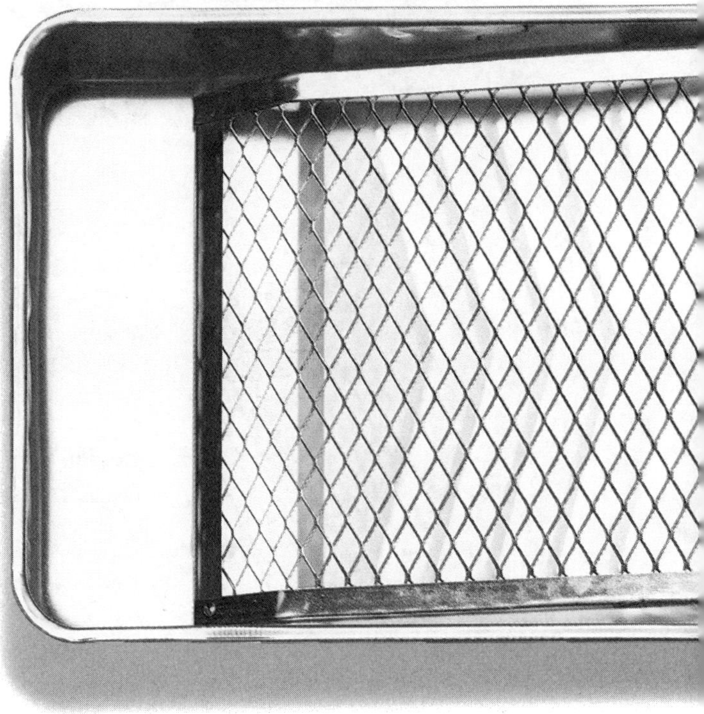

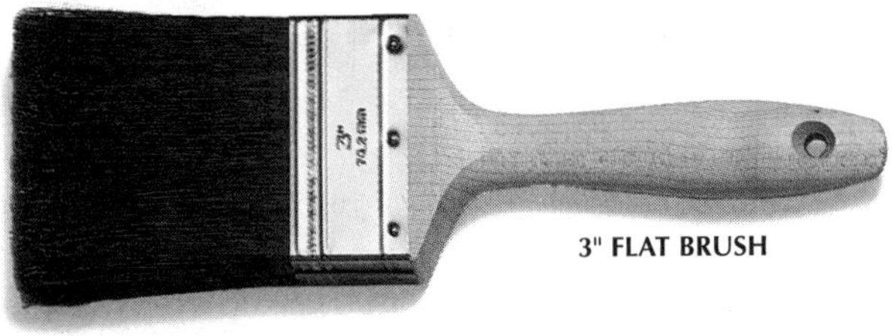

3" FLAT BRUSH

2" CHISEL-EDGE BRUSH

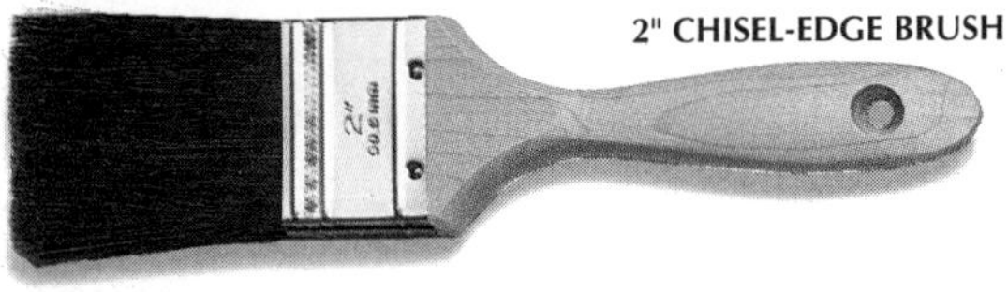

ANGULAR SASH BRUSH

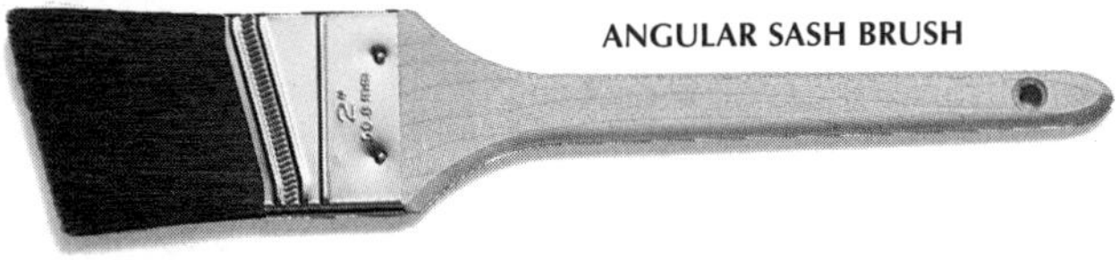

OVAL SASH BRUSH

9" SPRING ROLLER FRAME AND HANDLE

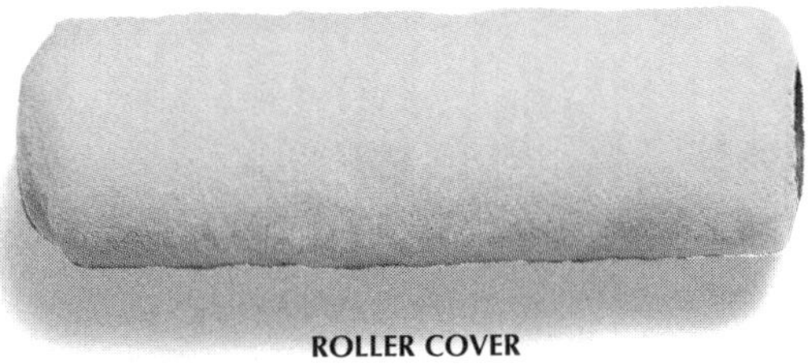

ROLLER COVER

Tools for applying paint.

Rollers and brushes are the main tools for painting interiors. Among the most useful brushes are a 3-inch flat brush for wide trim and flat areas, a chisel-edge brush for edges and corners, and sash brushes for narrow trim. A metal paint shield helps protect nearby surfaces from an errant brush. Rollers consist of a spring frame and a cover. The nap on the cover is loaded with paint from a roller tray; a grating serves to squeeze out excess paint.

WINDOW SCRAPER

PAINTBRUSH COMB

Cleanup tools.

This paintbrush comb cleans and aligns brush bristles and has a curved edge to scrape paint from rollers. The spin-drier slings solvent from rollers and brushes to help dry them. To peel dried paint from glass, use a window scraper.

SPIN-DRIER

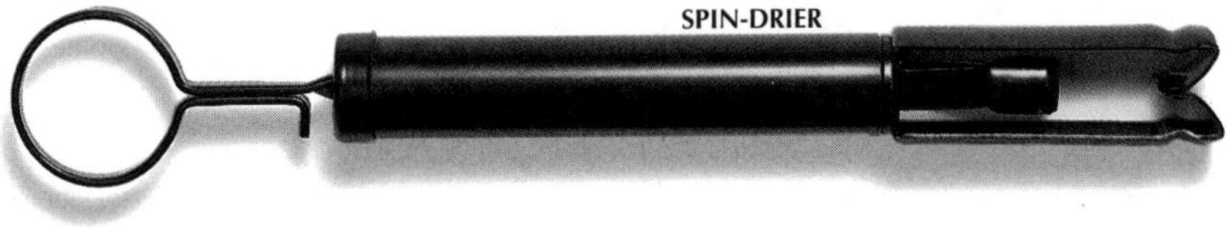

Preparing Interior Surfaces

The durability of any paint job depends largely on the care with which you have prepared the surfaces before you apply the paint.

For virgin wallboard, plaster, or wood, first dust the surface thoroughly, then brush a coat of primer on surfaces that you plan to paint.

If you are working with finished surfaces, try to ascertain whether the material beneath the finish is wallboard or plaster, and the type of surface covering that was used. Such information will help you determine how to proceed with preparation treatments and select the proper undercoatings, primers, and paints. Next, inspect the room thoroughly for damage that may call for repairs.

Dealing with Old Paint: Check for blistering, cracking, or peeling paint and scrape it off *(pages 83-84)* or remove it with a nylon paint stripper that is fitted to an electric drill. If it is necessary for you to remove many layers of paint, consider using a heat gun *(page 130)*. When the damaged paint is near window glass, strip it with a chemical paint remover rather than risk breaking the glass with a power tool *(page 84)*.

Concealing Flaws: Repair damaged wallboard or plaster *(pages 85-89)*, and fill in gouges, holes, and cracks in walls and trim. When choosing a filler, read the label to be sure the product is compatible with the finish you plan to use. Build up depressions and conceal nails with spackling compound. Use the same material to repair short open joints; longer gaps—along a baseboard, for example—are better caulked than patched with spackling compound.

On surfaces that are bare and those that have been painted, follow repair work with a thorough sanding. Electric sanders speed the work, but for small areas, a sanding block works well.

Special Surfaces: New paint will not adhere properly to glossy surfaces; dull such finishes by raising a nap with sandpaper or a liquid deglosser. Strip off wallpaper *(pages 95 and 98-99)*. If floor wax has adhered to baseboards, take it off with wax remover. Brush rust from radiators, pipes, and heat ducts, and clean mildew from damp places with a solution of chlorine bleach diluted in water.

Cleaning: Dirt, grease, and even fingerprints can prevent new paint from adhering firmly. A good washing down with a heavy-duty household detergent just before painting will usually suffice for finished walls and woodwork. Finally, be sure that surfaces are completely dry before painting.

⚠️ **CAUTION** *Paint strippers, solvents, and cleaning agents can give off harmful fumes. Keep children and pets out of the work area. Read labels of products for special requirements, and keep the labels on hand should you need to call a doctor. Work only in a ventilated room. Open doors and windows, and use fans to dispel fumes. Wash any coating off your skin as soon as you can, and scrub up carefully after each session. Dispose of all solvents and other toxic chemicals in an approved manner. Call your local sanitation department or environmental protection office for advice.*

 TOOLS

Putty knives
(flexible-and
stiff-blade)
Inexpensive
paintbrush

 **MATERIALS**

Sandpaper
(fine- and
medium-grit)
Spackling
compound
Primer
Paint remover
Paint solvent

 **SAFETY TIPS**

Protect your hands from cleaning agents and paint solvents. Wear rubber gloves and goggles to apply paint remover, and add a respirator if the product contains methylene chloride. When sanding, wear a dust mask.

CAUTION

Safety Measures for Lead and Asbestos

Lead and asbestos, known health hazards, pervade houses constructed, remodeled, or redecorated before 1978. Test all painted surfaces for lead with a kit, available at hardware stores, or call your local health department or environmental protection office for other options. Asbestos was once a component of wallboard, joint compound, acoustic or decorative ceiling and wall materials, duct insulation, and heatproofing materials. Mist such materials with a solution of 1 teaspoon low-sudsing detergent per quart of water to suppress dust, then remove small samples for testing by a National Institute of Standards and Technology-certified lab.

Paint preparation where lead or asbestos is present requires a tightly fitting respirator and protective clothing that's hot to wear. Hire a professional licensed in hazardous-substance removal if you suffer from cardiac or respiratory problems or don't tolerate heat well. And hire a professional for indoor jobs that require disturbing large areas of these materials.

When working with hazardous materials, take the following precautions:

❗ Keep children, pregnant women, and pets out of the work area.

❗ Indoors, seal off the work area from the rest of the house with 6-mil polyethylene sheeting and duct tape and turn off air conditioning and forced-air heating systems. Cover rugs and furniture that can't be removed with more sheeting and tape.

❗ Wear protective clothing (available from a safety equipment supply house or paint store) and a dual-cartridge respirator with high efficiency particulate air (HEPA) filters.

❗ If you must use a power sander on paint containing lead, get one equipped with a HEPA-filter vacuum, but never sand asbestos-laden materials or cut them with power machinery. Mist them with water and detergent, and remove with a hand tool.

❗ Avoid tracking dust from the work area into other parts of the house, and take off protective clothing (including shoes) before leaving the work area. Shower and wash hair immediately. Wash clothing separately.

❗ When you finish indoor work, mop the area twice, then run a vacuum cleaner equipped with a HEPA filter. Dispose of materials as recommended by your local health department or environmental protection office.

REPAIRING FLAWS IN PAINT

Scraping paint.
Insert the edge of a $1\frac{1}{4}$-inch-wide putty knife under the loose paint *(left)*, and being careful not to gouge the surface, scrape with a pushing motion. For more extensive areas, larger-sized scrapers are available.

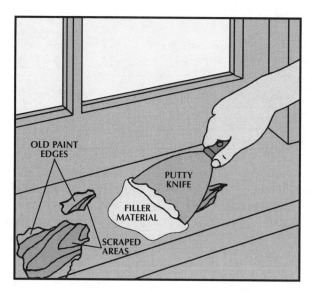

Filling in depressions.

◆ Apply spackling compound to a small depression with a flexible-blade putty knife; use a wide-blade putty knife for extensive filling *(left)*.

◆ When the filler has dried, sand it flush with the surface.

◆ Spot-prime all scraped or filled areas before repainting.

OLD PAINT EDGES

PUTTY KNIFE

FILLER MATERIAL

SCRAPED AREAS

STRIPPING PAINT

1. Applying paint remover.

On most surfaces, a paste-type, water-base remover is safest. However, water in the paint remover may lift or buckle a wood veneer; use a solvent-base remover instead.

◆ Protect the surrounding area with a thick layer of newspaper.

◆ With a clean, inexpensive paintbrush, spread a generous amount of remover on the area to be stripped *(above)*. Work with short strokes, brushing in one direction, and do not cover an area more than 2 feet square at one time.

2. Scraping off the paint.

◆ When the paint begins to blister and wrinkle, peel it off with a putty knife *(above)*.

◆ As you remove the paint, clean the knife frequently with newspaper.

◆ When all paint is off, clean the bare surface using a wash of water or solvent as the label directs.

◆ Wait for the surface to dry, then smooth it lightly with fine-grit sandpaper.

Making Old Walls As Smooth As New

Before painting a room, you must correct all defects in walls and ceilings. Explained here and on the following pages are repair techniques both for wallboard (nowadays the standard building material) and for plaster.

Wallboard Repairs: Although builders now use screws to fasten wallboard to studs and joists, at one time they attached it with nails, which can pull away and protrude over time. Any such "popped" nail must be reseated with a hammer and covered with joint compound.

Sometimes the taped seams between wallboard panels open up because of temperature changes or settling of a house. The gap can be closed with conventional paper tape or, in a step-saving method, with a fiberglass-mesh tape (*box, page 86*).

Tactics for dealing with holes depend on the scale of the damage. You can fill in nail holes simply by covering them with ready-mixed vinyl spackling compound. For holes up to 1 inch across, stuff a wad of newspaper into the hole to give the compound something to adhere to. Larger holes—up to 6

inches across—require the more substantial backing of wire screening fastened to the inside of the wallboard (*page 87*).

Patching Faults in Plaster: The basic strategy for plaster repairs is to clear away the damaged plaster, fill in the hole or crack, and sand the patch flush with the wall. For secure bonding of the patching material, large holes must be undercut so they are wider at the lath than at the surface. All plaster patches are topped with a layer of spackling or wallboard joint compound.

 TOOLS

Putty knives
Sanding block
Finishing knife (10")
Scissors
Can opener

 **MATERIALS**

Wallboard joint compound
Sandpaper (fine-grit)
Wallboard joint tape
Wire screening
String
Patching plaster

 SAFETY TIPS

To keep from inhaling dust while sanding, wear a cartridge-type respirator.

RETAPING WALLBOARD JOINTS

1. Filling the joints.
◆ Remove any loose or damaged tape and crumbled joint compound from between the sections of wallboard.
◆ Spread a $\frac{1}{8}$-inch-thick layer of joint compound directly over the joint with a 6-inch-wide putty knife, pressing the knife firmly against the wallboard to force the compound into the joint (*left*).

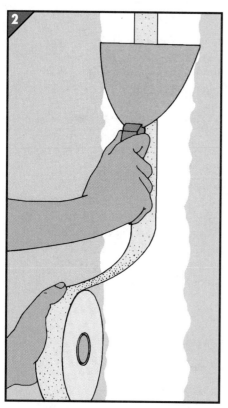

3. Covering the tape.
◆ Apply a thin, smooth layer of joint compound over the tape *(left)*. Use enough compound to extend this second layer about 1 inch beyond the edges of the layer applied in Step 1.
◆ Let the patch dry completely. Unless the weather is humid, this should take about 24 hours.

2. Applying the tape.
Before the joint compound dries, cover the filled seam with a single, unbroken piece of joint tape as follows:
◆ Roll out a 2-foot section of perforated paper joint tape.
◆ Center the end of the tape over the top of the joint, and press it into the joint compound.
◆ With the tape in one hand and the knife in the other, draw the knife over the tape at a 45-degree angle to embed it in the joint compound *(above)*. Unroll more tape in 2-foot sections as needed. If the tape wrinkles or veers away from the joint, lift it up carefully and recenter it.
◆ At the end of the seam, cut the tape from the roll.

When repairing only a short section of a joint, slightly overlap the ends of the old tape with the new tape.

A QUICKER JOINT WITH FIBERGLASS TAPE
Although perforated paper tape is the traditional material for covering wallboard joints, you can save some time by using fiberglass-mesh tape instead. Because this product is sticky on one side, you do not have to first apply joint compound to the seam for attachment. Simply stretch the mesh tape along the joint, pressing it down so that it adheres, then follow Steps 3 and 4 to finish the seam.

FIBERGLASS-
MESH TAPE

FINISHING KNIFE

4. Applying the final coat.

This completion of the repair goes fastest if you use a 10-inch finishing knife instead of the 6-inch putty knife.

◆ Smooth on a very thin finish coat of joint compound in a layer about 10 to 12 inches wide *(left)*.

◆ Let the patch dry.

◆ Sand the area with fine-grit sandpaper wrapped around a sanding block, feathering the edges.

FILLING HOLES IN WALLBOARD

1. Patching large holes.

◆ Remove the loose or torn wallboard around the opening.

◆ Cut a piece of wire screening that is slightly larger than the hole. Thread a length of string through the middle of the screen.

◆ Wet the inside edges of the hole with water and apply patching plaster to them. Then spread plaster on the inside of the wallboard, around the hole edge.

◆ Insert the screen through the hole *(right)*. Pulling the ends of the string gently, draw the screening flat against the inside of the hole and embed it in the fresh plaster.

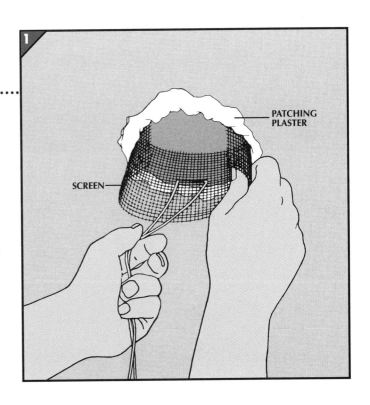

PATCHING PLASTER

SCREEN

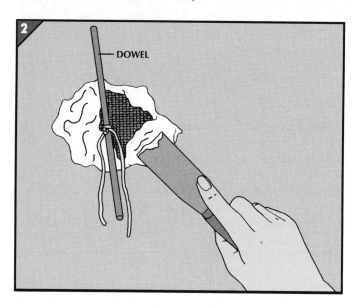

DOWEL

2. Initial filling.
◆ Secure the screen by placing a dowel across the opening and tying the ends of the string firmly around it.
◆ Fill the hole with plaster to a level almost—but not quite—flush with the wallboard surface *(left)*. Leave only a small gap around the string.
◆ Turn the dowel slightly to increase tension on the string and screen.
◆ Let the plaster set for 30 minutes.

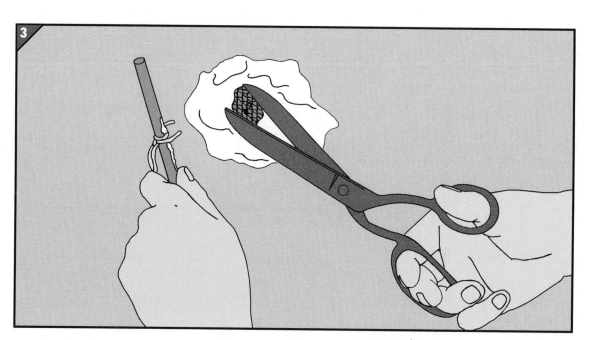

3. Removing the dowel.
◆ Cut the string as close to the screen as possible and then remove the dowel *(above)*.
◆ Wet the edges of the remaining gap and fill the gap with fresh plaster.
◆ Plaster over the entire patch to bring it flush with the wallboard surface.
◆ Allow the patch to set.

4. Final sealing.
◆ With a wide-blade putty knife, spread joint or spackling compound over the patch. Extend this final layer beyond the edges of the previous layer with long, smooth sweeps of the knife.
◆ Let the patch dry for about 24 hours.
◆ Finally, sand the patch with fine-grit sandpaper wrapped around a sanding block. Feather the edges of the patch.

REPAIRING A HAIRLINE CRACK IN PLASTER

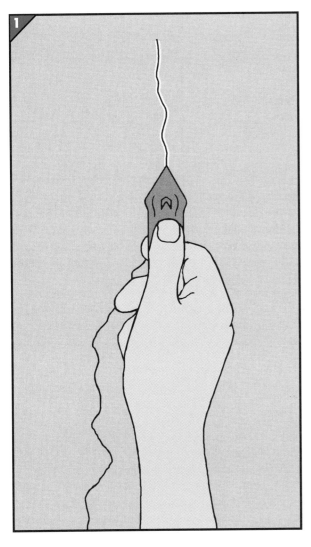

1. Cleaning.
◆ With the tip of a can opener, clear away loose plaster along the edges of the crack *(left)* so that the patching material will have a sound surface to grip.
◆ Remove a bit of the firm plaster at each end of the crack. This will keep the crack from extending farther in the future.
◆ Clear all dust out of the crack.

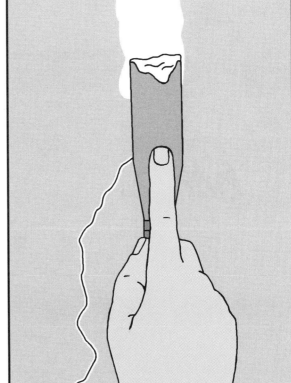

2. Sealing.
◆ Wet the crack and the surrounding area.
◆ Spread joint or spackling compound along the entire length of the crack. Make sure the patching material fills the crack completely and overlaps the solid edges.
◆ Let the patch dry for a day or so. If it shrinks, add another layer and allow it to dry.
◆ Sand the patch smooth.

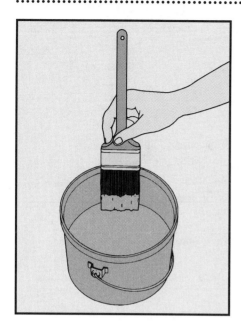

Loading the brush.

This technique helps prevent overloading and reduces the likelihood that paint will run under the ferrule, where dried paint can ruin the brush.

◆ Dip the bristles into the paint no more than halfway.

◆ Tap the ferrule gently against the rim of the pail *(left)* to remove excess paint. Do not wipe the brush across the pail rim; doing so removes too much paint.

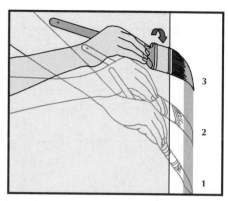

A feathered brush stroke.

Make the length of each stroke about double the length of the bristles. Wherever possible, end the stroke in the wet paint of a previously painted section.

◆ Start the brush stroke with the flat side of the brush angled low to the surface *(1)*.

◆ As you move the brush, increase the angle gradually *(2)*.

◆ End the stroke by drawing the brush up and off the surface with a slight twist *(3)*; the brush should leave a thin, feathered edge of paint.

◆ If one stroke covers the surface satisfactorily, move on to an adjacent area. Otherwise, repaint the area with a second stroke.

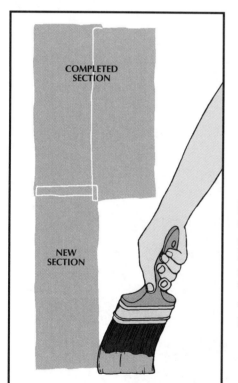

COMPLETED SECTION

NEW SECTION

Painting in sections.

Cover a large surface in sections, each about two brush widths across and two bristle lengths long. With slow-drying paints, you can experiment with painting larger sections.

◆ Paint the first section, using up-and-down strokes combined with the feathering technique shown above.

◆ Then move to an adjacent section, working toward and into the completed area of wet paint *(left)*.

PAINT SHIELD

Guarding as you go.

A metal or plastic paint shield, available where paint is sold, protects surfaces you do not want painted.

◆ Hold the edge of the shield against the surface you want to protect. If there is a gap at the boundary, such as often occurs between walls and baseboards or walls and carpets, gently push the shield into it.

◆ While holding the paint shield in place with one hand, paint along the length of the shield with the other hand *(left)*.

◆ Remove the shield and wipe it clean. Then reposition the shield and paint the next section.

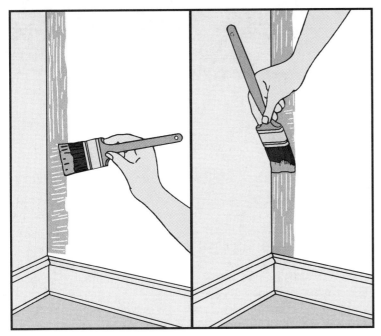

Cutting in.

◆ Make four or five 2-inch-long overlapping brush strokes perpendicular to the edge of the wall or ceiling *(far left)*. (At the bottom of the wall, make the last stroke about $\frac{1}{2}$ inch above the baseboard.)

◆ Smooth over the brush strokes with one long stroke. Wherever possible, end the stroke in an area of wet paint *(near left)* and use it to cover the small gap above a baseboard.

◆ Repeat this procedure along the edge of the adjacent wall or ceiling.

AN INITIAL ZIGZAG

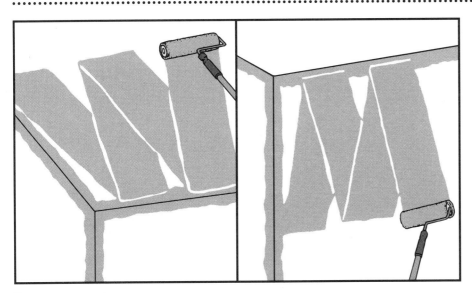

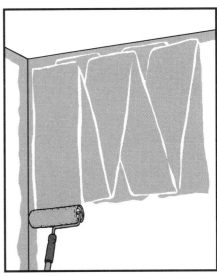

1. Starting a wall or ceiling section.

When painting with a roller, always make the first stroke away from you.

◆ To paint a ceiling, begin at a corner, about 3 feet away from one wall and overlapping the cut-in strip on the adjacent wall.

◆ Without lowering the roller from the ceiling, make three more strokes—alternately toward and away from you—to form a letter "W" about 3 feet square *(above, left)*.

On a wall, push the roller upward on the first stroke and then complete an "M" pattern *(above, right)*.

2. Completing the section.

Fill in the "W" or "M" pattern with crisscrossing strokes of the roller without lifting it from the surface. Use even pressure to avoid bubbles and blotches, and stop when the entire section is evenly covered with paint.

Reload the roller with paint, then repeat the preceding two-step sequence in the next section.

Painting a Room in Sequence

To minimize drips and smears, work systematically from the top to the bottom of a room: Paint the ceiling first, then the walls, then windows, doors, and other woodwork, and finally the baseboards.

Ceiling and Walls: Plan on painting the entire ceiling and each wall without stopping. A roller attached to a 4- or 5-foot extension pole is ideal for reaching a ceiling. On a textured surface, be sure to use a roller with a long nap.

On walls, some people prefer to paint in vertical portions from top to bottom. However, if you are using a roller on an extension pole to reach the top of the wall, you may find it easier to work horizontally, to avoid attaching the roller to—and removing it from—the pole more than once.

Windows and Doors: Painting double-hung windows in the sequence that is shown on the opposite page will solve the tricky problem of your having to move the sashes to paint surfaces that are obstructed by the lower sash. Paint the horizontal parts of the frame with back-and-forth strokes of the brush and the vertical parts with up-and-down strokes.

With doors, follow the techniques that are described on page 90 to achieve best results.

CEILINGS AND WALLS

A basic pattern.
Paint a 2-inch-wide strip around the edges of the ceiling using the cutting-in technique described on page 91. Start painting the ceiling at a corner (A or B), then work back and forth across the short dimension of the ceiling in 3-foot-square sections, as indicated by the arrows. To prevent lap marks caused when wet paint is laid over dry, blend the paint at the edges of adjacent sections before the paint on either dries. After coating the entire ceiling, check your work for missed or thin spots, and revisit them with a roller lightly loaded with paint.

Before painting a wall, cut in not only along the edges, but also around the entire frame of any door or window and along baseboards. Apply paint across the wall in tiers, beginning at corner A or B and alternating direction as with the ceiling. Check your work for missed spots.

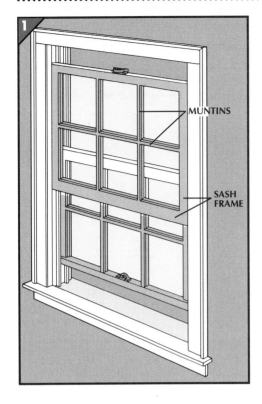

MUNTINS

SASH FRAME

1. Starting on the sashes.

◆ Raise the inside sash and lower the outside sash, leaving each open about 6 inches.

◆ Paint the inner sash first, omitting the top edge. Begin with the muntins (horizontals then verticals), followed by the sash frame (horizontals then verticals). Spread the paint onto the wood allowing a narrow strip—about $\frac{1}{16}$ inch wide—to flow onto the glass and form a seal between the two materials. This irregular edge of paint is best straightened during final cleanup with a window scraper.

◆ On the outside sash, paint the same parts in the same order as far as they are exposed—but do not paint the bottom edge until you paint the house exterior.

JAMB

2. Completing the sashes.

◆ Push up on the bottom of the outside sash and down on the unpainted top of the inside sash, positioning them about 1 inch from their closed positions.

◆ In the same order as in Step 1, paint the surfaces of the outside sash that were obstructed; also paint the top edge of the inside sash.

◆ Proceed to paint the wood framing of the window, starting with the top horizontal. Coat the two side pieces next and finish with the sill.

◆ Wait until all of the paint is thoroughly dry before proceeding to the jambs in Step 3; meanwhile, work on other windows or on doors (page 94).

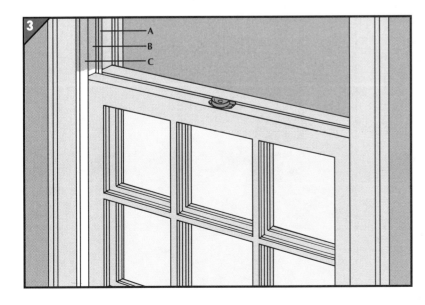

A
B
C

3. Finishing with the jambs.

◆ When the paint is dry to the touch, slide both sashes up and down a few times to make sure they do not stick. Then, push both sashes all the way down to expose the upper jambs (left).

◆ Paint the wooden parts of the upper jambs in the order shown by the letters A through C; metal parts are never painted. Avoid overloading the brush to prevent paint from running into the grooves of the lower jambs.

◆ Let the paint dry, then raise both sashes all the way and paint the lower halves of parts A through C.

◆ Wait for the paint to dry, then lubricate parts A and B of the jambs with paraffin or with silicone spray.

CASEMENT WINDOWS

Windows that open outward.
Casement and awning windows may be made of aluminum, steel, or wood. An aluminum window does not need to be painted, but to protect the metal against dirt and pitting, consider coating it with a metal primer or with a transparent polyurethane varnish. Coat a steel casement with both a metal primer and paint, or with a paint especially suitable to metal, such as an epoxy or polyurethane paint. Treat a wood case-ment the way you would any other interior woodwork—unless the wood is clad in vinyl, which requires no paint.

Before painting, open the window. Working from inside outward and always doing horizontals first and then verticals, paint the parts in this order: muntins, sash frame, hinge edge, window frame and mullion, and sill. Leave the window open until all the paint dries.

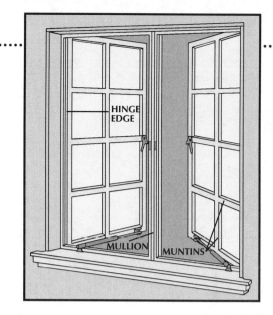

DOORS, CABINETS, AND LOUVERS

Hinged doors.
◆ Cover metal hinges, knobs, and latches with masking tape to protect them from paint spatters.
◆ Work from top to bottom when painting a door. On a panel door, shown at right, paint the panels first, the horizontal rails next, and finally the vertical stiles. The top and bottom edges of a door need be painted only once in its lifetime, to seal the wood and prevent warping.
◆ Paint the latch edge only if the door opens into the room you are painting. The hinge edge of a door is painted the color of the room it faces when the door is open.

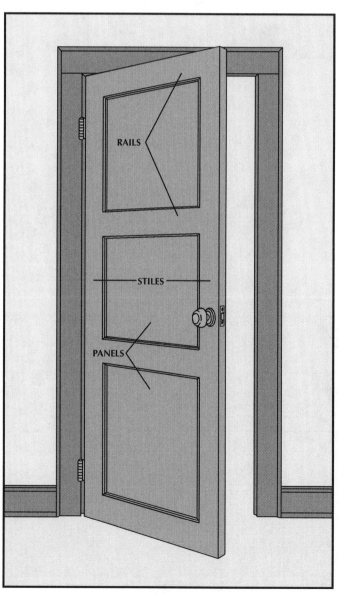

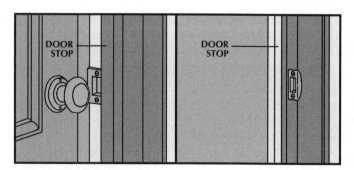

Doorframes and jambs.
◆ Paint the top of the door-frame, then the two sides, followed by the part of the jamb between the frame and the door stop.
◆ Paint the door stop as follows: If the door opens into the next room (*above, left*), paint the side of the door stop that directly faces you and the broad side that faces into the door opening.
◆ If the door opens into the room you are painting, paint only the edge of the door stop that the door closes against (*above, right*).

Preparing Walls for New Paper

Whatever type of surface you are papering over—wood, new wallboard or plaster, paint, a stripped wall, or existing paper—the wall must be properly prepared if the new paper is to adhere well.

Preparing a Painted Surface: Before papering over paint, wash the wall with a household cleaner to remove mildew, dirt, and grease, and rinse well. Lightly push a flexible putty knife along the walls to knock off any loose material and also to help you find popped nails or other imperfections in the wall. Repair damaged surfaces as described on pages 85 through 89, then coat the wall with an opaque all-purpose primer-sealer, which is compatible with all types of papers and adhesives.

Primer-sealer prevents paste from being absorbed into the wall and provides a surface for the new paper to glide onto easily. It binds chalking paint, eliminating the need to remove an old finish, and it roughens semigloss and satin paints for good paper adhesion.

Stripping Paper: Whenever possible, remove old paper; new coverings will always adhere better to a stripped wall. Vinyl or vinyl-coated coverings, which can be identified by their smooth, plastic textures, are called strippable papers because they are easily pulled from a wall. If a test pull at a top corner gets no results, you are probably dealing with a nonstrippable material or a strippable paper applied over unprimed wallboard. Try removing the paper by soaking *(pages 98-99)* or steaming.

If these methods fail—as may happen in a bathroom covered with a vinyl material stuck to the wall with waterproof adhesive—you can dry-scrape the wall *(page 98)*. Once you have stripped the paper, prepare the walls as you would a painted surface.

Papering over Paper: You may decide to apply new paper over an existing wall covering because the wall beneath is too fragile to withstand paper stripping, or because the time you save by leaving the old paper on the wall is more important than the long-term durability of the job.

Applying new wallpaper over old, however, is risky: The water in wallpaper paste can loosen old layers so they pull away from the wall. Make sure the old covering is firmly attached to the wall and as smooth as possible.

Never attempt to paper over more than three layers of paper, no matter how well they seem to be attached. The weight of the additional layer, plus wet wallpaper paste, can pull away the whole sheaf of papers.

Apply spackling compound to smooth the seams, and coat the old paper with opaque all-purpose primer-sealer. If you are applying new paper to vinyl, you must use a vinyl-to-vinyl adhesive, even if the new paper is prepasted.

Final Preparations: Before getting ready to apply new paper, refinish the trim and paint the ceiling if these are part of your redecorating plan. While it is simple to wipe wallpaper paste from woodwork, cleaning paint from new wallpaper is next to impossible.

 TOOLS

Flexible putty knife (3" or 4")
Utility knife
Wall scraper
Sponges
Cheesecloth

 **MATERIALS**

Water
Chemical stripping solution
Primer-sealer

 **SAFETY TIPS**

When you are working with chemical stripping solutions, rubber gloves and goggles are essential. A dust mask prevents droplets of the solution from getting in your mouth and nose.

Tool Kit for Paperhanging

The paperhanging tools shown here are grouped according to the various stages of preparing a room for a wall covering and hanging the paper.

Not every tool in this collection is necessary for every job. The water box, for example, is needed only for prepasted papers, and the artist's brush is used mostly for small repairs to damaged or peeling wallpaper. Tools like the trimming knife and the utility knife are inter-changeable. Some do double duty; a utility knife and the seam roller, for example, are as helpful for minor repairs on previously hung paper as they are in hanging new paper.

All these tools are available at home-improvement and decorating stores; many are packaged as a complete wall-covering tool kit. If you are acquiring tools separately, buy only those you need for your project.

Scraping and repairing.
A wall scraper is the tool used to remove paper without wetting it or to break the surface for soaking. A wide, flexible putty knife helps peel a soaked covering away from a wall. You need a narrower, rigid putty knife if the walls must be repaired before the new covering is applied.

Measuring and marking.
A metal straightedge at least 36 inches long takes measurements and guides long cuts. A plumb bob helps you establish a precise vertical line. The chalk line marks a straight line on a wall; the string coats itself with powdered chalk stored in the case.

FLEXIBLE PUTTY KNIFE

RIGID PUTTY KNIFE

PLUMB BOB

CHALK LINE

METAL STRAIGHTEDGE

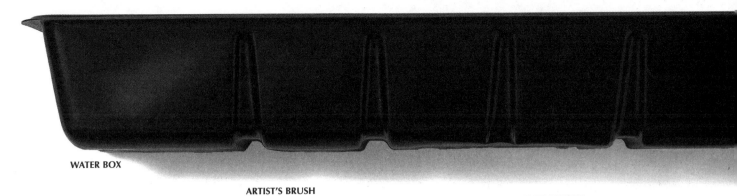

WATER BOX

ARTIST'S BRUSH

PASTE BUCKET

Pasting.

A paste bucket and brush are used to mix and apply adhesive. Water boxes come in several sizes; an extra-long one lets you soak two strips of prepasted paper at a time. The artist's brush is ideal for pasting small tears or peeling corners.

PASTE BRUSH

SEAM ROLLER

TRIMMING GUIDE

Cutting.

Wallpaper can be cut with scissors, a utility knife, or a trimming knife. This utility knife has a segmented blade; snap off the tip when it dulls. The trimming knife uses a single-edged razor blade.

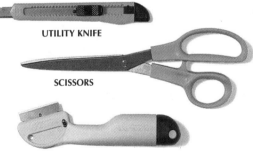

UTILITY KNIFE

SCISSORS

TRIMMING KNIFE

Edging and rolling.

The metal trimming guide creases paper against the wall at a ceiling or baseboard for cutting. A seam roller gives a final smoothing to edges.

SPONGE

SMOOTHING BRUSH

Smoothing and cleaning.

A smoothing brush fixes the paper firmly on the wall. The sponge is for wiping up stray adhesive. For prepasted papers, a sponge is recommended for smoothing instead of the brush.

STRIPPING AND SCRAPING OLD PAPER

Removing strippable wall coverings.
◆ With a fingernail or a utility knife, lift a corner of the covering at the top of a section.
◆ Carefully peel the covering downward, pulling it flat against itself *(left)* to minimize ripping of the paper backing.
◆ Remove any backing that remains stuck to the wall, but leave the fuzzy residue to help the new wall covering adhere.

If the paper surface of wallboard peels off with the wall covering, it was applied without a primer-sealer. Soak the material to remove it *(below)*, or repaste the corner and apply the new wall covering over the old.

Dry-scraping paper.
Nonstrippable papers that cannot be soaked off because of waterproof adhesives must be removed from the wall using a wall scraper.
◆ Hold the blade of the scraper perpendicular to the wall and slit the paper horizontally *(left)*. Apply gentle pressure to avoid damaging wallboard behind the paper.
◆ Slide the blade into a slit at an angle and loosen one section of paper at a time. Tear the loosened sections off with your fingers.

SOAKING PAPER TO REMOVE IT

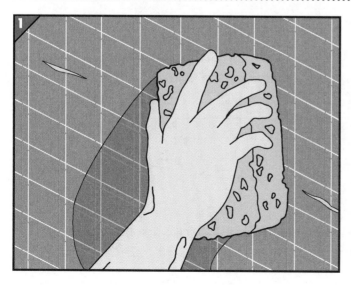

1. Wetting the paper.
A stripping solution of ethyl alcohol and other chemicals or a liquid containing enzymes that break down the organic materials in wallpaper paste works more quickly than plain water.
◆ Spray the paper with a small amount of water. If the water penetrates, there is no need to perforate the paper. Otherwise, you must puncture the paper so that stripping solution can get behind it. Use either the blade of the scraper *(above)* or the perforating tool shown opposite.
◆ With a large sponge or a garden sprayer set for a fine stream, not a mist, wet all the walls with stripping solution *(left)*.
◆ Wait 5 to 10 minutes—or the length of time recommended by the manufacturer—then wet the first wall again and proceed to Steps 2 and 3. (Always resoak a wall before beginning to strip paper.)

A Quick Way to Perforate Paper

Rolling this tool randomly across a wall makes the job of piercing wallpaper easier. Its six wheels, edged with sharp teeth that penetrate most wall coverings without damaging the wall beneath, make dozens of perforations in a single pass. This multitude of holes ensures good penetration by the stripping solution.

2. Loosening the paper.

Holding a putty knife at about a 30-degree angle, firmly push the wet paper up from one of the perforations in the paper. The paper should come up easily *(left)*. If it does not, resoak and try again. Where the stripping solution fails to soften the paste, you will have to use an electric steamer, which can be rented at most wallpaper dealers.

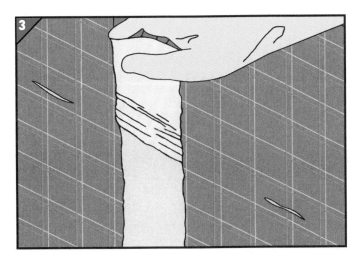

3. Stripping paper away.

◆ Grasp the loosened paper with your fingers and draw upward steadily and firmly *(left)*. To help prevent the paper from ripping, pull it parallel to the wall.
◆ After stripping off all the paper in the room, wash the walls with cheesecloth dipped in the stripping solution to remove any of the remaining scraps of wallpaper and paste.

Deciding Where to Start and Where to End

Wallpaper goes on the wall in consecutive strips, both clockwise and counterclockwise from the first one, with the pattern of each matching the previously completed section. Since the pattern unfolds from the starting point, the placement of the first strip affects the entire wallpapering job. Designs with narrow stripes and small random patterns match easily and can be begun conveniently alongside any door or window. But before you begin to hang a complex pattern, make sure you choose your starting point carefully.

Getting the Pattern Right: Complex patterns usually look best when the overall arrangement is symmetrical and the strips placed so the pattern draws a viewer's attention to a single part of the room—one wall, or the space above a fireplace, or the area surrounding one or more windows. When planning such an arrangement, try to avoid hanging strips whose width is less than 6 inches; they may be difficult to align and to affix.

Before putting up the first strip, inspect the wallpaper and note if the pattern is centered on the roll. If it is not, move the roll to the left or right to center the pattern on the wall rather than the roll.

Ensuring Alignment: When you hang the first strip and periodically thereafter, check to make sure that the paper is going on straight. Use a chalk line, metal straightedge, or carpenter's level to make vertical lines on the walls, and align the paper with them as you proceed *(page 103).*

A Suitable Finish: Unless the room contains an interruption on one wall such as a floor-to-ceiling storage unit or a built-in corner cabinet, a mismatch will occur along one edge of the last strip. Plan ahead to locate the mismatch in an inconspicuous place *(page 102).*

LOCATING THE FIRST STRIP

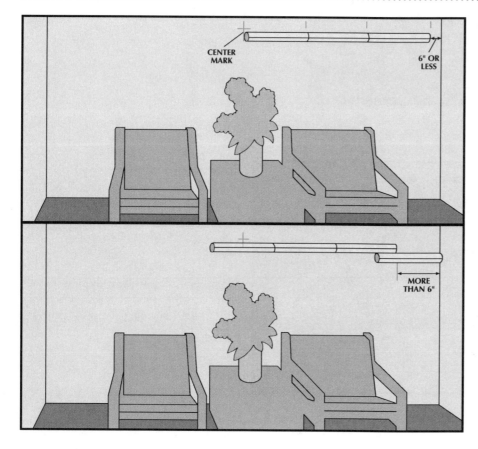

Centering the strip on a wall.
◆ Locate and mark the center of the wall. Then, using a roll of wallpaper, measure the distance to the nearest corner: place one edge of the roll against the mark and move the roll toward the corner, one width at a time, until less than the width of one roll remains.
◆ If the remaining distance is 6 inches or less *(left, top),* plan to center the first strip of paper over the mark *(left, bottom).* If the remaining distance exceeds 6 inches, hang the first strip of paper where you started measuring—with the left edge of the strip against the pencil mark.
◆ To center the pattern above a fireplace, make the pencil mark above the center of the mantel and proceed as for a wall.

Centering the paper between two windows.
The width of the wall between the windows determines the placement of the first strip of wallpaper.

◆ With a pencil, mark a spot that is halfway between the windows and then center a roll of paper on that mark.

◆ If centering the roll on the mark results in narrow strips at each window edge *(above, left)*, you may prefer to hang the first strip alongside the center mark *(above, right)*.

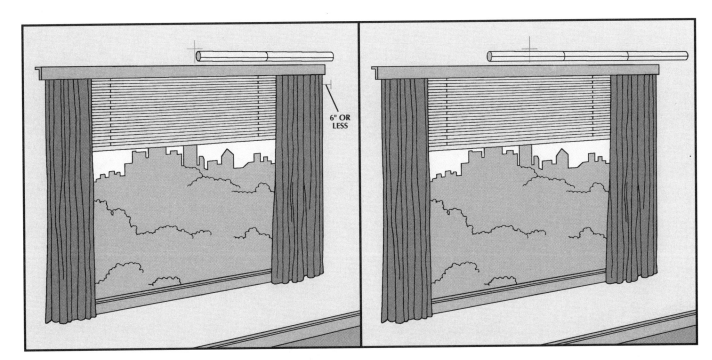

Centering above a window.
◆ Mark the center of the wall section above the window and measure as for walls *(opposite)*, moving the roll toward the window's right upper corner.

◆ If the last full roll of wallpaper extends 6 inches or less beyond the corner of the window *(above, left)*, plan to center the first strip on the mark *(above, right)*.

PLANNING THE LAST STRIP

Ending at an interruption.
If a wall you plan to paper contains a section of paneling, a fireplace, or a built-in cabinet or bookcase, as in the illustration at left, make this area the target of your final strip. After you choose the location of your first strip *(pages 100-101),* work from there both clockwise and counterclockwise, ending at the left and right sides of the interrupted area. In this way, there will be no mismatched strip anywhere.

Ending in a partly hidden area.
An unobtrusive corner is best for ending in mid-pattern. In the room above, for example, the shallow corner where the fireplace meets the wall gets no direct light from the nearest window and is inconspicuous from most directions. Another option might be a corner of the room that is obscured by furniture.

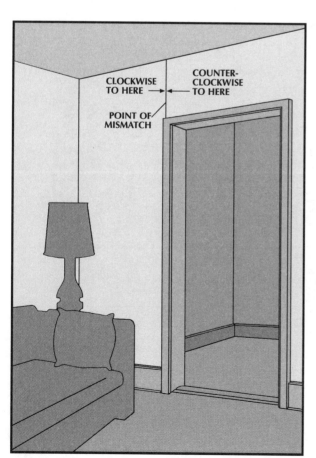

Ending above a door.
The narrow strip of wall above a door is a likely place to finish papering. Join the last two strips above the side of the door that is closer to the room's nearest corner *(left).* If the door is centered on the wall, consider the location of windows and lamps and choose the side of the door that receives less light.

GETTING THE PATTERN STRAIGHT

No house has truly vertical walls. If you hang strips of wallpaper by following the planes of the walls, the paper will be uneven by the time you finish the job.

To avoid slanted strips, draw a true vertical line and align the first strip with it. Recheck the alignment frequently, particularly after turning a corner; doing so enables you to move the paper before the adhesive dries. Two simple tools for marking a vertical line on a wall, a chalk line and a metal straightedge, are illustrated below.

Before putting up chalk lines, test one with your wallpaper; the chalk may show through some translucent or light-colored papers. You can substitute a carpenter's level for the straightedge; read both upper and lower vials to make sure that the level is truly vertical. Then press the level firmly against the wall and draw a pencil line along its side.

CHALK
LINE
CASE

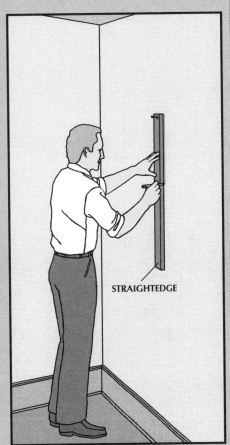

STRAIGHTEDGE

Snapping a chalk line.
◆ Tack the end of a chalk line high on the wall; when the case stops swinging, the string will be vertical.
◆ Without altering the position of the case, pull it slightly downward until the string is taut, press it firmly against the wall, and snap the string with the other hand *(above)*.

Using a metal straightedge.
◆ Tack a metal straightedge loosely to the wall through the hole in one end.
◆ When the straightedge comes to rest, hold it firmly against the wall and draw a light pencil line along its edge *(above)*.

A Mess-Free Pasting Method

Unless you use prepasted paper and a water box *(opposite, bottom)*, the choice of an adhesive and its correct application have much to do with the success of a wallpapering project. Purchase the one recommended by the wall-covering manufacturer; if no such instructions accompany the wallpaper, follow your dealer's advice.

Types of Adhesive: Whether organic or synthetic, adhesives are available in both liquid and dry form. Pour liquids directly into a bucket if you plan to apply with a paste brush, or into a roller tray for a paint roller. Dry adhesives must be mixed with water; directions on the package indicate how much. Approximately 30 minutes before use, pour the powder slowly into the water to minimize lumps. Mix thoroughly, making sure that you dissolve all lumps.

Applying the Paste: In order to spread adhesive evenly over the back of a strip of wallpaper, you'll need a table at least half as long as the strip. Neatness counts in pasting; avoid getting adhesive on the pattern side—or on the table where the next strip of wallpaper would come in contact with it. One way of achieving this is to spread several layers of kraft paper on the table, discarding the top layer after applying the paste to each strip. The method demonstrated here, however, eliminates waste by keeping the brush well away from the table surface during the entire operation.

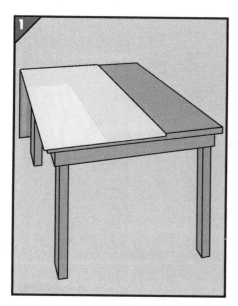

1. Pasting the lower left area.
◆ Measure and cut the wallpaper into strips *(page 106)*, then lay one strip on the table, pattern side down, so that the left and lower edges extend beyond the table $\frac{1}{4}$ inch or so.
◆ Apply paste to the lower left quarter, covering a little less than half the length of the strip.

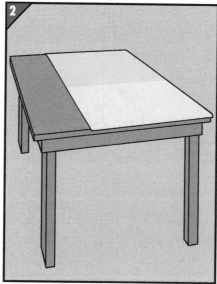

2. Pasting the lower right area.
◆ Shift the strip across the table, allowing the strip's right and lower edges to jut slightly beyond the tabletop.
◆ Paste the lower right quarter.

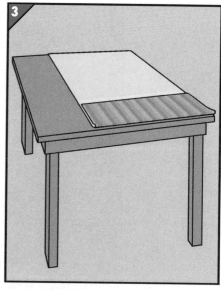

3. Making the lower fold.
Pull the strip toward you, and without creasing the paper, gently fold the pasted section onto itself, pattern side out. Make this fold somewhat shorter than the one you will make at the top *(Step 6)* so you can identify the top when you are ready to hang the strip.

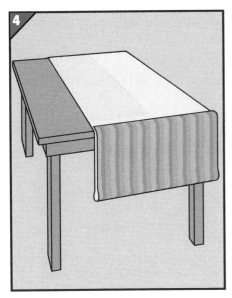

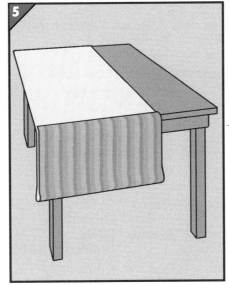

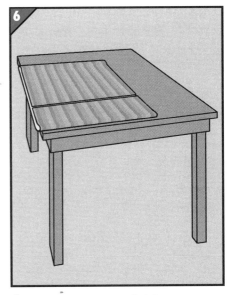

4. Pasting the upper right area.

◆ Slide the strip toward you until the upper edge of the paper barely overlaps the table. Let the folded section hang freely over the edge of the table, and make sure that the right edge of the paper still extends beyond the right edge of the table.

◆ Paste the upper right quarter of the wallpaper strip.

5. Pasting the upper left area.

◆ Shift the strip to the left across the table to position the strip's left and upper edges slightly beyond the edge of the table.

◆ Paste the upper left quarter.

6. Making the top fold.

◆ Fold the upper section onto itself as you did the lower section in Step 3, bringing the top edge just short of the bottom edge. Do not crease the fold.

◆ Set the pasted strip on a clean surface to cure for about 10 minutes; the strip will then be ready to hang *(pages 106-108)*. While you are waiting, apply paste to additional strips.

USING A WATER BOX

•••••••••••••••••••••••••••••••••••••••

Before hanging a prepasted paper, buy a special plastic container called a water box from your wallpaper dealer. An inexpensive item, it will simplify your job.

Set the box, two-thirds full of water, on newspaper directly below each section of wall as you work. After cutting a strip of wallpaper to the proper length, roll it loosely from bottom to top, with the pattern inside, then lay it in the box to soak for as long as the manufacturer recommends—usually 10 seconds to 1 minute. If the paper floats to the surface, slip an object without sharp edges—such as a wooden dowel—inside the rolled strip to weight it down.

Next, place a stepladder sideways in front of the water box. With the pattern facing you, draw the paper up as you climb the ladder *(above)*. Hang the paper immediately *(pages 106-108)*.

Hanging the Paper

After you have decided on a starting point and established a vertical guideline at that location *(pages 100-103)*, cut the first strip—a length of wallpaper at least 4 inches longer than the height of the wall. At the same time, cut as many additional strips as you plan to hang in one session, making sure that the patterns of successive strips will match. To do this for each new strip, unroll the paper alongside the previously cut strip and shift it up and down until the patterns align. When you cut the new strip, allow an extra 2 inches at each end.

Apply paste to the strips and let it cure *(pages 104-105)*. If the wallpaper has selvages—blank strips along both edges—remove them after pasting *(Step 1, below)*.

On the Wall: Hang the first strip as explained opposite and on page 108. As you smooth the paper, eliminate air bubbles, especially large ones. The brush strokes that are diagramed on page 108 will take care of most of them. Any small bubbles that resist smoothing will probably vanish as the paper dries. You can get rid of small bubbles that persist by making two cuts across them to let air escape and create flaps. Then apply adhesive to the underside of the flaps and the wall underneath with a thin artist's brush. Finally, pat the flaps down gently.

Trim the strip. Then, before the paste dries, wring a clean sponge in clear water and remove paste from the ceiling, the baseboard, and the face of the strip itself. Rinse the sponge often.

Making Seams: The usual way to join two strips is with a butted seam *(page 110)*; the edges of the wallcovering meet without any overlap. Only in special situations —such as turning corners or allowing for excessive shrinkage—will an overlap be necessary. In such cases, you can opt for either a lapped seam or a less noticeable wire seam, both of which are described on page 110.

Because a vinyl wallcovering will not adhere to itself, you must apply a vinyl-on-vinyl adhesive in order to make an overlapping seam.

Bonding the Seams: Avoid stretching edges when you join strips of any kind of material. Except for very fragile coverings, use a seam roller to get a strong bond *(page 111)*. Because seam rolling works best after the adhesive has begun to dry, you will save time if you hang four or five strips before starting to roll the seams.

 TOOLS

Straightedge	Scissors
Trimming or utility knife	Trimming guide
	Seam roller
Smoothing brush	Sponge

THE FIRST STRIP

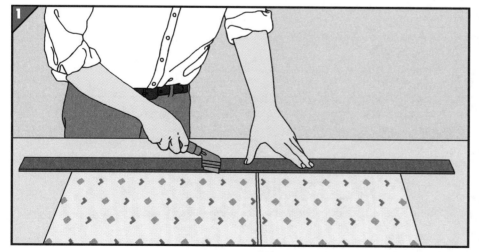

1. Trimming the selvages.

◆ If your paper has selvages, align the side edges of a pasted and folded strip, making sure that the visible portions of the selvages lie precisely over the selvages on the underside of the folds.

◆ Cover the visible selvage on one side with a straightedge. Using the straightedge as a guide, cut off the selvage with a firm, continuous stroke of your trimming knife or any sharp utility knife *(left)*.

◆ Repeat the procedure on the other side of the strip.

2. Starting the alignment.

◆ Unfold the top section of the strip. Starting at the ceiling line and allowing roughly 2 inches for final trimming along the ceiling, align one of the side edges of the paper with the plumb, or vertical, line *(left)*.

◆ As you align the paper, pat the top section into place with your hand, just lightly enough to make it hold on the wall. Because pasted wallpaper may stretch, be careful not to pull the edges of the strip.

3. Brushing at the ceiling line.

◆ Brushing with short, upward strokes, press the topmost few inches of paper against the wall, up to—but not beyond—the ceiling line *(above)*.

◆ Work in this fashion across the entire width of the strip, pressing the paper firmly with the smoothing brush into the angle formed between the ceiling and the wall.

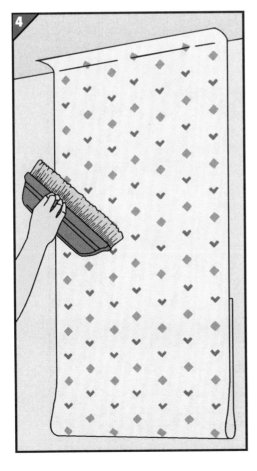

4. Brushing on the top section.

◆ With brisk, light strokes, press the entire top section of the strip against the wall *(left)*, stopping 1 inch or so from the upper edge of the lower fold. Do not worry at this stage about occasional air bubbles.

◆ To remove wrinkles, gently pull the lower part of the strip away from the wall up to the point where a wrinkle has formed, then brush the paper smooth.

5. Applying the lower section.

◆ Unfold the lower section of the strip and align it against the plumb line down to the baseboard.

◆ Press this part of the strip to the wall as in Step 4, using light brush strokes and removing wrinkles *(left)*.

6. Smoothing the strip.

◆ Remove all air bubbles and ensure a firm bond between the paper and the wall with firm brush strokes—using both hands on the brush if necessary. Smooth the paper from the middle of the strip toward its top and bottom edges, following the general direction of the arrows shown at right. Do not move the brush from side to side; this may stretch the paper.

◆ If any wrinkles appear while you are brushing, remove them as you did in Step 4.

◆ Finally, go over the entire surface of the strip with firm, vertical strokes.

1. Creasing the edges.

Press the wallpaper against the upper edge of the baseboard with the blunt side of a pair of scissors *(right)*. The scissors will form a crease along the line where the paper is to be trimmed.

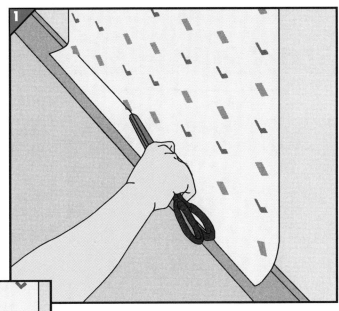

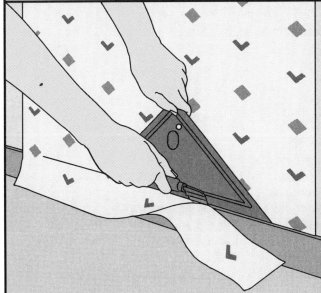

2. Trimming the paper.

◆ Gently lift the strip away from the wall and use scissors *(left, top)* to cut off the excess along the crease you made in Step 1 above.

◆ Brush the paper down again with your smoothing brush.

◆ Repeat Steps 1 and 2 along the ceiling line.

Instead of scissors, you can use a trimming knife *(left, bottom)* to trim the paper in places where pulling the strip away from the wall would be awkward, such as around windows. Another possibility is a utility knife with snap-off blades *(page 97)*. Be sure to change blades frequently. With either tool, a trimming guide (sold in paint stores) will ensure a straight cutting stroke.

TYPES OF SEAMS

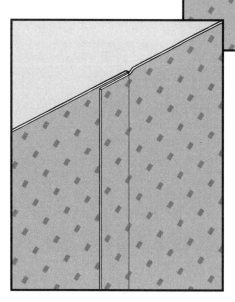

Butted.
For this seam, bring the adjacent edges of two strips of wallpaper firmly against each other until the edges buckle slightly. The buckling eventually flattens out against the wall as the paper dries and shrinks. This is the best-looking seam and the one most frequently employed when papering a flat expanse of wall.

Wire.
The edge of one strip of a wire seam overlaps the adjacent edge by no more than $\frac{1}{16}$ inch, hiding only a tiny portion of the pattern. Use this method if you have trouble butting paper or if the paper shrinks so much that the seams spread open.

Lapped.
In this type of seam, one strip overlaps the adjacent one by $\frac{1}{4}$ to $\frac{1}{2}$ inch. A lapped seam produces a noticeable ridge and is appropriate only in special cases—near corners, for example, where you must correct the alignment of the paper because the walls are not perfectly vertical.

JOINING SEAMS

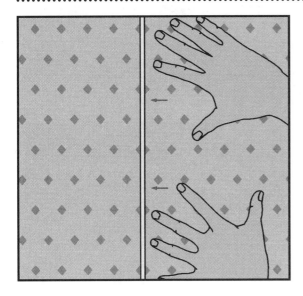

Positioning.
◆ For a butted seam, affix each new strip lightly on the wall about $\frac{1}{4}$ inch away from the previous strip. Keeping your hands flat and well away from the edge of the strip to avoid stretching it, move the strip until the pattern matches and the edges meet and buckle very slightly.
◆ For a lapped seam, affix the strip about $\frac{1}{4}$ inch (or $\frac{1}{16}$ inch for a wire seam) over the previous one instead of away from it. Using the same hand motions, adjust the position of the new strip until the pattern matches.

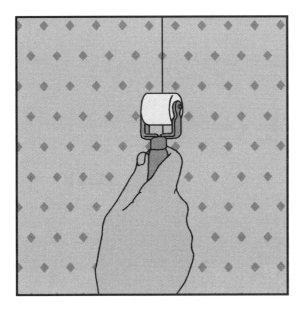

Rolling the seams.
When the adhesive is partly dry—10 to 15 minutes after you have hung a new strip—press the edges of the seam firmly together and against the wall with a seam roller, moving the cylinder against the seam with short up-and-down strokes *(left)*.

Do not use a seam roller on textured papers, foils, or other fragile coverings; they could be marred by the rolling action. Instead, press the seam with a sponge as shown below.

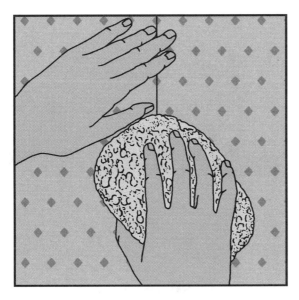

The sponge method.
To join the edges of fragile papers, press each seam gently together with your fingers and a damp sponge *(left)*.

4 CHAPTER

WINDOWS AND DOORS

It's not surprising that doors and windows require frequent maintenance; they are opened and closed countless times a year and often deal with the worst punishment the elements can dish out. The most common repairs, such as replacing a broken sash cord, are easy fixes, once you know how to get at the problem. More serious ailments can be cured with a variety of time-proven techniques.

This chapter will show you how to free tight window sashes, how to install new window channels, and how to replace a broken windowpane. You'll also find several simple remedies for binding doors.

For tips on painting windows and doors, refer to pages 93 and 94. Techniques for weatherproofing around windows and doors are presented on pages 294 to 303.

Most windows and doors pose little deterrent to intruders. Simple techniques for strengthening these vulnerable openings are described on pages 362 to 369.

▲

Most wooden windows anchor the glass in the sashes with glazier's points and glazing compound. Repairing a broken windowpane is seldom more complex than replacing the old glass, points, and compound with new ones.

Wear and tear combined with exposure to the elements can force a door out of shape. Planing an edge or shimming a hinge can provide the remedy.

▼

Paint buildup can cause an exterior door to bind. You can often solve this problem by scraping excess paint from the jamb surfaces that are touched by the door. ▶

Keeping double-hung sash windows working smoothly is often simply a matter of cleaning the sash channels. When the sash cord on one side of a double-hung window breaks, it's best to replace both.

A small hole in door screening can usually be plugged with a dab of glue or repaired with a patch. For large holes, however, you should replace the screening.

Why Windows Stick—and How to Free Them

The sashes of double-hung windows are sometimes difficult to operate. Many times, the repair is as simple as easing the sash channels; or you may need to replace part or all of the mechanism.

Binding Sashes: The most common cause of a sticking sash is a layer of paint and dirt that narrows the channels between the stops. This layer can be removed as explained opposite.

If the channels are clean, check the jamb with a straightedge to see whether the sash is bowed; slip a piece of paper along the joints between the stops and the sash to find where it is binding. You may be able to free it by forcing the jamb or stop away from it slightly *(opposite)*.

Sometimes the sash can be freed by removing one of the stops and repositioning it. To do so, score the joints between the stop and the jamb with a utility knife, then use a chisel and a mallet to pry the stop away from the jamb. Once the stop is freed, move it back slightly, and renail it to the jamb—but be sure to move it only a fraction of an inch or the sash will rattle. Never try to plane down the sides of a sash—no matter how little wood you remove, you will almost certainly end up with a rattling sash.

Frozen Sashes: A sash that will not budge at all may be painted shut and have to be pried open *(page 118)* or it may be nailed shut. To remove finishing nails,

drive them completely through the sash with a pin punch; pull any large-headed nails with carpenter's nippers; then try to free the sash by the techniques described on page 118.

Faulty Mechanisms: If the channel is clean and the jamb straight but the sash jams partway open, or if it falls when the window is opened, the mechanism is probably at fault and can be repaired or replaced.

Older double-hung windows are counterbalanced by a pulley and a cord with a weight. A broken cord can be replaced *(pages 119-120)*; do not use ordinary rope, which wears out too quickly. Newer wood double-hung windows often have window channels *(page 121)*.

 TOOLS

Wood chisel
Mallet
Hammer
Screwdriver
Wide-blade putty knife or window zipper

Utility knife
Shears
Pry bar
Carpenter's nippers
Pliers
Long-nose pliers
Diagonal-cutting pliers

 **MATERIALS**

Steel wool
Sandpaper (medium grade)
Paraffin block
Silicone spray lubricant

Galvanized nails $(1\frac{1}{2}")$
Galvanized wood screws $(\frac{3}{4}"$ No. 6, $\frac{1}{2}"$ No. 8, $2\frac{1}{2}"$ No. 12)
Replacement nails and screws
Sash cord or chain
Wire

 SAFETY TIPS

Wear goggles to protect your eyes from flying debris when scraping or prying.

⚠ **CAUTION**

Working Safely with Lead

The paint used in homes built or remodeled before 1978 may contain lead. Scraping or sanding this paint can release particles into the air, posing a health risk. To find out if your paint contains lead, use a home test kit available in hardware stores, or contact your local health department or environmental protection office for other testing options. If you suspect that the paint you are removing may contain lead, keep children, pets, and pregnant women away from the work area.

Cover the floors, then spray the paint with water before scraping it to keep dust down. Wear gloves and a high-efficiency particulate (HEPA) respirator while working, and set up a fan to blow the dust outside. When you are finished, mop the area twice and carefully sweep up any debris with a vacuum cleaner outfitted with an HEPA filter. Shower and wash hair, and launder clothing separately.

EASING A TIGHT SASH

Cleaning the channels.

◆ On wooden or metal channels, run a chisel, flat side out, along the surfaces touched by the sash. Work on the jambs first, then the sides of the stops and the parting strips, if any. If necessary, remove the sash *(page 119)* to do a thorough job. Weather stripping and plastic channels should be cleaned with steel wool since a chisel might damage the surfaces.

◆ Sand wood channels and paint them if you wish. Do not sand or paint metal or plastic channels.

◆ Lubricate wood jambs, stops, and parting strips by running a block of household paraffin up and down the channels three or four times. For metal and plastic jambs apply silicone spray, which is also suitable for wood.

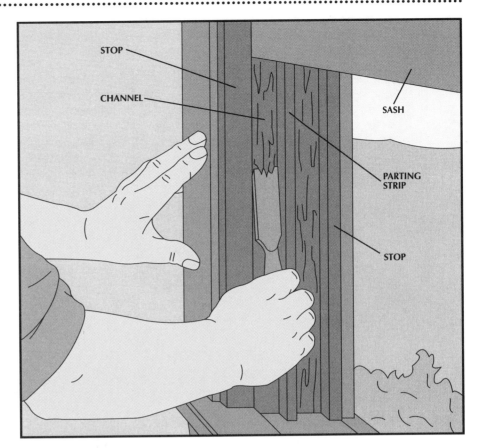

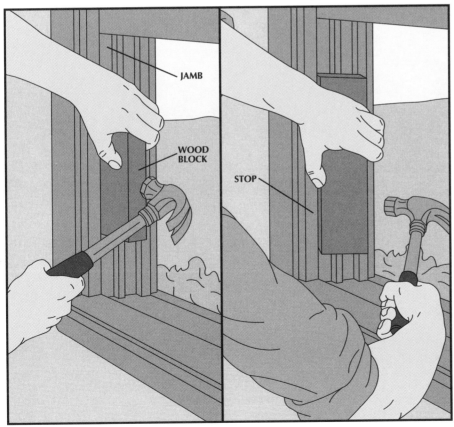

Straightening bowed jambs and stops.

◆ Set a wood block about 6 inches long against the back of the channel at the point where the sash sticks, and strike the block no more than five or six times with a hammer *(far left)*.

◆ If this treatment makes the sash slide more easily, drive $2\frac{1}{2}$-inch galvanized No. 12 flat-head screws about 3 inches apart through the jamb and into the jack stud behind it to straighten the jamb. If hammering the jamb does not make the sash slide more easily, do not repeat the procedure—continued pounding could damage the window frame. Instead, remove the sashes *(pages 119-121)* and straighten the jamb as you would for a door *(pages 124)*.

If a sash binds against a stop, set the block against the side of the stop and tap it with a hammer several times *(near left)*; do not drive screws into the stop.

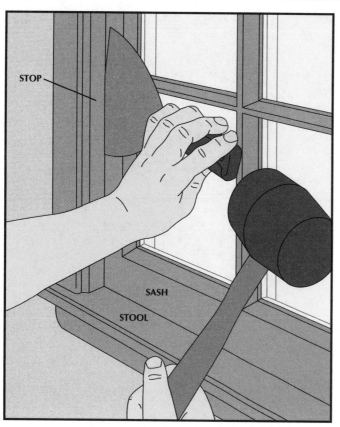

STOP

SASH

STOOL

Breaking a paint seal.

◆ Force a wide-blade putty knife or a window zipper (photograph) into the joint between the sash and the stop. Work the tool around both sides of the sash, then force it into the joint between the sash and the stool.

◆ If the sash still refuses to move, go outside the house and check the joint between the sash and the parting strip; repeat the procedure there if necessary.

SASH CORD

Prying open a double-hung window.

◆ Force the blade of a heavy screwdriver between the sash and the jamb; if the sash has a groove for a sash cord, use it as the point of entry for the blade (right).

◆ Pry the sash away from the jamb, then repeat the procedure at the other side of the sash. Continue to work the sash to the right and left until you can slide it open.

Prying the sash up from outside.

◆ If the window remains stuck, go outside the house and wedge a pry bar between the finish sill and the sash.

◆ Set a block of wood on the sill under the pry bar for leverage and, working first under the corners of the sash, pry the sash up (left).

REPLACING A BROKEN SASH CORD

1. Removing the lower sash.

The lower sash cord is generally the first to break; if the upper cord is broken, see page 121. In either case, replace the cord on the opposite side of the sash at the same time.

◆ Pry off the stop on the side of the window with the broken cord. Raise the sash slightly, angle it toward you, and pull it sideways to free the other side of its stop (right).

◆ Pull the knot at the sash end of the broken cord down with a pair of long-nose pliers and set the piece of cord aside.

◆ On the other side of the sash, pull the cord out of the sash. Tie a larger knot in the end of the cord and guide the knot up to rest against the pulley.

◆ Remove any weather stripping from the lower part of the jamb.

◆ If your window has interlocking metal weather stripping, which fits into a groove in the sash, remove the stop from the other side of the window and have a helper raise the sash and hold it at the top of the window frame.

◆ Using carpenter's nippers, remove the nails that fasten the weather stripping to the frame; then carefully angle both the weather stripping and the sash out of the window frame.

UPPER SASH · PULLEY · LOWER SASH · STOP · SASH WEIGHT

CASING · ACCESS PLATE · PARTING STRIP

2. Taking out the access plate.

If your window does not have an access plate, you will have to remove the casing with a pry bar to get at the sash weight.

◆ Remove the screws at the top and bottom of the access plate and pry the plate out of the jamb with an old chisel (left). If the parting strip covers one edge of the access plate, remove the strip (page 121) before prying out the plate. For an access plate that is concealed by paint, rap on the lower part of the sash channel with a hammer. When the outline of the plate appears, cut around it with a utility knife, then remove the screws and pry out the plate.

◆ Reach into the access hole, take out the sash weight, and untie the broken cord. Add 1 foot to the total length of the broken cord and cut a new cord with shears or a utility knife to this length. If you are using a chain, cut it with diagonal-cutting pliers.

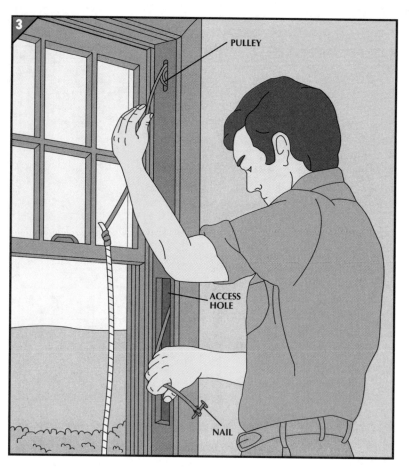

3. Putting in the new cord.

◆ Tie one end of a length of string to a bent nail and the other end to the new sash cord. Feed the nail over the pulley into the access hole; then pull the cord over the pulley and down to the access hole *(left)*.

◆ Untie the string and tie the cord to the sash weight, leaving about 3 inches of surplus cord.

◆ Rest the sash on the sill and refasten the undamaged cord on the opposite side.

If you are using a sash chain, put a nail through a link at one end to keep the chain from slipping through the pulley and feed the other end over the pulley until it appears at the access hole. Put the end of the chain through the eye of the weight and fasten the loop with thin wire or with clips provided by the manufacturer.

4. Attaching the new cord to the sash.

◆ With the sash resting on the sill, pull down on the new cord until the sash weight touches the pulley, then lower the weight about 2 inches.

◆ Thread the cord into its groove in the sash. Tie a knot in the cord at the level of the hole in the side of the sash, cut off any extra cord, and insert the knot in the hole.

◆ Hold the sash in its track and slide it all the way up; the bottom of the weight should be visible in the access hole, about 2 inches above the bottom of the window frame. If necessary, adjust the cord by retying it at the sash weight.

◆ Replace the access plate, any weather stripping, and the stop; use short nails or screws that will not obstruct the sash weight.

To attach a sash chain, thread the chain into the groove in the sash and drive ¾-inch No. 6 wood screws through two of its links into the sash *(inset)*.

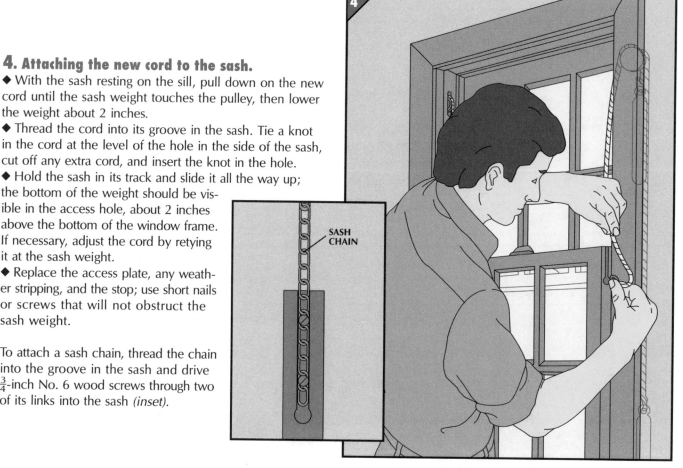

FIXING THE UPPER SASH CORD

Removing the upper sash.

◆ After removing a side stop and the lower sash *(page 119)*, lower the upper sash.

◆ Drill a pilot hole in the parting strip about 3 inches from the top and thread a short wood screw into it. Caution: Do not drive the screw clear through the strip into the jamb.

◆ Pull steadily on the screw with a pair of pliers until you can slip a chisel behind the end of the

parting strip. From this point, pry the strip out a little at a time with the chisel, moving the tool downward as the gap widens between the jamb and the parting strip.

◆ When the top half of the strip is free, slide the sash to the top of the window frame, then pry out the lower half of the parting strip.

◆ Follow the procedures outlined in Steps 2 to 4 on pages 119 and 120 to replace the sash cord.

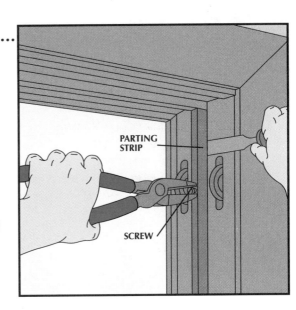

NEW WINDOW CHANNELS

1. Removing the channels.

Window channels rely on tracks with tabs and springs hidden behind the track to hold the sashes up.

◆ With carpenter's nippers, pull the nails or staples that fasten the channels to the side jambs. Remove any interior stops from the side and head jambs (and slide both sashes to the middle of the window.

◆ Working at one channel while a helper works at the other, tilt the tops of both channels inward *(left)*. Let the bottoms slide partway outdoors from the window, and remove both the channels and sashes as a single unit.

◆ Set the bottoms of the channels on the floor and, while your helper holds them upright against the sashes, slide the sashes up and out of the channels.

2. Installing new channels.

◆ Have your helper hold the new channels upright on the floor, with the angles cut by the manu-facturer at their bottoms matching the slant of the window's finish sill. Slide the bottom sash into the channel tracks, then the upper sash *(right)*.

◆ Together, lift the entire unit into the window frame, tilting it as described in Step 1 *(above)*.

◆ Position the channels against the blind stops and fasten them to the side jambs with $1\frac{1}{2}$-inch galva-nized nails or No. 8 wood screws at the top and bottom of each track. Replace the interior stops.

Doors often rattle, bind, or refuse to close. Rattles sometimes may be cured simply by installing weather stripping or repositioning the stops. Likewise, other simple repairs can improve a door's operation.

Paint Problems: Paint buildup can cause a swinging door to bind. Remove excess paint as you would for a sticking window *(page 117)*. If a door binds slightly at the top or bottom, plane or sand the point where it sticks *(pages 123)*; however, moisture can cause an unsealed door to swell, so paint or varnish any bare wood during a dry season.

Adjusting Hinges: Sometimes simply tightening the hinge screws will free a sticking door. If the screws turn but will not tighten, plug and redrill the holes *(page 123)*. When the door sticks along the lock side, recess the hinge leaves or remove the door and plane the hinge side. If the problem is at the top of the lock side, shim the bottom hinge *(page 124)* or cut a deeper mortise for the top hinge. Use the reverse procedure on a door that binds at the bottom of the lock side.

Warped Doors and Jambs: On a warped interior door with two hinges,

move the stop molding or the strike plate to accommodate the warp, then install a third hinge. Exterior doors generally must be replaced.

If the jamb bows outward, try the method shown on pages 124 and 125. To straighten a jamb that bows inward, adapt the procedure and place shims where needed. Do not try to straighten a bow of more than $\frac{1}{2}$ inch; instead, replace the jamb.

Realigning the Lock: When the bolt does not properly meet the strike, you can file the strike plate or reposition it *(page 124)*. If the hinges are too deeply recessed for the bolt to enter the strike, try placing cardboard shims beneath them.

Jammed Sliding Doors: Start by cleaning the track with a stiff brush and a vacuum cleaner. To replace broken rollers, you must remove the door. For a metal door, remove the bottom rail to get at the rollers; to do so, tilt the door out of its opening and lay it on a flat surface. Undo the bottom-rail retainer screw, clamp the door to a table, and tap a wood block against the rail with a mallet. Rollers for wooden doors can usually be replaced without removing the rail. A slightly dented track can be straightened by hammering a block of wood into the track; a badly damaged track must be replaced.

 TOOLS

Tape measure	Mini-hacksaw
2x4 or plywood straightedge	Utility knife
	File
Combination square	Jack plane
Hammer	Block plane
Mallet	Electric drill
Wood chisel	Counterbore bit
Handsaw	Pry bar
	Carpenter's nippers

 MATERIALS

Wood dowel	Galvanized finishing nails ($3\frac{1}{2}$")
Galvanized flat-head wood screws ($2\frac{1}{2}$" No. 12)	Shims
	Sandpaper (medium grade)

 SAFETY TIPS

Protect your eyes with safety goggles when pulling nails.

The Use and Care of a Plane

✔ For smooth cutting, lubricate the bottom of the plane, called the sole, with wax.

✔ Work with the grain and remove the wood in several thin shavings.

✔ Apply pressure to the toe or front of the plane at the beginning of each stroke, then gradually shift the pressure to the heel, or back, as you finish the cut.

✔ To protect the plane iron —or blades—always place the plane on its side when the iron is exposed.

✔ After the job is completed, retract the plane iron completely.

✔ When the cutting edge becomes dull or nicked, remove and sharpen the iron.

Planing the top or bottom of a door.

◆ To plane the top of a door, wedge the door halfway open. Lay a long, straight piece of lumber on the top edge of the door and mark any high points on the door.

◆ Hold a block plane by its wings, setting your index finger on the finger rest. Working from the sides of the door toward the center *(right)* to avoid splintering, plane until there is $\frac{1}{8}$-inch clearance between the top of the door and the head jamb.

◆ To check for squareness, slide a combination square along the face and edge of the door, and mark and plane any remaining high points.

To plane the bottom of the door, remove it as described below and shave the bottom edge until there is $\frac{1}{8}$-inch clearance between the door and the floor.

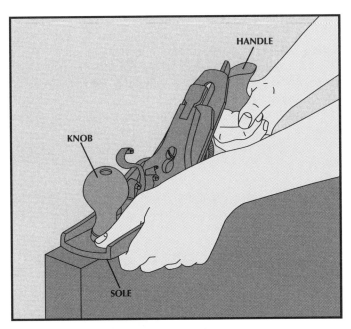

Planing the hinge or lock side of a door.

If less than $\frac{1}{8}$ inch of material must be removed, plane the lock side of the door; otherwise, plane the hinge side. If you are planing the lock side, maintain the bevel. When planing the hinge side, deepen the mortises if necessary before replacing the hinges.

◆ Starting with the bottom hinge and working up, take the door off the hinges by driving the pins up and out with a hammer and nail.

◆ Remove the hinges and support the door with a door jack or have a helper hold it on edge.

◆ Mark the edge of the door as described above.

◆ Grip the handle of a jack plane with one hand. Hold the thumb of the other hand against the knob and curl your fingers under the sole and against the board as a guide. (If the wood is rough, grip the knob.)

QUICK FIXES FOR DOORS

Tightening loose screws.

◆ Remove the door as described above, then take off the hinge.

◆ Enlarge the holes so a dowel will fit tightly in them.

◆ Cut lengths of the dowel to serve as plugs, then coat them with glue and tap them into the holes *(right)*.

◆ Let the glue set for at least an hour, then drill pilot holes through the plugs and screw the hinges back in place.

Shimming a hinge.
◆ Wedge the door open.
◆ Loosen the screws that fasten the hinge leaf to the jamb.
◆ Insert a cardboard shim, slotted at the level of the screws, behind the hinge leaf *(right)*, then tighten the hinge screws and test the door.
◆ Add a second shim if necessary.

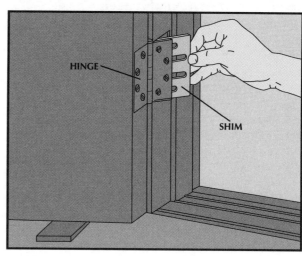

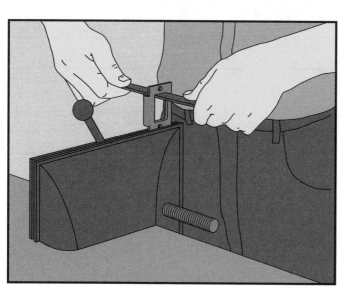

Filing a strike plate.
◆ If a strike plate is less than $\frac{1}{4}$ inch out of alignment with the bolt, remove the plate and secure it in a vise.
◆ Enlarge the plate opening $\frac{1}{16}$ inch at a time with a flat double-cut file *(left)* until the bolt fits.
◆ If necessary, enlarge the strike-plate hole in the jamb with a chisel.

For a larger misalignment, reposition the strike plate.

STRAIGHTENING A JAMB

1. Marking the bow.
◆ For an exterior door *(right)*, remove the casing inside the house. For an interior door, remove the casing on both sides of the partition. In either case, use a pry bar.
◆ Wedge the door open.
◆ Hold a long, straight scrap of plywood against the jamb and mark the high point of the bow.

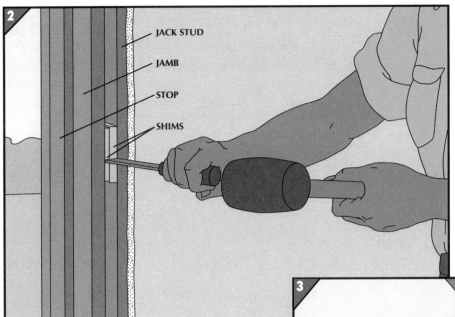

JACK STUD

JAMB

STOP

SHIMS

2. Removing the shims.

◆ Pry the entire length of the bowed jamb away from the jack studs just enough to loosen it.

◆ With a mallet and a $\frac{1}{4}$-inch wood chisel, split the shims *(left)* that are nailed between the jamb and the jack stud and pull out the fragments. If the shims do not split easily, cut the nails with a mini-hacksaw or pull them out with carpenter's nippers.

3. Eliminating the bow.

◆ At the high point of the bow, counterbore a pilot hole through the jamb for a $2\frac{1}{2}$-inch galvanized No. 12 flat-head wood screw.

◆ Drive the screw through the jamb into the jack stud, tightening the screw until the jamb is straight *(right)*.

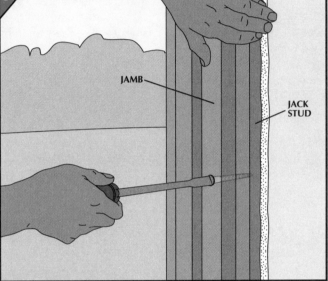

JAMB

JACK STUD

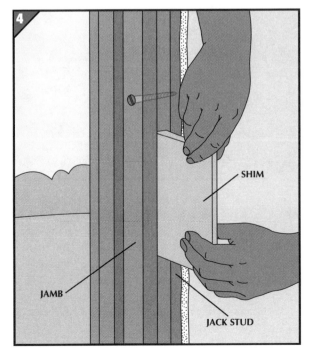

SHIM

JAMB

JACK STUD

4. Reshimming the jamb.

◆ On an exterior door, insert the butt end of a shim between the jamb and the jack stud just below the screw used to straighten the jamb *(left)*.

◆ Cut 3 inches from the thin end of a second shim and tap it in alongside the first shim.

◆ Drive two $3\frac{1}{2}$-inch galvanized finishing nails through the jamb and shims into the jack stud.

◆ Install a pair of shims at the level of each of the shims on the opposite side of the door, and add two more pairs in the unshimmed spaces.

On an interior door, insert full-sized shims, thin end first, between the jamb and the jack stud from opposite sides of the jamb. Nail through the jambs and shims into the jack stud, then score the protruding ends of the shims with a utility knife, and break them off.

Repairing Damaged Screens

Each of the two most common screening materials, aluminum and fiberglass, has its advantages. Aluminum is less likely to tear or sag, but unlike fiberglass it may corrode or oxidize. To restore rusted screening to its original condition, rub it with a wire brush, then vacuum it.

Simple Repairs: Repairing a very small hole may mean simply pushing the wires of the screening back into line with the tip of an awl. Other small gaps can be plugged with dabs of weatherproof glue or with patches glued in place. On aluminum screening, you can fasten patches by weaving the wires at the edges of the patch into the surrounding mesh, or you can use ready-made patches with edging wires prehooked to clip onto the screening. On fiberglass screening, simply set a fiberglass patch over the hole, cover the patch with a cotton rag, and run a hot iron over the rag, fusing the patch to the screening.

Replacing the Screening: If the holes are too large to patch, or so close to the frame that the screening sags, replace the screening. On all metal frames and some wooden ones, screening is secured with a spline *(below)*—a thin strip pressed down over the screening and into a channel at the inside edges of the frame. To replace the screening, you must pull out the old spline and screening, then put a spline back in place over new screening *(opposite)*.

On some wooden frames the screening is secured with tacks or staples. New screening is installed while the frame is bowed by clamps *(page 128)*. When the clamps are released, the frame tightens the screening as it straightens out.

Loose joints on wooden frames can easily be reinforced with corrugated fasteners, angle plates, or screws.

 TOOLS
Tape measure	Awl	Screen-spline roller
Hammer	Heavy-duty shears	Hand stapler
Screwdriver	Tin snips	C-clamps
Wire brush	Utility knife	

 **MATERIALS**
Brads ($\frac{3}{4}$")
Screening
Screen splines

A SPLINE FOR SCREENING ON A CHANNELED FRAME

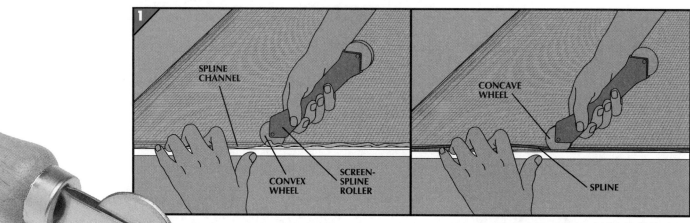

SPLINE CHANNEL · CONCAVE WHEEL · CONVEX WHEEL · SCREEN-SPLINE ROLLER · SPLINE

1. Securing a short side.

◆ With heavy-duty shears or tin snips, cut a piece of screening to the outer dimensions f the frame.

◆ If your screening is aluminum, crease it into the spline channel on a short side of the frame *(above, left)*, using the convex wheel of a screen-spline roller *(photograph)*; start at a corner and work in short back-and-forth strokes.

◆ Set the old spline in place, or if it is damaged, cut a length of new spline a bit longer than the channel. With the concave wheel, force the spline into the channel over the screening *(above, right)*. Cut new spline at the corners of the frame and tamp it into place with a screwdriver.

If you are installing fiberglass screening which will not crease, roll the spline over the screening in one step.

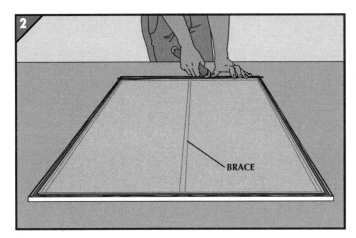
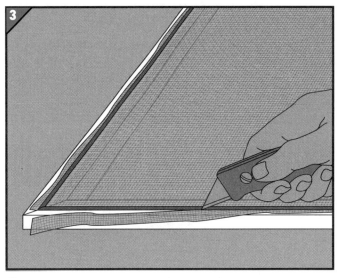

2. Completing the splines.
◆ Pull the screening taut at the opposite side of the frame, crease it if necessary, and roll a length of spline over it and into the channel *(above)*. If the frame bows inward, fit a board as a temporary brace to hold the sides parallel.
◆ With the screening pulled flat across the frame, add splines to the two remaining sides.

3. Trimming the excess screening.
With a utility knife, cut through the screening along the outer edges of the spline channels; slant the blade toward the outside of the frame to avoid cutting into the spline.

STAPLING SCREENING TO A WOODEN FRAME

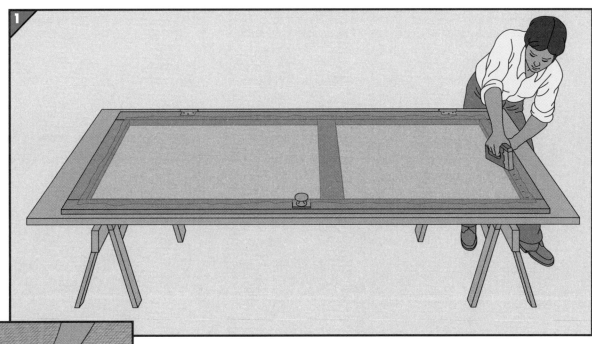

1. Fastening the first side.
◆ For aluminum screening, cut the material 2 inches larger than the frame opening.
◆ Staple the screening to a short side of the frame at 2-inch intervals, starting at a corner *(above)*. Angle each staple so it straddles several strands of the mesh.

For fiberglass screening, cut the material $\frac{1}{2}$ inch larger than the outside edges of the molding that will conceal the staples. To keep the screening from tearing along the line of staples, make a hem by folding the extra $\frac{1}{2}$ inch over as you staple the material *(inset)*.

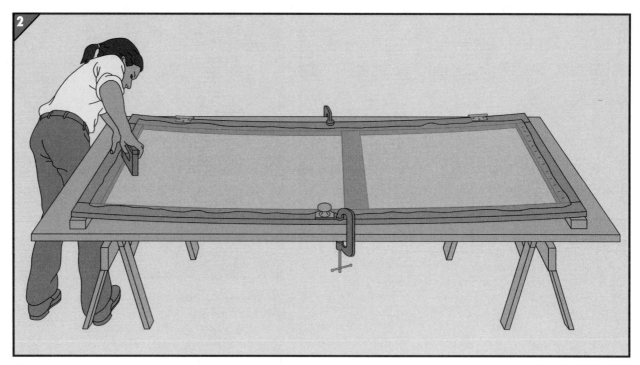

2. Attaching the remaining sides.

◆ Set blocks of scrap wood under the short sides of the frame and use a pair of C-clamps to force the centers of the long sides down about $\frac{1}{4}$ inch.

◆ Pull the screening taut along the unstapled short side, staple it and release the C-clamps.

◆ Staple the long sides, which are now stretched taut.

◆ Replace the molding, fastening it with $\frac{3}{4}$-inch brads every 6 inches.

◆ On metal screening, trim off the excess screening with a utility knife; the hem on fiberglass screening will be covered by the molding.

TRICKS OF THE TRADE

Stretching Screening

The setup at right is an alternative to bowing the frame to stretch the screening. Cut the screening a few inches longer than the size of the frame. After stapling one end of the material to the frame, staple the other end to a board held against the frame. Then push down on the board as you staple the screening in place.

Replacing a Windowpane

Windows are glazed either with a single pane of glass, or with double or triple panes for increased insulation. Shown here are techniques for replacing single panes. The same techniques can be used to refit single-pane windows with insulating panes; but these require a sash channel at least 1 inch wide.

Measuring the Glass: To determine the size of a single replacement pane, measure the inside of the frame after you have removed the old pane and putty, then subtract $\frac{1}{8}$ inch from each dimension to allow for expansion. Single-glazed panes will be cut to size by most glass and hardware stores, but you can do it yourself if the glass is less than 4 feet long. Insulating panes come in a range of pre-cut sizes; panes smaller than 12 by 12 inches generally must be custom-made. For the correct size of a replacement, consult a window dealer.

Installing the Glass: Before cutting a windowpane, practice on a piece of scrap glass to get a feel for the amount of pressure needed to score the glass for a clean cut. Brush linseed on the area to be cut and score the panel with a glass cutter guided by a straightedge. A rasping sound as you draw the cutter across the glass indicates that the pressure is right.

Single-pane glass is held in a wood frame with wedge-shaped glazier's points. For panes secured with points, glazing compound cushions the glass and forms a watertight seal.

Insulating glass is generally held in place by wood moldings in wood windows. If the glass is foggy the seal is broken and the unit must be replaced. Use a latex-based compound to glaze insulated glass—oil-based compounds will rot the sealant that holds the panes together.

 TOOLS

Straightedge
Wood chisel
Stiff-bladed putty
  knife
Wire brush
Small paintbrush
Long-nose pliers
Glass cutter
Dowel
Heat gun

 **MATERIALS**

Linseed oil
Light machine oil
Emery stone
Glazing compound
Sandpaper (coarse
  grade and 240-grit
  silicon-carbide)
Replacement glass pane
Glazier's points

 SAFETY TIPS

Wear heavy leather work gloves when handling loose panes or fragments of glass. If you are removing broken glass or cutting glass, protect your eyes with safety goggles. When using solvent-base glazing compound instead of a water-base or acrylic compound, wear rubber gloves.

Tips for Handling Glass

Working with glass is not dangerous if you take the following precautions:
✔ Work with a helper whenever you carry panes larger than 4 by 4 feet.
✔ Transport glass flat in several layers of newspaper or blankets on a padded surface (an old rug or piece of carpet will do).
✔ Have a professional deliver any glass pane you cannot lay flat in your car.
✔ Cut glass on a padded surface.
✔ Immediately after cutting glass, sweep up any fragments left from the work.
✔ If the window is hard to reach, remove the sash *(page 119)* and do the work on a flat surface.
✔ Before storing panes, mark them with a grease pencil or masking tape so they are easily seen.

1. Removing broken glass.
◆ Tape newspaper to the inside of the sash to catch glass fragments.
◆ From outside the house, work the shards of glass back and forth to free them. If the glass is only slightly cracked, tap it lightly with a hammer to break it.

2. Scraping off the glazing compound.
◆ Brush the old glazing compound with linseed oil to soften it.
◆ Let the oil soak in for a half hour, then scrape off the softened compound with an old chisel or a stiff-bladed putty knife.
◆ If oil does not soften the compound sufficiently, warm it with a heat gun *(photograph)* on a low setting. Be careful not to heat surrounding panes as this could crack them.

⚠ **CAUTION** *Old glazing compound may contain lead. When removing it, take the same precautions you would with lead paint* (page 116).

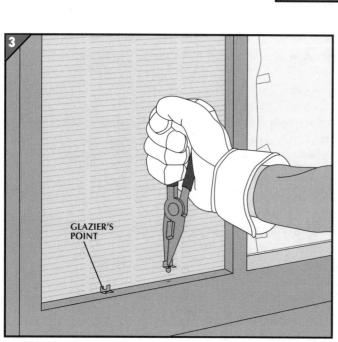

GLAZING COMPOUND

GLAZIER'S POINT

3. Smoothing the channel.
◆ Pull the glazier's points out of the frame with long-nose pliers and remove loose fragments of glass and glazing compound with a wire brush.
◆ Sand the channel smooth with coarse sandpaper and brush it with linseed oil. (Uncoated wood draws oil from the glazing compound and makes it brittle.)

SETTING A SINGLE PANE IN A WOOD FRAME

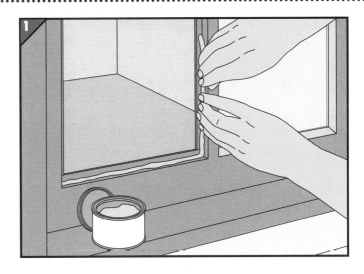

1. Lining the frame.
◆ Outside the house, roll glazing compound between your palms into strips about $\frac{1}{4}$ inch thick and press it into the channels in which the pane of glass will rest.
◆ Add compound until you have filled the channels completely.

GLAZIER'S POINT

2. Securing the glass.
◆ Press the pane of glass firmly into the glazing compound.
◆ Fasten the pane securely in place with glazier's points pushed into the frame with a putty knife. Use two points on each edge for a frame up to 10 inches square or one point every 4 inches for a larger frame.

3. Beveling the glazing compound.
◆ Press additional strips of glazing compound around the frame so the glass is sandwiched between two beads of compound.
◆ With a putty knife, smooth the strips into a neat bevel that runs from the face of a sash or a muntin (sash divider) to the glass. As you work, dip the knife in water periodically—or paint thinner if the compound is solvent-based—to prevent the knife from sticking. A glazier's knife has one end designed for removing old compound, driving in glazier's points, and applying new putty. The tool also has a V-blade end that serves to smooth and bevel the putty.
◆ When the compound has hardened—in five to seven days—paint it to match the frame *(page 93)*, extending the coat of paint $\frac{1}{16}$ inch onto the glass for a weathertight seal.

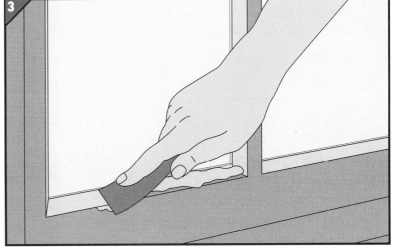

5 CHAPTER

FLOORS AND STAIRWAYS

Any flooring from attic to basement needs regular maintenance and occasional repair. Closely linked to the framing of a house, floors often suffer from shifts in the under-lying structure. Other enemies are moisture, abuse, and age. Whatever caused the damage, repairs are usually possible. Some, like replacing a joist, are major projects, but most require only a little time plus the right materials and approach.

This chapter includes a number of simple cures for wood floors, from silencing squeaks and patching holes to sanding away an old finish and applying a new one. You'll also find easy fixes for resilient surfaces—both tiles and sheet flooring—and ceramic tile floors.

Wall-to-wall carpeting is the flooring of choice in many homes—and for good reason. It soaks up sound and can be laid over almost any surface without special preparation. Maintenance is simple, and most rips, burns, or other damage can be concealed.

Stairways of all shapes and sizes share one trait: Whether plain or elaborate, they must be sturdy. The most common problems—squeaky treads, loose or broken balusters—are minor and easily corrected using the techniques shown on pages 166 to 173.

With regular cleaning and a protective finish, hardwood flooring can easily last a lifetime. To preserve a wood floor's beauty, you occasionally need to sand off the old finish and apply a new coating. ▶

This resilient sheet floor evokes the richness of terra cotta without the expense or trouble of installing individual tiles. In the event of damage, blemishes in such flooring are easy to conceal or patch.
▼

▲

Bright, durable, and available in dozens of shades and patterns, no-wax vinyl flooring is easy to maintain, making it an ideal choice for high-traffic areas of the house.

Ceramic tiles give bathrooms beautiful, durable, and water-resistant flooring. Filling the spaces between new or replacement tiles with fungicidal grout will help prevent mildew from forming, easing cleanup.

▼

▲

Stairways are built to survive as long as the homes they serve. But wear and tear can give rise to squeaky treads, shaky handrails, and broken balusters. All these problems are simple to repair.

Quick Cures for Wood Floors

Although durable, wood floors are subject to a variety of ailments—among them, squeaks, bouncing, cracks, stains, and burns. Most maladies can be easily remedied. If the damage is serious, you can replace boards without leaving visible scars.

Problems beneath the Floor: Squeaks are usually caused by subflooring that is no longer firmly attached to the joists or by the rubbing of finish floorboards that have worked loose from the subfloor. Retightening either can be done in a number of ways, explained opposite and on page 138.

Squeaks, along with bouncing, may also indicate a lack of bridging—diagonal braces between joists, needed for any joist span of 8 feet or more. If this reinforcement is missing, install prefabricated steel bridging.

Sealing Cracks: Cracks between boards open when humidity and temperature changes cause uneven shrinkage. Plug them with a mixture of sawdust from the floor itself and penetrating sealer. Gather the dust by sanding boards in a corner of a closet. Work 4 parts sawdust and 1 part sealer into a thick paste and trowel it into the crack.

Surface Defects: Stains and burns, if not too deep, can be erased by sanding. To determine the extent of the damage, go over the blemished area with a wood scraper. If the defect starts to lift out, the board can be saved by sanding and refinishing; otherwise, you will have to replace it.

Patching a Damaged Floor: Replacement of ruined boards is best done in the winter, when dry furnace heat will shrink the wood and ease the job of fitting in new pieces. Inspect for decay in the subfloor if you see any sign of rot in the floorboards: With an ice pick or awl, pry up some wood; if it feels spongy or cracks across the grain, rot has set in. Treat lightly decayed subfloors with a preservative containing pentachlorophenol. If the rot has penetrated through the wood, replace the subflooring.

 TOOLS

Hammer
Stud finder
Electric drill
Nail set
Screwdriver
Putty knife
Mallet
Wood chisel
Pry bar

 **MATERIALS**

Construction adhesive
Finishing nails or trim head screws (3")
Wood shingles
Screws and washers
Glazier's points
Steel bridging
Replacement boards
Flooring nails (3")

 SAFETY TIPS

When hammering nails, wear safety goggles to protect your eyes from flying debris.

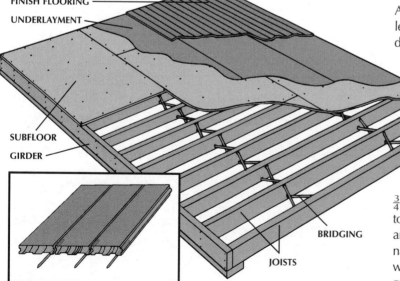

FINISH FLOORING
UNDERLAYMENT
SUBFLOOR
GIRDER
BRIDGING
JOISTS

Anatomy of a wood floor.

A typical wood floor is constructed in layers. Parallel 2- by 8-inch joists, laid on girders and braced by diagonal bridging, provide structural support. In older homes, the subfloor is often wide planks or tongue-and-groove boards laid diagonally for extra stability. Today, sheets of $\frac{3}{4}$-inch plywood are preferred; they are usually glued as well as nailed to the joists. A moistureproof and sound-deadening underlayment of heavy felt or building paper is laid atop the subfloor. The finish flooring, most commonly strips of oak, $\frac{3}{4}$ inch thick and $2\frac{1}{4}$ inches wide, has interlocking tongues and grooves on the sides and ends. They are attached by driving and setting 3-inch flooring nails at an angle above the tongues, where the nails will be concealed by the upper lips of the adjoining grooves *(inset)*.

Shimming the subfloor.

If the subfloor is accessible from below, have someone walk on the floor while you look for movement in the subfloor over a joist. To eliminate movement, apply a bead of construction adhesive to both sides of the tapered edge of a wood shingle and wedge it between the joist and the loose subfloor *(left)*. Do not force the subfloor upward or you may cause boards in the finish floor to separate.

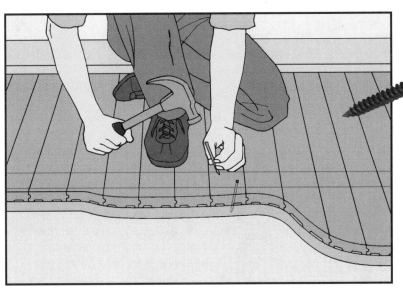

TRIM HEAD SCREW

Securing inaccessible subfloors.

If the ceiling beneath the floor is finished, refasten the loose section of subfloor to the nearest joist through the finish floor above.
◆ Use a stud finder to locate the joist. Then drill pairs of pilot holes angled toward each other and drive 3-inch finishing nails *(left)* or trim head screws *(photo)* into the subfloor and joist below.
◆ Set the nailheads or countersink the screws and cover them with wood putty that has been tinted to match the color of the boards.

Anchoring floorboards from below.

◆ Select screws that will reach to no more than $\frac{1}{4}$ inch below the surface of the finish floor.
◆ Drill pilot holes through the subfloor, using a bit with a diameter at least as large as that of the screw shanks, so that the screws will turn freely. Avoid penetrating the finish floor by marking the subfloor's thickness on the drill bit with tape.
◆ Drill pilot holes into the finish floor with a bit slightly narrower than the screws.
◆ Fit the screws with large washers, apply a bit of candle wax to the threads to ease installation, and insert them into the pilot holes. As you turn the screws *(right)*, their threads will bite into the finish floorboards, pulling them tight to the subfloor.

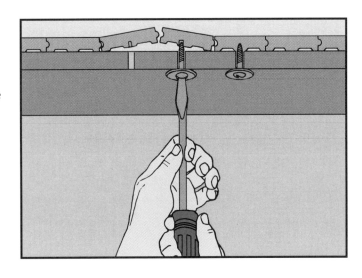

Silencing finish flooring from above.

◆ First, try remedies that do not mar the finished surface. Force powdered graphite or talcum powder into the joints between boards.

◆ If the squeak persists, insert glazier's points—the triangular metal pieces that secure glass into frames—every 6 inches and set them below the surface with a putty knife *(right)*. If the pressure of the knife is insufficient to push the points down, use a hammer and small piece of scrap metal to tap them into place.

◆ Should these solutions fail, drive finishing nails or trim head screws through the floorboards and into the subfloor, angling and concealing them as explained on page 137.

GLAZIER'S POINT

Installing steel bridging.

Prefabricated steel bridging comes in sizes to fit between joists spaced at 12, 16, and 24 inches. To install the braces, hammer the straight-pronged end into a joist near the top *(left)*. Then pound the L-shaped claw end into the adjacent joist near the bottom. Alternate the crisscross bridging pattern from joist to joist, making sure the pieces do not touch each other.

138

CUTTING OUT A DAMAGED AREA

1. Making end cuts.

◆ Remove boards in a staggered pattern, with adjacent end joints at least 6 inches apart. At the end of a damaged board, make a vertical cut with a sharp 1-inch wood chisel, keeping its bevel side toward the portion of the board to be removed *(right)*.

◆ Working back toward the vertical cut, angle the blade and drive the chisel at about 30 degrees *(inset)* along the board.

◆ Repeat this sequence until you have cut all the way through the board. Repeat at the other end.

2. Splitting the board.

◆ With the chisel, make two parallel incisions a little less than 1 inch apart along the middle of the board from one end to the other *(right)*.

◆ Use the chisel to pry up the board between the incisions just enough to split the wood.

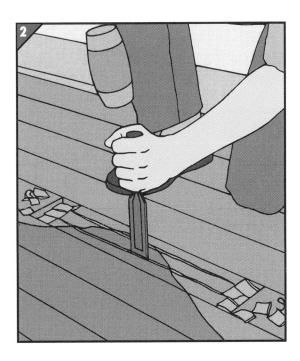

3. Prying the board out.

◆ Working on a board at the center of the damaged area, insert a pry bar into the lengthwise crack created with the chisel *(right)*. Pry the middle strip out, then the groove side of the board, and finally the tongue side.

◆ Remove adjacent boards in the same way, working toward the edge of the damaged area and taking care not to harm any good boards. Remove exposed nails or drive them down with a nail set.

◆ Take a sample of the flooring to a lumberyard to get matching replacement boards.

PATCHING THE HOLE

REPLACEMENT BOARD

HAMMERING BLOCK

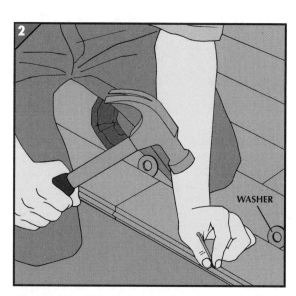

WASHER

1. Inserting a new board sideways.

Cut a replacement board to fill the outermost space on the tongued side of the damaged area. Using a scrap of flooring with a groove that fits the tongue of the replacement piece as a hammering block, wedge the new board securely into place *(above)*.

2. Blind-nailing a board.

Drive and set 3-inch flooring nails at a 45-degree angle through the corner of the tongue of the replacement piece. Pilot holes are not essential but may be helpful. If existing boards around the repair have separated slightly, try to match their spacing by inserting thin shims such as metal washers between the new board and the old one while driving the nails *(above)*.

3. Inserting a new board lengthwise.

To slide a replacement between two boards, lay it flat on the subfloor and work the tips of its tongue and groove into those of the existing pieces. Using a scrap hammering block *(left)*, tap it all the way in.

4. Inserting a new board from above.

◆ For the last few spaces where you cannot slide the pieces into place, lay a replacement board upside down on a piece of scrap wood and chisel off the lower lip of the groove as indicated by the blue line on the board at right.

◆ Turn the board faceup and gently tap it into place from above.

5. Face-nailing.

◆ To fasten the last replacement boards, which offer no access for blind-nailing, drill angled pilot holes every 12 inches about $\frac{1}{2}$ inch from the edges of the face. Drive 3-inch finishing nails or trim head screws into the holes *(right)*.

◆ Set the nails or countersink the screws and cover them with wood putty that has been tinted to match the color of the boards.

Repairing a Sagging Floor

A small dip in a floor is irritating but not necessarily dangerous. If less than $\frac{3}{4}$ inch deep and 30 inches long, the dip can be repaired with hardwood wedges driven between a joist and the subfloor *(page 137)*.

A larger sag, in conjunction with other symptoms such as a sticking door, cracked plaster, or leaky plumbing, may indicate structural damage in the supporting framework of joists, girders, and posts.

Pinpointing the Problem: Inspect the framework underneath the floor *(below)* for structural members that are defective. If you have a second-story sag, an entire floor or ceiling may have to be torn out before you can get at the trouble and repair it.

Test for rot and insect damage by stabbing the wood with an awl. Rotted wood feels spongy and does not splinter. A honeycomb of small holes signals termites or carpenter ants; if you find such holes, call an exterminator at once.

A sound joist can be straightened permanently by having a new joist nailed to its side, a technique called doubling *(page 144)*. A slightly rotted joist can also be doubled if it will hold a nail—and if you first coat it liberally with a penetrating wood preservative. Always replace a joist that is thoroughly rotten or insect infested *(pages 145-146)*.

Where a drooping girder is the cause of a sagging floor, the repair may entail the substitution of a

steel column for a wood post *(pages 147-149)*, the installation of a new girder, or both.

Jacking Up the Floor: In order to make any of these repairs, you'll need to jack up the joists or girder under the sag. The jacking techniques shown here for an unfinished basement also apply to finished areas of the house, once you have exposed the supporting framework of the floor.

Always use a screw jack; the hydraulic type is neither as strong nor as reliable. If you are working in a basement, rent a house jack; in a crawl space, use a contractor's jack. In either case, grease the jack threads before you begin.

 TOOLS

Straightedge (8')
Telescoping house jack
Contractor's jack

 **MATERIALS**

Pad (4 x 8)
Beam (4 x 6)
Blocks (2 x 6)
Timbers (6 x 6)

 SAFETY TIPS

A hard hat guards against painful encounters with joists, girders, and exposed flooring nails.

What holds up a floor.

At the ground floor of a typical house, joists are laid across the shorter dimension of the foundation. Outer joist ends rest on the foundation sills; inner ends rest on a girder supported by posts anchored in concrete footings that may include raised piers. The built-up girder shown here, made of lengths of lumber cut to overlap atop a post, rests in pockets in the foundation wall. Cross members called bridging strengthen the joists and keep them in alignment. Other elements called trimmer joists and headers frame a stairwell opening. Trimmers and headers consist of two boards nailed together to carry the extra weight of the stair and of joists cut short of the foundation sill.

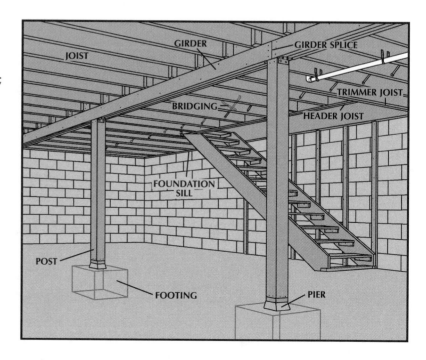

JACKING UP JOISTS

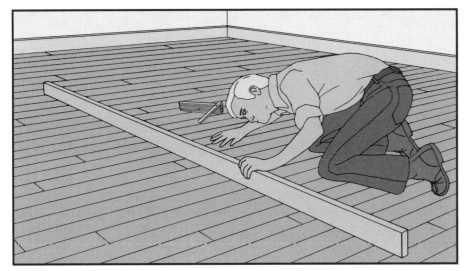

Measuring a sag.

◆ Lay an 8-foot straightedge—either a 2-by-4 or the factory edge trimmed from a sheet of plywood—across the sagging area *(left)*. Measure the gap between straightedge and floor and mark the floor where the sag is deepest.

◆ Measure from the mark on the floor to two different reference points—walls or stairways, for example—that lie at right angles to each other and that are visible in the basement. There, take measurements from the reference points to position the jack.

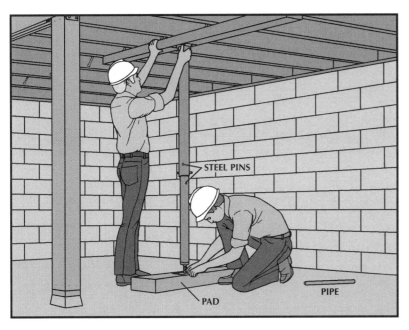

Jacking from a basement.

◆ Extend the jack to fit between the joist and the floor with about 12 inches to spare, and lock the tube at that length with the steel pins provided.

◆ Set the bottom plate on a length of 4-by-8 lumber. While a helper steadies a 4-by-6 beam at least 4 feet long between the joists and the jack's top plate *(left)*, screw the jack until the beam presses against the joists. Plumb the jack with a level, then nail the plates to the beam and pad.

◆ Remove the bridging between a joist to be doubled or replaced and its neighbors. To keep the joists parallel, cut 2-by-6 spacers to fit snugly between them and insert as shown on page 144.

◆ Once a day raise the jack no more than $\frac{1}{16}$ inch, about a half-turn. If necessary, slip an 18-inch pipe over the jack handle for leverage. Because the floor will settle after the jacks are removed, raise it $\frac{1}{4}$ inch higher than level.

Jacking from a crawl space.

◆ Assemble a pyramidal framework, called cribbing, from hardwood 6-by-6 timbers, available from dealers in structural timber. Stack the timbers as shown at right, placing the ones at the top of the structure about 18 inches apart.

◆ Atop the cribbing, set a 4-by-8 pad for the jack, then raise the jack to meet a 4-by-6 beam held across the joists.

◆ Install spacers as described above, then raise the jack $\frac{1}{16}$ inch a day—one-eighth turn on most contractor's jacks—until the floor is $\frac{1}{4}$ inch above level.

Reinforcing Weakened Framing

Once you have decided whether to double a joist or replace it *(page 142)*, proceed as described on these pages. In either case, electrical cables, pipes, and ventilating ducts that run perpendicular to joists can be substantial hurdles.

Circumventing Obstacles: You can get around one or two such roadblocks when doubling a joist by using the technique shown at the top of the next page. But in some instances of doubling—and often when replacing a joist—it may be more practical to temporarily remove a section of ductwork or to unstaple electrical cables from joists to improve access. When a pipe intrudes, the simplest solution is to notch the joist to fit around it.

One-for-one replacement of an unsalvageable joist is usually suffi-

cient. However, if the old joist has sagged badly enough that the subfloor above it has split or broken, you'll need to install a second new joist for added support.

Choosing Lumber: Buy doublers and replacement joists to match the old joist in every dimension. The single exception is the height of doublers that you plan to use for reinforcing a notched joist. All of the boards should be straight and free of cracks or large knots; if rot has been a problem, use pressure-treated lumber. Before you install a doubler or a new joist, find the crown, an edge with a slightly outward, or convex, curve. Install the board with the crown facing upward, against the subfloor; the joist will be forced straight by the weight that it bears.

 TOOLS

Floor jack
Plane
Pry bar
Reciprocating saw

Saber saw with
   flush-cutting
   blade
Carpenter's nippers
Wood chisel
Cat's paw

 **MATERIALS**

2 x 4s
2 x 6s
Joist lumber
Steel bridging

Construction
   adhesive
Common nails
   ($2\frac{1}{2}$", $3\frac{1}{2}$")
Finishing nails (3")

 SAFETY TIPS

Protect your eyes with goggles when hammering or pulling nails, using a hammer and chisel, or sawing wood with a power saw. Add a dust mask when cutting pressure-treated lumber, and wash hands thoroughly after handling it. Wear a hard hat when handling heavy objects overhead.

DOUBLING A JOIST

Attaching the new joist.

◆ Remove bridging, insert spacing blocks, and jack up the floor *(page 143)*.
◆ Plane a $\frac{1}{4}$-inch-deep, 18-inch-long notch in the new joist's ends *(inset)*. Remove a spacer and test-fit the joist. Deepen the notches as needed.
◆ Lay a bead of construction adhesive on the top edge of the new joist. While a helper holds it tight against both the old one and the subfloor, fasten the doubler to the joist with $3\frac{1}{2}$-inch common nails, staggered top and bottom every 12 inches *(right)*. Hammer the protruding nail points flat.
◆ Trim $1\frac{1}{2}$ inches from the spacer removed earlier, and toenail it between the doubler and the neighboring joist.
◆ Remove the other spacing block and install new bridging *(page 138)*.

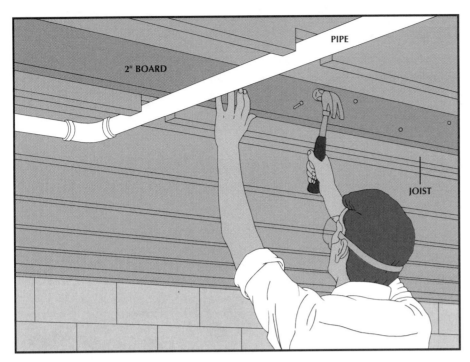

Doubling a notched joist.
◆ To reinforce a joist notched to make way for a pipe, measure the distance between the top of the obstacle and the subflooring.
◆ From the widest 2-inch lumber that will fit in the space, cut two pieces the same length as the weak joist.
◆ With a helper to hold the boards against the subflooring, fasten one of them to each side of the weak joist with $2\frac{1}{2}$-inch nails. If no helper is available, support the boards on nails driven partway into the old joist *(left)*.

REPLACING A JOIST

1. Mounting a new joist.
◆ Plane or chisel the ends of the new joist to make notches *(opposite, inset)*.
◆ Remove bridging, insert spacing blocks, and then jack up the floor *(page 143)*.
◆ Take out any nails and blocks holding the old, weak joist to the girder and the sill plate. Remove the spacing blocks that are next to the weak joist.
◆ Apply construction adhesive to the new joist's top, then position it so the weak joist is sandwiched between the new one and the sound existing joist that extends to the opposite sill plate.
◆ Force the new joist tightly against the subfloor by driving hardwood shims at the notches *(above)*.

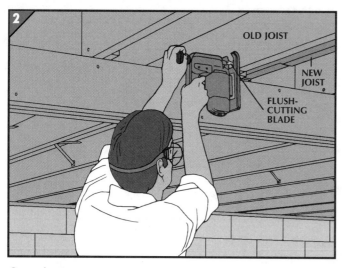

2. Removing the old joist.
◆ Cut through the weak joist at points near the girder and the sill plate with a reciprocating saw or a saber saw fitted with a flush-cutting blade *(above)*.
◆ With a pry bar, lever the joist away from the nails that hold it to the subfloor.
◆ Trim protruding nail points with a plierslike cutter called a carpenter's nippers.

THE RECIPROCATING SAW
With a fast, pistonlike motion, a reciprocating saw can rough-cut wood, metal, plaster, and PVC pipe. When fitted with a long wood-cutting blade, this heavy-duty tool is ideal for cutting out old floor joists. Some models allow you to mount the blade teeth up, a feature that makes for easy overhead cutting and allows you to cut a joist all the way to the subflooring.

3. Splitting out the joist ends.
◆ With a wood chisel, split the ends of the joist that remain on the girder and sill plate *(right)*. Remove the pieces and protruding nails with a pry bar. Drive the claw of a cat's paw beneath any embedded nailheads with a hammer, and then pull on the bar to withdraw the nail.
◆ If there are breaks in the subfloor, install and shim a second new joist in the old one's place *(Step 1)*.

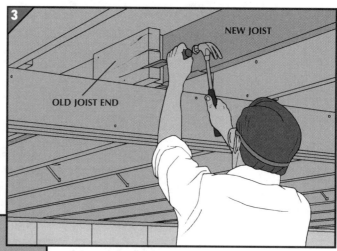

4. Nailing the joists.
◆ With $3\frac{1}{2}$-inch common nails, nail the new joists to the one they sandwich at the girder.
◆ Then nail 2-by-4 spacers every 3 feet between the new joists *(left)*.
◆ Toenail the new joists to the girder and sill plate.
◆ Trim the spacing blocks *(page 144)* to fit in the space that lies between each new joist and its neighbor, then toenail the spacers in place.
◆ Drive 3-inch finishing nails, spaced 8 inches apart, through the finish floor and into each joist.

Replacing a Failing Post

When a girder sags at the top of a wood post, the trouble is in the post, not the girder. Either the post's concrete footing has sunk or the post itself has been attacked by rot or termites. Both problems have the same solution: Replace the post with a steel column that is supported by a new footing.

You will need a building permit, and some of the work involved is strenuous: removing the old wood post, breaking through the basement slab with a rented electric jackhammer, digging a hole, and pouring a new footing.

If your house is built on fill or if the span between posts is more than 12 feet, consult an architect or a civil engineer before undertaking this project.

A Steel Replacement: Adjustable steel columns, available at lumberyards and building-materials dealers, are made of 11-gauge, 3-inch

pipe fitted with a threaded base like that of a telescoping jack. Get a column 4 inches longer than the distance between the basement slab and the bottom of the girder, so the base will be anchored in concrete when you patch the slab.

The Key to a Sturdy Post: A post is only as strong as its footing. The size and depth of the footing depend on the load it must bear, on soil conditions and, in unheated basements or crawl spaces, on the depth of the frost line—the point of deepest penetration of frost below ground level.

A footing that is 2 feet square and 22 inches deep is typical, but check your local building code for the required dimensions and whether steel reinforcement is mandatory. Either rent a concrete mixer or, if you are pouring more than one footing, have concrete delivered in a ready-mix truck.

TOOLS

House jacks	Masonry trowel
Hacksaw	Shovel
Electric jack-	Electric drill with
hammer	$\frac{3}{8}$" bit
	Carpenter's level

MATERIALS

	Adjustable steel
	column
Plywood ($\frac{1}{2}$")	Lag screws (3" x $\frac{3}{8}$")
Common nails	and washers
($2\frac{1}{2}$")	Epoxy bonding
Concrete	agent

SAFETY TIPS

When operating a jackhammer, wear goggles, gloves, ear protection, and a dust mask.

1. Removing the old post.

◆ To make way for the new column, set up telescoping house jacks *(page 143)* 3 feet to either side of the post. Raise the girder $\frac{1}{16}$ inch a day until the post no longer supports any weight.
◆ Remove the nails or lag screws that fasten the post to the girder. With a helper, tilt the top of the post clear of the girder and lift the post off the vertical steel dowel that connects it to the concrete *(right)*.

If the girder is spliced over the post, reinforce the splice before jacking the girder. Using a hacksaw, cut away any metal splice reinforcement, and nail a 3-foot length of $\frac{1}{2}$-inch plywood across the splice, on both sides of the girder. Secure each plywood piece with 30 $2\frac{1}{2}$-inch common nails.

DOWEL

2. Digging the footing.

◆ On the basement floor, mark off a footing of the size that is required by your building code. Rent an electric jackhammer to break through the concrete slab.

◆ Beginning inside one of the footing marks and working toward the line, break out easy-to-handle chunks of concrete with a series of cuts. Hold the jackhammer perpendicular to the slab at the start of each cut; then, when you have chiseled out a groove, tilt the handles slightly toward yourself and lean firmly *(left)*.

◆ When you have broken up the slab and the old concrete footing within the marks, dig a hole of the depth required by the code.

3. Pouring the footing.

◆ Clean out all loose dirt from the hole and spray it with a hose.

◆ While the hole is still wet, fill it with concrete *(above)* to a point 4 inches below floor level. Drive a shovel into the wet concrete several times to eliminate air bubbles, then level the surface with a masonry trowel.

◆ The concrete must cure for about 2 weeks: Cover it with polyethylene sheeting, and keep the surface wet by sprinkling it with water twice a day.

4. Bolting the column.

◆ Set the steel column on the new footing. Holding the bottom plate with your toe, turn the column on its threaded base to raise the top plate tightly against the girder.

◆ Center the plate at the marks left by the old post. Using the holes in the plate as a guide, drill $\frac{3}{8}$-inch pilot holes into the girder *(above)*.
◆ Attach the plate loosely to the girder with 3-inch lag screws and washers.

5. Making the column fast.

◆ Tap the base of the column with a hammer as needed to make the column plumb, checking all sides with a level *(left)*, then tighten the lag screws.
◆ Lower the temporary jacks $\frac{1}{16}$ inch a day until they can be removed.
◆ To finish the floor around the column, coat the footing and the edges of the slab with an epoxy bonding agent. Then fill the hole with concrete to the level of the surrounding floor, and trowel it smooth.

A New Face for a Wood Floor

Restoring the natural beauty of a wood floor, whether it is varnished or painted, necessitates removal of the old finish before the new one can be applied. The first step is to take all furniture out of the room and to seal drapes in plastic bags. Lift off floor registers and cover the vents with plastic.

Fasten loose boards and replace badly damaged ones *(pages 139-141)*. Drive protruding nailheads $\frac{1}{8}$ inch below the floor surface with a nail set. Beginning at a door, remove shoe moldings from baseboards by driving the nails through the molding with a pin punch no larger than the nailhead.

Getting to Bare Wood: Some laminated floorboards are too thin to sand; remove the old finish with a chemical stripper. On thicker boards, use a drum sander *(below)*. Multiple sandings are required.

For rough or painted floorboards, begin with 20-grit sandpaper, then proceed to 36-grit, 50-grit, and finally 80-grit. Varnished or shellacked floors need only three sandings beginning with 36-grit. Sand parquet floors first with 50-grit followed by 80- and 100-grit.

Removing Stains: First try to remove a stain by hand-sanding. If it remains, apply a small amount of wood bleach to its center. Let the spot lighten, then apply enough bleach to blend the treated area with the rest of the floor. Rinse away the bleach with a vinegar-soaked rag. If the stains remain even after bleaching, replace the boards *(pages 139-141)*.

A Two-Step Glaze: To protect the wood and emphasize the grain, apply a sealer, which is available in both natural wood hues and a clear, colorless form *(page 152, bottom)*. For a final protective glaze over the sealer, select a urethane floor finish, which becomes exceptionally tough as it hardens.

Both oil- and water-based sealers and finishes are available. If you plan to stain the floor, oil-based products provide richer, more even color than water-based products, which dry faster and are easier and safer to handle.

If you choose water-based products, apply and smooth them with tools made of synthetic material, avoiding natural-bristle brushes and steel wool. Use a synthetic abrasive pad instead. Clean the floor with a lint-free rag rather than a tack cloth.

⚠️ **CAUTION** *Sanding produces highly flammable dust. Seal the doorways into the work area with plastic, and ventilate the room with a fan* (opposite).

TOOLS

Nail set
Pin punch
Drum sander
Edging machine
Floor polisher
Paint scraper
Paintbrushes
Lambs wool applicator
Putty knife

MATERIALS

Sandpaper
Wood bleach
Vinegar
Tack cloth
Lint-free rags
Sealer
Urethane floor finish
Abrasive pads (steel-wool or synthetic)
Tinted wood putty

SAFETY TIPS

Sand floors wearing goggles, ear protection, and dust mask. When applying wood bleach, sealer, or finish, put on goggles and rubber gloves, as well as long pants and a long-sleeve shirt.

TOOLS TO RENT

A refinishing job calls for professional equipment. One such tool is a drum sander *(right)*. Make sure the machine has a tilt-up lever for lifting the spinning drum from the floor (not all have this feature). The second is an edging machine, a sander with a rotating disk for working along baseboards and other places that the drum sander cannot reach. Finally, to smooth each coat of sealer or new finish, rent a commercial floor polisher. Fit it with a round pad of steel wool—or a synthetic abrasive pad if using a water-based finish.

Before leaving the shop, check that the machines are working and that their dust bags are clean. Take with you any special wrenches for loading the drum sander and plenty of sandpaper—at least 10 drum-sander sheets and 10 edger disks of each grit for an average room. Because sanders need grounding, they must have three-pronged plugs; if your house has two-slot receptacles, you will need grounding adapters.

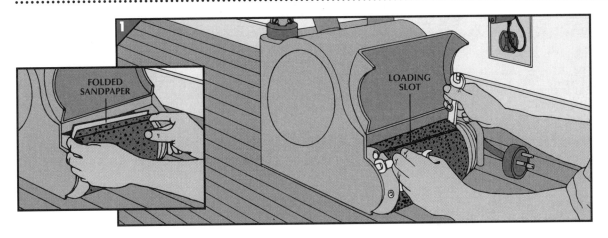

1. Loading the drum sander.

◆ With the sander unplugged, thread a sheet of sandpaper into the loading slot, turn the drum one full revolution, and slip the other end of the sheet into the slot.
◆ To secure the paper, tighten the drum's internal clamp by turning the boltheads at both ends of the drum with the wrenches provided by the dealer *(above)*. With fine-grit sandpaper, fold a strip of the material in half, grit exposed, and slip it into the slot between the two ends to keep them from slipping out *(inset)*.

Filtered Ventilation

A window fan with a furnace filter helps clear the air in a room while you are sanding. Buy a filter large enough to cover the entire fan, and tape it to the intake side; duct tape works well for the purpose. Place the fan in a window with the intake side inward, and turn it on. The filter will catch a large portion of the dust so it does not collect in your fan or blow into the neighborhood.

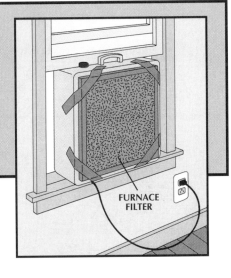

FURNACE FILTER

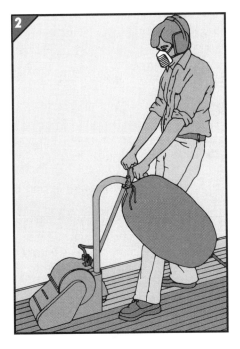

2. The first sanding.

◆ Standing with a wall about 3 feet behind you, lift the drum from the floor with the tilt-up lever, start the sander, and when the motor reaches full speed, lower the drum to the floor. Let the sander pull you forward at a slow, steady pace *(left)*. Sand boards along the wood's grain unless they undulate slightly. In that case, or if the floor is patterned with varying grain directions, do the first sanding diagonally.
◆ At the far wall, raise the drum from the floor, move the cord behind you to one side, then lower the drum and pull the sander backward over the area you just sanded.
◆ Lift the drum and move the machine to the left or right, overlapping the first pass by 2 or 3 inches.
◆ Continue forward and backward passes across the room, turning off the sander occasionally in order to empty the dust bag, then turn the machine around and sand the area next to the wall.

⚠ **CAUTION** *Keep the sander in motion to prevent it from denting or rippling the wood.*

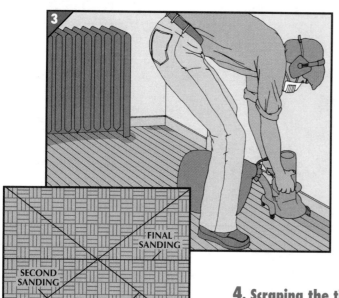

3. Completing the sanding.
◆ Sand areas missed by the drum sander with the edger, loaded with coarse-grit paper *(left)*.
◆ Repeat both the drum and edge sandings, with successively finer sandpaper. On floorboards, these sandings, like the first, should be made with the grain. On parquet floors, do the second sanding on the opposite diagonal to the first, and the final sanding along the length of the room *(inset)*.
◆ Smooth the floor with a floor polisher *(opposite)* and a fine abrasive pad, suited to sealer and finish. This will lessen the boundary between drum- and edge-sanded areas.

4. Scraping the tight spots.

In areas that neither the drum sander nor the edging machine can reach, remove the finish with a paint scraper *(right)*. At a radiator, remove collars from around the pipes for a thorough job. Always pull the scraper toward you, applying firm downward pressure on the tool with both hands. Scrape with the grain wherever possible, and replace the blade when it gets dull. Sand the scraped areas by hand.

APPLYING PROTECTIVE COATS

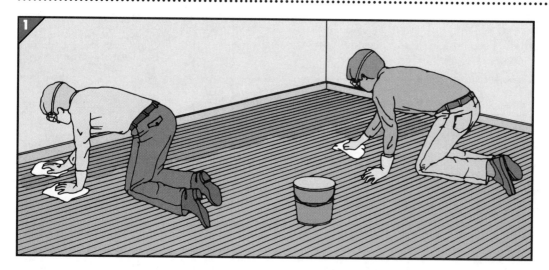

1. Spreading sealer.
◆ Ventilate the room. Vacuum the floor and pick up dust with a tack cloth, or a dry rag if using water-based sealer.
◆ Starting next to a wall and away from the door, apply sealer liberally over a 3-foot-wide strip of floor with a rag. Use long, sweeping strokes along the grain of the wood or along the length of the room if the grain directions vary.
◆ Between 8 and 20 minutes after it is applied, the sealer will have penetrated the wood, leaving shallow puddles of the liquid on the surface. Have a helper, using rags in both hands, mop up the excess sealer.
◆ As your helper works on the first strip, start applying sealer to the second strip *(above)*. Try to work at a pace that keeps both of you moving together with your knees on dry floor until the job is almost finished. On the last strip, the helper will have to back across wet sealer to the door.
◆ Finally, allow the sealer to dry according to the manufacturer's specifications.

ABRASIVE PAD

SCRUB BRUSH

2. Smoothing the sealed wood.
◆ Fit a floor polisher with a heavy-duty scrub brush and press a fine abrasive pad into the bristles of the brush *(inset)*. Run the polisher over the floor to smooth irregularities in the surface caused by tiny bubbles in the sealer coating *(left)*.
◆ Scour the edges and corners of the floor by hand with a small abrasive pad, then vacuum the entire floor and go over it thoroughly with a tack cloth or damp rag, according to the finish, to pick up any remaining dust.

3. Finishing the floor.
◆ Apply the finish slowly and evenly with a wide brush *(right)*. With oil-based finish you may use a lambs wool applicator *(photograph)*. Work along the grain. If grain directions vary, work along the room's length. Stroke in one direction and do not go back over finish that has begun to set. If working alone, do edges and corners first with a small brush, then work on the rest.
◆ When the first coat is dry, smooth the surface *(Step 2, above)*.
◆ Clean the floor with a vacuum and tack cloth or damp rag. Force wood putty, tinted to match, into cracks and nail holes with a putty knife.
◆ Apply a second coat of finish in the same way. Water-based urethane, thinner than oil-based, needs a third coat.
◆ After 24 hours replace shoe moldings, registers, and pipe collars.

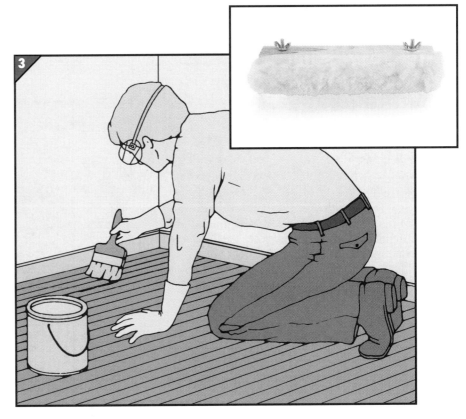

Mending Resilient Floors

The tough surface of resilient flooring—typically vinyl tiles or sheet flooring—will resist wear and stains for many years. If damage does occur, you can usually repair it yourself, or at least reduce the visibility of the scars.

Common-Sense Precautions: A resilient floor should be kept as dry as possible, even when being cleaned, so that water does not get underneath and destroy the bond of the adhesive that holds it in place.

Resting furniture feet on plastic or rubber coasters will help protect the floor from punctures and gouges. When heavy furniture or appliances must be moved across the floor, slide them over pieces of plywood.

Curing Minor Ailments: To conceal a shallow scratch in a vinyl floor, gently rub it lengthwise with the rim of an old coin. This will press the edges of the scratch together so only a thin line remains. Deeper cuts can be closed by carefully heating the vinyl with an iron and aluminum foil, as explained on page 157.

If a tile has come loose, first determine whether water from leaking plumbing is the cause; if it is, repair the leak *(pages 56-63)* before fixing the floor. Use water-based latex adhesive to glue the tile down.

Mending Major Flaws: The best remedy for a ruined tile is a replacement; similarly, a badly damaged section of sheet flooring will need a patch. But before removing any resilient flooring or adhesive, read the asbestos warning on page 156.

If you cannot find any spare matching tiles or sheet flooring, look for replacements in inconspicuous areas of your floor—under a refrigerator or at the back of a closet, for instance. Cut and remove the section from the hidden area and substitute a nonmatching material of equal thickness.

If your resilient floor is glued to an asphalt-felt underlayment, the felt may tear as you remove damaged flooring. Usually you can glue the felt back together with latex adhesive; allow the adhesive to dry before continuing the job. If the felt is too badly torn, cut out the damaged section and glue down enough replacement layers of 15-pound asphalt felt to maintain the same floor level.

 TOOLS

Putty knife
Utility knife
Iron
Notched trowel
Metal straightedge

 **MATERIALS**

Latex adhesive
Replacement vinyl tiles or sheet flooring

 SAFETY TIPS

Protect your hands with rubber gloves when working with adhesive.

SIMPLE FIXES

Securing a loose tile.
◆ Lift the loose portion of the tile and spread a thin coat of latex adhesive on the underside of it with a putty knife. If only a corner of the tile has come unstuck, loosen more of it until you can turn the tile back far enough to spread the adhesive.
◆ Press the tile into place, so that it is level with those tiles that surround it. Hold it down with a 20-pound weight for at least an hour.

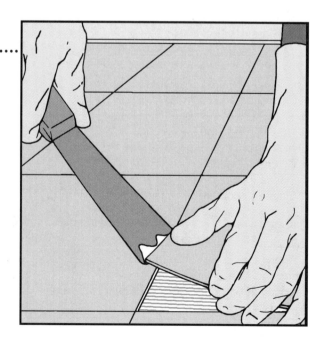

Deflating a blister.

◆ Following a line in the flooring pattern if possible, score then slice along the length of a blister with a utility knife *(right)*. Extend the cut $\frac{1}{2}$ inch beyond the blister at both ends.

◆ With a putty knife, spread a thin layer of latex adhesive through the slit onto the underside of the flooring.

◆ Press the vinyl down; if one edge overlaps because the flooring has stretched, use it as a guide to trim the edge beneath. Remove trimmed-off scrap, then press the edges together and put a 20-pound weight on the repaired area for at least 1 hour.

Dealing with Stains

Most resilient flooring today has a permanent finish as hard, smooth, and shiny as wax, protecting it against stains and dirt. Daily sweeping plus occasional damp-mopping is usually sufficient to remove grime. Limit washing with detergent and water to every 3 to 6 weeks. Over time, some spillage and staining is almost inevitable. The following treatments are recommended for stains caused by common substances:

STAIN	REMEDY
Alcoholic beverages	Go over the spot with a cloth that has been dampened with rubbing alcohol.
Blood	Sponge with cold water; if that does not work, sponge with a solution of 1 part ammonia to 9 parts water.
Candle wax, chewing gum, or tar	Cover with a plastic bag filled with ice cubes. When the material becomes brittle, scrape it off with a plastic spatula.
Candy	Rub with liquid detergent and grade 00 steel wool unless the floor is a "waxless" vinyl; in that case use a plastic scouring pad, warm water, and powdered detergent.
Cigarette burns	Rub with scouring powder and grade 00 steel wool.
Coffee or juice (canned or frozen)	Cover for several hours with a cloth saturated with a solution of 1 part glycerine (available at drugstores) to 3 parts water. If the stain remains, rub it gently with scouring powder on a damp cloth.
Fresh fruit	Wearing rubber gloves, rub with a cloth dampened with a solution of 1 tablespoon oxalic acid, a powerful solvent available at hardware stores, and 1 pint water.
Grease or oil	Remove as much as possible with paper towels, then wash the stain with a cloth dampened in liquid detergent and warm water.
Mustard or urine	Cover for several hours with a cloth soaked in 3 to 5 percent hydrogen peroxide, and cover that cloth with another soaked in household ammonia.
Paint or varnish	Rub with grade 00 steel wool dipped in warm water and liquid detergent.
Leather and rubber scuff marks	Scrub with a cloth soaked in a solution of 1 part ammonia to 9 parts water.
Shoe polish or nail polish	Rub with grade 00 steel wool soaked in warm water and scouring powder.

REPLACING A DAMAGED TILE

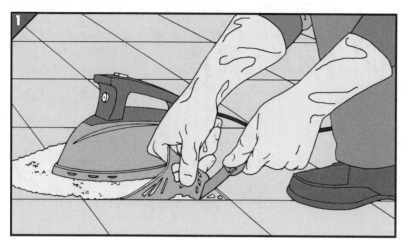

1. Removing a tile.

◆ Lay a towel on the tile and warm it with an iron at medium heat until the adhesive softens and you can lift one corner with a putty knife.

◆ Pull up the corner and slice at the adhesive underneath with the putty knife *(left)*, reheating the tile with the iron if necessary, until you can take out the entire tile.

◆ Scrape the remaining adhesive from the subfloor *(box, below)*.

2. Installing a replacement.

◆ Spread a thin layer of adhesive—not more than half the thickness of your tile—on the subfloor with a notched trowel, then butt one edge of the new tile against the edge of an adjoining tile, aligning the pattern.

◆ Ease the tile into place *(above)*. Make sure it is level with surrounding tiles; if it is too high, press it down and quickly wipe away excess adhesive before it dries; if the tile is too low, gently pry it out with a putty knife and add more adhesive beneath it. Rest a 20-pound weight on it for the length of time specified by the adhesive manufacturer.

⚠ **CAUTION**

Asbestos Warning

If your resilient floor was installed before 1986, the flooring or the adhesive underneath may contain asbestos. When damaged, these materials can release microscopic asbestos fibers into the air, creating severe, long-term health risks. Unless you know for certain that your floor does not contain asbestos, assume that it does, and follow these precautions when making any repairs:

❗ *Always wear a dual-cartridge respirator. Asbestos fibers will pass right through an ordinary dust mask.*

❗ *Never sand resilient flooring or the adhesive that lies under it.*

❗ *Try to remove the damaged flooring in one piece. If it looks likely to break or crumble, wet it before removal to reduce the chance of raising dust.*

❗ *When scraping off old adhesive, always use a heat gun to keep it tacky or a spray bottle to keep it wet.*

❗ *If vacuuming is necessary, rent or buy a wet/dry shop vac with a HEPA (High Efficiency Particulate Air) filtration system.*

❗ *Place the damaged flooring, adhesive, and HEPA filter in a polyethylene trash bag at least 6 mils thick, and seal it immediately.*

❗ *Contact your local environmental protection office for guidance as to proper disposal.*

PATCHING SHEET FLOORING

1. Cutting the patch.

◆ Place over the damaged spot a spare piece of matching flooring larger than the area to be patched, aligning the design of the replacement piece with that of the floor. Secure it in position with tape *(left)*.

◆ With a metal straightedge and a utility knife, score the top piece, following lines in the pattern where possible. Using the scored line as a guide, cut through the replacement piece and the flooring underneath. Keep slicing along the same lines until you have cut through both sheets.

◆ Set the replacement piece aside and loosen the adhesive under the section you are replacing as shown in Step 1 on page 156. Remove the damaged section and the old adhesive.

2. Installing the patch.

◆ Spread adhesive over the exposed subfloor with a notched trowel and set the replacement patch in position as you would a tile *(page 156, Step 2)*.

◆ Hide the outline of the patch by a careful application of heat: Cover the edges of the patch with heavy aluminum foil, dull side down, and press the foil several times with a very hot iron *(inset)*. This will partly melt the cut edges of the flooring so they form a solid and almost undetectable bond.

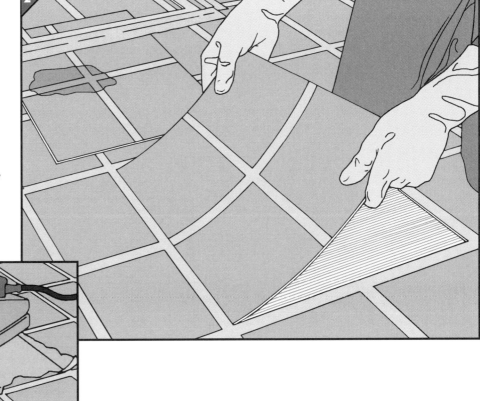

Easy Repairs for Hard Surfaces

Ceramic, marble, or slate tiles make the most durable floors. They are also the most inflexible and brittle. All of them can be cracked by the fall of a heavy weight. They can also be pulled apart by the normal expansion and contraction of a house.

Underlying Problems: A floor that is cracked throughout a room is usually a sign of trouble in the structure beneath it. If your subflooring is less than $1\frac{1}{8}$ inch thick, you may have to replace it.

When subflooring has localized damage, you can usually tighten or patch problem areas. Repair the cause of any water damage before installing new flooring. Dampness in concrete slabs may not be curable; dry the area as much as possible, and use a waterproof epoxy adhesive to hold the finish surface in place.

Ceramic Tiles: The techniques for replacing a tile at the base of a toilet *(below and opposite)* work for repairing damage around any permanent fixture, such as a tub or kitchen cabinet. To cut a tile for installation around a pipe, outline the pipe diameter on the tile and drill a hole through the tile at the outline with a carbide-tipped hole saw. Using a glass cutter, score the tile through the center of the hole, then set the tile on a pencil and break the tile by pressing on both sides.

Use organic adhesives to lay new tile on a wood subfloor or on smooth, dry concrete, and epoxy adhesive on a floor that is moist or uneven. Fill joints between tiles with color-matched silicone grout, which comes premixed in squeeze tubes, cures quickly, and adheres to both old and new tile.

Marble and Slate: These tiles are normally butted tightly against each other in a bed of mortar. To cut them, use a saber saw with a tungsten carbide blade instead of scoring the tile as a prelude to fracturing it or shaping it with tile nippers. Otherwise, replacing them involves only slight variations in the procedure for ceramic tiles shown here.

TOOLS

Grout saw	Cold chisel
Straightedge	Putty knife
Glass cutter	Compass
Electric drill	Grease pencil
Masonry drill bit	Tile nippers
Hammer	Adhesive spreader

MATERIALS

Replacement tile
Emery cloth
Tile adhesive
Grout
Length of 2 x 4

SAFETY TIPS

Safety goggles will protect your eyes when you remove tiles or grout. Wear rubber gloves when you are spreading adhesives.

A TIGHT FIT AROUND A FIXTURE

1. Removing the grout.
◆ Run a grout saw along the joints bordering the damaged tile, applying firm pressure as you move the saw back and forth *(right)*.
◆ To remove grout from very narrow joints, unscrew one of the twin blades supplied with the saw. For extra-wide joints, add a third blade.
◆ Clean fine debris and dust from grooves with a brush or shop vacuum.

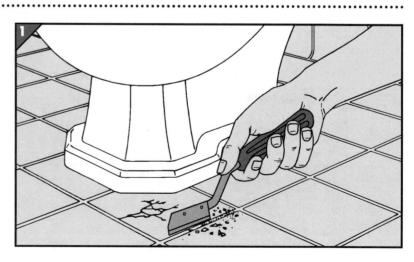

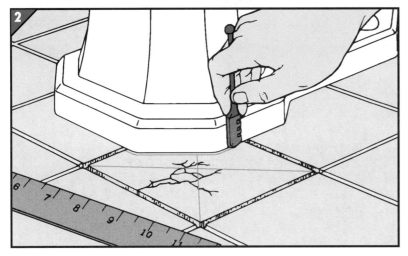

2. Taking out the tile.

◆ For ceramic tile, score an X on the damaged piece with a glass cutter and straightedge, then score along the base of the fixture *(left)*.

◆ Drill a hole through the center of the X with a $\frac{1}{4}$-inch masonry bit. Hammer a cold chisel into the hole, and working toward the edges, break the tile into small pieces. Remove the tile fragments, and scrape off the old adhesive beneath them with a putty knife.

On marble or slate tile, mark an X with a grease pencil. With a masonry bit, drill $\frac{3}{4}$-inch holes every $\frac{1}{2}$ inch along the X and the fixture's base. Break out the tile with a hammer and chisel.

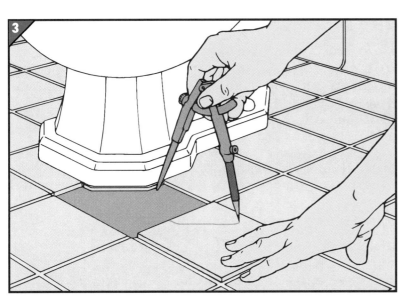

3. Marking and cutting the new tile.

◆ Lay a new tile over the tile adjacent to the space you have cleared.

◆ Replace the pencil in a school compass or scribe with a grease pencil, and open the compass to the width of a tile.

◆ Set the pencil at the edge of the new tile and the point of the compass or scribe at the corresponding point on the base of the fixture.

◆ Holding the new tile securely, move the compass slowly along the base of the fixture to mark the shape of the base on the new tile *(left)*.

◆ Score the fixture outline with a glass cutter, then score a crisscross pattern in the area to be cut away. Cut the tile to fit with nipper blades.

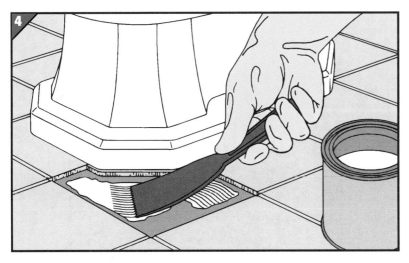

4. Setting the tile in place.

◆ With a notched plastic spreader, apply adhesive to the subfloor or mortar bed *(left)*. If the new tile has tabs on its back, also add a thin coat of adhesive to the bottom.

◆ Apply enough adhesive to raise the tile slightly higher than the ones around it. Use toothpicks or coins set on edge as spacers to keep the joints between ceramic tiles open and even.

◆ Lay a 2-by-4 across the tile, and tap it down with a mallet or hammer.

◆ Let the adhesive set for 24 hours, remove the spacers, and fill the joints with silicone grout.

Dealing with Carpet Stains and Tears

The most carefully tended carpets can suffer accidental damage such as burns, rips, and stains. But with a few scraps of matching carpet and some inexpensive tools and materials, you can make durable, almost invisible repairs.

Set scraps aside when the carpet is laid or ask for some from the seller when you buy a carpeted house. If no scraps have been saved, take them from unseen areas such as a closet floor.

Carpet Repair Basics: Many repair jobs call for a tuft-setter, a special tool for embedding bits of pile yarn in the carpet backing. If you cannot find one at a carpet supplier, you can make your own *(opposite)*.

Before you begin to repair a damaged carpet, familiarize your-

self with its special characteristics. Loop pile, for example, may require a different cutting technique from the one that is used for cut pile, and the repairs for carpeting installed over padding are different from those for cushion-back carpeting *(page 165)*.

Always use the smallest piece of scrap carpet first, so that if you make a mistake there will be larger scraps available to correct it. Practice on carpet scraps before tackling the actual repair.

Cushion-Back Considerations: This type of carpet is glued to the floor instead of being stretched over tackless strips, so some techniques cannot be used. For example, cushion-back carpet has only a single layer of woven backing (convention-

al carpet has two), so mending a surface tear, as shown on page 164, will not work; the tear must be repaired by patching.

Cushion-back carpet is different in another way, as well: Although pile rows run straight along its length, as on a conventional carpet, the rows of pile running across the width of the roll sometimes meet the long rows diagonally.

Before cutting a patch, run the tip of a Phillips screwdriver along the crosswise rows at various angles until you can easily clear pathways for a utility knife. The resulting shape may be a parallelogram instead of a rectangle. Cut out the damaged area to fit the patch as you would on conventional carpet *(page 162)*, slicing through the cushion back all the way to the floor.

 TOOLS

Nail scissors
Tweezers
Cotton swabs
Tuft-setter
Hammer

Utility knife
Knee-kicker
Awl
Putty knife
Notched trowel
($\frac{3}{32}$")

 **MATERIALS**

Scrap carpet
Latex cement
Nails (1$\frac{1}{2}$")
Seam tape

Latex seam
   adhesive
Multipurpose
   flooring adhesive
Cushion-back seam
   adhesive

 SAFETY TIPS

Rubber gloves protect your hands when you are working with liquid adhesives.

RESTORING A SMALL AREA

1. Removing damaged pile.
Using nail scissors *(right)*, cut the damaged pile down to the carpet backing, then pick out the stubs of the tufts or loops with tweezers. For replacement pile, pick tufts or unravel lengths of looped yarn from the edge of a carpet scrap.

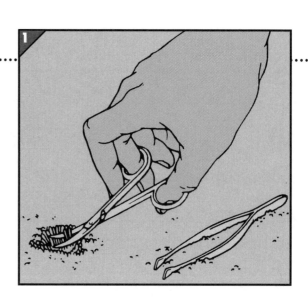

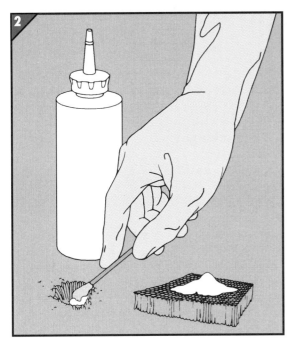

2. Applying the cement.

Squeeze a small amount of latex cement onto the back of a carpet scrap, dip a cotton swab into it, and lay a spot at the point where you will begin setting new tufts or loops *(left)*. The cement dries rapidly—apply it to one small area at a time, and avoid getting it on the carpet pile.

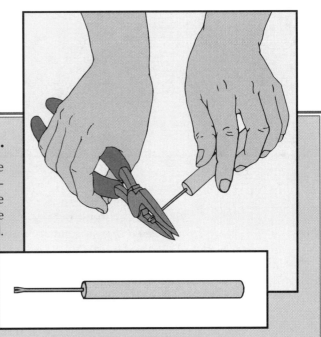

A TOOL FOR SETTING CARPET TUFTS

The makings of a tuft-setter consist of a large needle of the type used for sewing squares of knitting together and a $\frac{3}{8}$-inch wooden dowel. Cut a 4-inch length of dowel and drill a $\frac{1}{16}$-inch hole about 1 inch deep into one end. Insert the needle point into the hole and tap it with a hammer, driving the point into the wood. Using wire cutters or the cutting section of a pair of long-nose pliers *(right)*, clip most of the eye from the needle, leaving a shallow V-shaped end *(inset)*. To complete the tuft-setter, round and smooth this end with a small file or sharpening stone.

3. Replacing the pile.

◆ For cut-pile carpet, fold a tuft into a V over the tip of the tuft-setter and punch it into the latex-swabbed backing with one or two light taps of a hammer *(right)*.

◆ Repeat the process, setting the tufts close together and spreading more cement as needed. For best results, set the new pile so that it protrudes above surrounding fibers, and trim it flush with scissors.

◆ For loop-pile carpet *(inset)*, punch one end of a long piece of yarn into the backing with a tuft-setter, then form successive loops from the same piece and set the bottom of each loop.

◆ Check each loop to be sure it is the same height as the existing pile. Pull a short loop up with tweezers; punch a long one farther into the backing with the tuft-setter.

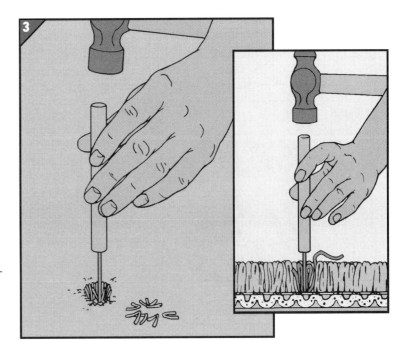

PATCHING A LARGE AREA

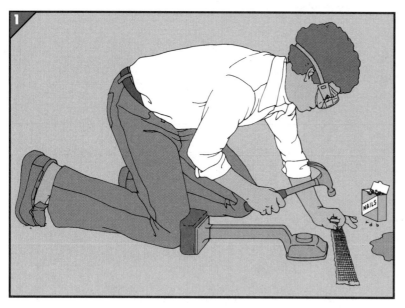

1. Stay-tacking.
◆ To reduce carpet tension for patching, set the teeth of a knee-kicker about 1 foot from the area to be patched and push the kicker forward. Be careful not to raise a hump in the carpet.
◆ Lay a strip of scrap carpet upside down just ahead of the knee-kicker and tack it to the floor with $1\frac{1}{2}$-inch nails at 3- to 4-inch intervals *(left)*. Later, this strip of scrap carpet simplifies pulling out the nails without damaging the carpet.
◆ Release the knee-kicker and repeat the process on the other three sides of the damage.

2. Cutting a patch.
◆ From scrap carpet, measure out a patch slightly larger than the damaged area.
◆ Open a pathway through the pile with a blunt tool, such as a Phillips screwdriver, then pull the pile away from the cutting line with your fingers as you cut with a utility knife *(right)*.

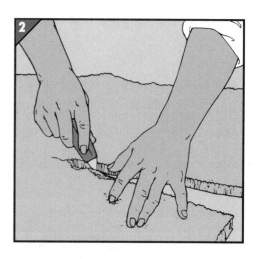

A COOKIE CUTTER FOR SMALL REPAIRS

If the damaged area is less than 4 inches in diameter, rent a tool like that at left, which cuts both a hole in the carpet and a patch to fit, consolidating Steps 2, 3, and 4.

Four spikes penetrate the backing to hold the tool in place as you twist it to work the sharp, serrated edge through. Do not cut the underlying carpet pad except with cushion-back carpet *(page 165)*. Use the same technique to cut a matching patch, then glue it in place as explained in Step 6 on page 164.

3. Cutting a hole.

◆ Place the patch over the damaged area, matching pattern and pile direction.
◆ With one edge of the patch acting as a guide, cut through the carpet and backing to a point about $\frac{1}{2}$ inch from each edge of the patch. Open a pathway for the knife between rows of pile as you cut. Do not cut the pad beneath the carpet.
◆ Lift the patch and cut completely around the damaged area to create a hole about $\frac{1}{2}$ inch smaller than the patch on three sides, as shown by the light gray lines in the illustration *(right)*.

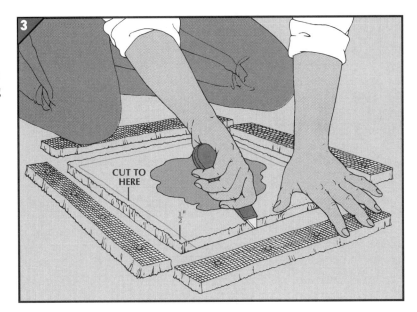

4. Trimming the hole.

◆ Position the patch to overlap the hole evenly on three sides, and stay-tack the edge used in Step 3 as a guide for the first carpet cut *(left)*.
◆ Cut around the anchored patch to enlarge the hole in the carpet to fit snugly around all sides of the patch.
◆ Pull the nails used to secure the patch and remove it from the hole.

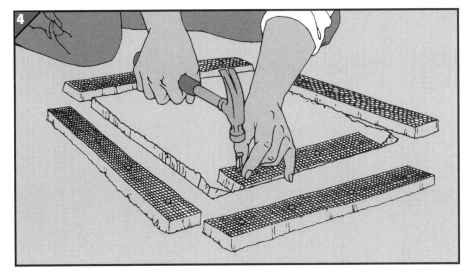

5. Placing seam tape.

◆ Cut four strips of seam tape about an inch longer than the sides of the hole, and spread each strip with a thin layer of latex seam adhesive—just enough to fill in the weave of the tape.
◆ Slip each strip beneath an edge of the hole so that the cut edge of the carpet lies on the centerline *(right)*.
◆ Squeeze a thin bead of adhesive along the edges of the carpet backing; avoid getting any adhesive on the pile.

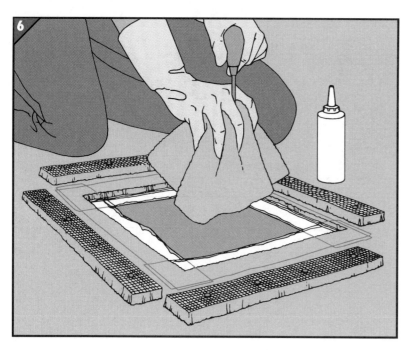

6. Putting in the patch.

◆ Cup the patch in your hand if it is small enough. Otherwise, push an awl through the center of the patch, then fold the patch downward into a tent shape *(left)*.

◆ Position the patch over the hole, and push it off the awl. As the edges of the patch move toward the sides of the hole, they will pick up small amounts of adhesive from the tape.

◆ Push the edges of patch and carpet together and press on the seam around the patch with the heel of your hand. With the awl, free tufts or loops of pile crushed into the seam, and brush your fingers back and forth across the seam to blend the pile of carpet and patch.

◆ After about 5 hours, tug the carpet scraps to remove nails from around the patch, and restore the overall tension on the carpet by using the knee-kicker opposite the patch at all four walls of the room.

MENDING A SURFACE RIP

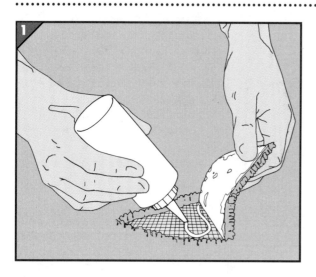

1. Sealing the flap.

◆ If the backing is undamaged, lift the torn section of carpet pile and clean out any loose pile or dried cement.

◆ Apply latex seam adhesive to the exposed backing *(left)*, then spread it in a thin coating over the backing.

2. Hiding the seam.

◆ Press the ripped pile against the adhesive and hold it in place with one hand while you rub the carpet surface with a smooth object, such as the bottom of a glass bottle *(right)*. Rub firmly from the rip toward the sound carpet to work the adhesive into the backing. If any adhesive oozes to the surface, clean it off immediately with water and detergent.

◆ After 4 or 5 hours, when the adhesive has dried, replace any pile that is missing *(page 161)*.

REPAIRS FOR CUSHION-BACK CARPET

1. Applying floor adhesive.

◆ After cutting out the damaged area and a patch to fit, scrape any dried cement from the floor with a sharpened putty knife.

◆ Spread multipurpose flooring adhesive on the clean floor using a $\frac{3}{32}$-inch notched trowel. Press firmly on the trowel to leave a pattern of adhesive ridges separated by bare floor *(right)*.

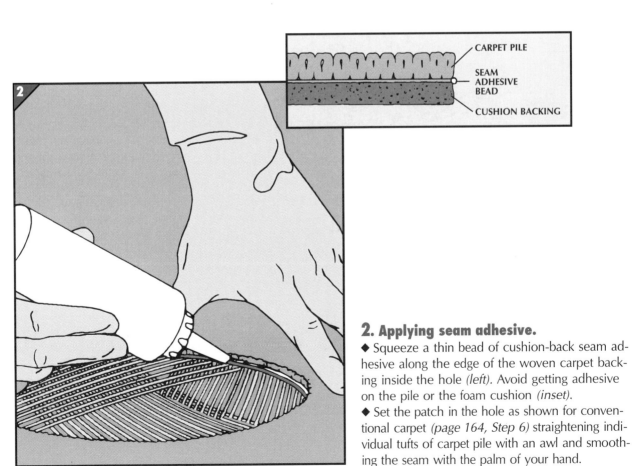

CARPET PILE

SEAM ADHESIVE BEAD

CUSHION BACKING

2. Applying seam adhesive.

◆ Squeeze a thin bead of cushion-back seam adhesive along the edge of the woven carpet backing inside the hole *(left)*. Avoid getting adhesive on the pile or the foam cushion *(inset)*.

◆ Set the patch in the hole as shown for conventional carpet *(page 164, Step 6)* straightening individual tufts of carpet pile with an awl and smoothing the seam with the palm of your hand.

Easy Stairway Repair

Building a stairway and balustrade goes beyond simple carpentry to include elegant techniques of cabinetwork and ingenious joinery. For this reason major problems are rare and usually caused by settling of the floor at one or both ends of the stairway, throwing it out of plumb and level and skewing its right-angle joints.

Jacking up the floor *(page 142)* may restore the stairway's health, but if the damage is extensive, have a contractor raze the old one and install a new stairway.

Common Ailments: The following pages offer simple solutions to squeaks, broken parts, or wobbly newel posts. For many of these repairs you need to know how your stairway was built. Among finished interior stairways made of wood there are only two basic types *(below and opposite, top)*, defined by the way the treads are supported—rough stairways, such as a cleat stairway for the basement, are sometimes made by simpler methods. Metal spiral stairs are a special case.

Open-sided stairways with more than three steps require a post-and-railing fence, or balustrade *(opposite, bottom)*, to provide a handhold. A balustrade's many components are susceptible to minor damage and loosening over time but can also be mended easily *(pages 171-173)*.

Protecting the Wood: Two precautions are in order when repairing finished-wood stairways. Treads, risers, balusters, newel posts, railings, and moldings are made of hardwood—usually oak, birch, poplar, or beech—and will split unless pilot holes are bored for all nails and screws.

Also, glue, used to repair treads and balusters, will not bond to dried glue; old joints must be scraped before reassembly. Glue can also mar any wood finish it drips onto; wipe it away immediately with a damp cloth, let the area dry, and sand it.

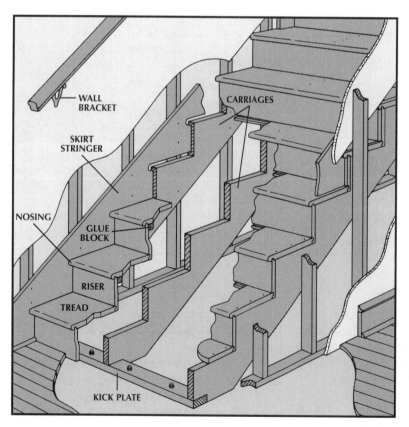

WALL BRACKET
SKIRT STRINGER
CARRIAGES
NOSING
GLUE BLOCK
RISER
TREAD
KICK PLATE

A carriage-supported stairway.

In most older stairways and in a few newer ones, thick sawtooth-notched boards called carriages *(left)* support the treads and provide surfaces for nailing the risers, the vertical boards between treads.

At the bottom, the carriages fit over a kick plate nailed to the floor to keep them from sliding. Each tread has a tongue on its back edge that fits into a groove in the riser behind it and a groove under the front edge that drops over a tongue on the riser below. The treads are also nailed to the carriages. Each tread projects beyond the riser beneath it and ends in a rounded edge called a nosing. Glue blocks are used to reinforce the joints between the treads and risers, and nails through the back of the riser into the tread strengthen that joint.

In this example, the stairway is enclosed by walls on both sides; wall brackets support handrails. Where the stairway meets the wall, a baseboard of finish softwood called a skirt stringer, carefully sawed to fit against the treads and risers, covers and hides their ends.

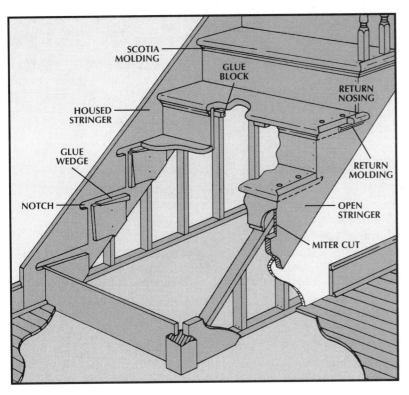

SCOTIA MOLDING

GLUE BLOCK

RETURN NOSING

HOUSED STRINGER

GLUE WEDGE

RETURN MOLDING

NOTCH

OPEN STRINGER

MITER CUT

A prefabricated stairway.

In the modern prefabricated stairway, the functions of the carriage and the skirt stringer are combined in one board, the housed stringer. Glue wedges clamp the ends of the treads and risers in V-shaped notches, which are routed into the side of the housed stringer. The treads and risers usually meet in rabbet joints and are glue-blocked and nailed.

A walled stairway would use housed stringers on both sides, but an open-sided stairway like the one at left supports the outer ends of the treads on an open stringer cut like a carriage. Since it is too light to serve as a true carriage, the studding of the wall beneath it must be used to provide extra support.

The vertical cuts on the open stringer are mitered to match a miter at the end of the riser, concealing the end grain. The end of each tread has a return nosing nailed on, also hiding end grain. A return molding at the end and a scotia molding at the front complete the tread trim.

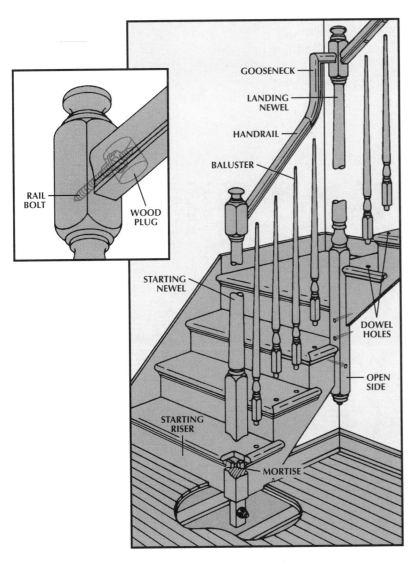

GOOSENECK

LANDING NEWEL

HANDRAIL

BALUSTER

RAIL BOLT

WOOD PLUG

STARTING NEWEL

DOWEL HOLES

OPEN SIDE

STARTING RISER

MORTISE

The parts of a balustrade.

Newel posts provide structural support for the railing. At its base the starting newel has slots called mortises to receive the ends of the starting riser and the open stringer. The newel sometimes extends through the floor to be bolted to a joist. Landing newels, also mortised, are bolted to the header joists behind them.

The railing is joined to the newels with rail bolts *(inset)*. The lag-bolt end is screwed into the newel post, and the machine-screw end runs into a hole in the end of the railing. A washer and a nut are attached to the machine screw through an access hole bored from underneath the rail. Then the hole is plugged. Some railings rise to the upper newel in a curved piece called a gooseneck.

Vertical balusters are installed between treads and the railing, usually with dowels. Often the tops of the dowels are press-fitted into their holes to keep glue from dripping down the balusters.

In an adaptation of a traditional form, many stairways use a longer starting tread, called a bull-nose, and a spiraled railing end called a volute.

Silencing a Squeaky Tread

Squeaks, a common problem in older, carriage-supported stairways *(page 166)*, are caused by treads that have separated slightly from the carriage or by the riser's rubbing against other stair parts when stepped on. You can stop the squeak by making the separated portion stay down or by inserting a thin wedge as a shim underneath it.

The repairs described on these pages will also work on modern prefabricated stairways *(page 167)* with housed stringers, though they develop squeaks far less frequently. A special technique for replacing a glue wedge that has worked loose from the tread and housed stringer is shown on page 170.

Locating the Squeak: Use a carpenter's level to find warps, twists, or bows in the treads. While a helper climbs the stairs, listen, watch for rise and fall, and—resting your hand on the tread—feel for vibration.

If the tread spring is minimal, you can eliminate it with angled nails *(below)* or trim head screws. If the tread movement is substantial, use wedges *(opposite, top)*.

Such repairs from the top are usually sufficient. But if you can get to the stairway from underneath you can make a sound and simple fix, preferable because it is invisible, by adding glue blocks to the joint between the tread and the riser, the most common source of squeaks. If the tread is badly warped or humped in the center, rejoin it with a screw through the carriage *(page 170)*.

 TOOLS

Carpenter's level
Electric drill with bits ($\frac{1}{8}$", $\frac{1}{4}$", $\frac{3}{32}$")
Hammer
Nail set
Utility knife
Screwdriver
Putty knife
Chisel

 MATERIALS

Finishing nails ($2\frac{1}{2}$")
Wood putty
Trim head screws ($2\frac{1}{2}$")
Hardwood wedges
Glue
Common nails (2")
Construction adhesive
Wood screws (3" No. 12)

 SAFETY TIPS

Goggles protect your eyes from dust and flying debris while you are hammering, chiseling, or drilling.

WORKING FROM ABOVE

Nailing the tread down.
◆ With a helper standing on the tread, drill $\frac{3}{32}$-inch pilot holes angled through the tread and into the riser at the point of movement. If the squeak comes from the ends of the tread, angle the holes into the carriage.
◆ Drive $2\frac{1}{2}$-inch finishing nails into the holes, sink the heads with a nail set, and fill with wood putty.

If the tread spring is too great for nails to close, drill pilot holes as above and secure the tread with $2\frac{1}{2}$-inch trim head screws. Apply paraffin wax to the threads to make the screws turn easily in oak. Countersink the heads and fill the holes with wood putty.

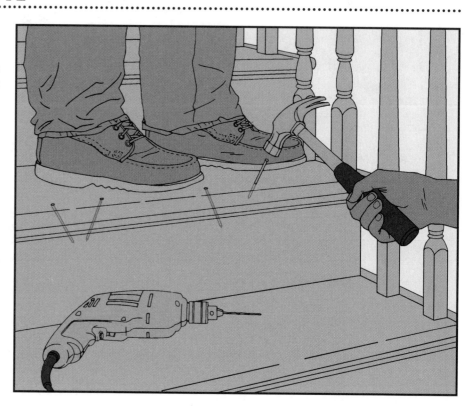

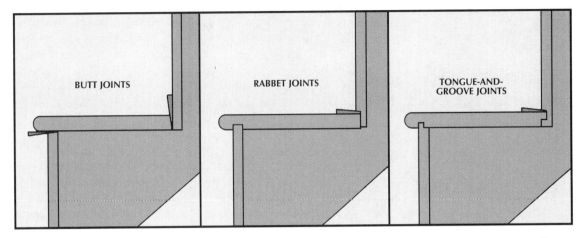

BUTT JOINTS   RABBET JOINTS   TONGUE-AND-GROOVE JOINTS

Wedging treads tight.

◆ Remove the scotia molding under the tread nose and insert a knife into the tread joints in order to discover the kind of joints that were used. With butt joints, the knife will slip vertically into the joint behind the tread and horizontally under the tread; with rabbet or tongue-and-groove joints, the knife-entry directions are reversed.

◆ Drive sharply tapered hardwood wedges coated with glue into the cracks as far as possible in the indicated directions.

◆ Cut off the wedges' protruding ends with a utility knife; replace the scotia molding. Use shoe molding to cover joints at the back of the treads.

WORKING FROM BELOW

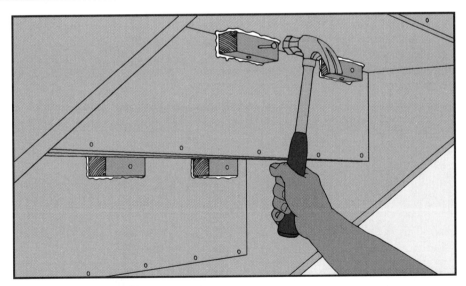

Installing glue blocks.

◆ If the joint has old blocks that have come partly unstuck, pry them off with a screwdriver or putty knife and scrape the dried glue off the tread and riser.

◆ Spread glue on two sides of a block of wood $1\frac{1}{2}$ inches square and about 3 inches long. Press the block into the joint between the tread and the riser and slide it back and forth a little to strengthen the glue bond.

◆ Then fasten the block with a 2-inch common nail in each direction. Add two or three more blocks to each joint.

Drilling through the carriage.

◆ About 2 inches below the tread, chisel a shallow notch into the carriage. With a helper standing on the tread, drill a $\frac{1}{8}$-inch pilot hole angled at about 30 degrees through the notch and $\frac{3}{4}$ inch into the tread *(left)*. Then enlarge the hole through the carriage with a $\frac{1}{4}$-inch bit.

◆ With the helper off the tread, spread a bead of construction adhesive along both sides of the joint between the tread and the carriage, and work it into the joint with a putty knife.

◆ Have the helper stand on the tread again and install a No. 12 wood screw 3 inches long.

RE-SHIMMING A PREFAB STAIRWAY

Replacing loose wedges.

◆ Split out the old wedge with a chisel *(below)*, and pare dried glue and splinters from the notch.

◆ Plane a new wedge from a piece of hardwood to fit within 1 inch of the riser. Coat the notch, the bottom of the tread, and the top and bottom of the wedge with glue.

◆ Hammer the wedge snugly into the notch, tap it along the side to force it against the notch face, then hit the end a few more times to jam the wedge tightly under the tread.

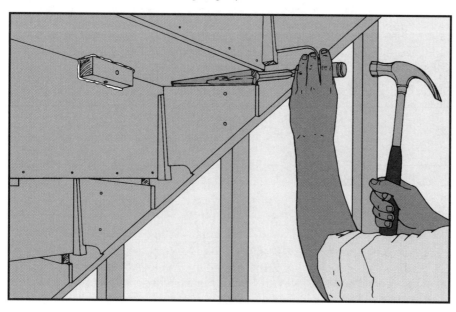

Repairing a Balustrade

The stairway balustrade is an elegant piece of carpentry that is also essential for safety. A broken baluster or a shaky railing should be fixed without delay, in order to preserve both the balustrade's appearance and its stability.

Three Types of Baluster: Tighten a loose baluster with glue, nails, or small wedges; but if it is cracked, dented, or badly scraped, replace it. First, determine how your balusters are fastened. Square-topped balusters usually fit into a shallow groove in the railing. Blocks of wood called fillets are nailed into the grooves be-

tween balusters. Sometimes balusters also end at the bottom in the groove of a lower rail, called a buttress cap, that lies on top of a stringer nailed to the ends of the treads and risers *(page 173)*.

Balusters with cylindrical tops fit into holes in the railing. If they do not overlap the return nosing, balusters are also doweled at the bottom, even though a square section may abut the treads. Balusters that overlap the return nosing are probably joined to the tread by a dovetail joint, and you will have to remove the return nosing to make the replacement.

Obtaining a New Baluster: Save the broken baluster as a pattern for a new one. If you cannot match it, have a cabinetmaker turn one. Instead of cutting a dovetail, pin a doweled baluster into the dovetailed tread with a nail *(page 172)*.

Cures for a Shaky Railing: The cause of a wobbly railing is usually a loose starting newel post. For a post in a bullnose tread, run a lag screw up through the floor into the foot of the post. Where there is no bullnose, the solution is to drive a lag screw through the newel and into the boards behind it *(page 173)*.

 TOOLS

Compass saw or keyhole saw
Pipe wrench
Electric drill with bits ($\frac{7}{32}$", $\frac{5}{16}$")
Spade bit
Folding rule
Chisel
Pry bar
Forstner bit ($\frac{3}{4}$")
Hammer
Miter box
Socket wrench

 MATERIALS

Glue
Finishing nails ($1\frac{1}{2}$")
Lag screws ($\frac{5}{16}$" x 3" and 4") and washers
Scrap wood for pry block
Putty
Scrap 2 x 4 lumber for gauge block

 SAFETY TIPS

Protect your eyes with safety goggles when you are hammering nails, using a hammer and chisel, drilling at or above waist level, or levering wood with a pry bar.

REPLACING A DOWELED BALUSTER

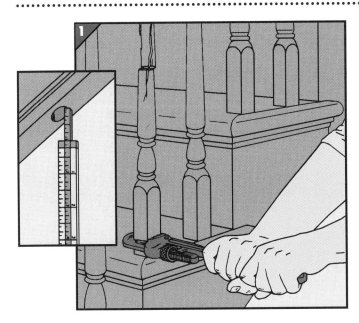

1. Removing the damaged baluster.
◆ Saw the baluster in two and sharply twist the bottom piece with a pipe wrench to break the glue joint at the base *(left)*. Then remove the top piece; if it is stuck, use the wrench.
◆ If the joints do not break, saw the baluster flush, using cardboard on the tread to guard it from the saw. Then drill out the dowel ends with spade bits the size of the dowels on the new baluster.
◆ Trim the bottom dowel to a $\frac{3}{16}$-inch stub.
◆ With a folding rule, measure from the high edge of the dowel hole in the railing to the tread *(inset)* and add $\frac{7}{16}$ inch. Cut off the top dowel to shorten the new baluster to this length.

2. Installing the new baluster.

◆ Smear glue in the tread hole, angle the top dowel into the railing hole, and pull the bottom of the baluster across the tread, lifting the railing about $\frac{1}{4}$ inch *(right)*.

◆ Seat the bottom dowel in the tread hole. If the railing will not lift, bevel the top dowel where it binds against the side of the hole.

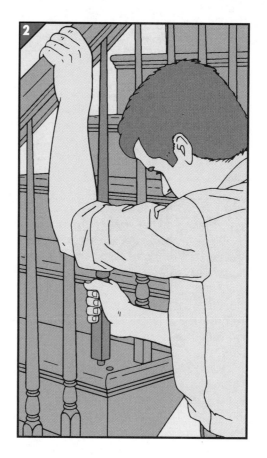

DEALING WITH A DOVETAILED BALUSTER

1. Removing the return nosing.

◆ Use a chisel to crack the joints.

◆ While protecting the stringer with a pry block, insert a pry bar and remove the return molding and return nosing *(below)*.

◆ Saw through the old baluster and hammer it out of the dovetail.

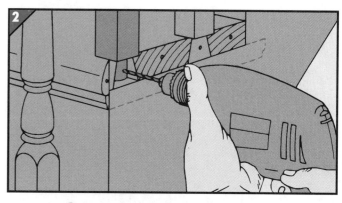

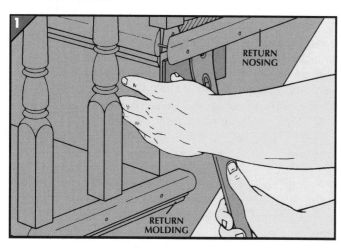

RETURN NOSING

RETURN MOLDING

2. Securing the new baluster.

◆ Insert the top of a cut-to-length doweled baluster into the railing hole and set its base in the tread dovetail. Shim behind the dowel, if necessary, to align it with its neighbors.

◆ Drill a $\frac{1}{16}$-inch pilot hole through the dowel into the tread *(above)*, and drive a $1\frac{1}{2}$-inch finishing nail through the hole into the tread.

◆ Renail the return nosing and return molding through the old holes; putty over the nailheads.

A NEW FILLETED BALUSTER

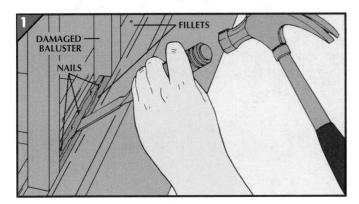

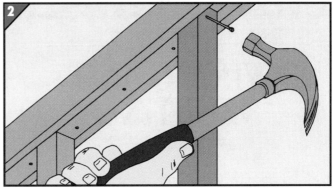

1. Taking out the old baluster.
◆ With a chisel, remove the fillet in the buttress cap on the downstairs side of the damaged baluster *(above)*. Then chisel out the railing fillet on the upstairs side of the baluster.

◆ Hammer each end of the baluster toward the chiseled-out fillet grooves to remove the baluster. Pull any nails left behind and scrape old glue from the grooves.

◆ Obtain the angle for the new baluster ends and fillets by placing the old baluster on top of the new one. Mark the angle on the new baluster and saw it to length.

2. Fastening the new baluster.
◆ Set the baluster against the existing fillets and toenail it to the railing and buttress cap with two $1\frac{1}{2}$ inch finishing nails through each end *(above)*. Start the nails where the new fillets will hide them, and set the heads.

◆ Measure the length of each new fillet, mark the angle cuts using the old baluster, and cut with a miter box.

◆ Coat the backs with glue and fasten them in the railing and buttress-cap grooves with $1\frac{1}{2}$-inch finishing nails.

TIGHTENING A SHAKY NEWEL

Installing a lag screw.
◆ Hold a gauge block *(box, right)* against the newel, 4 inches from the floor, the hole centered on the post. Guide a $\frac{3}{4}$-inch Forstner bit through the block, and drill a hole $\frac{3}{4}$ inch deep in the newel *(below)*. Extend the hole through the newel with a $\frac{5}{16}$-inch bit and into the carriage with a $\frac{7}{32}$-inch bit.

◆ With a socket wrench, drive a $\frac{5}{16}$-inch lag screw 4 inches long fitted with a washer *(overhead view, inset)*. Plug the hole with a dowel, then cut it flush.

To steady a newel set in a bullnose tread, drive two nails through the flooring near the newel. From beneath, measure from the nails to locate the center of the newel dowel. Drill shank and pilot holes and install a $\frac{5}{16}$-inch lag screw 3 inches long. Pull the nails and putty the holes.

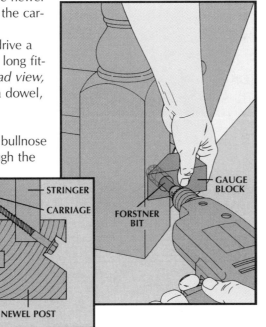

A GAUGE BLOCK FOR ANGLED DRILLING

A gauge block like the one shown in the photograph above simplifies the drilling of an angled hole into a newel post. To make a gauge block, use a Forstner bit to bore a $\frac{3}{4}$-inch hole through the edge of a block of 2-by-4. Then cut the block through the hole at the angle you wish to drill.

6 CHAPTER

WIRING AND LIGHTING

Many homeowners think of wiring as difficult to understand and even dangerous. In reality, most electrical jobs are straightforward, safe, and often surprisingly easy. Learning how electricity works and becoming familiar with its standardized procedures and equipment will give you the confidence to tackle almost any repair or installation.

From repairing a lamp to installing an up-to-date receptacle or light fixture, many electrical projects around the house require little more than turning off the power, detaching wires from the old, and connecting them to the new. Taking on such tasks not only saves the cost of an electrician but provides an opportunity to customize your electrical system and even to improve its safety.

To bring electricity and lighting where it is lacking is often simply a matter of making electrical connections. The following pages illustrate ways to install a variety of conveniences, from additional receptacles and track lighting to ceiling fans and dimmer switches. Techniques for installing low-cost, low-voltage lighting outdoors are presented on pages 356 to 361.

By installing light fixtures outdoors, you can lengthen recreational time in the yard and garden and provide lighting for safety and security. Outdoor wiring techniques are no different from those used indoors, but special fittings are needed as protection against the weather.

◄ An overhead fixture splashes light where it is needed, such as over a bank of shelves. A wall light can be wired to virtually any 15-amp circuit with a wall switch.

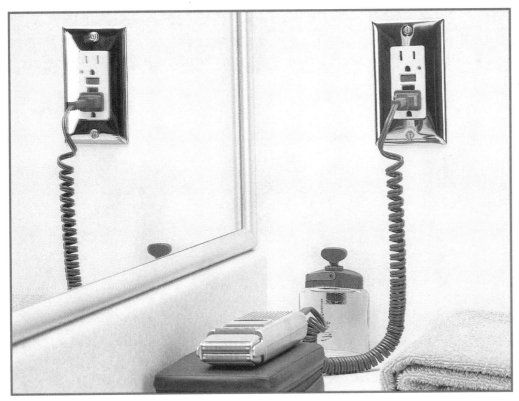

Protection against electrical leaks and ground faults is required for new receptacles in several areas of a home, including bathrooms. You can satisfy this requirement by installing ground-fault circuit interrupters, or GFCIs.

Simple to install, track lighting offers unmatched flexibility. In most systems the fixtures can be moved individually along the track strip as needs change.

Hanging lamps help focus light on a countertop or range. Augmenting the recessed fixtures in the ceiling, the overhead lighting makes the kitchen more pleasant and safer to work in.

A Tool Kit for Basic Wiring

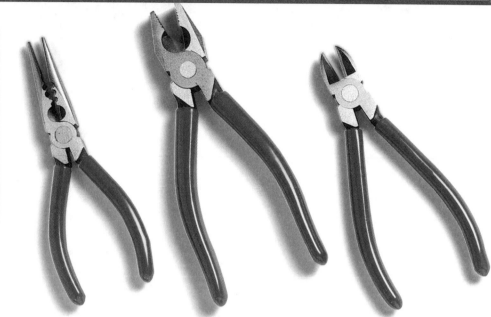

The full range of electrical repairs and improvements described in this chapter require a wide variety of tools, from hammers and screwdrivers to a stud finder and a star drill. If you have built or fixed things around the house, you probably already own some of these items.

When undertaking electrical work, consider the dozen tools shown here as potential additions to your tool kit. Not only do they speed the task and improve results, the majority have no satisfactory substitute.

Even so, few jobs require all these devices. Buy them as you need them. In short order, you will assemble an electrical tool kit tailored to the kind of work that appeals to you.

Long-nose pliers.
Handy in tight spaces, this tool has rounded jaws to aid in bending wires to fit around screw terminals.

Receptacle analyzer.
Plugged into a receptacle, this device tests for electrical faults in the circuit. Three lights at the bottom of the tester glow in different combinations to diagnose several problems.

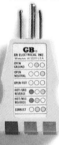

Lineman's pliers.
This heavy-duty tool is used for pulling cable into fixture boxes, bending wire, and twisting knockouts from metal boxes.

Diagonal-cutting pliers.
The narrow tip and angled jaws of this tool let you snip wires in tight spaces such as small fixture boxes.

Voltage tester.
A neon bulb glows when the two probes are touched to a live circuit. Voltage testers are used to check that the current is off inside an electrical box before you begin a job and to determine which is the incoming hot wire in a circuit.

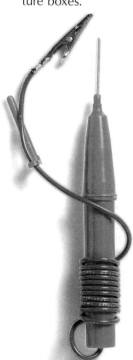

Conduit bender.
Fitted with a long pipe handle for leverage *(not shown)*, a conduit bender turns metal conduit around a corner without crimping. This model has built-in spirit levels. They indicate 45-degree and 90-degree bends.

Continuity tester.
This device, used only when the power is turned off, detects interruptions in the path of current. Connected to a switch in the on position, for example, the tester lights if the switch is good.

Cable ripper.
A short tooth inside the tool slits plastic sheathing on electrical cable without damaging the wires inside.

Fuse puller.
This tool, made of plastic, is used to extract cartridge fuses from a service panel. The small jaws on one end fit fuses up to 60 amps; the other end is for fuses of higher capacity.

Multipurpose tool.
Three tools in one, the jaws of a multipurpose tool cut wires, strip insulation from wire ends, and squeeze crimp fittings tightly around wires.

Fish tape.
The flat, springy metal band of fish tape is used to pull—or "fish"—cables and wires through walls, ceilings, and other enclosed spaces.

Tin snips.
Useful for cutting plastic cable sheathing and the sheet metal from which many electrical boxes and fixtures are made, tin snips come in right-cutting, left-cutting, and straight-cutting varieties. Straight-cutting snips, shown here, are best for electrical work.

The Electrical System

Evaluating the electrical system of your house involves determining whether the power supply is adequate, checking the condition of the wiring and whether it is safe for rated loads, and testing receptacles to see if they work.

How Much Power: The amount of electricity entering the house is measured in amperes (amps). Older houses may have a service capable of supplying only 60 or 100 amps—too little to operate a collection of power-hungry appliances such as clothes dryers and ranges, which require 150- or 200-amp service.

Check the amperage rating on the service panel; it is commonly printed on the inside of the door on panels with fuses, or on the main breaker in a panel with circuit breakers. If you see no rating, look for it inside the glass housing on the electric meter, which can reveal service capacity even if it isn't marked there *(opposite, bottom)*.

Older houses tend to have fewer circuits than newer ones, but an electrician can add additional circuits up to the limit of the service. For example, 150-amp service can supply as many as 30 circuits; 200 amps support up to 40 circuits. Note also the number and positions of electrical receptacles in each room. If some walls have no receptacles, it's a good idea to add some.

Examine the Wiring: Since most wiring is hidden inside walls, a complete inspection is never possible, but you can get a general idea of its condition by scrutinizing wires in the attic and basement *(opposite, top)* and near fixtures.

Turn off power to a circuit at the service panel and remove the cover of a receptacle or switch on the dead circuit to check the condition of wires inside the box; frayed or cracked insulation around the wires there indicates that new wiring is probably needed in places, though not necessarily throughout the house.

In some cases improvements in the electrical system must meet the requirements of modern building codes. And if you rewire part of the house, there is a possibility in some locales that the inspector may require you to bring the entire house up to electrical-code minimums.

TOOLS Screwdriver
Voltage tester
Receptacle analyzer
Three-prong
   receptacle adapter

Evaluating a service panel.

Power enters the house through a service-entrance cable located at the top of the main service panel. In a fuse-protected panel of the type shown here or on page 183, the electricity passes through the main fuse block—which cuts off power to the entire house when it is removed—and to the fuses to house circuits that exit from the sides of the box. The system is grounded by means of a bare copper wire that is clamped either to a nearby cold-water pipe at least $\frac{3}{4}$ inch in diameter or to a copper rod driven several feet into the ground outside. In a panel that contains circuit breakers *(page 182)*, a main breaker takes the place of a fuse block, and individual breakers control the circuits.

An old panel may be overloaded by modern appliances; if so, it poses a fire hazard and should be replaced as soon as possible. Signs of overloading include the presence of many 20- and 30-ampere fuses or circuit breakers, a burning smell near the panel, fuses that are warm to the touch, or darkened and discolored copper contact points under the fuses.

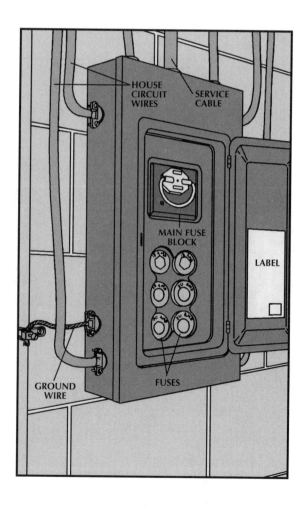

HOUSE CIRCUIT WIRES
SERVICE CABLE
MAIN FUSE BLOCK
LABEL
GROUND WIRE
FUSES

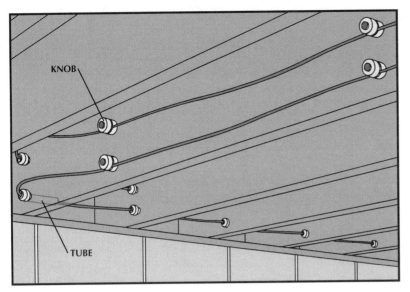

KNOB

TUBE

Evaluating the wiring.

If the basement or attic joists are exposed, check the wiring. Outdated knob-and-tube wiring, illustrated here and identified by its paper insulation and the porcelain insulators from which it gets its name, must be entirely replaced. This old system is ungrounded and therefore unsafe.

With other types of electrical wiring, check the insulation for fraying or cracking. Insulation problems indicate that rewiring is probably needed, although minor repairs are possible in some instances.

Evaluating receptacles.

Test all receptacles with a plug-in receptacle analyzer as shown on page 186. To adapt a two-slot outlet, remove the center screw from the cover plate, attach the adapter's ground contact to this screw, then plug in the analyzer and retighten the screw. Depending on the type of tester used, one or more test lights will glow if the outlet is functioning and safely grounded—check the manufacturer's instructions. If you find ungrounded outlets, consider replacing the first receptacle on the circuit with one containing a ground-fault circuit interrupter (GFCI), as shown on pages 192 to 194. This tactic is just as safe as a grounded circuit and protects all receptacles downstream on the circuit. Bathroom receptacles and those within 6 feet of a kitchen sink should also be protected by a GFCI.

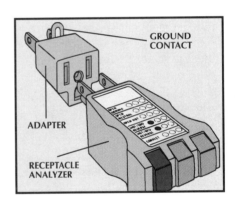

GROUND CONTACT

ADAPTER

RECEPTACLE ANALYZER

A Clue to Incoming Power

When all else fails, compare the electric meter outside a house with the photographs shown here to gauge how many amps the electric service provides. An old, 60-amp meter *(far left, top)* sits on a round socket that is barely larger than the glass housing. A 100-amp meter *(far left, bottom)* is fastened to a rectangular box little wider than the meter's glass bubble, while a 150- or 200-amp meter *(near left)* is fastened to a box that is much larger.

Never break the seal on an electric meter or otherwise disturb it; the meter belongs to the electric utility, and tampering with it is a criminal offense in some jurisdictions.

TRICKS OF THE TRADE

The Service Panel

Each branch circuit from the main service panel is protected against overloads by an individual circuit breaker or fuse. These safety devices cut off power to defective circuits at the service panel. By preventing the flow of excessive current, they reduce the risk of fires resulting from overheated wires.

A circuit breaker is a sort of switch that "trips," turning itself off, when current exceeds the breaker's maximum amperage. In a fuse, too-high amperage causes a metal element to melt or to break, cutting off the current.

Causes and Cures: A tripped breaker or blown fuse always indicates a problem in its circuit, which must be fixed as soon as possible. The most common cause, and the easiest to remedy, is that the various devices on the circuit draw too much current. Reduce the load before replacing the fuse or resetting the breaker. If there appears to be

no overload, check for malfunctioning appliances, which may draw more power than normal.

A circuit overload is more dangerous when it results from a short circuit—for example, when one bare wire touches another or touches a metal electrical box that allows the current to flow to ground. In such cases, the current meets almost no resistance, because it does not pass through an appliance or a light. The result is a surge of amperage that quickly overloads the circuit.

Circuit breakers and fuses protect only wires, not you. If you cause a short circuit by touching a wire (hot or neutral; both carry current) while you are grounded, a potentially fatal current can flow through your body in the split second before the breaker or fuse detects the overload. Only a GFCI circuit breaker *(page 195)* can respond quickly enough to protect both you and the wires.

Safety While Working: Breakers and fuses serve another important safety function, allowing you to turn off power to an individual circuit while you work on it. You can also shut off power to the entire house from the service panel, by switching one or more breakers or by pulling out a block of fuses.

⚠ **CAUTION** *Never try to solve a continuing overload problem by replacing a fuse with one of a higher amperage rating. It will allow the wires to overheat and create a fire hazard.*

⚠ **CAUTION** *Tripping the main breaker or pulling the main fuse block turns off power throughout the house, but these actions do not completely kill power within the service panel. Only the power company can completely shut off power to the panel. Always exercise extreme caution when working around the service panel.*

SAFEGUARDS OF THE ELECTRICAL SYSTEM

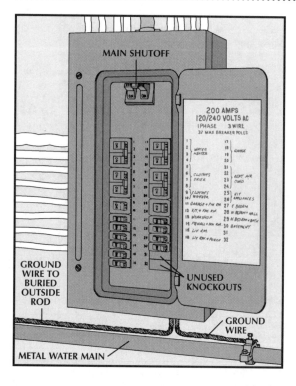

MAIN SHUTOFF

200 AMPS
120/240 VOLTS AC
1PHASE   3 WIRE
32 MAX BREAKER POLES

GROUND WIRE TO BURIED OUTSIDE ROD

UNUSED KNOCKOUTS

GROUND WIRE

METAL WATER MAIN

A straight-bus circuit breaker panel.

One large breaker on this panel serves as a main shutoff as well as limiting the total amperage of current flowing into the house through the service head. The panel shown at left has a 200-amp main breaker; similar panels in older houses may have a lower amperage rating.

◆ Circuits that carry 240 volts to appliances such as a water heater or a clothes dryer are protected by two linked breakers. Single

breakers or small, space-saving breakers control the 120-volt circuits. Each breaker's amperage rating is marked on the end of the switch.

◆ The unused space at the bottom right of the panel contains knockouts that allow later installation of more circuits and breakers.

◆ When a circuit breaker trips, it is reset by flipping the switch back to the on position. Some models require that the switch be pushed firmly to the off position before resetting.

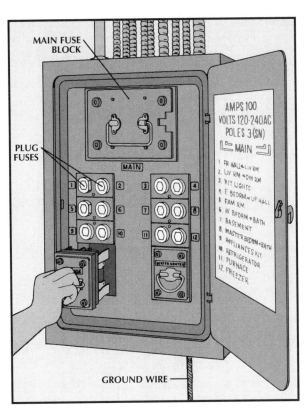

A straight-bus fuse panel.
This type of panel contains a main fuse block with knife-blade fuses *(page 184)* that each control power to the circuits. Turning off all power to the house requires pulling the entire block out of the panel.

◆ Below the main block are screw-in plug fuses *(below, bottom)*, rated for 15 amps or 20 amps, which protect the individual 120-volt circuits.

◆ Blocks at the bottom of the panel each contain two cartridge fuses *(page 184)*, which protect 240-volt circuits.

◆ Before removing a fuse for any reason, ensure that no current is flowing through it by turning off all electrical devices on that circuit.

◆ To change a cartridge fuse, pull its block completely out of the panel *(left)*.

◆ To change a plug fuse, unscrew it while touching only the insulated rim. Do not stand on damp ground and do not touch any other object while you are removing or replacing the fuse.

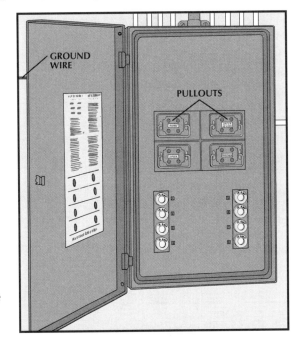

A split-bus panel.
This type of panel, found in some houses built before the early 1980s, has no main shutoff. Instead, blocks of high-amp breakers or fuses control different groups of circuits; all must be tripped or removed to shut off power in the house.

◆ The split-bus fuse panel shown at right has four pullout blocks to control all power to the house. A split-bus breaker panel may have as many as six heavy-duty circuit breakers to do the job.

◆ Split-bus panels have been banned in construction since 1984.

TYPES OF FUSES

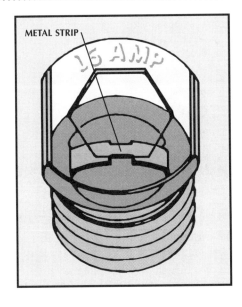

Plug fuse.
The plug fuse is the most common type. It screws into the panel in the same way that a light bulb screws into a socket. Current flows through a narrow metal strip—zinc in the United States—which melts through when overloaded, breaking the circuit. In Canada, the strip is made of copper, which melts at a lower temperature, making the fuse more sensitive.

Time-delay fuse.
Similar in shape to a plug fuse, this type also screws into the service panel. Its design allows it to withstand the momentary surge of current caused by the starting of a motor in an appliance such as a power tool or a refrigerator compressor. The zinc strip softens but does not melt through unless the surge continues. The larger current typical of a short circuit, however, melts the zinc immediately. The plug-type time-delay fuse cannot be used in Canada.

Type S fuse.
Also known as a tamper-proof fuse, a Type S provides time-delay protection and prevents the use of fuses of the wrong amperage rating for a given circuit. A Type S fuse cannot be screwed directly into the service panel; instead, it fits an adapter that locks into the panel socket. Each adapter is sized for only one amperage rating. A fuse rated for 20 amps, for example, will not fit into an adapter for a 15-amp fuse. In Canada, this kind of fuse is designated Type D. A similar Canadian tamper-proof fuse, Type P, does not have a time-delay function.

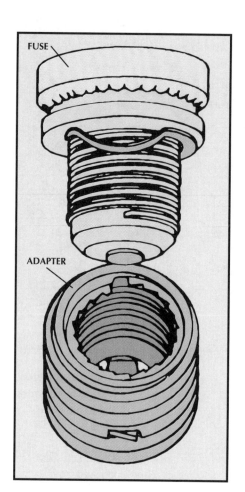

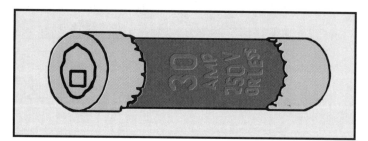

Cartridge fuse.
The metal-capped ends of a cartridge fuse, called ferrules, snap into metal spring-clip contacts. Often found in auxiliary fuse boxes *(opposite, top)*, cartridge fuses are rated from 10 to 60 amps. They are generally used to protect circuits that are dedicated to large appliances such as ranges, dryers, or central air conditioners.

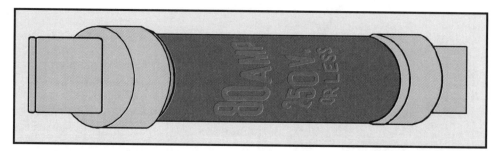

Knife-blade fuse.
Another type of cartridge fuse, a knife-blade fuse is distinguished by metal blades at each end that snap into spring clips within a fuse block. Knife-blade fuses are rated for more than 60 amps and may be used in the main fuse block of the service panel.

CHECKING AND REPLACING CARTRIDGE FUSES

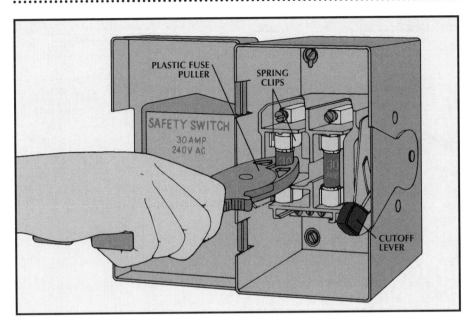

Changing a cartridge fuse.

◆ Before replacing a cartridge fuse (shown above in an auxiliary fuse box), first cut off power from the main service panel.

◆ Open the box and flip the cutoff lever inside to the off position.

◆ Use a plastic fuse puller to grasp the center of the fuse, pulling sharply to release it from the spring clips. In a recently used circuit, the metal caps of the fuse may be hot to the touch.

◆ Carefully push the replacement cartridge fuse into the spring clips with the fuse puller.

◆ To change fuses in a fuse block, pull the block from the service panel, then remove the fuses in the same manner.

⚠️ **CAUTION** *Be careful not to touch the metal spring clips in an auxiliary fuse box—they might still carry current—and never pull a fuse with metal pliers.*

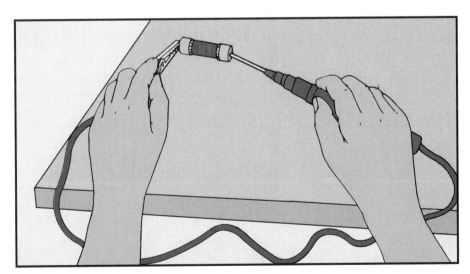

Testing a cartridge fuse.

Because a cartridge fuse or a knife-blade fuse gives no visible sign that it has blown, it must be checked with a continuity tester (*page 178*).

◆ Remove the fuse and touch each of the metal end caps or blades with a continuity tester (*above*). If the bulb lights, the fuse is good and the trouble is in the appliance it protects. If the bulb does not light, the fuse has blown and must be replaced with a new one.

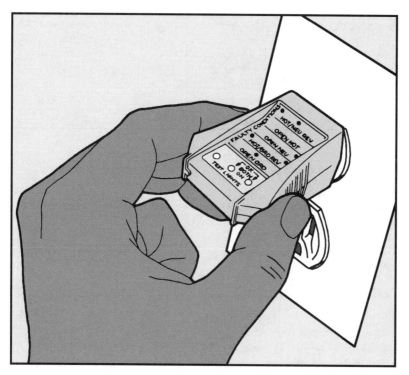

Verifying receptacle wiring.

A receptacle analyzer *(page 178)* detects several wiring problems when plugged into a live circuit, identifying the difficulty with different combinations of three glowing lights. Typically, wiring is correct when all three lights glow. No lights means that power is not reaching the receptacle. A guide printed on the analyzer explains other combinations of lights.

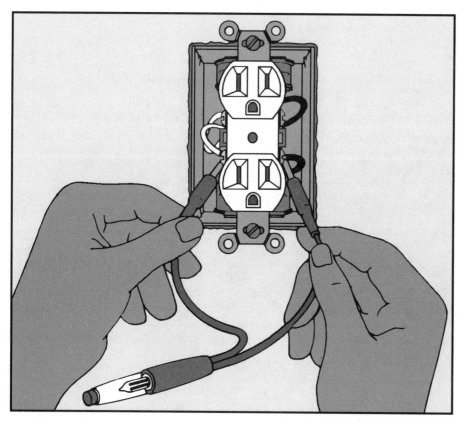

Testing a receptacle for power.

Before working, turn off power to the circuit at the service panel and make the following checks with a voltage tester. If the tester's neon bulb glows at any stage of the process, the circuit still has power; stop and try a different fuse or circuit breaker at the service panel.

◆ Before removing the cover plate, check that power is off by inserting the probes of a voltage tester into the receptacle's vertical slots.

◆ Remove the cover plate. Touch the probes to the terminal screws where the black and white wires attach to the receptacle *(left)*. On a dual receptacle, test both pairs of terminals.

◆ Test from each black wire to the ground wire to check for defects or improper wiring in the neutral circuit.

Checking a light fixture.

◆ Turn off power to the fixture at the service panel. Flip the wall switch to OFF.

◆ Unscrew the fixture and pull it away from the box to expose the wires.

◆ Hold the fixture in one hand and remove wire caps with the other. Keep black and white wires away from each other and the box if it is metal.

◆ Gently loosen each fixture wire from the corresponding house wire. Set the fixture aside.

◆ In the following checks, a voltage tester will not glow if the power is off. Touch one probe of the tester to the black wire in the box and the other to ground—the box if it is metal (left), or the ground wire in a plastic box. Check also for voltage between the black wire and the white wire and between the white wire and ground.

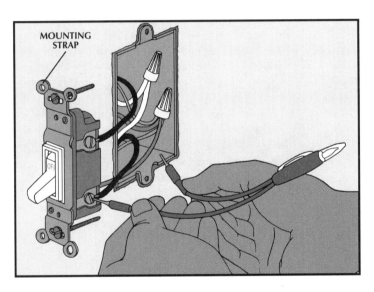

Testing a switch for power.

◆ To verify that electricity to a switch has been shut off, unscrew the cover plate, then the switch. Pull the switch from the box by the mounting strap.

◆ While touching one probe of a voltage tester to the outlet box if it is metal—or to the ground wire if the box is plastic—touch the other probe to each of the brass terminals on the switch (left). If the switch has push-in terminals (page 191), insert the probe into the release slots. The tester's bulb will not glow if electricity to the switch has been turned off.

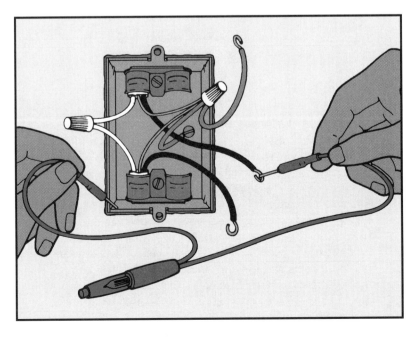

Identifying a feed wire.

◆ To find out which of the black wires in a box supplies current from the service panel, first cut power to the box.

◆ Pull the fixture or other device from the box, and confirm with a voltage tester that the electricity is off.

◆ Disconnect all black wires and arrange them so they are not touching each other, the fixture, or the box.

◆ Have a helper restore power to the circuit.

◆ Touching nothing but the insulated leads of a voltage tester, hold one probe against the box or ground wire, and the other against each black wire in turn (left). The tester will glow when the probe touches the feed wire.

◆ Have your helper turn off the power. After verifying that the feed wire is no longer hot, mark it with tape.

Basic Skills

Almost every household wiring job entails a few basic tasks such as stripping cable sheathing and wire insulation, joining wires with wire caps, and connecting wires to switches and receptacles. Once you have become familiar with these easily learned skills, your home wiring projects will proceed more quickly and easily.

Taking Care with Cable: It is critical when stripping cable sheathing that you avoid damaging the insulation on the wires inside. Even a small nick on a wire's insulation can become an electrocution or fire hazard.

Likewise, avoid excessive marring of bare wires as you work with them. Minor scratches and nicks from tools are unavoidable, but badly damaged wires increase resistance, which can cause overheating.

Leave Enough Slack: When extending or adding a circuit, don't stint on cable. Two or three extra feet of cable provide a margin for error when stripping sheathing from cable or insulation from the wires inside. If you damage a wire or make some other mistake, you can cut off the error and proceed. Excess cable remains hidden inside the wall or ceiling.

Leave No Bare Wire Exposed: Strip $\frac{3}{4}$ inch of insulation or less from the ends of wires. Following this rule will, in most cases, ensure bare wire ends long enough for making connections to fixtures or to other wires, yet short enough that no bare wire can be seen after connection is made. If the shine of copper is visible, undo the connection and trim the ends of the wires.

The Remarkable Wire Cap

Wires are connected to each other with a conical plastic fastener called a wire cap. Hollow at its base, a wire cap contains a copper coil. When the wire cap is tightened like a nut onto two or more wires, the coil binds them securely together.

Wire caps used in house wiring come in a variety of sizes. A wire cap that is too large or too small will result in an unreliable connection. The one to use depends on the number of wires in the connection and their gauge. Keep several sizes on hand; the best way to find the right one is to experiment.

WORKING WITH CABLE AND WIRE

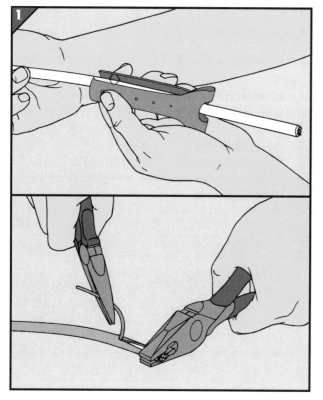

1. Exposing the wires in cable.

◆ With NM-B cable—the plastic-sheathed cable used for ordinary indoor wiring—insert 10 to 12 inches of cable into a cable ripper and squeeze the tool to force a tooth inside the tool through the sheathing. Pull the ripper toward the end of the cable *(left, top)*.

◆ When stripping UF, or underground feeder, cable—used for outdoor circuits buried in soil—cut a 3-inch slit alongside the ground wire with diagonal cutters. Grasp the wire with long-nose pliers and the end of the cable with lineman's pliers. Pull the ground wire through the sheathing to expose 10 to 12 inches of bare copper *(left, bottom)*. Repeat for the insulated wires if necessary.

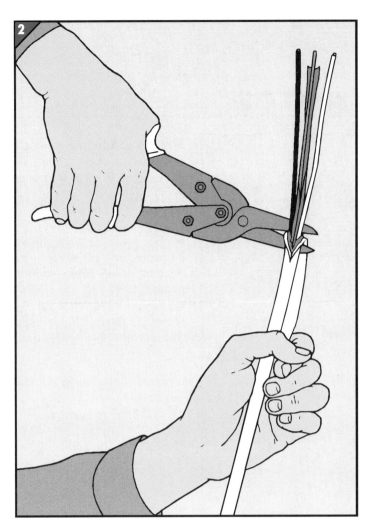

2. Removing cable sheathing.

With both types of cable, bend back the sheathing—and in the case of NM-B cable, its paper liner—then cut off the insulation with tin snips *(left)*. Also tear off the brown paper wrapped around the ground wire in NM-B cable.

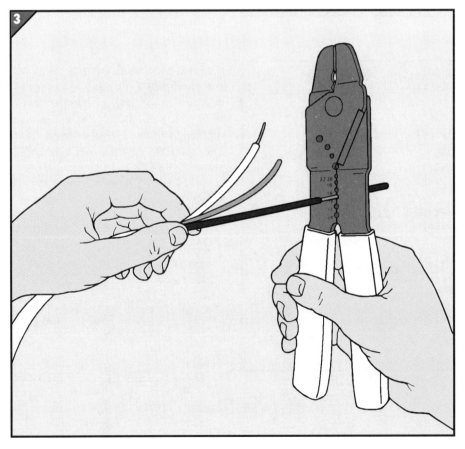

3. Stripping insulation.

◆ Match the gauge of wire you are working with—it is embossed on the plastic sheathing of the cable—to the corresponding wire-stripping hole in a multipurpose tool *(left)*.

◆ Close the multipurpose tool over the wire $\frac{1}{2}$ inch to $\frac{3}{4}$ inch from the end and rotate the tool a quarter-turn in each direction.

◆ Without opening the tool, pull the severed insulation off the wire to expose the bare metal.

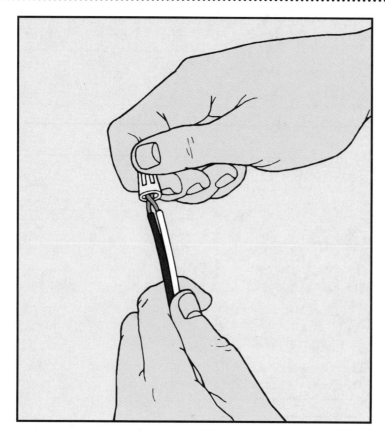

Making solid-wire connections.
◆ After stripping the insulation from the wires, hold them next to each other with long-nose pliers and twist the exposed metal ends together clockwise with lineman's pliers.
◆ Place a wire cap over the wires. If bare metal is visible *(left),* trim the ends of the wires without untwisting them.
◆ Push the wires firmly into the base of the cap as you twist the cap clockwise until the connection is tight.

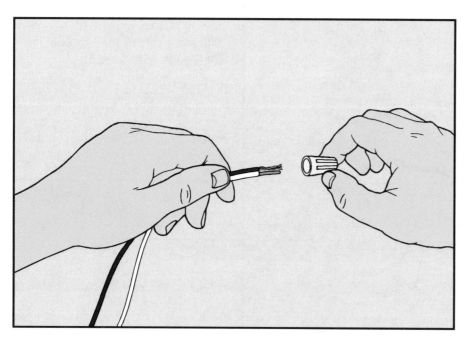

Making stranded-wire connections.
◆ When connecting stranded wire to solid wire, strip about $\frac{1}{8}$ inch more insulation from the stranded wire than from the solid wire. Do not twist together the individual strands.
◆ Hold the two wires side by side as shown at left, then check the fit of a wire cap, making sure that it encloses every filament of the stranded wire.
◆ While pushing the wires firmly into the wire cap, twist it clockwise until the connection is tight.

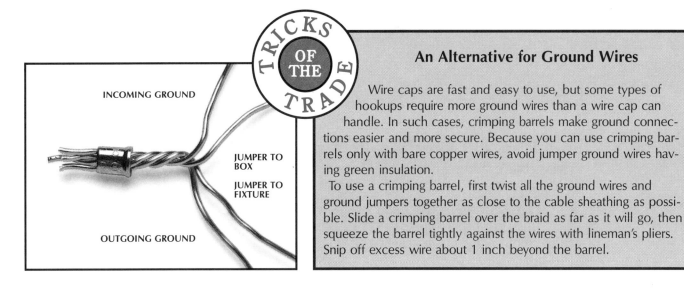

INCOMING GROUND

JUMPER TO BOX

JUMPER TO FIXTURE

OUTGOING GROUND

An Alternative for Ground Wires

Wire caps are fast and easy to use, but some types of hookups require more ground wires than a wire cap can handle. In such cases, crimping barrels make ground connections easier and more secure. Because you can use crimping barrels only with bare copper wires, avoid jumper ground wires having green insulation.

To use a crimping barrel, first twist all the ground wires and ground jumpers together as close to the cable sheathing as possible. Slide a crimping barrel over the braid as far as it will go, then squeeze the barrel tightly against the wires with lineman's pliers. Snip off excess wire about 1 inch beyond the barrel.

TWO KINDS OF TERMINALS

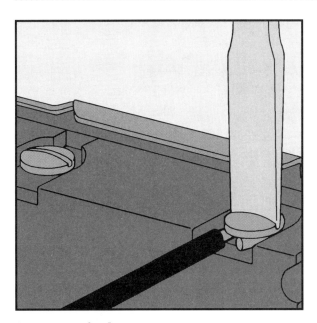

Screw terminals.
◆ With long-nose pliers, form a partial hook in the stripped end of the wire.
◆ Loosen the terminal and fit the hook under the screwhead in the direction shown above.
◆ Bend the wire around the screw with long-nose pliers, then tighten the screw.

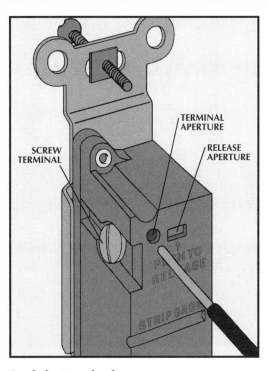

SCREW TERMINAL

TERMINAL APERTURE

RELEASE APERTURE

Push-in terminals.
Some fixtures offer the alternative of a push-in terminal.
◆ Trim the wire or remove additional insulation as necessary to make the bare end of the wire fit the strip gauge on the back of the fixture.
◆ Push the wire into the terminal aperture as far as it will go, leaving no bare wire exposed.
◆ To disconnect a wire, push the blade of a small screwdriver into the release aperture while pulling on the wire.

Protecting Circuits with GFCIs

Electricity can be deadly in very small doses. A current not much larger than 5 milliamps—$\frac{5}{1,000}$ ampere, or about $\frac{1}{3,000}$ the amperage required to trip a 15-amp circuit breaker—can fatally disrupt the rhythm of your heart.

Deviant Currents: The potential for danger arises when electricity leaks from a hot wire inside an electrical box or within an appliance or tool to a cover plate or casing. These accidentally energized elements may well pass unnoticed—unless you happen to touch one of them while working outdoors in bare feet or otherwise connected to ground.

Under such circumstances, your body can become a conductor for a minuscule but potentially deadly current. Such a shift from the current's usual path through the house wiring is called a ground fault.

An Electronic Sentinel: Since the middle of the 1970s, electrical codes have required safety devices called ground-fault circuit interrupters (GFCIs) in locations around the house where you might cause a ground fault *(box, opposite)*.

A GFCI compares the amperage in a circuit's hot wire with that in the neutral wire. In a circuit without a ground fault, the two currents are identical. When a ground fault occurs, however, they differ by a small amount. A detector in the GFCI notes the discrepancy, and if the difference reaches 5 milliamps, the device will interrupt the circuit within $\frac{1}{40}$ second. Either style—receptacle or circuit breaker—will protect the circuits in most homes. In circuits containing more than 200 feet of cable, however, tiny leakages can add up to trip the device and make the circuit unnecessarily troublesome.

Two Types of Protection: GFCIs are available as receptacles that fit an ordinary outlet box and as circuit breakers for the service panel. A receptacle-style GFCI *(opposite)*, in addition to offering protection where it is installed, also covers the circuit downstream from that point. The circuit breaker variety *(page 195)* protects every point on a circuit. When replacing a circuit breaker with a GFCI, buy one of the same capacity.

A Monthly Checkup: GFCI receptacles and circuit breakers both have a test button that simulates a ground fault. Push the button monthly and immediately replace any GFCI that fails to trip.

 TOOLS

Screwdriver
Long-nose pliers
Wire stripper
Voltage tester

 **CAUTION**

A GFCI Limitation

! A ground-fault circuit interrupter offers no protection if you touch both the hot and neutral wires at the same time.

! Hire an electrician to install any GFCI on a circuit having aluminum wires, even if they are clad in copper.

INSTALLING A GFCI RECEPTACLE

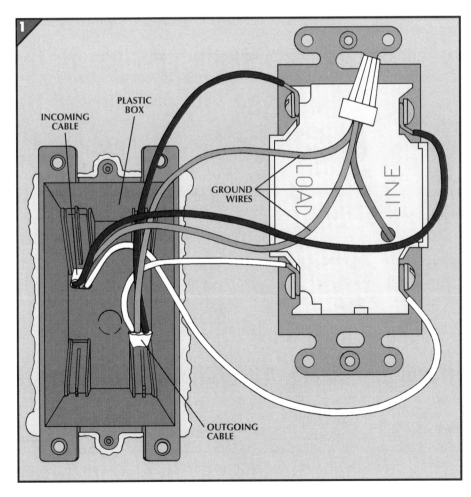

PLASTIC BOX

INCOMING CABLE

GROUND WIRES

LOAD

LINE

OUTGOING CABLE

1. Wiring the receptacle.

◆ Determine which is the incoming cable using the procedure described on page 187, then turn off power to the circuit at the service panel.

◆ Connect the insulated wires of this cable to the "line" side of the receptacle, black wire to the receptacle's brass-colored screw as shown at left—or to the black wire that some GFCIs offer instead of a terminal—and the white wire to the silver-colored screw (or white wire).

◆ In the same manner, attach the wires of the outgoing cable to the "load" side. With no outgoing cable and a GFCI having wires instead of terminals, cover the bare ends of the unused wires with wire caps.

◆ In a plastic box, join the bare copper ground wires in the cables to the ground wire of the receptacle with a wire cap. If the box is metal, run a grounding jumper from the box to the wire cap.

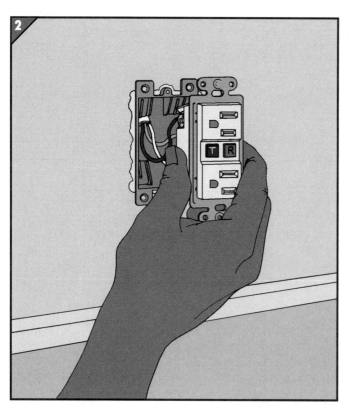

2. Mounting the receptacle.

◆ After making all connections, tuck the wires into the outlet box, being careful not to loosen any connections.

◆ Push the receptacle into the box *(left)* and secure it with mounting screws.

◆ Screw the cover plate in place.

3. Testing the receptacle.

◆ Restore power at the service panel and plug a radio into the first protected receptacle on the circuit. Turn on the radio, then push the GFCI test button T *(right)*. If the reset button R pops out and the radio goes off, the GFCI is working correctly.

◆ Press the reset button and repeat the test with other receptacles downstream from the GFCI.

If you get other results, turn off power at the service panel and confirm that you have connected the incoming and outgoing wires correctly. Next, try a replacement GFCI. If the problem persists, call an electrician.

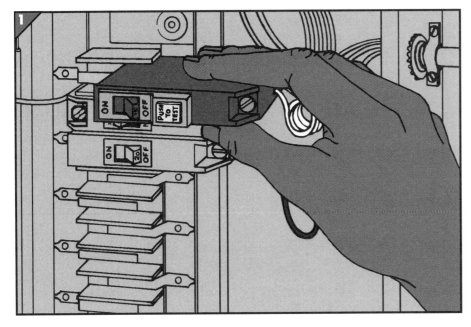

1. Mounting a GFCI breaker.

◆ Turn off power to the panel at the breaker marked MAIN or, in a split-bus panel, at the high-voltage breakers *(page 183)*. Remove the face of the panel to expose the circuit breakers.

◆ Detach the black wire from the existing breaker and pull the device from the panel.

◆ Turn the GFCI off, then insert it into the now vacant slot *(left)*.

For a new circuit, choose an unoccupied slot and remove the corresponding knockout in the panel face. Insert the GFCI breaker in the slot and wire it as described below.

2. Wiring the GFCI breaker.

◆ Attach the black wire in the circuit to be protected to the terminal on the GFCI marked "load" or "load power."

◆ Connect the white circuit wire to a terminal or white wire marked "load neutral" on the GFCI.

◆ Screw the GFCI wire labeled "panel neutral" or "neutral bus" to any vacant terminal on the neutral bus bar.

◆ In a new circuit, connect the ground wire to the panel grounding bar.

◆ Restore power to the panel and push the test button on the GFCI. If it does not trip, try the remedies in Step 3 on the preceding page. Otherwise, reset it as you would an ordinary circuit breaker *(page 182)*.

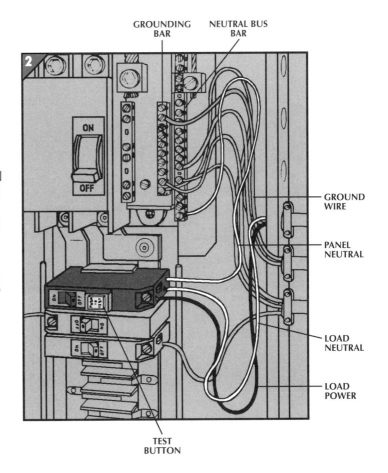

GROUNDING BAR

NEUTRAL BUS BAR

GROUND WIRE

PANEL NEUTRAL

LOAD NEUTRAL

LOAD POWER

TEST BUTTON

Repairing a Lamp

Despite the great variety of lamp shapes and sizes, almost all incorporate a few standard electrical components—a switch, one or more bulb sockets, a cord, and a plug. You can usually fix a lamp that will not light by replacing one or more of these parts. You should also install a new cord or plug when one appears worn, even if the lamp is in working order.

Switch and Socket Repairs: The lamp part that is most prone to failure is the switch, which is typically built into the socket. To determine whether a socket with a switch needs replacement, remove and test it using the procedures shown on pages 197 and 198.

The procedure is the same whether the switch control is a pull chain, a knob, or a push button.

New Cords and Plugs: When putting in a new lamp cord *(pages 198-199)*, make sure it has the same wire size and thickness of insulation as the old one. To upgrade two components at once, buy a cord with a molded-on polarized plug.

A plug should be replaced whenever its casing is cracked or its blades are too loose to make a solid connection in the wall receptacle. For a house with polarized receptacles—those with one vertical slot wider than the other—choose a polarized plug *(page 199)*.

 TOOLS

Screwdriver   Long-nose pliers
Continuity tester   Wire stripper
Utility knife   Wire cutters

 MATERIALS

Lamp socket   Standard polarized
Lamp cord   plug
Strain-relief bushing   Quick-connect
Glue   polarized plug

The Importance of Polarity

In a properly wired lamp, the hot components—those that carry current to the bulb—are connected together, as are the neutral components, which complete the circuit. If this arrangement, known as polarity, is not maintained, a short circuit can result. If the polarity is accidentally reversed, so that the elements designated as neutral become hot, an exposed socket can deliver a shock even when the switch is off.
To avoid these dangers, manufacturers code each component so that you can easily determine whether it is hot or neutral. As illustrated at right, the narrow slot of the wall receptacle is hot, and so is the narrow blade of the plug. The hot wire in the lamp cord is smooth—that is, it has no ridges molded into its plastic insulation. This wire attaches to the hot socket terminal, which is brass colored. The neutral components of the lamp consist of the wide blade of the plug (which matches the wide slot of the receptacle), the ridged wire in the cord, and the silver-colored terminal.

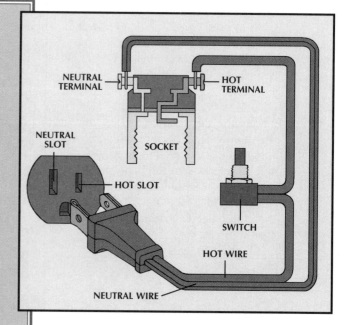

1. Removing the socket.

◆ Unplug the lamp and remove the shade and bulb. Before testing the socket, try adjusting the brass tab inside it by raising the tab slightly with a screwdriver. Put in the bulb, plug in the lamp, and check whether it lights. If it does not, unplug the lamp once again, remove the bulb, and proceed with the repair.

◆ Push with your thumb on the socket's outer shell where it says PRESS. Tilt the shell out of the socket cap.

◆ Lift away the shell and its sleeve.

◆ Loosen the terminal screws. Pull the wires off the screws to free the socket.

Remove a socket cap if it is bent or corroded, or later if you need to install a new socket that will not fit it. To do so, pull the cord out of the cap and unknot it. Loosen the cap setscrew, and then unscrew and remove the cap.

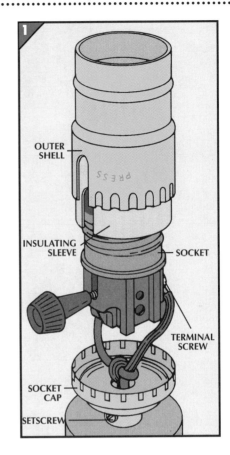

2. Testing the socket.

◆ Attach the alligator clip of a continuity tester to the socket's screw shell, which is the part that holds the light bulb. Then touch the tester's probe to the neutral (silver-colored) terminal screw on the socket.

◆ If the tester lights *(left)*, the electrical connection is unbroken between the terminal and the shell; proceed to Step 3.

◆ Otherwise, replace the socket, making sure to connect the smooth lamp cord wire to the brass terminal screw and the ridged cord to the silver one.

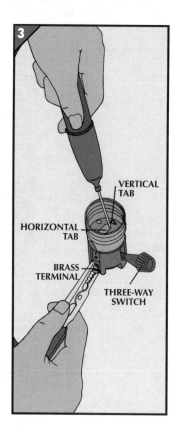

3. Testing the switch.

◆ For a simple on/off switch, clamp the alligator clip to the brass terminal screw on the socket and touch the tester probe to the brass-colored tab inside the socket.

◆ Turn the switch. If the tester does not light in either switch position, replace the socket.

In a three-way switch, attach the clip to the brass terminal and test both the vertical and horizontal tabs inside the socket.

◆ Turn the switch until the tester lights when the probe touches the vertical tab but does not light when the probe touches the horizontal tab. If the tester does not light at all, replace the socket.

◆ Advance the switch one position; the tester should light with the probe on the horizontal tab *(left)*.

◆ In the next position, it should light when the probe touches either tab. If the tester does not light as expected, the socket must be replaced.

VERTICAL TAB
HORIZONTAL TAB
BRASS TERMINAL
THREE-WAY SWITCH

REPLACING AN OLD LAMP CORD

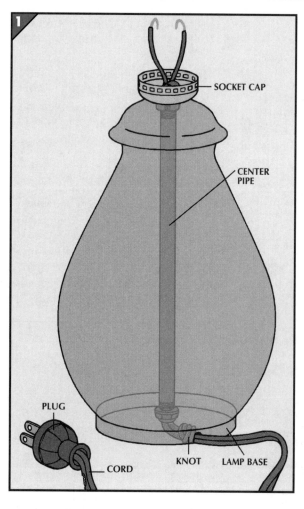

SOCKET CAP
CENTER PIPE
PLUG
CORD
KNOT   **LAMP BASE**

1. Taking out the old cord.

◆ Unplug the lamp and remove the shade and bulb.

◆ Take out the socket *(page 197)*. If the wires of the lamp cord are knotted in the socket cap, untie them.

◆ Turn the lamp on its side. With a utility knife, peel away the felt base covering.

◆ Pull the cord out of the center pipe into the base. If it is knotted inside the base, as in the example at left, untie the knot. Then pull the cord out through the hole in the base.

◆ In newer lamps, there may be a plastic strain-relief bushing in the hole in the base. Working from inside the base, squeeze the bushing with long-nose pliers and push it out the hole.

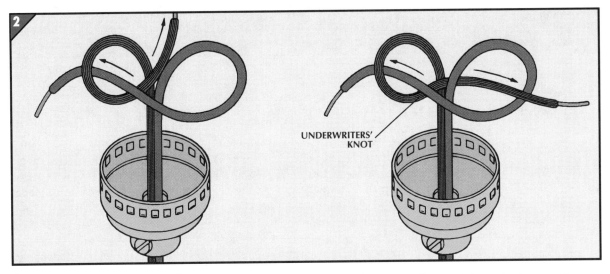

2. Putting in the new cord.

◆ Push enough new cord through the hole at the lamp base to reach the socket with 4 inches to spare. Put a strain-relief bushing on the cord at the hole and squeeze it into place.

◆ Snake the cord through the pipe and into the socket cap. Separate the wires in the last 2 inches of the cord and strip $\frac{1}{2}$ inch of insulation from each.

◆ Tie the ends of the wire into an Underwriters' knot as shown

above. Tighten the knot so it nestles in the socket cap.

◆ Reglue felt to the base, rewire and reattach the socket, and put in a bulb.

◆ Plug in the lamp.

ATTACHING A NEW PLUG

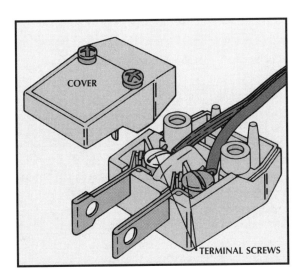

Installing a polarized plug.

◆ Unplug the lamp, then cut off the old plug.

◆ Separate the wires $1\frac{1}{8}$ inches from the cord's end. Strip $\frac{1}{2}$ inch of insulation from each wire.

◆ Remove the cover from the new plug and loosen the plug's terminal screws.

◆ Twist together the strands at the stripped end of the ridged wire, then loop them clockwise around the silver terminal. Tuck any loose strands under the terminal before tightening the screw.

◆ Fasten the smooth wire to the brass terminal in the same way (above).

◆ Reattach the plug cover and plug in the lamp.

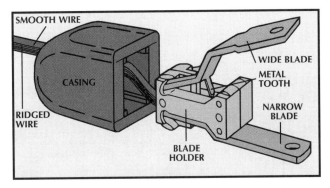

Installing quick-connect plugs.

◆ Unplug the lamp, then cut off the old plug. Make sure the exposed cord is cut cleanly, with no stripped wire or protruding strands; trim if necessary.

◆ Lightly press the blades of the plug together and pull the blade holder out of the casing.

◆ Thread the lamp cord through the back of the casing. Pull the blades apart and push $\frac{7}{8}$ inch of the cord into the holder (above), orienting the lamp cord so that the ridged wire aligns with the tooth in the wide blade and the smooth wire with the narrow blade's tooth.

◆ Squeeze the blades together, forcing the tooth on each into the cord insulation. Slide the blade holder back into the casing and plug in the lamp.

Changing Light Fixtures

TOOLS

Utility knife
Screwdriver
Wire stripper
Adjustable wrench

MATERIALS

Coat hanger wire
Light fixture
Wire caps
Crossbar
Nipple
Reducing nut
Hickey

A new light fixture can both enhance a room's look and save energy. While incandescent bulbs produce softer and more natural light, fluorescent fixtures *(pages 202-203)* comsume less wattage, give off less heat, and last much longer. The procedures below and on the following page apply to almost any incandescent fixture mounted on a wall or ceiling.

Removing the Old Fixture: With the power turned off, remove the bulbs or tubes. Free a fixture stuck to the wall or ceiling with paint or caulk by cutting around the decorative cover, or canopy, with a utility knife. Unscrew any mounting screws or cap nuts, then pull the fixture away from the box and hang it from the box with a

hook that is made of coat hanger wire. Disconnect the wiring.

If the exposed ends of house wires have cracked insulation, cut them back and strip off $\frac{1}{2}$ inch of insulation to reveal bright, clean wire. If necessary, strip the new fixture wires to the same length.

Mounting a Fixture: Most new fixtures come with mounting hardware and instructions. If not, and if the new fixture is similar in size and weight to the old one, you may be able to reuse some of the old hardware.

Every light fixture must be fastened securely to a ceiling or wall box. Moreover, heavy fixtures such as chandeliers must have additional support and should be attached to a box stud *(opposite)*.

HANGING LIGHTWEIGHT FIXTURES

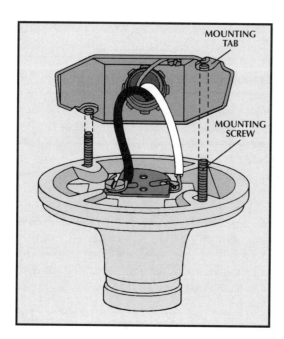

MOUNTING TAB

MOUNTING SCREW

Connecting a simple fixture.

A single-bulb porcelain fixture, typically used in garages and basements, connects to house wiring by means of terminals.

◆ To install this type of fixture, connect the black house wire to the brass-colored terminal and the white house wire to the silver-colored terminal.

◆ Secure the fixture to the threaded mounting tabs of the box with screws. Tighten the mounting screws gingerly; overtightening can crack the ceramic.

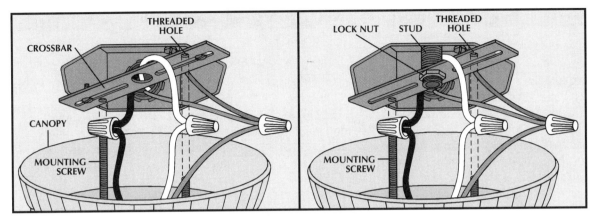

Attaching a fixture with an adapter.

Light fixtures are often fastened to outlet box mounting tabs with screws, typically through holes in the canopy.

◆ Where canopy holes do not align with the tabs, adapt the box with a slotted crossbar. Screw the crossbar to the tabs *(above, left)*, or for box with a stud in the center, slip the crossbar onto the stud and secure it with a lock nut *(above, right)*.

◆ Fasten the canopy to the threaded holes in the crossbar with screws trimmed, if necessary, so they do not press against the back of the box.

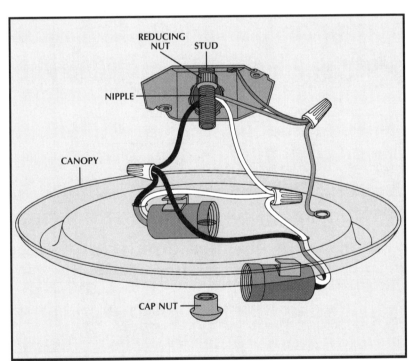

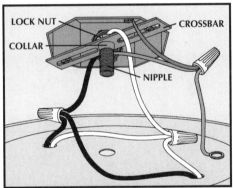

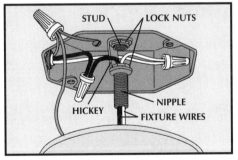

Securing center-mounted fixtures.

If the box has a built-in stud, extend it with a smaller-diameter nipple held to the stud by a reducing nut *(above, left)*.

If the box has no stud, use a crossbar with a threaded collar in the center *(above right, top)*. Screw a nipple into the collar and secure it with a lock nut so the nipple protrudes through the canopy just far enough to engage the cap nut. Fasten the crossbar to the box tabs.

To hang chandeliers or other fixtures whose wires pass through the canopy *(above right, bottom)*, attach a nipple to the stud with a C-shaped adapter called a hickey. Secure both nipple and hickey with lock nuts.

Pass the fixture wires through the nipple into the box.

◆ With the nipple in place, connect the fixture's white, black, and ground wires to the house circuit's corresponding wires. Fold the wires into the box or under the canopy.
◆ Fasten the fixture to the nipple with the cap nut, drawing the canopy against the wall or ceiling.

Installing Fluorescent Fixtures

Although the cost of bulbs and installation may be greater, fluorescent lighting gives more uniform illumination than incandescent lighting and is more efficient in its use of energy. Using the hardware that comes with a new fixture, you can mount fluorescents quite easily with an electric drill and spade bit. Follow the procedures on page 200 to remove old incandescent or fluorescent fixtures.

The heart of every fluorescent fixture is the ballast, a device that provides a quick surge of voltage to start the tube, then limits the current while the tube is lit. After 10 or more years, a ballast will wear out, but often it is more economical to install a new fixture than to replace a ballast.

Types of Fixtures: Fluorescents come in a variety of shapes and sizes, but most of them fall into three categories:

Rapid-start fixtures, which light after a few seconds' delay, often are used in home workshops and laundry rooms. These fixtures may malfunction if turned on and off frequently in a brief period of time.

Instant-start fixtures turn on at the flick of a switch but wear out quickly because of the high-voltage surge when switched on.

Compact fluorescent bulbs are self-contained fixtures that have the ballast or an adapter in the base. More efficient and versatile than fluorescent tubes, compact fluorescents screw into ordinary incandescent bulb sockets.

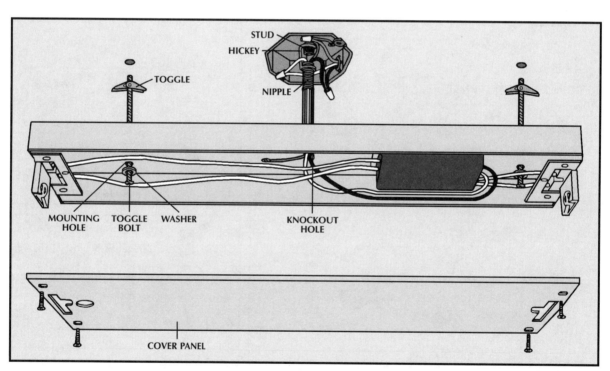

Mounting a one-tube fixture.

◆ Position the fixture with the knockout hole for the wires centered on the ceiling box, and mark the ceiling through the fixture-mounting holes. Lower the fixture and, with a spade bit, drill $\frac{5}{8}$-inch holes at the marks.

◆ Slip a toggle bolt and washer through the fixture-mounting holes and screw a toggle onto the end of each of the bolts.

◆ Thread a hickey to the stud and a nipple to the hickey; if there is no stud, attach a crossbar to the box tabs and a nipple to the crossbar *(page 201)*.

◆ Have a helper support the fixture or hang it from the box with a wire hanger, then lead the fixture wires through the nipple and connect them to those that are in the box, black to black and white to white. Connect the ground wires from the fixture and the house circuit to each other and to the grounding jumper in the box if it is metal.

◆ Raise the fixture. While folding the wires into the box, push the toggles through the ceiling holes and guide the fixture onto the nipple. Tighten the toggle bolts.

◆ Finally, install the cover panel and the tube.

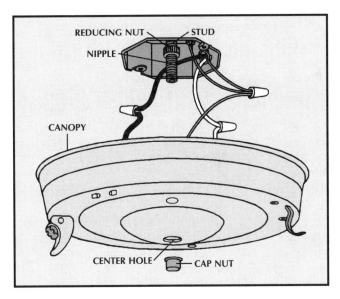

Hanging a circular fixture.

◆ Thread a reducing nut onto the stud and screw a nipple into the nut.

◆ Connect the fixture wires to the house wires—black to black and white to white. Join the ground wire in the fixture to the circuit grounding wire and to a jumper in the box if it is metal. Fold the wires into the box.

◆ Raise the fixture to the box so that the nipple protrudes through the center hole of the canopy. Thread the cap nut onto the nipple and tighten to secure the fixture against the ceiling.

Troubleshooting Guide

PROBLEM	REMEDY
Tube will not light.	Replace fuse or reset circuit breaker. Replace tube. Rapid-start: Rotate tube on holder. Instant-start: Make sure pins are fully seated in sockets. Check that tube wattage equals that shown on ballast.
Ends of tube glow but center does not light.	Check attachment of fixture's ground wire and circuit ground.
Tube flickers, blinks, or spirals.	Normal with new tube. Should improve with use. Rapid-start: Rotate tube on holder. Instant-start: Make sure pins are fully seated in sockets. Replace tube.
Fixture hums or buzzes.	Tighten ballast connections.
Blackening at end of tube.	Tube worn out. Replace tube.

Replacing a Switch

Electrical switches are inexpensive and easy to replace, but before swapping a switch that you suspect is faulty, first check the light bulb or appliance that the switch controls and the circuit breaker or fuse that protects the circuit.

If those are operating properly, it is time to test the switch itself *(opposite and page 206)*. If the switch passes the tests, the problem is elsewhere in the circuit and it is best to call in an electrician to diagnose the cause of the failure.

Such mysterious—and potentially dangerous—problems are rare, however. Chances are, if the fuse or circuit breaker is operating properly and no electricity is reaching an operative bulb or appliance, the switch has failed and must be replaced.

There are reasons other than failure to replace a switch, the most common being the desire to install a dimmer or timer. Although installing any replacement switch is a fairly simple task, several factors must be considered if the job is to be successful.

Type and Location: No matter what type of new switch you are putting in, you must first know the type you are replacing and where in the circuit it is located. Some switches, such as a timer, can only replace a single-pole switch installed in the middle of a circuit run *(below)*. A three-way switch *(page 206)* can be replaced only by another three-way switch or a three-way dimmer.

You can tell the type of switch by examining it. The arrangement of wires within the box tells where on the circuit the switch is located.

Keep Track of the Wires: When replacing a simple single-pole switch, there are only two hot wires, and they can be hooked up in any order. But installing other kinds of switches can be more complicated. If you fail to identify or lose track of the wires for a three-way switch, for example, you can wind up with a device that does not work and a tedious chore making things right.

Switch Swapping Basics: As with any other electrical work, turn off power to the circuit at the service panel and then test to make sure it is off *(page 187)*. Remove the switch cover plate and loosen the two screws that hold the switch in the box. These screws will not fall free of the mounting strap; small fiber washers hold them in place. After loosening the screws, gently pull the switch out of the box until the wires are fully extended.

Many switches made before the 1980s will not have grounding terminals. When replacing one, always use a grounded switch.

TOOLS

Lineman's pliers
Screwdriver

Wire stripper
Continuity tester

SINGLE-POLE SWITCHES

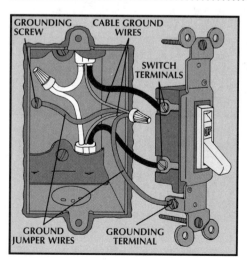

GROUNDING SCREW   CABLE GROUND WIRES

SWITCH TERMINALS

GROUND JUMPER WIRES   GROUNDING TERMINAL

Middle-of-the-run switch.
Found anywhere between the beginning and the end of a circuit, a middle-of-the-run switch can be identified by the two or more cables that enter the box. In a metal box, as shown here, the ground wires are joined with jumper wires to the grounding terminal on the switch and the grounding screw in the box. A plastic box requires no grounding jumper to the box. The switch shown has two black wires, both hot, attached to its terminals. In some hookups, you might find a black and a red hot wire.

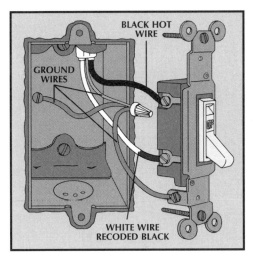

Switch loop.

One cable enters the box in a switch loop. The cable runs between a fixture and the controlling switch. The white wire carries current from fixture to switch; therefore it is a hot wire, and the end of the wire is recoded black. Although codes do not require this, electricians consider it good practice that will help avoid confusion. The black wire carries current back to the fixture when the switch is on. Electricians use an expression to remember this scheme: "White down, black back."

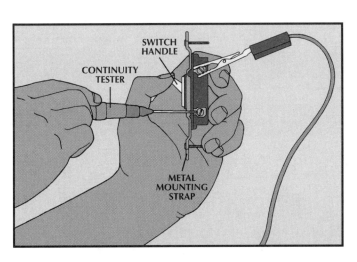

Testing a single-pole switch.

There are two tests you can perform on a suspect switch. If the switch fails either test, it is defective.
◆ Apply the clip of a continuity tester to one switch terminal and touch the other terminal with the probe *(above)*. Operate the switch handle; the tester should light when the switch is on but not when it is off.
◆ Fasten the clip to the metal mounting strap of the switch. Touch the probe to each terminal and operate the switch as you do. The tester's bulb should not light in either position.

Mounting a single-pole switch.

◆ Connect the two hot wires to the switch terminals, in either order.
◆ With the switch handle in the off position, push the switch into the box, carefully tucking in the wires.
◆ Fasten the mounting strap to the box with its screws. Maneuver the switch within the box so that it is perfectly vertical, even if the box is not, before tightening the screws. If the box is flush with the wall but the plaster ears get in the way, twist them off with lineman's pliers.

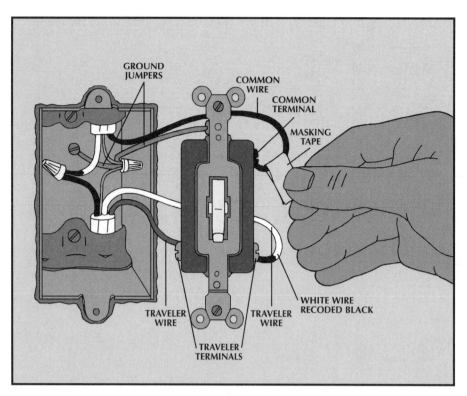

Replacing a three-way switch.

◆ Turn off the power at the service panel and test to see that the power is off at the switch *(page 187)*.

◆ Pull the old switch out of the box, but before you disconnect any wires, mark the common wire with masking tape *(left)*. The common wire is connected to a terminal that is black or otherwise darker than the two brass traveler terminals.

◆ Once the common wire is marked, disconnect all wires and remove the old switch. Connect the common wire to the dark common terminal on the new switch, then fasten the two other wires, called travelers, to the brass traveler terminals, in either order. Recode the white wire to indicate that it is hot. Mount the switch in the box.

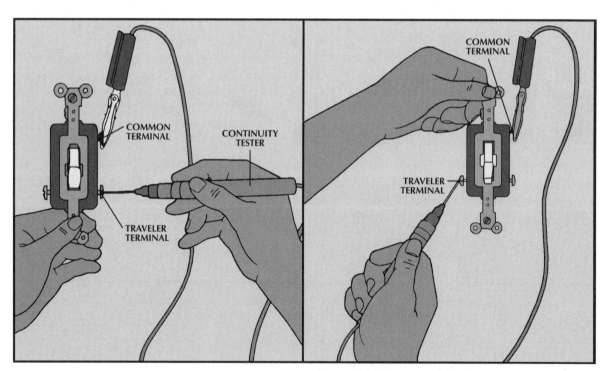

Testing a three-way switch.

◆ Once the circuit is turned off and the switch is removed, place the clip of a continuity tester on the common terminal.

◆ Place the tester's probe on one traveler terminal *(above, left)* and flip the switch up and down. The tester should light when the switch is in one position only.

◆ When the tester lights, leave the switch there and touch the probe to the other traveler terminal. The tester should not light.

◆ Without moving the probe, now flip the switch to the opposite position. The tester should light *(above, right)*. If the switch passes both tests, it is good. Remove the other switch in the circuit and test it.

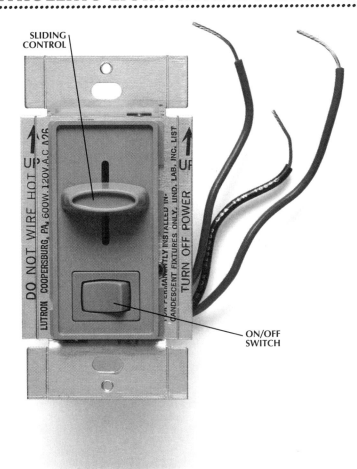

SLIDING CONTROL

DO NOT WIRE HOT · LUTRON COOPERSBURG, PA. 600W. 120V.A.C. A26

UP

UP

TURN OFF POWER

FOR PERMANENTLY INSTALLED IN-CANDESCENT FIXTURES ONLY. UND. LAB. INC. LIST

ON/OFF SWITCH

How dimmer switches work.

A dimmer switch controls the voltage of the electrical current reaching a light fixture, allowing you to vary the light level from very dim (when the sliding control is at the bottom of the slot) to bright (at the top). The small rocker button at the bottom turns the light on or off.

Wiring a three-way dimmer.

A three-way dimmer is wired the same as any other three-way switch, but you can use only one dimmer in a three-way hookup (page 206).

◆ Mark the common wire as you did for a three-way switch on page 206.

◆ Use a wire cap to connect the black common lead of the three-way dimmer to the common wire.

◆ Connect the two remaining switch leads to the traveler wires, in any order.

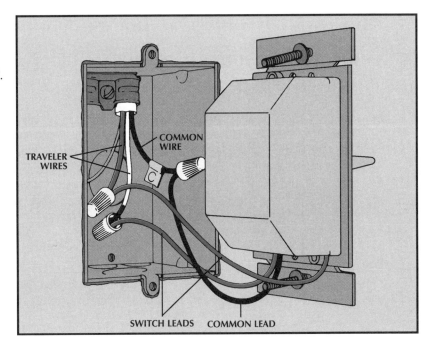

COMMON WIRE

TRAVELER WIRES

SWITCH LEADS   COMMON LEAD

Replacing Plugs and Receptacles

Swapping a new receptacle for a defective one is an inexpensive and easy home repair. It also may be necessary in some houses. Before the early 1960s, it was common practice to install ungrounded receptacles. Modern electrical codes require that ungrounded receptacles be replaced with grounded ones, the only exception being in a two-conductor system, where there is no separate ground wire. In such a case, you can obtain an extra measure of protection by replacing an old, ungrounded receptacle with a GFCI receptacle *(box below, and pages 192-194)*.

When you replace any receptacle, make sure the new one is rated for the correct voltage and amperage *(page 211)*.

Double Duty: Receptacle installations can do more than provide electricity. A switch-controlled receptacle offers easy control of plug-in fixtures; a light-receptacle fixture *(page 213)* provides light and a handy place to plug in an appliance.

Special Situations: Other receptacles are available for special locations. One recessed unit provides room for the cord of a plug-in wall clock and even a hook on which to hang the clock.

Floor receptacles are designed for large rooms so you can plug in a lamp or appliance that will not reach a wall receptacle.

A locking receptacle prevents a plug from being pulled out accidentally, and several varieties of safety receptacles prevent toddlers from inserting objects into them.

Replacing a Plug: This is even easier than installing a new receptacle. A new three-prong terminal plug is connected by attaching the black appliance cord wire to the brass screw, the white wire to the silver screw, and the green wire to the green screw. Lamps and many small appliances use cords with molded plugs permanently attached. If one of these is damaged, do not splice a cord to a molded plug. Instead, snip off the plug and replace it with a terminal plug, which is attached to the wires by screw terminals, or with a quick-clamp plug.

⚠ **CAUTION** *Modern polarized plugs have one wide blade to ensure correct polarity for the light or appliance* (opposite), *and many appliances and tools use cords with plugs featuring a grounding prong. These are important safety features, even though they are a nuisance when they won't fit into an older receptacle.*

Do not try to do a quick fix by filing down the wide blade or snipping off the grounding prong. It's far safer to replace the receptacle instead.

Substituting GFCIs for Ungrounded Receptacles

The national electrical codes in both the United States and Canada forbid replacing a two-slot receptacle on an old ungrounded system with a new three-slot variety because, with no ground wire present, the receptacle cannot be grounded. But the codes provide an easy solution: the substitution of a ground-fault circuit interrupter (GFCI) receptacle for a two-slot receptacle. Although the GFCI is not itself grounded in this situation, it protects users by shutting off the current in the event of a ground fault *(box, page 193)*. In addition to providing safety, the device features a third, grounding slot so you can use three-prong plugs in it. Moreover, the GFCI protects all receptacles downstream. The codes allow you to replace downstream outlets with regular, three-slot non-GFCI receptacles, even though they are not individually grounded, thus giving you three-slot receptacles on the entire circuit.

GFCI manufacturers package several stickers reading "GFCI Protected" with each unit. The codes require that all downstream receptacles protected by the one GFCI be so marked.

TYPES OF SLOTS AND PRONGS

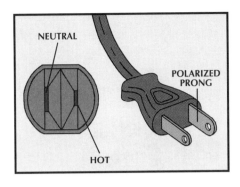

120-volt, 15-amp, ungrounded.

This receptacle is found only in older houses built before the mid-1960s. When it is wired correctly, the wide slot on the left is neutral, the narrow slot is hot.

An appliance or lamp with a polarized plug will fit only one way into this receptacle, ensuring correct polarity. In some two-slot receptacles, both slots are the same size, and polarized plugs will not fit them.

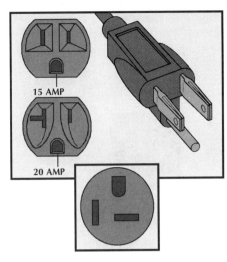

120-volt, grounded.

A modern 15-amp receptacle and a 20-amp one have a U-shaped slot for the grounding prong of the plug shown. They also have wide and narrow slots for correct polarity of two-prong plugs. The Canadian requirement for 20-amp receptacles is shown in the inset. In the United States, 20-amp receptacles require 20-amp circuits. Certain appliances have plugs that fit this shape receptacle only.

120/240-volt, 30-amp.

This receptacle and plug are designed especially for electric clothes dryers. They supply 240 volts for the heating coils and 120 volts for dryer accessories such as the timer and pilot light. The red and black wires in the plug and cord act as returns for each other as the electricity cycles 60 times a second. The white wire carries the 120 volts. The receptacle is grounded in its box with a ground wire. The Canadian receptacle *(inset)* and plug have a fourth slot that accommodates a separate ground besides the two hot and one neutral wire.

120/240-volt, 50-amp.

This receptacle and plug combination is used for an electric range. It supplies the oven and cooktop burners with 240 volts and the oven light, timer, and built-in receptacles with 120 volts. The Canadian-style receptacle *(inset)* and plug feature a fourth slot and prong for a ground.

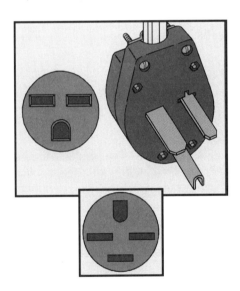

240-volt, 30-amp, grounded.

This receptacle supplies only 240 volts and is used for appliances such as window air conditioners. The black and white wires act as returns for each other as the electricity cycles 60 times a second, and the plug and receptacle have separate ground wires. The Canadian receptacle *(inset)* contains a fourth slot for a ground.

RECEPTACLE TERMINALS

Side-wired and back-wired receptacles.

A side-wired receptacle *(left)* features two brass-colored terminals on one side for the hot wires and two silver-colored terminals on the other side for the neutral wires. A small metal tab joins the upper and lower terminals. A back-wired receptacle *(right)* is connected by pushing the wires into spring-loaded grippers through holes in the back. A "strip gauge" molded into the back shows how much insulation must be removed to ensure proper wire contact. Both receptacles have green grounding terminals at one end. Back-wired receptacles often come with side-wiring terminals for versatility in installation.

GROUNDING TERMINAL

WIRE HOLES

TWO SAFETY RECEPTACLES

Childproof outlets.

Safety receptacles have spring-loaded covers that keep small children from inserting objects, which is dangerous. One type *(near right)* features a spring-loaded, slotted guard; a plug is inserted in the guard, then moved sideways to expose the receptacle slots. When the plug is removed, the guard face snaps back to cover the receptacle slots. Another type *(far right)* uses sliding plates to cover the entire receptacle. When you insert a plug, one or both plates slide vertically out of the way and are held open by the plug. When the plug is removed, the plate snaps back to cover the receptacle.

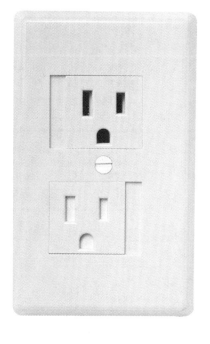

READING A RECEPTACLE

Facts to look for.

All receptacles must be marked with certain data to indicate their operating limitations and safety certifications. The receptacle at right is rated for 15 amps and 125 volts maximum. The "UL" mark indicates that it has been tested and certified by Underwriters Laboratories, an independent testing agency. The "CSA" logo shows the certification of the Canadian Standards Association. The statement "CU OR CU CLAD ONLY" on the metal strap indicates that only copper wire can be used with this receptacle. The abbreviation CO/ALR (sometimes "CU-AL" or "AL-CU" on older receptacles) would indicate that solid aluminum wire is also acceptable.

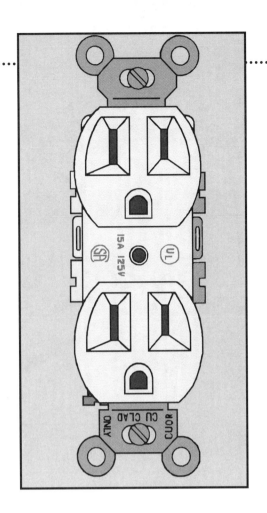

REPLACING 120-VOLT RECEPTACLES

Middle-of-the-run, plastic cable.

Two cables enter a box in the middle of a circuit run, each containing black, white, and bare copper wires.

◆ Connect each black wire to a brass-colored terminal in any order.

◆ Attach the white wires to the silver-colored terminals.

◆ In a metal box, attach a short jumper to the back of the box with a machine screw and attach another jumper to the green grounding terminal on the receptacle.

◆ Fasten these jumpers and the two bare copper wires from the cables with a wire cap *(right)*. For a plastic box, there will be no jumper needed to the box.

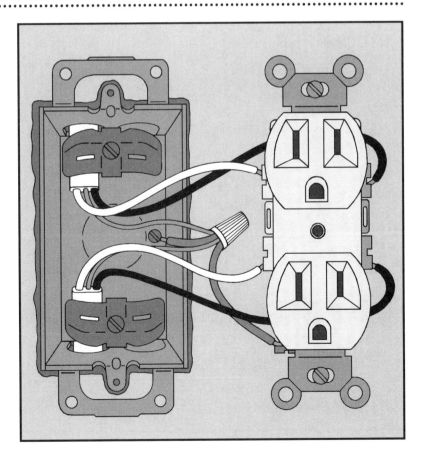

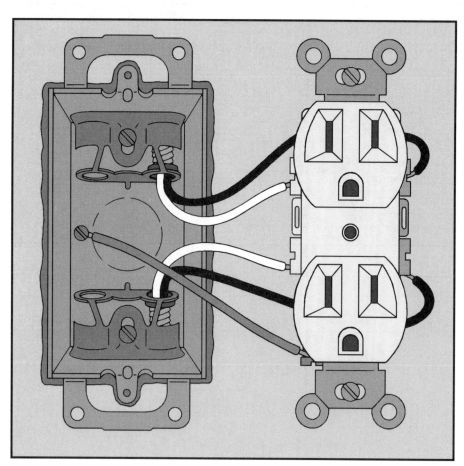

Middle-of-the-run, armored cable.

Wiring is the same as for plastic cable, with the exception of the grounding connections, because the metal cable jacket serves as the ground conductor.

◆ Connect each black wire to a brass-colored terminal and each white wire to a silver terminal.

◆ Run a jumper wire from the green grounding terminal on the receptacle to the back of the box and attach it with a machine screw.

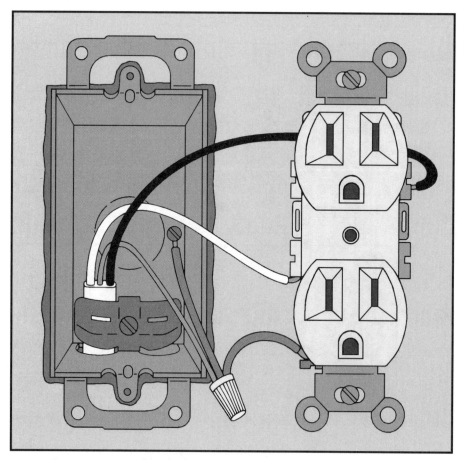

End-of-the-run, plastic cable.

Only one cable enters an end-of-the-run box.

◆ With plastic-sheathed NM-B cable, connect the one black wire to either brass-colored terminal and the white wire to either silver terminal.

◆ With a metal box, attach ground jumpers to the box and receptacle, and connect them to the bare copper wire with a wire cap. With a plastic box, there is no jumper to the box.

◆ Armored cable has no bare copper wire. Connect a jumper from the receptacle's grounding terminal to the back of the box.

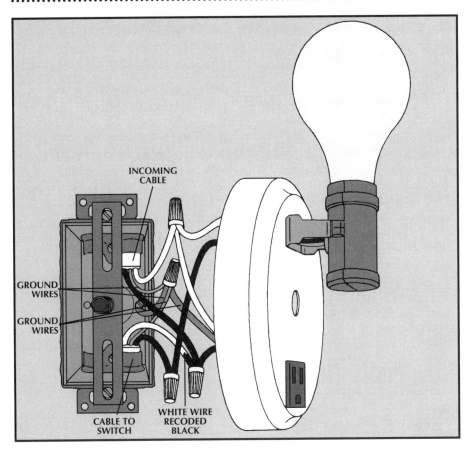

INCOMING CABLE

GROUND WIRES

GROUND WIRES

CABLE TO SWITCH

WHITE WIRE RECODED BLACK

Middle-of-the-run installation.

This is ideal for this fixture because, with two cables entering the box, you can wire the fixture so that the switch controls only the light while the receptacle remains always hot.

◆ The white wire in the switch cable should be recoded black to indicate that it will be hot (page 205).

◆ Using a wire cap (page 190), connect the black wire from the receptacle half of the fixture to the incoming black wire and white wire recoded black (page 205).

◆ Connect the black wire from the light half of the fixture to the black switch wire.

◆ Connect the two white wires from the fixture to the incoming white wire. Attach ground wires to the fixture, cables, and box as shown.

Note: If you are installing a sconce or other light-only wall fixture, the connections are as shown on this page, except that there will not be any leads from a receptacle to be connected.

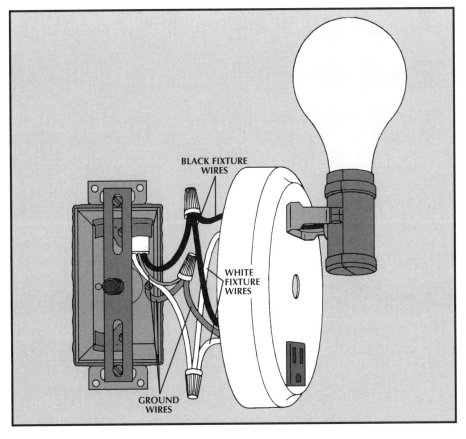

BLACK FIXTURE WIRES

WHITE FIXTURE WIRES

GROUND WIRES

End-of-the-run installation.

When only one cable enters the box, the switch will control both the receptacle and the light of the combination fixture.

◆ Connect the two black wires from the fixture to the incoming black wire with a wire cap, making sure no bare wire is exposed below the cap.

◆ Connect the two white fixture wires to the incoming white wire in the same way.

◆ Connect the green fixture wire and a jumper wire from the back of the box to the bare copper cable wire.

⚠ *Electrical codes require that this type of combination fixture not be installed in a bathroom unless the incoming cable is protected by a GFCI upstream.*

CAUTION

Installing a Ceiling Fan

Easy to install and modest in electricity consumption, a ceiling fan can be useful all year round. Most fans have reversible action to draw cool air upward in the summer and send warm air downward in the winter, abetting the work of your heating and cooling system. Some ceiling fans, such as the one shown here, can also accommodate a light fixture.

Proper Support: Because ceiling fans may weigh anywhere from 35 to 50 pounds, sturdy mounting is essential. The outlet box that the fan will be hung from must be metal—and it should be secured directly to a joist or suspended between joists by a crosspiece known as a bar hanger.

Placement Considerations: Fan blades must be at least 7 feet from the floor and 24 inches from the nearest obstruction. Where there is only a small amount of vertical room, choose a fan that mounts against the ceiling. For a higher ceiling or one that is angled or vaulted, hang the fan from an extension called a downpipe, available in several lengths. Never mount a fan where it may become wet—on an open porch, for example.

Installation: Fans are sold in kits, which include all the necessary parts. Before beginning work, turn off the electricity to the outlet at the service panel, and check that it is off with a voltage tester *(page 186)*. Although the fan is heavy, it can be installed by one person: A hook on the plate attached to the outlet box serves to support the fan while you connect the wires. Do not operate the fan motor until the blades have been attached.

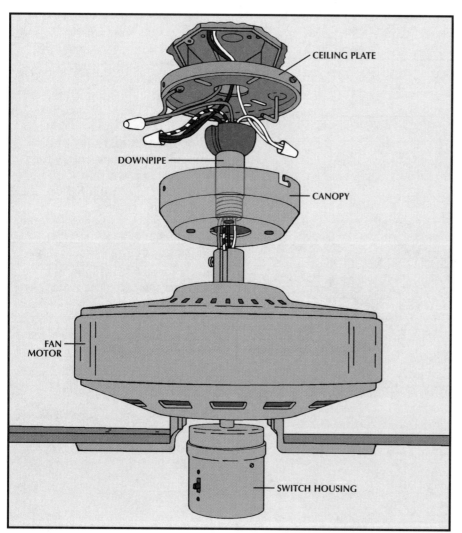

Anatomy of a ceiling fan.
Electricity for the ceiling fan at left is supplied through an outlet box that is braced above the ceiling to support the weight of the fan motor. The fan hangs from a ceiling plate that is fastened to the outlet box. Often, a downpipe is used to lower a fan for better air circulation. A light kit *(opposite)* that works independently of the fan motor can be attached to the switch housing so that a ceiling fan can double as a light source.

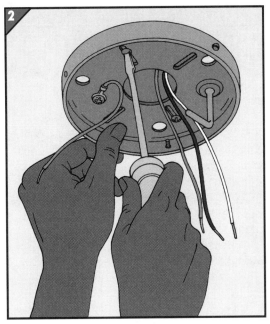

1. Assembling the fan.

◆ Insert the downpipe in the canopy, and feed the fan wires through the pipe *(above)*.
◆ Screw the downpipe into the fan, and tighten the setscrew securing the fan to the pipe.

To omit the downpipe, feed the wires through the canopy and fasten it to the fan motor with the screws provided.

2. Attaching the ceiling plate.

◆ Feed the electrical wires from the outlet box through the ceiling plate.
◆ Position the plate on the outlet box and fasten it to the ears of the box with the screws that come with the box *(above)*.

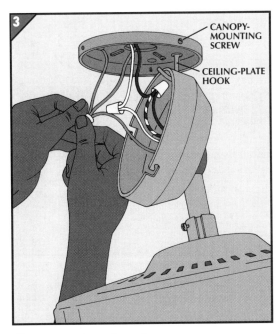

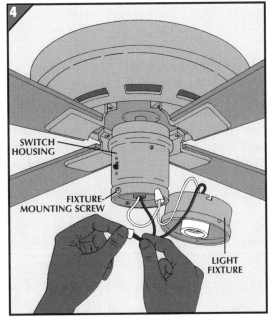

3. Connecting the wires.

◆ To support the fan, hang the canopy from the hook in the ceiling plate.
◆ Connect the black and black-and-white fan motor wires to the black ceiling-box wire.
◆ Join the two white wires, then connect the three ground wires *(above)*.
◆ Hook the canopy onto mounting screws in the ceiling plate and tighten them.

4. Attaching a light fixture.

◆ Remove the cover plate from the bottom of the switch housing.
◆ Connect the wires in the switch housing to those of the light fixture, black to black *(above)* and white to white.
◆ Mount the fixture to the switch housing with the screws provided.

Overhead Light, Exactly Where It Is Needed

For concentrated illumination from above, nothing surpasses a track light system and recessed fixtures. Track lighting, shown on these pages, is the more flexible of the two, but recessed units are a less obtrusive option.

Purchasing: Both types of equipment are sold in kits or as separate components. Track is available in 2-, 4-, and 8-foot sections that can be snapped together with connectors to form straight, right-angled, T-shaped, or X-shaped arrangements. Installation methods vary, and units from one manufacturer may not fit those of another.

Some recessed fixtures are designed specifically for finished or unfinished ceilings; others, like the unit shown on pages 218-219, can be adapted to either situation. For insulated ceilings, choose fixtures with an IC rating; these may be safely buried in insulation.

Wiring Requirements: A 15-amp circuit with a wall switch is adequate. A track system can be wired to a ceiling box at any point along its length by means of a special connector called a canopy. Recessed fixtures come with their own wiring boxes attached. When installing several such units on a single circuit, make sure that all but one are rated for "through-wiring" with two cables; the last fixture needs only a single cable.

TOOLS

Nail set
Hammer
Screwdriver

Drill with $\frac{3}{4}$-inch bit
Tin snips
Electronic stud finder
Drywall saw
Fish tape

MATERIALS

Track lighting kit
Canopy kit
Light fixtures for track
Electrician's tape
Wire caps
Bulbs

Recessed lighting kits
Cardboard
Plastic-sheathed cable
Patching materials for ceiling

WIRING TRACK LIGHTS TO A CEILING BOX

1. Removing the knockouts.
◆ Holding a length of track against the ceiling box, mark the large circular knockout nearest the center of the box *(right)*.
◆ Lay the track section upside down across two lengths of scrap lumber. With a nail set and hammer, remove the marked knockout and the small circular knockout next to it.
◆ In the same manner, remove a keyhole-shaped mounting knockout near each end of the track section.
◆ If you plan to install a single section, install the plastic end caps provided with the kit; otherwise, place caps on end sections before installing them.

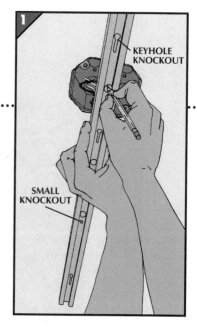

KEYHOLE KNOCKOUT

SMALL KNOCKOUT

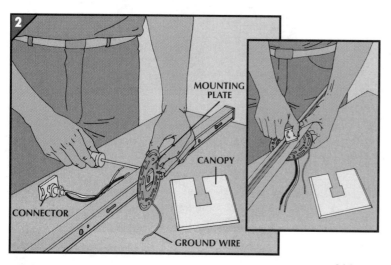

MOUNTING PLATE

CANOPY

CONNECTOR

GROUND WIRE

2. Attaching the mounting plate.
◆ Hold the plate against the ceiling side of the track, ground wire on top. Position the center hole at the large knockout opening, and align one of the threaded holes in the plate with the smaller knockout. Fasten the pieces together loosely with the screw provided *(far left)*, leaving a $\frac{1}{8}$-inch space between plate and track for the canopy.
◆ Thread the connector wires through the large track knockout and mounting plate. Lock the connector to the track by turning it clockwise *(inset)*.

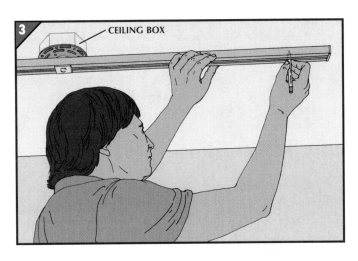

3. Marking the ceiling.

◆ Fasten the plate to the ceiling-box mounting tabs temporarily, using the screws provided with the box.

◆ Pivot the track on the loosely fastened mounting plate screw to align the track parallel to a nearby wall, and mark the ceiling at the midpoint of each keyhole slot *(right)*.

◆ Unscrew the mounting plate from the ceiling box and drill holes for toggle bolts at the marks. Assemble two bolts and push their toggles into the holes.

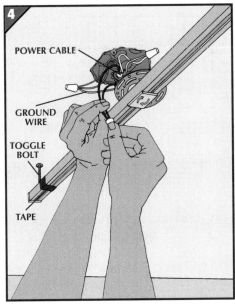

4. Wiring the track.

◆ Suspend the track from the toggle-bolt heads. Wrap tape around the track to prevent it from accidentally slipping off the boltheads.

◆ Connect the connector wires to the wires of the cable entering the ceiling box, black to black and white to white *(left)*.

◆ Connect the ground wire from the mounting plate to the ground wire in the power cable and to the ceiling box, if it is metal.

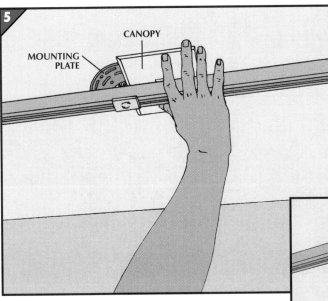

5. Adding the canopy.

◆ Tuck all wiring connections into the ceiling box, and screw the mounting plate securely to the box.

◆ Slide the canopy between the mounting plate and the track to conceal the plate and ceiling box *(left)*. Tighten the mounting plate screw.

◆ Unwrap the tape from the ends of the track and tighten the toggle bolts to hold the track against the ceiling.

◆ Extend the track as desired, using toggle bolts to secure each section of it to the ceiling.

◆ Fit light fixtures to the track *(inset)*, and then lock them in place.

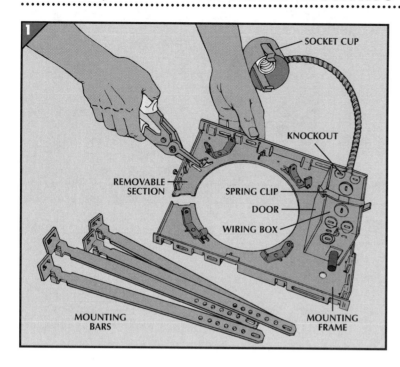

1. Preparing the mounting frame.

◆ Remove the frame's mounting bars and place the frame on a piece of cardboard. Outline the frame and circular opening with a pencil, then cut along the lines to create a template.

◆ With tin snips, cut out the removable section of the frame opposite the wiring box *(left)*.

◆ Lift the spring clip on top of the wiring box and remove one of its two detachable doors. Unscrew the two cable clamps that are inside and modify them for use with plastic-sheathed cable by using tin snips to cut off the strips that connect the extra metal loops to the main part of the clamps.

◆ Reinstall the clamps and remove one knockout above each clamp.

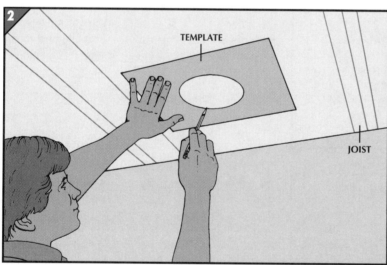

2. Cutting a ceiling opening.

◆ With a stud finder, locate the ceiling joists. Using the template, mark fixture locations on the ceiling between joists.

◆ Drill a small hole in the center of each circular mark. Bend hanger wire to a 90-degree angle, insert one end through the hole, and rotate the wire to check for obstructions. If you find any, relocate the fixtures.

◆ At each joist running between fixtures, cut an access opening in the ceiling for the cable. Drill a $\frac{3}{4}$-inch hole through the center of each joist.

3. Wiring connections.

◆ Fish a two-conductor cable from a junction box to the first fixture opening, followed by another cable from the second fixture opening to the first- and so on downstream.

◆ At the first ceiling opening, rest a fixture-mounting frame atop a stepladder, and clamp the cable ends to opposite sides of the box.

◆ Red wire caps *(right)* indicate the connections to be made between the cable and fixture wires. Connect black to black, white to white, and the ground wires.

◆ Reattach the box door.

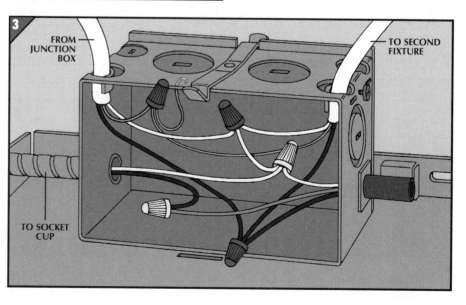

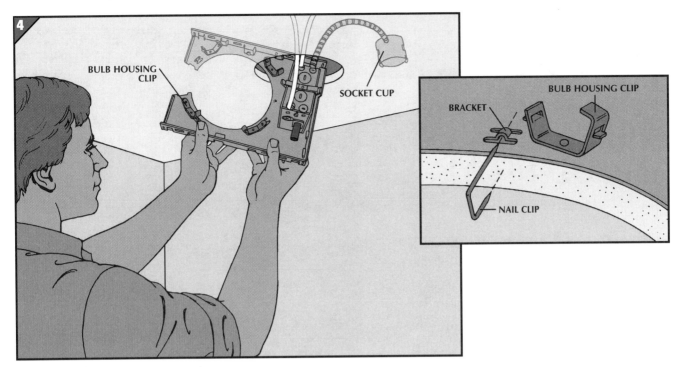

4. Securing the mounting frame.

◆ Push the socket cup through the ceiling opening and set it beside the lip of the hole.

◆ Beginning at the opening cut in the frame in Step 1, work the frame through the hole *(above)*, and rest it on the ceiling with the opening in the frame aligned with the ceiling hole.

◆ Slide the long ends of the four nail clips provided with the fixture partway into the brackets at the frame's edge *(inset)*. Align the short ends of the nail clips with the center of the ceiling material, then tap them into the ceiling with a hammer.

5. Installing the bulb housing.

◆ Bring the socket cup back through the opening. Rotate the bulb housing clips inward.

◆ Insert the socket cup into the top of the bulb housing so that tabs in the cup snap into slots in the housing.

◆ Push the assembly into the frame *(right)* until the bulb housing flange rests against the ceiling, completing the installation.

◆ At the second fixture opening, connect cables from the first and third fixture openings to the second fixture in its wiring box, and complete the installation as described above.

◆ When all the fixtures are in place, patch the access holes at each joist *(pages 87-88)*.

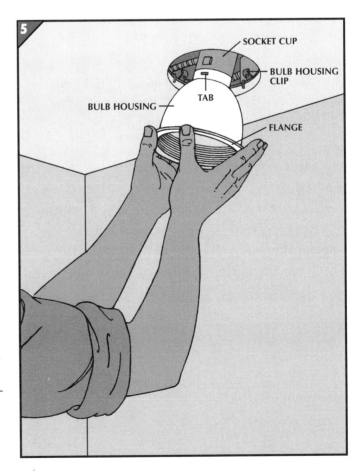

CHAPTER 7

FIREPLACES AND WOOD STOVES

A roaring fire in a fireplace has a voracious appetite for both air and wood, but it can also devour heat. By drawing warm air from the rest of the house, a fire can actually raise heating bills. But you can make fireplaces and wood stoves more efficient by performing some simple measures such as installing glass doors, adding a chimney cap, extending the flue, and sealing cracks in the firebox. And, as shown on pages 214 and 215, you can also put in ceiling fans to improve air circulation.

One of the best ways to heat a home with wood is with a modern wood-burning stove. This chapter will show you how to install a fireplace insert in an unused fireplace—an alternative that combines the look of a fireplace with the efficiency of a stove.

Keeping a home heated with a fireplace or wood stove takes a bit of work. But the tasks involved, such as cleaning the flue, are actually not as difficult or as time-consuming as you might think. Your job will be easier if you have the right knowledge and tools.

A fire needs enough air for full combustion. A wide iron grate will support the logs and allow air to circulate around and under the fire. ▶

The average chimney needs cleaning once every two years, but a monthly inspection for soot and creosote deposits is a good idea. When the build-up of these substances exceeds $\frac{1}{8}$ inch, the flue needs sweeping.

▼

The fireplace was once an integral part of domestic life, used for cooking as well as for heating. With its smaller, shallower firebox and a separate air intake, the modern version focuses on heating efficiency. By installing glass doors on a fireplace, you can reduce the loss of heated air up the chimney.

A modern wood stove can ▶ supply the heating needs of an old farmhouse, provided cracks and other flaws in the stove are corrected.

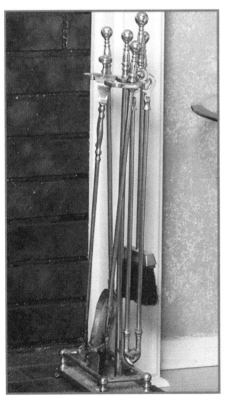

Equipped with basic accessories— a poker, tongs, a shovel, and a brush— a fireplace can keep fires safely contained and make them easy to manage.

Making a Fireplace More Efficient

The efficiency of a fireplace depends largely on the proper functioning of the firebox. Problems generally result from either structural damage or flaws in the design. Fortunately, many problems can be easily remedied.

Improving Airflow: Poor air intake can cause a fire to smolder and die. Check for a faulty damper *(below)*; if the damper is in good working order, you can alleviate the problem by supplying a source of outside air *(opposite)*. A smoky fireplace is often due to faulty draft—the airflow up the chimney is not strong enough to pull up all the smoke. Install glass doors to regulate airflow and reduce the loss of heated air up the chimney *(opposite)*. Decreasing the size of the firebox opening with a smoke guard can help *(page 226)*; or you can increase the draft by extending the chimney *(pages 230-231)*.

Refurbishing the Firebox: Crumbling mortar joints in the firebox are easy to fix *(page 227)*. If the damper frame breaks, consult a chimney professional—the frame is usually anchored in the masonry. Or, you can substitute a top-sealing damper *(pages 229-230)*. To help prevent future damage, keep the weather out with a chimney cap *(page 229)*. Poor design can be partially offset with a fireback—a decorative cast-iron plate mounted on the back wall of the firebox to absorb heat and radiate it into the room.

 TOOLS

Wire brush	Wrench	Ball-peen
Pliers	Electric drill	hammer
Screwdriver	Masonry bit	Caulking gun
Putty knife	Cold chisel	

 **MATERIALS**

Lead anchors	Fireplace
Smoke guard	mortar
Glass fireplace	cartridge
doors	

 SAFETY TIPS

When using an electric drill or chipping out mortar, wear safety goggles. Add a dust mask when cleaning soot from the damper.

MAINTAINING A DAMPER

Variations on a common design.

The damper controls the size of the opening between the firebox and the smoke chamber *(right)*. Some dampers have three movable parts —the damper plate, a ratcheting arm, and a handle *(left inset)*. With others, only two parts move: the plate and a ratcheted handle *(right inset)*.

With a powerful flashlight, check whether the plate is out of its track. If so, take it out by removing the cotter pins or bracket bolt, and clean debris and soot from the damper frame groove with a wire brush. If necessary, use a soot-cleaning product.

Where you cannot return the damper plate to its track, install a top-sealing damper *(pages 229-230)*, or consult a chimney professional.

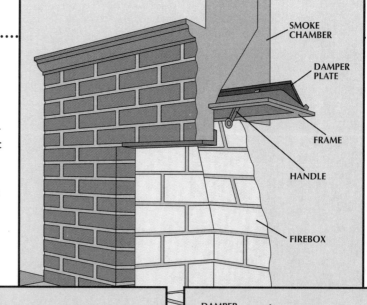

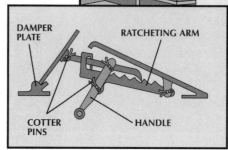

IMPROVING THE DRAFT WITH GLASS DOORS

1. Positioning the frame.
◆ Attach the mounting brackets and lintel clamps to the glass door frame with the screws provided.
◆ Holding the frame at an angle (*left*), slip the lintel clamps under the lintel—the metal or masonry beam that supports the bricks above the firebox opening.
◆ Push the bottom of the frame into position so the top and sides are flat against the face of the fireplace, making sure the frame is centered over the firebox opening. Push any protruding fiberglass insulation back behind the edges of the frame with a putty knife.

2. Anchoring the frame.
◆ If the frame has bottom brackets, drill holes for lead anchors in the floor of the firebox with a masonry bit. Insert the anchors and fasten the brackets to the anchors with the screws provided.
◆ At the top of the frame, slide the lintel clamps against the lintel, then use a wrench to tighten the pressure bolts against the lintel.

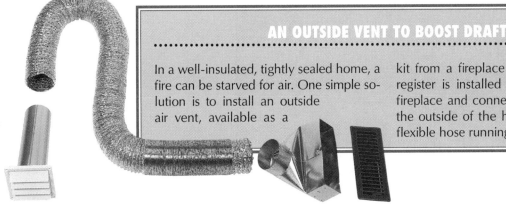

AN OUTSIDE VENT TO BOOST DRAFT

In a well-insulated, tightly sealed home, a fire can be starved for air. One simple solution is to install an outside air vent, available as a kit from a fireplace specialist. The floor register is installed within 3 feet of the fireplace and connects to an air inlet on the outside of the house by means of a flexible hose running under the floor.

1. Establishing the lintel height.

◆ Tape a sheet of aluminum foil across the fireplace just above the lintel so the sheet overhangs the firebox opening by about 4 inches *(above)*.

◆ Light a small smoky fire in the firebox —one fed by newspaper or dry leaves.

◆ If smoke still enters the room, tape another sheet of foil across the opening about 4 inches below the first. Repeat, if necessary, until smoke no longer spills into the room.

◆ Leave the foil in place during several fires to check the adjustment.

2. Installing a smoke guard.

◆ Buy a smoke guard sized to match the combined width of the foil strips taped to the fireplace in Step 1. Choose a spring-loaded model you can custom-fit to the width of your firebox opening.

◆ Compress the smoke guard against one side of the opening, then release it slowly *(left)*, making sure that its top edge fits tightly against the lintel.

REPAIRING FIREBRICK MORTAR JOINTS

1. Applying fresh mortar.
◆ Chip away any damaged mortar with a cold chisel and ball-peen hammer.
◆ Clean soot and debris from the damaged joints with a wire brush.
◆ Dampen the joints and surrounding area with a wet rag.
◆ Using a caulking gun loaded with a cartridge of fireplace mortar, fill the damaged joints *(right)*.

2. Smoothing the mortar.
◆ With a putty knife, smooth the mortar flush with the surrounding fire-bricks *(left)*. Scrape excess mortar from the bricks.
◆ Let the mortar cure for 24 hours before lighting a fire. The first fire will darken the new mortar to match the color of the old.

Chimney Repairs

Inspect your chimney annually for obstructions. Before lighting the first fire of the season, open the damper and shine a strong flashlight up the flue. If you see any debris, clean the chimney *(pages 238-242)*. A chimney cover *(opposite)* will help keep debris out. Also clean and adjust the damper *(page 224)*. If it is broken or cannot be adjusted properly, you can install a top-sealing damper *(pages 229-230)*.

Extending the Chimney: When a fireplace lets smoke drift into the house, it is because the draft is poor. The chimney should extend at least 3 feet above the point where it passes through the roof—and stand at least 2 feet above the next-highest structure within 10 feet, such as a dormer or tree. If yours does not meet these criteria, you can extend it with terra-cotta flue liners and bricks *(pages 230-231)*.

Or, the chimney's crown may not be properly beveled so as to direct air currents upward over the flue. A crown can be reshaped or rebuilt with mortar as you would when extending the chimney.

Sealing Smoke Leaks: Leaking smoke anywhere along the length of the chimney is a serious problem; it signals cracks in the masonry—a potential fire hazard. If you suspect your chimney is leaking, perform this simple test: Cover the top of the chimney with a towel, then place a smoke bomb or a smoky flare—available at fireplace supply stores—on the smoke shelf and close the damper. Examine the exterior of the chimney for smoke—from outside, and inside on each floor and in the attic. If smoke is seeping through, do not use the fireplace until you remedy the problem. For an unlined chimney, install a stainless-steel flue liner *(pages 232-234)*. If the chimney has a terra-cotta liner, the leak may be the result of structural damage or deteriorating mortar joints in the liner. Since the repair may involve tearing down the chimney's outer wall, consult a professional.

 TOOLS

Wrench
Wire brush
Electric drill
Masonry bit
Ball-peen hammer

Screwdriver
Wire cutters
Cold chisel
Caulking gun
Handsaw
Hammer
Mason's trowel

 MATERIALS

Chimney cover
Top-sealing damper
Fireplace mortar cartridge
Terra-cotta flue liners
Bricks

Mortar ingredients
  (Portland cement,
  hydrated lime,
  masonry sand)
2 x 6s
Common nails (3")
Plastic sheeting

 SAFETY TIPS

Wear goggles and gloves when mixing, applying, or chipping out mortar.

SAFETY AT HEIGHTS

Safety is the overriding concern when you are working on the roof. While the slope of your roof is the main factor in determining whether you need special equipment, your personal tolerance for heights is also important: if you don't feel comfortable on a gently sloping roof, consider hiring a professional.

If your roof slopes less than 4 vertical inches for every 12 inches of horizontal run, you can work on it observing common-sense precautions and wearing rubber-soled shoes. On steeper roofs, create temporary footholds by hanging a ladder from the ridge with ladder hooks *(page 323)*. For added safety and convenience, you can set up roof scaffolding. Ridge hooks *(below)*, which adjust to any roof slope, can be used to support roof scaffolding and are secured to the roof without having to nail through the roofing material.

Whatever the slope of your roof, you'll need a ladder to reach it; tying it to the eaves helps *(opposite)*. Make sure the ladder is level; place the feet on a board, if necessary.

Never prop the ladder against a window or door, and install a stabilizer *(page 322)* on it to keep it from slipping sideways on the wall. When climbing a ladder, don't carry anything in your hands; wear a tool belt containing your tools and supplies instead. For more information on ladder safety and on working safely at heights, refer to page 321.

SECURING A LADDER TO THE EAVES

If you will be going up and down the ladder a lot to get on and off the roof, you may find it worthwhile to fasten it to the eaves.

If the ladder rests against a gutter, fit a block of wood in the gutter to keep it from being crushed. Fasten a screw eye in the fascia opposite each ladder side rail.

Tie each side rail to a screw eye with good-quality nylon rope and a slip-proof knot.

PROTECTING A FLUE WITH A CHIMNEY COVER

Securing a chimney cover.
◆ Buy a prefabricated chimney cover to fit the size and shape of your flue liner.
◆ Slip the base of the cover over the top of the flue liner, then tighten the bolts against the liner to hold the cover in place, as shown at right.

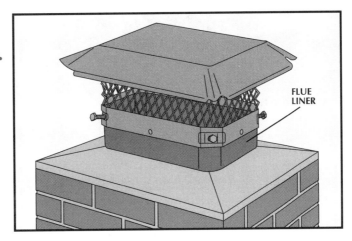

FLUE LINER

INSTALLING A TOP-SEALING DAMPER

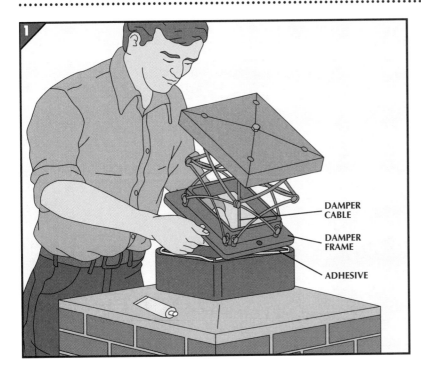

DAMPER CABLE

DAMPER FRAME

ADHESIVE

1. Securing the damper.
◆ Clean the top edges of the flue with a wire brush, then apply along the edges a $\frac{1}{4}$-inch bead of the adhesive supplied with the damper.
◆ From the top of the chimney, drop the damper cable down the flue (left). Have a helper inside the house check to make sure that the cable extends all the way down into the fireplace.
◆ Press the damper frame firmly against the flue to seat it in the adhesive.

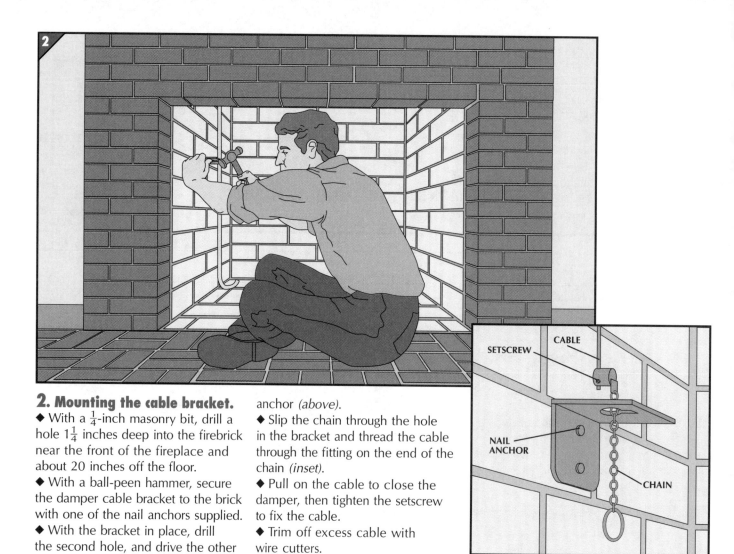

2. Mounting the cable bracket.

◆ With a $\frac{1}{4}$-inch masonry bit, drill a hole $1\frac{1}{4}$ inches deep into the firebrick near the front of the fireplace and about 20 inches off the floor.

◆ With a ball-peen hammer, secure the damper cable bracket to the brick with one of the nail anchors supplied.

◆ With the bracket in place, drill the second hole, and drive the other anchor *(above)*.

◆ Slip the chain through the hole in the bracket and thread the cable through the fitting on the end of the chain *(inset)*.

◆ Pull on the cable to close the damper, then tighten the setscrew to fix the cable.

◆ Trim off excess cable with wire cutters.

EXTENDING THE FLUE

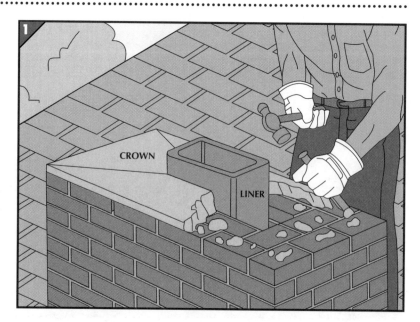

1. Removing the old crown.

With a ball-peen hammer and a cold chisel, break away the masonry crown around the flue liner *(right)*, angling the tip of the chisel away from the liner to avoid damaging the liner. Do not let chips fall down the flue.

LINER
EXTENSION

MORTAR

2. Installing a flue extension.

◆ Clean the top edge of the flue liner with a wire brush, then apply fire-place mortar with a caulking gun along the edge.

◆ Position a terra-cotta liner extension squarely on top of the existing liner *(left)*.

◆ Build up the walls of the chimney with bricks to the height of the new liner. Add more liner sections and bricks, if necessary, ending the chimney walls 8 inches below the top of the flue.

3. Filling the crown form with mortar.

◆ With 3-inch common nails, build a form of 2-by-6s around the top of the chimney so that the form hugs the sides of the chimney tightly and the boards' top edges extend about $3\frac{1}{2}$ inches above the uppermost bricks.

◆ Prepare a batch of stiff mortar according to manufacturer's instructions.

◆ Moisten the bricks, then pour the mortar into the form *(right)*, overfilling it near the flue.

CROWN
FORM

4. Shaping the crown.

◆ As the mortar begins to stiffen, use a mason's trowel to slope the crown up toward the flue liner on all four sides, leaving at least 4 inches of the liner exposed *(left)*.

◆ Mist the mortar with a garden hose, then tape plastic sheeting over the mortar to keep it damp over the next four days.

◆ Remove the frame when the mortar has cured.

A Stainless-Steel Chimney Lining

Adding a liner to an unlined chimney can stop smoke leaks from the mortar joints and improve the draft. You may choose to have a chimney professional install a cast-in-place liner system, but a less costly solution—and one you can undertake yourself—is putting in a stainless steel liner. If you choose this option, first verify that your house insurance policy and local building code permit installation by a nonprofessional.

A Tailor-Made Liner: Liners usually come in 3-foot lengths that must be assembled on site. Begin by measuring from the top of the flue to the point where the flue meets the smoke chamber. Next, measure the length, width, and depth of the firebox, and the width of the chimney in both directions. Take your measurements to a fireplace supplier for a liner of the correct shape and size.

Anchoring the Liner: You will need to cut an access hole through the chimney to mount the bottom plate that secures the liner in place. For the plate, buy a sheet of 24-gauge stainless steel at least 4 inches wider and longer than the flue opening from a sheet-metal fabricator.

 TOOLS

Tape measure
Electric drill
Masonry bit
Cold chisel
Ball-peen
   hammer
Compass
Tin snips
Screwdriver
Caulking gun
Mason's trowel

 **MATERIALS**

Stainless steel chimney
   liner (24 gauge) and
   sheet-metal screws
Stainless steel sheet
   (24 gauge)
Masonry screws (2")
Fireplace mortar cartridge
Mortar ingredients
   (Portland cement, hydrat-
   ed lime, masonry sand)
Chimney-lining insulation
Flashing metal
Chimney-rated caulk

 SAFETY TIPS

Wear safety goggles when drilling into masonry or chipping out mortar, and gloves when handling or cutting sheet metal.

ACCESS HOLE OUTLINE

1. Making an access hole in the chimney.
◆ At the top of the chimney flue feed a tape measure down to measure the distance from the top of the flue to the top of the smoke chamber. Have a helper shine a flashlight up the flue from inside the house to see when the tape reaches the smoke chamber. Transfer your measurement outside to mark the top of the smoke chamber on the chimney.
◆ Outline the access hole on the chimney from the mortar joint closest to the top of the smoke chamber to a height of two brick courses. Make the outline as wide as the inside width of the chimney—usually three brick lengths.
◆ Loosen the bricks within the outline by drilling through the mortar surrounding them with a masonry bit *(left)*. Pull out the bricks and set them aside.
◆ With a ball-peen hammer and cold chisel, chip off any mortar adhering to the bricks framing the access hole. Brush away any debris.

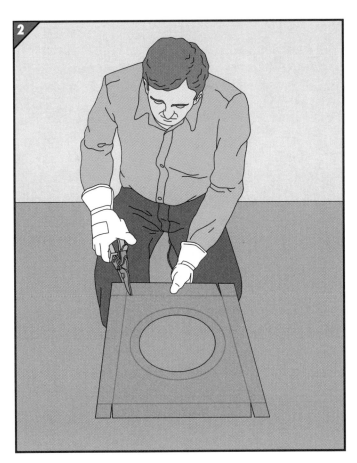

2. Sizing the bottom plate.

◆ Measure the inside dimensions of the flue at the top of the chimney and draw a matching rectangle on a sheet of 24-gauge stainless steel.

◆ Draw a second rectangle, 2 inches longer and wider, around the first.

◆ At the center of the rectangles, draw a circle of the same diameter as the chimney liner; then center a second circle, 2 inches smaller, inside the first.

◆ Cut around the outside rectangle and the inner circle with tin snips.

◆ At each corner, cut a slit from the edge to the inner rectangle, forming four parallel tabs *(left)*.

3. Shaping the plate.

◆ Make cuts at 1-inch intervals around the inside of the plate from the edge of the inner circle to the rim of the larger circle *(right)*, forming a series of tabs.

◆ Bend up the tabs at a 90-degree angle. Bend up the edges of the rectangle as well, wrapping the four tabs around the corners to form a flange around the plate *(inset)*.

◆ Working outside, slide the plate, flanges and tabs pointing upward, into the access hole in the chimney. The flanges should sit snugly against the walls of the chimney—bend the edges again, if necessary. Then position the plate in the chimney so the top edges of the flanges are flush with the tops of the bricks at the bottom of the access hole.

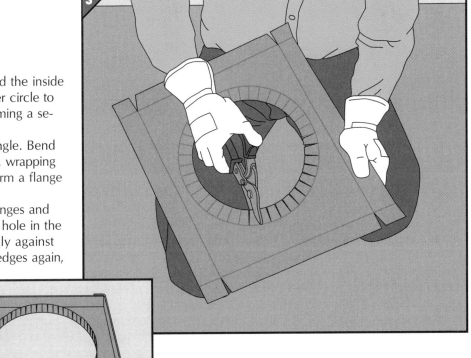

FLANGE

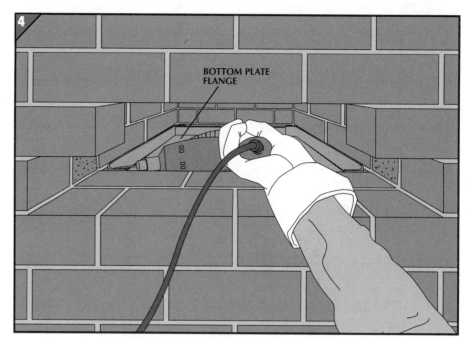

4. Anchoring the plate.

◆ Drill two $\frac{1}{4}$-inch holes through each flange *(right)*—one at the front and one at the back of the chimney; be sure to indent the bricks behind the flanges.

◆ Fasten the flanges to the bricks with 2-inch masonry screws. Caulk any gaps between the plate and the chimney walls with fireplace mortar.

BOTTOM PLATE FLANGE

LINER

5. Installing the chimney liner.

◆ Working on the roof with a helper, assemble the liner sections together; at each connection, use four of the screws supplied. Flexible flue liners are available for curving flues *(photograph)*. Lower the liner down the chimney until it contacts the bottom plate.

◆ Have a helper at the access hole apply fireplace mortar with a caulking gun around the inside of the bottom end of the liner and slip the liner over the tabs on the plate *(above)*.

◆ Replace the bricks in the access hole, mortaring them in place.

◆ To insulate the liner, buy chimney-lining insulation and pour it down the chimney, filling the space around the liner from the bottom plate to the top of the chimney.

◆ Seal the gap between the liner and the flue at the top of the chimney with a cap made from a piece of flashing metal cut 1 inch longer and wider than the flue opening. Cut a hole through the cap for the liner and run a bead of chimney-rated caulk around the top edge of the flue. Slip the cap over the liner and press it down onto the flue. Caulk the joint between the cap and the liner.

Restoring a Vintage Stove

Returning an old wood-burning stove to good working order can be gratifying, but keep in mind that its performance will pale in comparison to that of a modern advanced-combustion or catalytic stove. If you plan to use a stove or heater as a primary heat source, a modern one with superior heating efficiency is a wise choice.

Inspecting the Exterior: Before buying a secondhand stove, examine it thoroughly. Check the bottom to make sure that the legs provide stable support and the stove sits firmly on its base. Missing bolts or cracks in the legs are not fatal flaws—bolts can be replaced and a cracked leg can be welded at a foundry. Although cracks in the body of a stove can be repaired *(below)*, avoid purchasing a stove with anything larger than a hairline crack.

An Internal Exam: Inside the stove, check the floor lining—either firebricks or metal—for wear. On a stove with a circular floor, a castable lining will work best; buy the mix from a chimney-supply store and pour it onto the stove's floor. Otherwise, replace or add firebricks *(page 237)*.

Check the stove's movable parts—baffle, door handles, and draft controls. If parts are sluggish, a thorough cleaning of the stove's interior may restore them to order. Missing door glass *(page 237)* or gaskets *(page 237)* are easy to replace, but if anything else is missing from the stove, think twice about buying it; replacement parts are nearly impossible to find and costly to have made.

If the stove comes with a house you are planning to buy, inspect the installation. It should meet the same standards that apply to a new setup.

 TOOLS

Work light	Ball-peen
Wire brush	hammer
Putty knife	Screwdriver
Shoe brush	Tape measure
Brick set	Heavy-duty
	scissors
	Utility knife

 **MATERIALS**

	Firebricks
Furnace cement	Ceramic stove
Stove blacking	window
Metal polish	Stove door gaskets
	Gasket cement

 SAFETY TIPS

Wear gloves when removing a broken stove window; add goggles when cutting firebricks.

SEALING CRACKS IN A FIREBOX

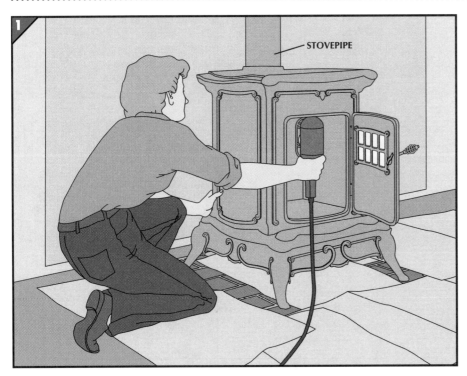

STOVEPIPE

1. Locating the cracks.
◆ Place newspaper on the floor around the stove. Remove any grates, baffles, or movable linings from the stove's interior, then hang a work light in the firebox *(left)*.
◆ Close the stove's door, turn off the room lights, and check the seams between sections of the stove body for leaking light.
◆ Disconnect the stovepipe, then have a helper tilt the stove so you can inspect the underside for leaks. To check for cracks that are too fine to pass light, rub chalk lightly over the stove's surface; the chalk will fill any crack, leaving a visible line. Or, you can light a small fire in the stove and watch for wisps of smoke seeping out.

FURNACE
CEMENT

2. Caulking a crack.

◆ With a wire brush, remove any rust or loose dirt from around the crack both inside and outside the stove.

◆ On the outside, outline the crack with masking tape to protect the surrounding surface from the furnace cement.

◆ Inside, dampen the damaged area with a wet cloth or sponge, then pack furnace cement into the crack with a putty knife. Repeat on the outside *(above)*.

◆ Remove the tape and let the cement dry for 24 hours. When using the stove next, keep a small kindling fire going for 2 hours to check the repair.

CORRECTING MINOR FLAWS

Polishing a worn stove.

◆ Remove encrusted dirt and rust from the stove's exterior by scrubbing the surface with a wire brush.

◆ For cast-iron sections, rub a light coat of stove blacking over the surface with a soft cloth *(right)*. Once the blacking dries, buff the metal with a shoe brush.

◆ Restore the shine to any nickel-plated parts with ordinary metal polish.

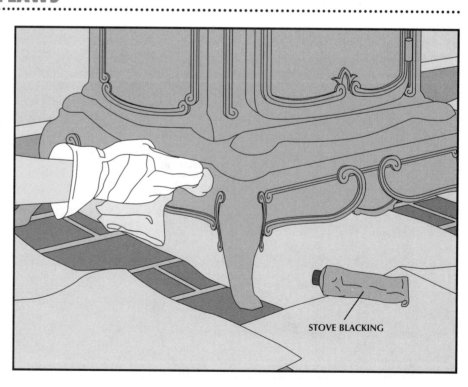

STOVE BLACKING

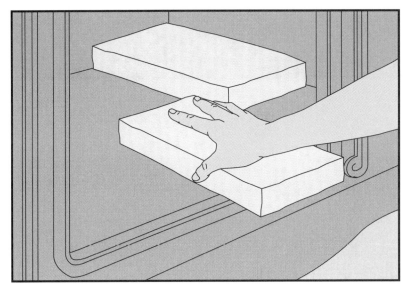

Lining a stove.

◆ Starting at the back and working toward the door, lay a dry run of firebricks on the firebox floor. Place the bricks in rows, spacing the units $\frac{1}{8}$ inch apart *(left)*. With a brick set and a ball-peen hammer, cut bricks as necessary to cover the floor, but don't try to fill small, irregular spaces at the edge of the firebox.

◆ Remove the bricks, noting their position in the stove. With a putty knife, apply furnace cement to the edges that will contact other bricks—don't apply cement to brick surfaces that will abut the floor or walls of the stove. Reposition the bricks in the stove.

◆ Let the cement dry for at least 24 hours before lighting a fire in the stove.

Replacing a stove window.

◆ Remove the screws securing the back plate over the window, and slip out the old pane.

◆ Order a clear-ceramic pane to fit the door—it should be about $\frac{1}{4}$ inch wider and longer than the opening.

◆ Center the pane over the opening, reposition the back plate over the glass *(right)*, then fasten the back plate in place.

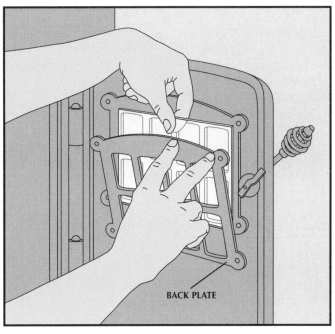

BACK PLATE

GASKET CHANNEL

Replacing a gasket.

◆ Pull off the old gasket around the stove's door opening. Clean out the gasket channel with a wire brush or a putty knife.

◆ Buy a length of tubular or flat fiberglass gasket that matches the original. Measure and cut four strips of the gasket to span the edges of the opening, making each piece about 1 inch longer than the actual measurement.

◆ Beginning at the top of the opening, squeeze a bead of gasket cement into the channel and press the gasket into place *(left)*.

◆ Repeat on the other sides, mitering the ends of the strips with a utility knife so they meet squarely at the corners.

◆ Let the cement dry for 24 hours before using the stove.

Keeping the Flue Clean

When a fire burns, residues in the form of soot and creosote are deposited inside the flue. These substances—both of which are flammable—are a major cause of chimney fires. Regular cleaning is crucial in eliminating the deposits.

Inspecting the Flue: Though the average chimney needs sweeping only once every two years, the flue of a fireplace that gets heavy and continuous use, or of a stove that is airtight, may need cleaning much more often. A monthly inspection is a good idea, at least until you become familiar with the rate at which your stove or fireplace collects deposits. When the buildup is more than $\frac{1}{8}$ inch thick, the flue needs cleaning, as well as the smoke chamber of a fireplace.

Working Safely and Efficiently: Cleaning tools are available at fireplace supply stores. For the chimney brush to work well, get one that matches the flue's inside dimensions. Fireplace chimneys can be swept from inside the house *(below and page 239)*, while vertical metal flues can be cleaned only from above *(pages 241-242)*. If you have to work on the roof, observe the safety measures outlined on page 228.

 TOOLS

Wrench
Pliers
Utility knife
Screwdriver
Flue brush with
  flexible rods

Steel flue
  scraper
Long-handled
  pot brush
Dustpan
Weighted
  flue brush
  with rope

 **MATERIALS**

Polyethylene
  sheeting
Duct tape

Heavy plastic
  garbage bags
Newspaper
Large paper
  bags

 SAFETY TIPS

Wear goggles, gloves, and a dust mask when removing the damper or inspecting the flue.

SWEEPING A MASONRY CHIMNEY FROM BELOW

1. Accessing the flue.
◆ Remove the damper plate *(page 224)* by detaching the handle from the plate and tilting the plate out of the frame *(right)*. If a cotter pin anchors the lever to the plate, remove it and lift the plate from the frame. If the plate cannot be removed, swing it open as wide as possible and determine if there is enough room for the sweeping brush. If not, you will have to clean the chimney from the top or have a professional do the job.
◆ Look inside the smoke chamber—wearing goggles or using a mirror—to establish the size and shape of the flue, and obtain a flue brush of appropriate size.

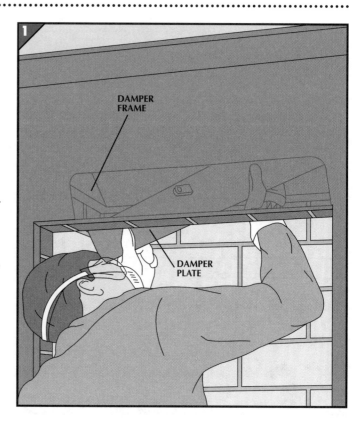

2. Sealing the fireplace opening.

◆ Cut a piece of polyethylene sheeting slightly larger than the fireplace opening. Seal it against the fireplace with continuous strips of duct tape along its top, bottom, and sides *(right)*.

◆ With a utility knife, make an inverted T-shaped cut 15 inches wide and 10 inches high in the center of the plastic. Watch the flaps created by the cut—they should be pulled into the fireplace, indicating the presence of an updraft that will carry loosened soot up and out the flue. If there is no updraft, create one by closing off the room, opening a window, and pulling air into the room with a fan.

◆ Cover the area in front of the hearth with newspaper or a drop cloth.

3. Sweeping the flue.

◆ Attach one rod section to the flue brush *(photograph)*, then slip the brush through the opening in the plastic, past the damper, and into the flue *(left)*.

◆ Work the brush up and down until the noise of falling debris subsides.

◆ Attach another section of rod to the bottom of the first and push the brush up to clean the next section of flue.

◆ Continue adding rods and sweeping the flue until the brush reaches the top of the flue.

◆ Pull the brush down to the smoke chamber and detach all but the first rod section.

4. Cleaning the smoke chamber.

◆ Scrub the walls of the smoke chamber vigorously, first with the flue brush then with a pot brush *(left)*, to loosen deposits from the surface.

◆ Slip a large doubled paper bag through the opening in the plastic. Holding the bag open with one hand, sweep in debris from the smoke shelf. With a dustpan, remove debris from the firebox floor.

◆ Inspect the flue for glazed creosote; if there is any, remove it *(page 241)*.

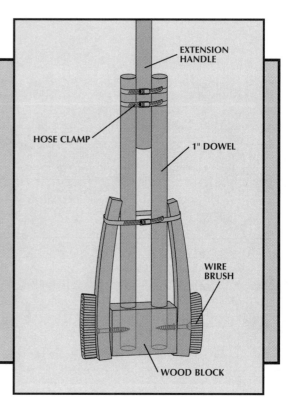

TRICKS OF THE TRADE

A Shop-Made Flue Brush

A brush like the one at right can effectively scour a flue from above. Cut a 4-inch-wide block to length so a wire brush attached to each end will make the assembly $\frac{1}{2}$ inch wider than the flue width. To assemble the unit, drill two 1-inch-diameter holes into the top edge of the block and glue a 1-inch dowel into each hole. To make a handle, fasten a third dowel to the first two with hose clamps. Pull bristles from a hole near the center of each wire brush and drill pilot holes through this hole and into the block; secure the brushes to the block with 2-inch No. 8 screws, and clamp the top ends of the brushes to the dowels. Extend the flue brush by clamping additional lengths of dowel to the handle.

EXTENSION HANDLE

HOSE CLAMP

1" DOWEL

WIRE BRUSH

WOOD BLOCK

REMOVING A COATING OF GLAZED CREOSOTE

Scraping the creosote.

◆ Attach the steel flue scraper to a rod section and slip it through the plastic sheet, up into the flue. Add rod sections to extend the scraper to the top of the flue.

◆ Scrape the flue with an up-and-down motion, rolling your wrists clockwise on the upstroke, then pulling the scraper straight down *(right)*.

◆ Once the noise of falling debris subsides, detach a rod section and work on the next section. Work your way down the flue, scraping until you reach the bottom.

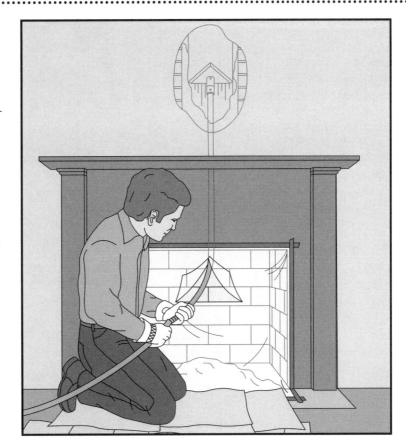

CLEARING A VERTICAL FLUE PIPE

1. Opening the flue.

◆ Spread newspapers on the floor under the flue pipe.

◆ For a stove with a flue collar at the back, remove any screws securing the pipe to the appliance and pull it off *(left)*; detach the elbow. If the collar is on top of the stove, unless you have a telescoping section, remove any screws holding the pipe to the collar and to the chimney-pipe support at the ceiling; detach the bottom section of pipe. Push up the upper part of the pipe enough to allow you to remove the bottom section, then lower it and have a helper reattach it at the chimney-pipe support.

◆ With duct tape, fasten a large double-thick paper or plastic bag to the open end of the pipe to catch debris.

2. Sweeping the flue.

◆ Observing the precautions for safety at heights *(page 228)*, climb to the roof and remove the chimney cap. If the stovepipe extends too high above the roof for you to work comfortably, remove a section of pipe.

◆ Lower a weighted brush *(right)*, or a brush extended by rods, to the bottom of the flue. Have a helper inside warn you just before the brush reaches the catch bag.

◆ Pull the brush up the flue gradually, using up-and-down strokes as you go.

◆ When you have finished sweeping the main portion of the flue, take the dismantled elbow or pipe segment outside and clean it.

◆ Carefully remove the catch bag and reassemble the flue.

◆ Clean the interior of the firebox with a pot brush.

WEIGHT

CLEANING A HORIZONTAL PIPE

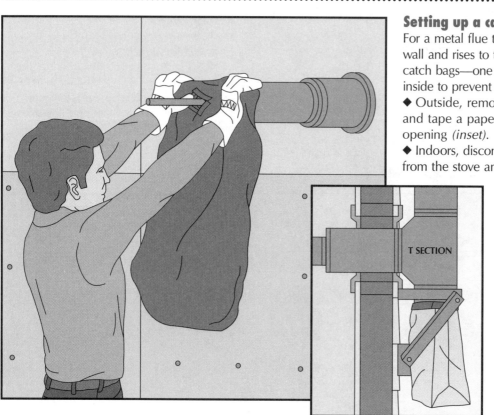

T SECTION

Setting up a catch-bag system.

For a metal flue that passes through an exterior wall and rises to the roof outside, you'll need two catch bags—one outside to collect debris, and one inside to prevent soot from entering the house.

◆ Outside, remove the cap from the T section and tape a paper or plastic bag around the opening *(inset)*.

◆ Indoors, disconnect the vertical pipe and elbow from the stove and horizontal pipe *(page 241, Step 1)*; clean them outside.

◆ Insert a flue brush and one section of rod in the horizontal pipe.

◆ Cut a slit for the rod through a heavy plastic garbage bag, reinforce the slit with duct tape, and tape the bag to the pipe *(left)*.

◆ Working slowly, push the brush back and forth, directing the debris into the outside catch bag. When you're finished, slide the brush into the garbage bag before untaping it from the pipe.

Recycling an Unused Fireplace

An unused fireplace can be salvaged to provide supplementary heat. The fireplace itself presents a ready-made cavity for a fireplace insert *(below and pages 244-245)*, or you can tap the old chimney to serve as a flue for a freestanding stove. For either of these projects, observe all code and safety requirements that apply to fireplaces or freestanding stoves.

Clearances: Before buying a fireplace insert, measure the height, width, and depth of the firebox. Inserts need minimum clearances, specified by the manufacturer, between the appliance and the firebox walls. Clearances to combustibles—such as a wooden mantel—must also meet the minimum. Since inserts produce more heat than an open fireplace, have the firebox and chimney inspected before beginning, to ensure they are in perfect repair.

Flue Liners: Fireplace inserts require a direct connection to the flue with a flexible liner running from the appliance collar through the damper and smoke chamber. The best method is to remove the damper and run the liner all the way up the chimney. Not only will the liner create better draft, the system can also be cleaned with less effort.

Freestanding Stoves: To vent a stove into an existing chimney, you must cut a hole in the chimney and anchor a stovepipe adapter called a thimble in the opening. Again, have a professional assess the project before you begin, to determine whether your existing chimney is adequate.

⚠️ **CAUTION** *Before cutting through your walls, ceilings, or roof, take precautions against releasing lead and asbestos particles into the air* (page 83).

 TOOLS

Carpenter's level
Pliers or wrench

Tin snips
Electric drill
Screwdriver
Caulking gun

 MATERIALS

Flexible flue liner
Flashing/chimney
  cap assembly

Flue collar adapter
Chimney-rated caulk

 **SAFETY TIPS**

Goggles protect your eyes when you are cutting into or chiseling masonry.

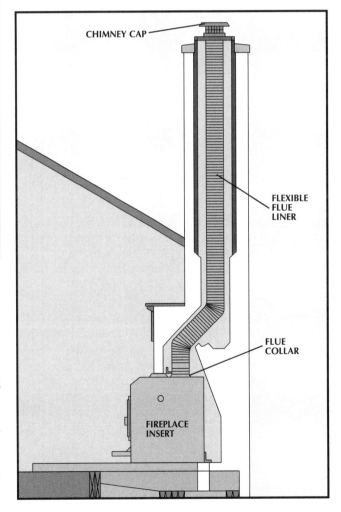

Anatomy of a fireplace insert.

The insert sits in the firebox of the existing fireplace, and the flue liner is attached to the insert's flue collar at the bottom and to a chimney cap at the top. A flexible stainless steel liner is well suited to snaking around bending flues *(right)*. The insert can be repositioned slightly after the liner has been attached to the flue collar.

PUTTING IN A FIREPLACE INSERT

FLUE COLLAR

FIRE-
BOX

CARDBOARD

1. Positioning the new firebox.
◆ Protect the hearth with a piece of heavy cardboard. Then, working with a helper, lift the insert onto the cardboard and slide it toward the rear wall of the fireplace *(left)*, observing any clearances specified by the manufacturer.
◆ Center the unit in the opening and check whether it is level; some models have adjustable legs.
◆ Buy a flexible flue liner and a flashing and chimney cap assembly sized to fit your chimney flue *(page 232)*; you'll also need an adapter to attach the liner to the firebox's flue collar.
◆ Remove the damper *(page 238)* and slide the flue liner down through the top of the chimney. Have a helper fit the bottom end into the flue collar adapter on the firebox.
◆ At the top of the chimney, trim off the excess flue liner with tin snips.
◆ Drill pilot holes through the flue liner and cap assembly, then attach the pieces with the screws supplied.

2. Adding the extenders.
◆ With chalk, mark lines along the top and sides of the insert in line with the front of the fireplace opening. Then, pull out the insert just enough to access the predrilled holes on the top and sides.
◆ Loosely fasten the top extender panel to the insert with the screws supplied. Position the panel so it just covers the chalk line, then tighten the screws *(right)*. Attach the side panels the same way, lining them up with the top panel.

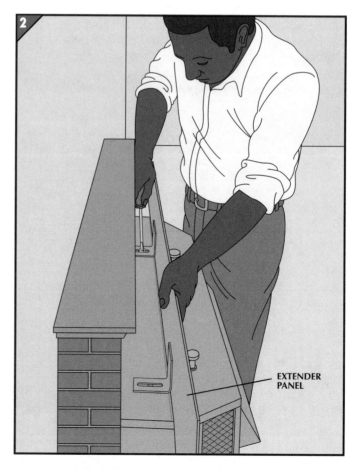

EXTENDER
PANEL

3. Caulking and insulating.

◆ Apply a bead of chimney-rated caulk along the joints between the insert and the three extender panels. Also caulk the seams between the top and side panels.

◆ Attach the insulation strips supplied to the back of the panels, $\frac{1}{2}$ inch inside their outer edges *(right)*. On some models, the extender panels have special channels for these bands of insulation.

◆ Slide the insert back in the fireplace so the extender panels rest flat against the front of the opening. For an irregular hearth, it may be necessary to add insulation for a snug fit.

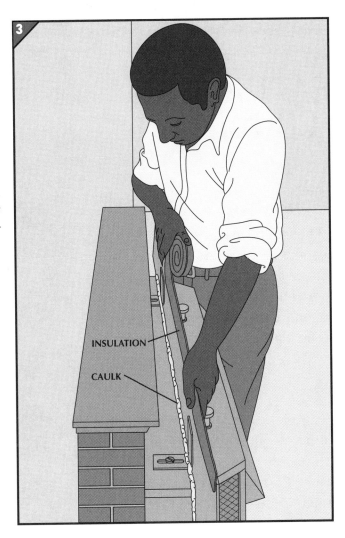

INSULATION

CAULK

GAS FIREPLACE INSERTS

Clean, reliable, and readily available, natural gas is a popular alternative fuel to wood. Fireplace inserts that burn gas *(right)* are installed much like the wood-burning insert described above, but a separate vent must be added for air intake. Some models, called "direct vent," can expel exhaust through the wall only a few feet above the fireplace, eliminating the need to pass a long liner through the chimney. Avoid any model that does not have a dedicated means to vent exhaust gases.

8 CHAPTER

HEATING AND COOLING

The goal of any heating or cooling system is to provide a comfortable environment in every room of the house. The most common defect—too much heat in one place and not enough in another—may be corrected by merely adding a damper to a duct or replacing a valve in a hot-water convector. Effective control of the system is also essential; a properly functioning thermostat will keep the temperature where you want it.

Furnaces and their system of pipes and ducts look forbidding, yet much furnace maintenance is surprisingly easy, and doing it yourself saves more than the cost of a service call. Some repairs and modifications to a system—maintaining a burner firing assembly, for instance—can also be undertaken with basic tools and techniques shown on the following pages.

Central air conditioning may seem the logical choice to fend off uncomfortably hot weather, but there are other options available as well. For a house without an existing duct system, room air conditioners can prove more economical to install and simpler to maintain.

Keep in mind that any improvements you make to the insulation in your home, as detailed in Chapter 9, will enhance your heating and cooling systems.

The Louvre

DECORATING WITH FABRIC LIBERTY STYLE · WATKINS · SIMON AND SCHUSTER

EQUUS · ROBERT VAVRA · MORROW

IMPRESSIONISM

247

A forced-air system, which carries heat ▶
from the furnace through ducts and fi-
nally to registers in the floor and walls,
is easy to adjust. Balancing the system
will provide each room in the house
with just the right amount of warmth.

Whether a gas furnace is a mid-
efficiency or standing-pilot type,
many upkeep and repair opera-
tions are safe and uncomplicated.
▼

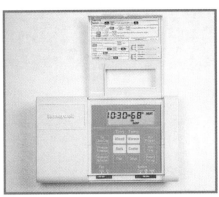

▲

A thermostat, the nerve center of a home's heating system, can malfunction with time and use. These devices are simple to service, and it's worthwhile to replace an older, manually set model with a fuel-saving programmable one.

▲

With proper maintenance—cleaning or replacing the air filter, cleaning the coils, and unclogging the drain hole—a window air conditioner can provide many years of trouble-free service.

◄ *A hot-water system should be tuned up at the beginning of every heating season. The only tool needed to bleed the air out of radiators is a screwdriver. Use a cup or a rag to catch any water that spurts out during the adjustment.*

Balancing a Forced-Air System

A heating system should provide each room in the house with just the right amount of warmth. This does not necessarily mean uniformity: You may want more heat delivered to bathrooms or a nursery, and less to bedrooms and the kitchen. Adjusting a forced-air system is easy if there are dampers—the movable metal plates in ducts that lead from the furnace to the room registers.

Adjusting the Dampers: Depending on the duct pattern, dampers may be clustered close to the furnace or scattered widely, as in the example shown below. Whatever the arrangement, all dampers work alike: When the damper handle parallels the duct path, the duct is wide open; when the handle is perpendicular, the duct is closed; and when the handle is in between, the duct is partially closed, or damped.

Balancing is simple, but it may take several days. Start by damping the duct to a room that seems too

hot—preferably one that lies close to the furnace. Wait 6 to 8 hours, then check the temperature of the room, by "feel" and with a thermometer held 4 or 5 feet above the floor. Repeat this process, one room at a time, until you have worked your way through the house.

You may find that the room containing the thermostat heats up so quickly that the furnace shuts down before other rooms are fully heated. The solution is to damp the duct leading to the thermostat room—almost completely, if necessary. More difficult is the situation in which the rooms farthest from the furnace never reach a comfortable temperature even with their ducts wide open. Try stepping up the speed of the furnace fan *(page 274)* to send more air to these distant rooms.

Fine-Tuning Your System: When balancing is complete, you will almost certainly have to make minor adjustments, since increasing or

decreasing the amount of air flowing into one room affects all the others. Go through the rooms again, adjusting one damper at a time and observing the 6- to-8-hour waiting period. Finally, when every room is getting the right amount of heat, mark the damper settings with a felt-tip pen. (If you have central air conditioning, repeat the entire operation in the summer and label the different settings HEAT and A/C.)

Installing Your Own Dampers: If your heating system lacks dampers, you can add them yourself. For round duct, buy a matching 2-foot-long section with a factory-installed damper. With the furnace off, insert the new section at the beginning of a duct run.

Ready-made damper sections for rectangular ducts are harder to find because the ducts come in many sizes. The steps opposite show you how to make and install your own.

TOOLS

Tin snips   Screwdriver
Broad-billed pliers   Pliers
Ball-peen hammer   Electric drill

MATERIALS

Sheet metal
Spring-loaded clips
Duct tape

SAFETY TIPS

When you are cutting and handling sheet metal, wear heavy work gloves to protect yourself against sharp edges.

Anatomy of a forced-air duct system.

Duct runs begin at the plenum, a large chamber attached to the furnace. An extended-plenum system *(below)* has a main duct (or ducts) running from the plenum, and branch ducts running from a main to the registers

in each room. You can usually detect the route and destination of a duct run by visual inspection; if necessary, close a damper to see which room turns cold. Dampers are found near the starts of the Branches.

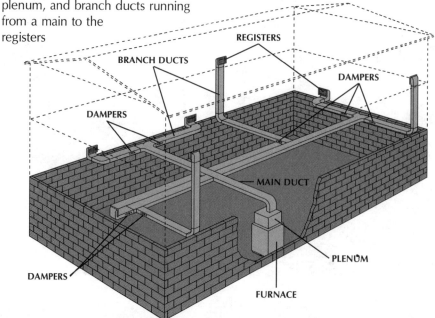

1. Making the damper.
◆ Measure the height and width of the duct.
◆ Wearing work gloves, use tin snips to cut a rectangle of sheet metal 1 inch longer and wider than these dimensions.
◆ Mark the dimensions of the duct within this rectangle, snip off the corners at about a 45-degree angle, and with broad-billed pliers fold the edges of the metal back along the marked lines to form rounded edges that are two layers thick.
◆ Hardware for the damper is available at heating-supply and hardware stores; buy the type with two spring-loaded clips that do not require welding or riveting.
◆ Slide the clips over the short edges of the damper, lining them up at the exact center. Set the damper on a firm surface and drive the clip prongs through the damper with a ball-peen hammer.

2. Opening the duct.
◆ Turn the furnace off and let it cool for an hour or so.
◆ Remove any duct tape over a connection of the branch duct, just past the point where the branch leaves the main duct, and open this connection.
◆ If the duct does not simply snap apart, remove the horizontal S clips and vertical drive clips. With a screwdriver, open the tabs at the tops and bottoms of the drive clips, then pull the clips down and off the duct connection with pliers. Separate the duct sections by pulling them out of the S clips.
◆ Remove the hanger supporting the duct section that lies farther from the main duct, and carefully lower the free end of this section until it is clear; support it in this position on a convenient prop—the rung of a ladder, for example.

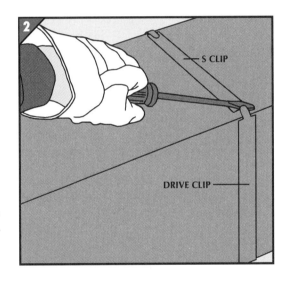

S CLIP

DRIVE CLIP

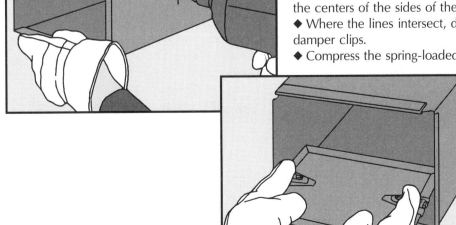

3. Installing the damper.
◆ Mark dots on the sides of the lowered duct section at a distance from its end that is equal to half the height of the damper plus 2 inches. Draw vertical lines through the dots. Draw horizontal lines along the centers of the sides of the duct.
◆ Where the lines intersect, drill holes the size of the bolts on the damper clips.
◆ Compress the spring-loaded clips, slide the damper into the duct, and release the bolts into the drilled holes. Install the damper handle.
◆ To rejoin the ducts, slip their edges into the S clip. Fold the bottom tabs of the drive clips, tap these clips lightly into place with a hammer, then fold the top tabs. Cover the connection with duct tape.

Balancing a Hot-Water System

The strategy for tuning the temperatures of individual rooms heated by hot-water convectors is much the same as that for balancing a forced-air system *(pages 250-251)*. The major difference is that hot-water systems cannot be balanced as precisely.

Directing the Flow: If your house has more than one thermostat, the system probably balances itself automatically. Otherwise, your system will have valves: balancing valves in the basement that correspond to warm-air dampers, or inlet valves at the convectors that correspond to the movable vanes of registers.

Tuning Up the System: At the beginning of the heating season—and always before adjusting a manually balanced system—vacuum convector fins and straighten them if they are bent. Then bleed the air out of the convectors to ensure that each is completely full of water for efficient heating. During the season, bleed any convector that seems cooler than normal.

TOOLS Screwdriver
Broad-billed pliers
Felt-tip pen

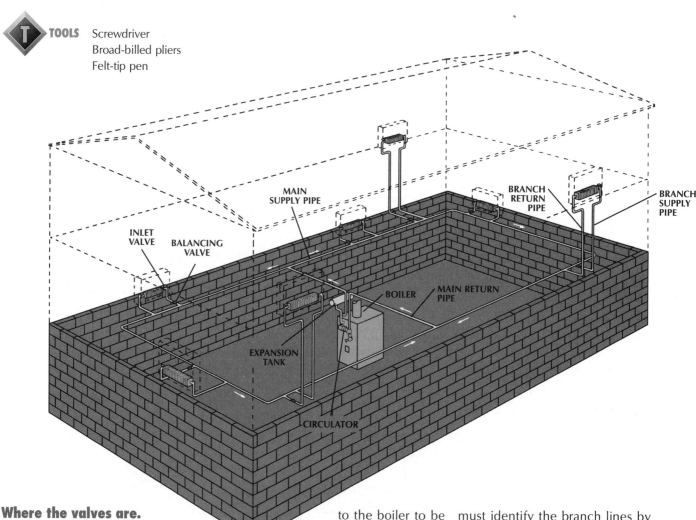

Where the valves are.
In a typical one-pipe hot-water system like the one above, a circulator pump draws hot water from a boiler and distributes it through main and branch supply pipes to baseboard heaters (or, in some systems, to taller units called convectors). Return pipes carry cooled water back to the boiler to be reheated. If your system has balancing valves *(red)*, you will find them wherever the main line branches to a convector; inlet valves *(blue)* are located at one end of each convector. Either can be used to balance the system, but if you have balancing valves you must identify the branch lines by room. To do so, close all the valves on a cool day and set the thermostat at 68°F. Open a valve and wait about an hour while the convector it serves warms up. Tag that valve with the name of the room, then open the others, one by one, until the valves are all tagged.

Straightening convector fins.

The metal fins on convectors should provide straight, smooth paths for air rising through the fixture. If a fin is bent, twist the metal back into shape with a pair of broad-billed pliers.

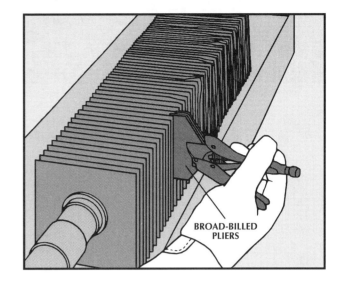

BROAD-BILLED PLIERS

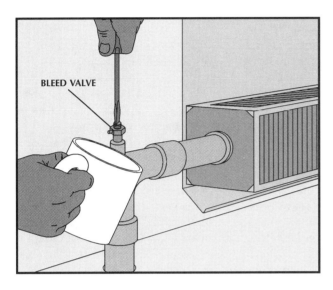

BLEED VALVE

Bleeding a convector.

With the system running, hold a cup or absorbent rag under the bleed valve, and unscrew the valve slowly until you hear air hissing out. When all of the air is discharged, hot water will spurt out quickly; close the valve immediately.

TRICKS OF THE TRADE

Quieting a Convector

Convector fins expand and contract with changes in temperature, causing them to rub noisily against the support brackets. To reduce this, place a piece of plastic—cut from an empty milk jug, for example—between the fins and the support bracket *(below)*. The plastic will prevent the rubbing while allowing the fins to expand and contract.

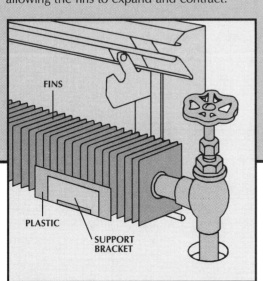

FINS

PLASTIC

SUPPORT BRACKET

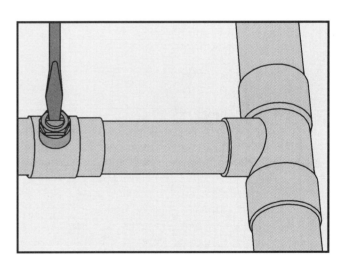

Adjusting a balancing valve.

The screwdriver slot that controls this valve also indicates its setting: The valve is wide open when the slot is parallel to the path of the pipe *(above)*, closed when the slot is perpendicular to the path. To regulate the flow of hot water to a convector, set the valve between these extremes, and when you have made all your balancing adjustments, mark the setting of the valve slot with a felt-tip pen.

Fixing and Replacing Thermostats

Most home thermostats operate on low voltage and consist of three sections: a cover, a middle segment containing the temperature-sensing and -control mechanism, and a base plate or wall plate. Wire terminals and switches are typically located on the base plate or on the temperature-control section.

With time and use, all thermostat parts can malfunction. Often you need only adjust a jammed cover to get a balky furnace or air conditioner going again. Wires can work loose, and switches can acquire a coat of dust and lint.

High-Voltage Thermostats: Controls that are designed to regulate electric baseboard heaters operate on the same current as the heaters,

usually 220 volts. Known as line voltage thermostats, these models, which mount on a standard electric switch box, have just two parts: a removable cover and a control section with terminals. If your baseboard system has a wall switch, you can easily replace it with a line-voltage thermostat *(page 256)*. Otherwise, you will need to reroute the heater's power cable through a switch box before adding the thermostat.

Upgrading: Although simple repairs can keep a thermostat functioning for years, you may prefer to replace an older, manually set thermostat with a fuel-saving programmable model that can be set for different day- and nighttime temperatures

(page 257). In most cases, this is a simple operation that involves little more than removing color-coded wires from the old thermostat and attaching them to color-coded terminals of the new one.

However, if you decide to change the location of a thermostat—to avoid drafts, for example—you will also need to run low-voltage cable containing the necessary number of 18-gauge wires to the new site.

Thermostats for furnaces and air conditioners usually have no more than five wires attached. A thermostat that has six or more wires is often connected to a heat pump, which requires a special thermostat. Contact your heat pump dealer for advice on a programmable replacement model.

 TOOLS

Screwdriver	Electric drill
Long-nose pliers	Hammer
Torpedo level	Wire strippers

 **MATERIALS**

Alligator clips	18-gauge wire
Nonsilicone switch	Insulation
cleaner	Wall anchors
Spackling	Wire caps
compound	

SIMPLE REPAIRS

Tightening wire connections.

◆ Set the thermostat's main switch to the off position.
◆ Pull the cover gently from its support clips to reveal the temperature-control section. Tighten any terminal screws that you see.

◆ Remove the mounting screws that are holding the temperature-control section to the base plate, disclosing four or five additional terminal screws. Tighten them.

[Diagram labels: BASE PLATE, ON·FAN, TERMINAL SCREW, SUPPORT CLIP, COOL·OFF·HEAT, 80, 50, TERMINAL SCREW, TEMPERATURE-CONTROL SECTION]

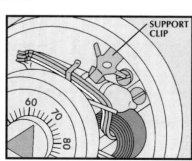

[Diagram labels: SUPPORT CLIP, 60, 70, 80]

Releasing jammed parts.

◆ When a thermostat dial binds, turn off the main switch. Remove the cover.
◆ Inspect the metal support clips that hold the cover in place. If one of the clips is bent *(left)*, use long-nose pliers to restore it to its original po-

sition or shape, as shown above.
◆ Replace the cover and set the switch for heating or cooling. Rotate the dial to be sure that it moves freely and turns the system on and off. If it does not, replace the thermostat *(page 257)*.

Bypassing a Faulty Thermostat

Thermostats often fail at inconvenient times. To keep your house reasonably comfortable until you can replace the faulty control, bypass it with a jumper wire fitted with an alligator clip on each end. Remove the thermostat cover and the temperature-control section as shown opposite. Next connect one end of the jumper to the terminal marked R or Rh and the other to terminal W. If the thermostat is at fault, the system will turn on. Turn it off when the temperature is comfortable by removing the jumper. Should the system not start with the jumper wire in place, look beyond the thermostat for the underlying difficulty.

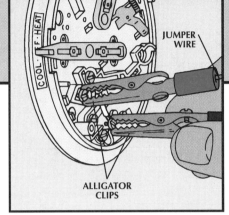

JUMPER WIRE

ALLIGATOR CLIPS

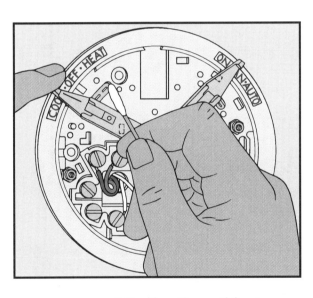

Cleaning thermostat switches.

◆ Turn off power to the heating and cooling systems. Remove the thermostat cover and unscrew the temperature-control section from the base.

◆ Saturate a cotton swab with a nonsilicone switch cleaner, available at electronics stores, or a strong (50/50) vinegar-and-water solution, and clean the contacts near the switch levers. Move the levers from side to side to expose all the contacts.

◆ Remount the temperature-control section and attach the cover.

Adjusting the anticipator.

This device, which contains an adjustable heating coil, keeps a thermostat from raising room temperature above the thermostat setting and keeps the furnace from turning on and off too often. To fix either problem, remove the thermostat cover and adjust the anticipator as follows (let the system adjust for a few hours after each change of setting):

◆ To correct swings of temperature more than 2°F above the thermostat setting, move the pointer of the anticipator down with the tip of a pencil, 0.1 ampere at a time.

◆ If the furnace starts and stops too frequently, move the pointer to a higher setting, 0.1 ampere at a time.

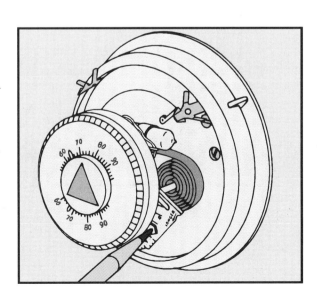

Installing a line-voltage thermostat.

◆ At the service panel, shut off power to the baseboard heater.

◆ Remove the switch mounting screws and pull the existing switch from the box.

◆ Label the switch wires with the markings on the terminals: L1 and L2 for the wires to the service panel, T1 and T2 for wires to the heater. Disconnect the wires and set the switch aside.

◆ Locate the matching terminals on the back of the line-voltage thermostat and connect the wires as shown at right.

◆ Remove the cover, mount the thermostat on the box, and replace the cover.

> **!**
> **CAUTION** *To avoid damaging fragile thermostat components, leave the cover in place while connecting wires.*

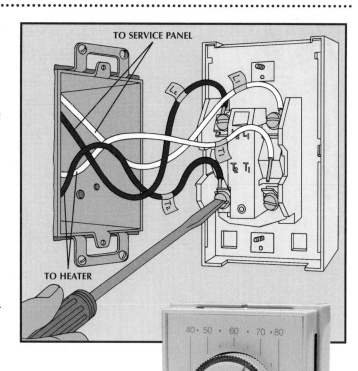

TO SERVICE PANEL

TO HEATER

TRICKS OF THE TRADE

Fine-Tuning an Erratic Thermostat

Drafts can cause a thermostat to misread the temperature in a home's living spaces. A thermostat should be mounted on an interior wall where sunlight cannot strike it and away from direct air flow from windows, doors, and supply registers. However, even a properly located thermostat may still be exposed to drafts coming from inside the wall.

If your thermostat operates erratically, unscrew the base plate from the wall and fill unused mounting holes with spackling compound. Gently pack the hole around the low-voltage wiring with fiberglass or rock wool insulation *(below)*. Do not substitute caulk for insulation; you may need to pull the wires a little farther out of the wall later if you install a new thermostat.

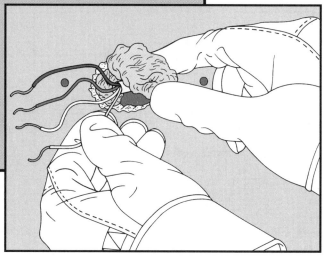

1. Mounting the base.

◆ Unscrew the old thermostat from the wall and label each wire with the color code of the terminal to which it is attached. (These codes may not always match the color of the corresponding wire's insulation.)

◆ Position the new base plate on the wall, with the wires centered in the plate's wiring opening. Level the top of the plate with a torpedo level, and mark two mounting holes with a pencil *(right)*.

◆ Set the base aside and drill $\frac{3}{16}$-inch holes at the marks. Tap wall anchors into the holes and screw the base to the wall.

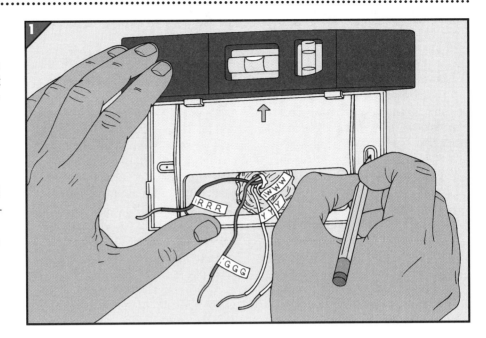

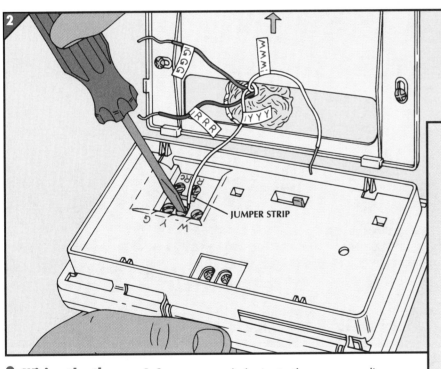

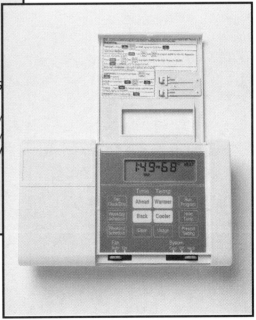

2. Wiring the thermostat.

◆ Holding the new thermostat next to the base plate, check that the wires are long enough to reach the new terminals. If they are not, cut 6-inch jumpers from 18-gauge thermostat wire. Strip insulation from both ends of the jumpers and join them to the existing wires with wire caps.

◆ Loosen all the thermostat terminal screws. Holding the unit in one hand, use the other to attach each coded wire to the corresponding terminal, then tighten the screw. If there is a fifth wire instead of four as shown here, break off the factory-installed jumper strip between the R and Rc terminals with a pair of long-nose pliers.

◆ Tuck in the wires and snap the thermostat onto the base plate. Install batteries and program the thermostat according to the manufacturer's instructions.

Maintaining a Gas Furnace

Gas furnaces, although extraordinarily reliable, require upkeep and occasional repair. Although many operations are best left to a professional, the ones shown in the chart opposite—and explained on the following pages—are safe and uncomplicated.

A Constant Pilot: Originally, all gas furnaces had standing-pilot ignition—a small flame that lights the burners *(below, right)*. On this type of furnace, maintenance involves turning off the pilot in the spring to save energy and relighting it in the fall. Occasionally, the thermocouple—a sensor that detects whether the pilot is lit—may require replacement and the pilot and burner flames may need adjustment.

Electronic Ignition Systems: Instead of a standing pilot, new furnaces are likely to have an intermittent pilot—in which the flame is lit by a spark and burns only long enough to light the furnace—or by a heating element called a hot-surface igniter. If an intermittent-pilot system fails to spark, call for service. However, you can test and replace a hot-surface igniter that does not glow when the heating cycle starts *(page 261)*.

A periodic task necessary for so-called mid- and high-efficiency furnaces is checking the temperature rise—the difference between the air temperature in the supply and return ducts. Too high a difference may crack the heat exchanger,

which transfers furnace heat to the air; condensation may corrode the system if the difference is too low.

Diagnosing a Problem: Furnaces with electronic ignition are regulated by a control center rather than by a series of relays and switches. Many centers have a red light that flashes a fault code to help in the diagnosis of problems. If the control center itself is faulty, it is easily replaced *(page 261)*.

⚠️ **CAUTION** *If you smell gas, turn off the supply at the meter, ventilate the room, and do not touch electrical outlets or switches. If the odor persists, evacuate the house and call the gas company.*

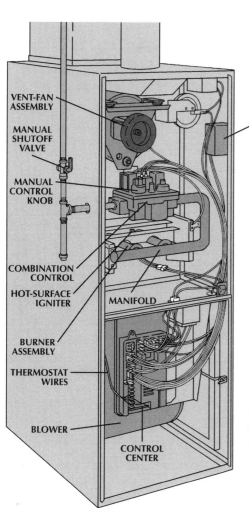

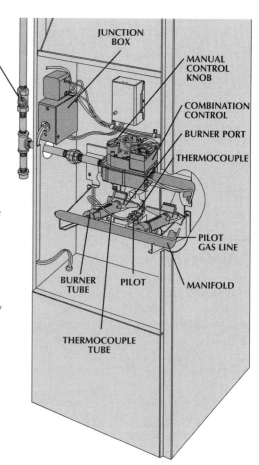

Two gas furnaces.

With the burner access and blower compartment panels removed on these mid-efficiency *(left)* and standing-pilot *(right)* furnaces, their differences are readily apparent. Their basic operation is the same: A valve in the combination control releases gas, which travels through the manifold to burners, then a blower circulates warmed air through the house. Features such as a hot-surface igniter allow mid- and high-efficiency furnaces to make more heat with less fuel. A control center oversees lighting the burners and monitors safety features. It also regulates the vent-fan assembly, which draws off combustion by-products and disposes of them outside.

TOOLS

Screwdriver
Pocket thermometer
Nutdriver
Wrench
Hex wrench
Multitester

 **MATERIALS**

Hot-surface
  igniter
Control center
Vent-fan motor
Long match or
  soda straw

Thermocouple
  tube
Cloth

 **SAFETY TIPS**

When adjusting the air shutter on a burner, wear gloves to protect your hands from heat.

Troubleshooting Guide

PROBLEM	REMEDY
No heat.	Replace fuse or reset circuit breaker. Check control center for flashing fault code. Replace hot-surface igniter *(page 261).* Replace vent-fan motor *(page 262).* Replace control center *(page 261).* Relight pilot *(page 263).*
Insufficient heat.	Increase blower speed *(page 274).* Adjust burner air shutter *(page 265).*
Hot-surface igniter does not glow.	Test and replace hot-surface igniter *(page 261).* Replace control center *(page 261).*
Pilot does not light or does not stay lit.	Tighten or replace thermocouple *(pages 264-265).*
Pilot flame flickers.	Adjust pilot flame *(pages 263-264).*
Exploding sound when burner ignites.	Adjust pilot flame *(pages 263-264).*
Burner takes more than a few seconds to ignite.	Adjust pilot flame *(pages 263-264).*
Burner flame too yellow.	Adjust burner air shutter *(page 265).* Provide air from outside by opening vents in furnace room.
Noisy furnace: rumbling when burners off.	Adjust pilot flame *(pages 263-264).*
Noisy furnace: rumbling when burners on.	Adjust burner air shutter *(page 265).*

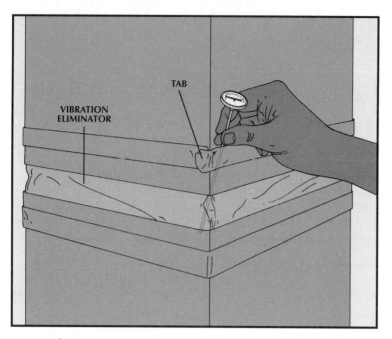

TAB

VIBRATION
ELIMINATOR

Measuring temperature rise.

◆ With a screwdriver, loosen a slip and drive connector at a joint in the supply duct close to the furnace and insert a pocket thermometer *(above)*. (Alternatively, poke the thermometer through a canvas vibration eliminator between ducts; the hole will reseal itself.) Note the temperature.

◆ In the same manner, check the temperature in the return duct.

◆ Subtract the lower temperature from the higher one. If the difference falls below the range indicated on the information plate in the burner compartment, decrease blower speed *(page 274)*. For a result above the range, increase blower speed.

◆ If changing the blower speed does not rectify the problem, call a professional.

Sequence of Furnace Operation

If you don't have a flashing fault code light to indicate where the heating cycle is interrupted, you can sometimes pinpoint a problem simply by watching and listening to learn where the furnace falters in its cycle, recounted here for a healthy mid-efficiency model.

✔ When the thermostat turns the furnace on, the vent-fan motor starts.

✔ After several seconds, the control center triggers the ignition system, causing the hot-surface igniter to glow or the spark igniter to flash.

✔ Gas is released from the combination control with an audible click. Normally the burners light.

✔ The flame sensor confirms that the burners have fired and allows the flow of gas to continue.

✔ When the furnace has warmed up, a temperature-sensitive switch or a timer turns on the blower, circulating air through the ducts.

INSTALLING A HOT-SURFACE IGNITER

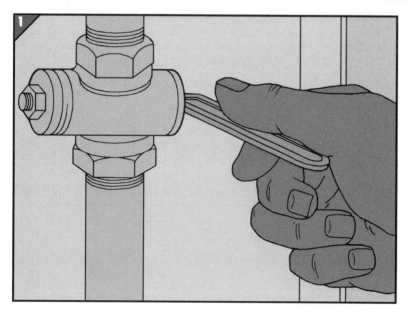

1. Shutting down the furnace.

◆ Turn off the gas to the furnace by closing the manual shutoff valve. The valve is closed when the handle is at right angles to the gas line *(left)*.

◆ Turn off power to the furnace at the master switch located on or near the furnace or, if there is no master switch, at the service panel.

2. Replacing the igniter.

◆ Take off the burner access panel.
◆ Unplug the igniter *(photograph)* and test it with a multitester *(page 29)*. Set the multitester to RX1 and attach an alligator clip to each prong in the igniter's plug. If the multitester registers between 45 ohms and 90 ohms, replace the control center *(below)*. Otherwise, install a new igniter.
◆ Unscrew or unclip the defective igniter and remove it.
◆ Screw or clip the new igniter in place; plug it in.
◆ Remount the access panel and restore power and gas to the furnace.

⚠️ **CAUTION** *A hot-surface igniter is fragile and should be handled with care.*

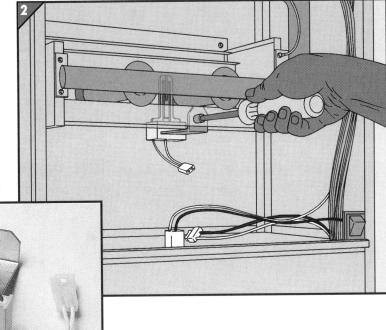

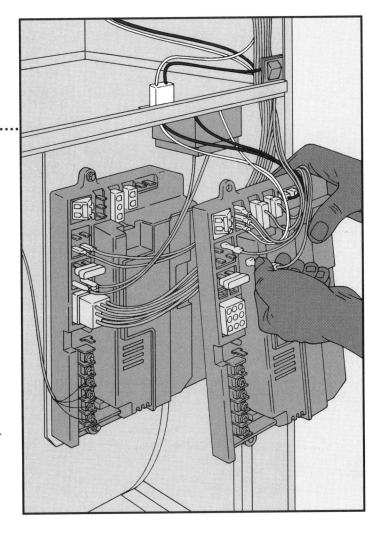

A NEW CONTROL CENTER

Transferring the wires.
◆ Shut down the furnace *(opposite)*.
◆ Take off the blower access panel, removing the burner access panel first if necessary.
◆ With a nutdriver, remove the screws securing the control center. Leave the wires attached.
◆ Screw the new control center in place.
◆ Transfer the wires from the old center to the new, one at a time and in an orderly sequence.
◆ Remount access panels and restore power and gas to the furnace.

REPLACING A VENT-FAN MOTOR

1. Removing the fan assembly.

◆ Shut down the furnace *(page 260)*.

◆ Remove the burner access panel and unplug the fan motor.

◆ Test the motor with a multitester *(page 29)* set to RX1. Attach an alligator clip to each prong on the plug. If the multitester registers any resistance at all, the motor is good; replace the control center *(page 261)*. Otherwise, install a new motor.

◆ With a nutdriver, remove the screws holding it in place. You may have to loosen the junction box or other components to reach all of the screws.

◆ Pull out the fan assembly.

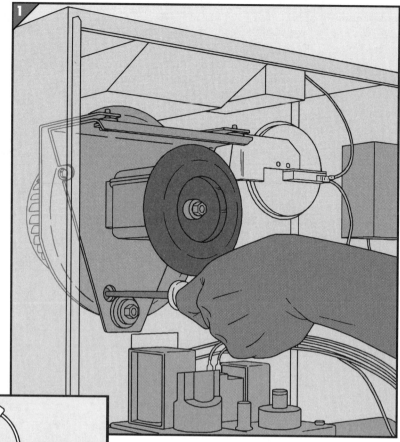

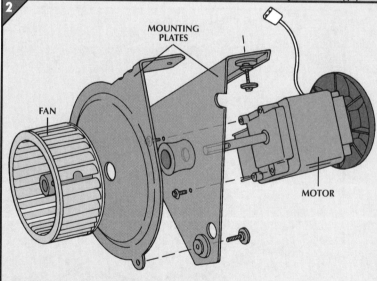

2. Installing the new motor.

◆ Slip a hex wrench through the slot provided in the fan, loosen the setscrew, and pull the fan off the shaft. If the fan is damaged or rusty, buy a new one.

◆ Remove the screws holding the two mounting plates together and separate the plates.

◆ Unscrew the motor from its mounting plate.

◆ Fasten the new motor to the mounting plate, then screw the two plates together. Slip the fan wheel onto the motor shaft and tighten the setscrew.

◆ Install the assembly in the furnace and plug it in.

◆ Remount the access panel and restore power and gas to the furnace.

TRICKS OF THE TRADE

Getting at Hard-to-Reach Screws

The flexible shaft of this tool, called a spinner *(below)*, makes it possible to reach screws that are somewhat obstructed by other components. Fitted with a socket of the appropriate size, the shaft of the tool can bend slightly around an obstacle, often eliminating the need for disassembly.

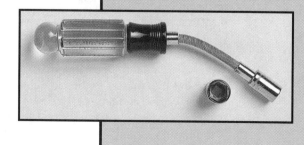

LIGHTING A PILOT

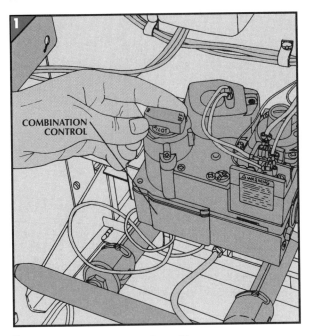

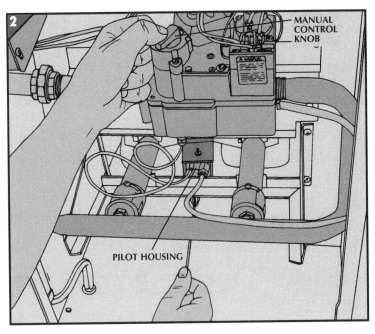

1. Turning off gas to the pilot.
◆ Turn off power to the furnace at the master switch or control panel.
◆ Set the manual control knob, located on the combination control, to the off position *(above)* and wait 10 minutes for any gas to dissipate.

CAUTION *If the smell of gas persists, do not attempt to relight the pilot; call for service.*

2. Relighting the pilot.
Follow the manufacturer's instructions for relighting the pilot—usually labeled on, or near, the combination control. In the absence of instructions, use the procedure explained here. If the pilot does not stay lit, the thermocouple may be faulty *(pages 264-265)*.
◆ Turn the manual control knob to the pilot position.
◆ While depressing the control knob or pilot ignition button, light the pilot burner located under the pilot housing with a long match *(above)* or a lit soda straw. Continue depressing the knob for 1 minute.
◆ Release the control knob, check the flame, and adjust as necessary *(Steps 1-2, below and page 264)*.
◆ Turn the control knob to the on position, then restore power to the furnace.

ADJUSTING THE PILOT FLAME

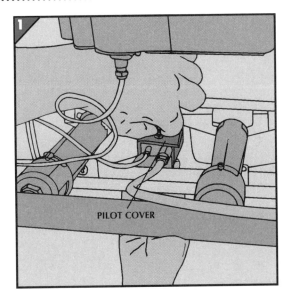

1. A view of the flame.
◆ Turn off power to the furnace at the master switch or control panel.
◆ If you can see the pilot flame clearly, go to Step 2. If, however, the pilot housing has a metal cover, first turn the manual control knob on the combination control to OFF. Wait a few minutes for the cover to cool. Unscrew and remove the cover *(left)*, then relight the pilot *(above)*.

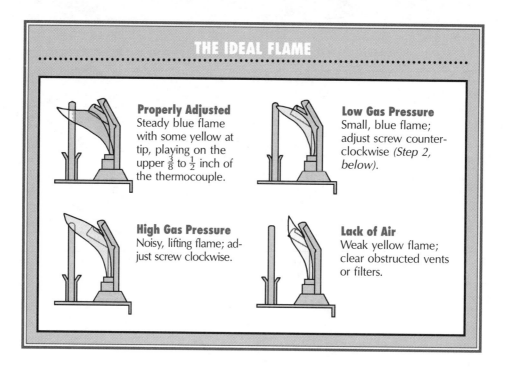

THE IDEAL FLAME

Properly Adjusted
Steady blue flame with some yellow at tip, playing on the upper $\frac{3}{8}$ to $\frac{1}{2}$ inch of the thermocouple.

Low Gas Pressure
Small, blue flame; adjust screw counter-clockwise *(Step 2, below)*.

High Gas Pressure
Noisy, lifting flame; adjust screw clockwise.

Lack of Air
Weak yellow flame; clear obstructed vents or filters.

2. Adjusting the pilot screw.

◆ Find the pilot-adjustment screw on the combination control. On some models the adjustment screw is recessed and covered by a cap screw that must first be removed.

◆ To increase the height of the flame, turn the adjustment screw counterclockwise; lower the flame by turning the screw clockwise.

If you removed a pilot cover in Step 1, turn the manual control knob on the combination control to OFF, replace the cover, then relight the pilot *(page 263)*.

ADJUSTMENT SCREW

COMBINATION CONTROL

EXCHANGING THE THERMOCOUPLE

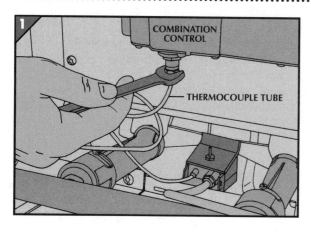

COMBINATION CONTROL

THERMOCOUPLE TUBE

1. Removing the thermocouple tube.

◆ First, shut down the furnace as described on page 260. A standing-pilot furnace may have a separate gas supply for the pilot; if so, also close the manual valve on this line. Allow a few minutes for metal parts to cool.

◆ Detach the thermocouple tube from the combination control by unscrewing the nut that secures the tube *(left)*.

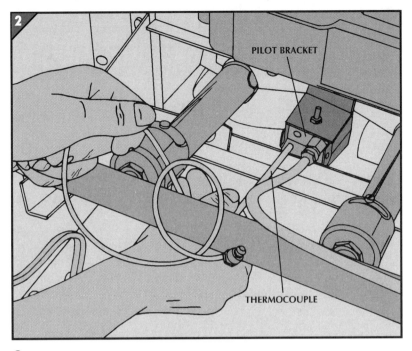

PILOT BRACKET

THERMOCOUPLE

2. Installing the new sensor.
◆ Slide the defective thermocouple out of the bracket that holds it in place next to the pilot burner *(above)*.
◆ Use a cloth to clean the fitting on the combination control, and screw a new thermocouple tube into the fitting. After tightening the nut by hand, turn it a quarter-turn with a wrench.
◆ Being careful not to crimp the tubing, insert the thermocouple into the pilot bracket.

ADJUSTING A BURNER FLAME

Rotating the air shutter.
The burner may have an adjustable shutter, held in position by a lock screw on the end of the burner tube; or a fixed air shutter, which must be adjusted by a professional; or no air shutter at all. To adjust a movable shutter:
◆ Turn the thermostat to its highest setting to start the burner and keep it running. Allow 5 minutes for the burners to heat up, then remove the burner access panel and loosen the shutter lock screw *(inset)*.
◆ Slowly rotate the shutter open *(right)* until the blue base of the flame appears to lift slightly from the burner surface. Then close the shutter until the flame reseats itself on the surface. The flame should appear blue with a soft blue-green core and occasional yellow streaking. If not, call for service.
◆ Tighten the lock screw, then repeat the process for the remaining burners.
◆ Reset the thermostat.

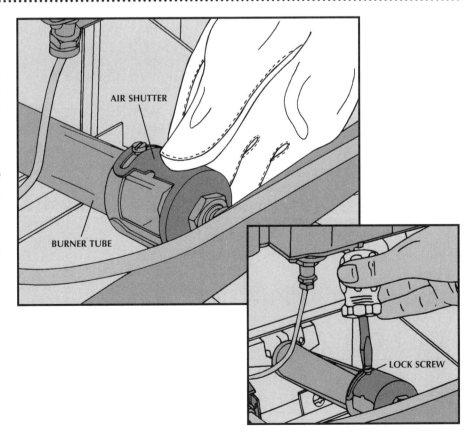

AIR SHUTTER

BURNER TUBE

LOCK SCREW

Cleaning and adjusting an oil burner before the heating season starts can cut fuel bills and extend the life of the burner. Moreover, the trouble-shooting chart opposite shows which of the procedures on the following pages can prevent costly service calls. Once a year, however, have a professional check the efficiency of the burner, a job that requires costly test instruments.

Before Beginning Work: Use newspapers to protect the floor, a pan of sand or cat litter to catch drips, and a bucket to dispose of sludge and excess oil. Turn off the burner master switch and cut power to the circuit that governs the burner by switching off the circuit breaker or pulling the fuse. Then shut down the oil line at the valve between the filter and the storage tank.

If your oil line has a special fire safety valve at the pump, turn the handle clockwise to push the stem down. The valve is closed when the handle slips off the stem. To seat the valve completely, give the stem a light tap with a wrench.

When the job is done, reopen the oil line before restoring power to the burner. Doing so prevents air pockets in the oil supply.

Repairing the Furnace: An air leak, a dirty heat exchanger, soot in the flue and the chimney, or a crumbling combustion chamber all affect burner efficiency. You can seal leaks with furnace cement *(page 272)* and clean heat exchanger or boiler surfaces with a stiff brush and a vacuum cleaner.

A bag of sand loosens soot, removable through a cleanout door at the base of the chimney. To dislodge soot in the stack leading from the furnace to the chimney, dismantle it and rap each section against a floor covered with newspapers.

Renewing a Combustion Chamber: After much intense heat and expansion and contraction, a combustion chamber's lining may crumble or burn up. If a firebrick lining crumbles in large chunks, furnace cement can bond the pieces back in place.

But the best repair for any combustion chamber retaining its shape

is to reline it. Available from heating and refrigeration suppliers, liners are made of heat-resistant fibers, kept moist and flexible in a plastic bag until heat is applied after installation. Before buying one, make sure the modification will not void your furnace or boiler warranty.

To get the right liner, you will need the firing rate and the spray pattern of your nozzle *(page 270, Step 3)* and the dimensions of the combustion chamber *(page 273, Step 2)*. The dealer may suggest a different nozzle, one more compatible with the new liner.

An Uncontaminated Oil Tank: Water or rust in the fuel line can cause burner problems. To keep moisture from condensing inside the oil tank and rusting the bottom, fill the tank at the end of the season.

You can detect water in the tank with gray litmus paste (from a heating or plumbing supplier) smeared on the bottom of the dipstick used to gauge fuel level. If the paste turns purple, water has pooled in the bottom of the tank. Drain water more than 1 inch deep from the bottom of the tank.

 TOOLS

Screwdriver
Shallow pan
Bucket
Small toothbrush
Long, narrow brush
Wrenches
Wire brush
Putty knife
Tape measure
Scissors

 **MATERIALS**

Cat litter or sand
Oil filter cartridge
Filter-bowl gasket
Nondetergent
 electric-motor oil
Clean rags
Solvent
Stiff paper
Furnace cement
Combustion-
 chamber liner

How an oil burner works.

When the thermostat calls for heat, the burner's relay box, or primary control, turns on the burner motor, which pumps oil to the burner nozzle and blows air into the combustion chamber. The pump draws oil from a storage tank through a shutoff valve and filter, then blasts it out the nozzle in a fine mist that mixes with blower air entering the combustion chamber through the burner air tube. Simultaneously, an ignition transformer boosts household voltage from 120 volts to 10,000 volts and sends it to the electrodes, causing a spark that ignites the oil-air mixture. Combustion gases exit through a stack at the back of the furnace (not shown). In the event of a misfire, a light-sensitive photoelectric cell shuts down the system until a reset button on the relay box is pressed.

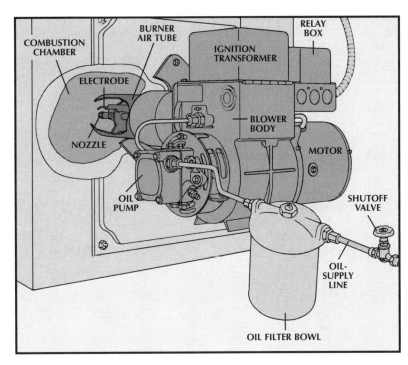

Troubleshooting Guide

PROBLEM	REMEDY
No heat or insufficient heat.	Check oil level in the fuel tank; have it refilled if necessary. Press reset button. (If the system doesn't start after two attempts, call for service.) Check electrodes; adjust if necessary. Clean or replace nozzle (pages 270-271). Clean photocell (page 269); replace if necessary. Replace oil filter (page 268). Clean strainer (page 268); replace if necessary.
Intermittent heat.	Check oil level in the fuel tank; have it refilled if necessary. Press reset button. (If the system doesn't start after two attempts, call for service.) Replace oil filter (page 268). Clean strainer (page 268); replace if necessary. Replace nozzle (pages 270-271). Clean or replace photocell (page 269).
High fuel consumption.	Replace nozzle (pages 270-271).
Burner system noisy.	Lubricate motor (page 269).
Diesel fuel odor from burner system.	Tighten oil line fittings. Check electrodes (page 270); adjust if necessary.

UNCLOGGING THE FILTER SYSTEM

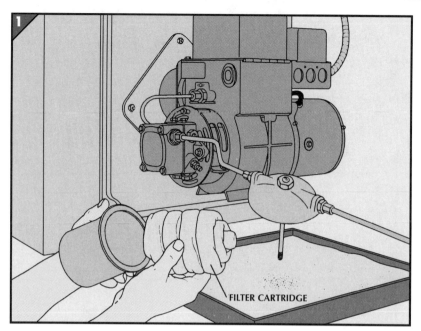

FILTER CARTRIDGE

1. Changing the oil filter.

◆ Switch off the burner, shut off the burner circuit, and close the supply valve. Set a pan filled with cat litter or sand under the oil filter.

◆ Unscrew the bolt on the cover above the filter bowl. Remove the bowl and upend it into a bucket, letting the filter cartridge inside fall out.

◆ Wipe the bowl and peel off the old gasket.

◆ Insert a new cartridge and place a new gasket on the lip of the filter bowl, then reattach the bowl to the cover.

2. Cleaning the pump strainer.

If your pump has a rotary-blade filter instead of a strainer—your oil dealer can tell you—skip this step. Otherwise, proceed as follows:

◆ Unbolt the pump cover and set it aside, without disconnecting the oil line. Discard the thin gasket around the cover rim.

◆ Remove the cylindrical wire-mesh strainer. Replace a torn or bent strainer; soak one that passes inspection in solvent for a few minutes to loosen sludge buildup. Then clean the mesh gently with an old toothbrush.

◆ Reinstall the strainer, place a new gasket on the cover rim, and bolt the cover in place.

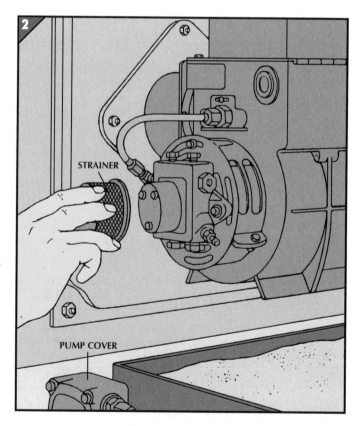

STRAINER

PUMP COVER

CHECKING THE FAN AND MOTOR

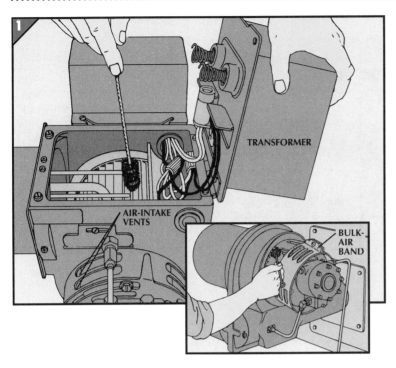

1. Cleaning the fan.
To maintain burner efficiency, clean the fan and air-intake openings every month during the winter as follows:
◆ First, sweep out the air-intake vents on the fan housing with a long, narrow brush.
◆ Unscrew the transformer atop the burner and swing it out of the way to expose the fan. Brush the fan blades *(left)* and wipe the interior of the fan housing with a rag.

To reach the fan on an old-style burner *(inset)*, mark the position of the slotted bulk-air band that surrounds the housing. Loosen the screw holding the band and slide the band back. After cleaning the fan, reposition the band in its original location and tighten the screw.

2. Lubricating the motor.
◆ On a burner motor with small oil cups at each end—the absence of oil cups indicates a permanently lubricated motor—lift the lids or plugs from the cups.
◆ Dribble 4 or 5 drops of 10- to 20-weight nondetergent electric-motor oil in each cup and replace the lids or plugs.
◆ Lubricate the motor every 2 months, or at the intervals specified by the manufacturer.

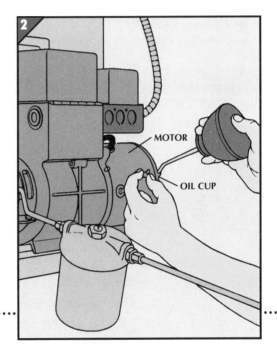

CLEANING THE FLAME SENSOR

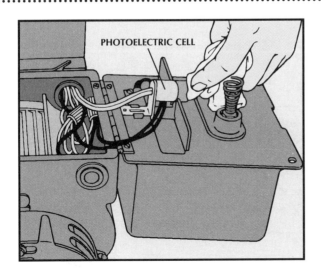

The light-detecting cell.
◆ Unscrew the transformer atop the burner and lift it up. Most often, the photoelectric cell that shuts off the motor when ignition fails is mounted on the underside of the transformer or attached to the burner housing near the end of the air tube.
◆ Wipe dirt from the cell with a clean rag, then resecure the transformer.

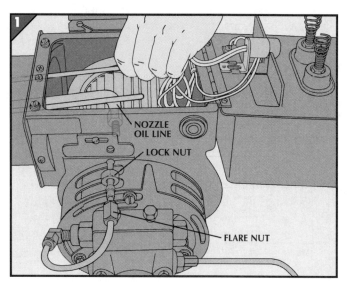

1. Removing the firing assembly.

◆ After moving the transformer out of the way, mark the position of the firing assembly in the air tube.

◆ Disconnect the nozzle oil line from the pump oil line, first loosening the flare nut then the lock nut.

◆ Pull the entire firing assembly—electrodes and nozzle oil line—out of the air tube.

You may need to twist the assembly as you pull it, but be careful not to knock the electrodes or nozzle against the burner housing.

◆ With the firing assembly removed, clean the air tube with a cloth or a brush. If there is a flame-retention device—a circular metal piece with fins or vanes—at the end of the tube, clean it as well.

2. Cleaning the ignition system.

◆ With a cloth dipped in solvent, wipe soot off the electrodes and their insulators, as well as the electrode extension rods or cables and the transformer terminals.

◆ If the insulators are cracked or the cables frayed, take the entire assembly to a professional for repair.

◆ Measure the spacing of the electrode tips, which should exactly match the manufacturer's specification—usually about $\frac{1}{8}$ inch apart pointed toward each other, no more than $\frac{1}{2}$ inch above the center of the nozzle tip, and no more than $\frac{1}{8}$ inch beyond the front of the nozzle (inset). If necessary, loosen the screw on the electrode holder and gently move the electrodes into place.

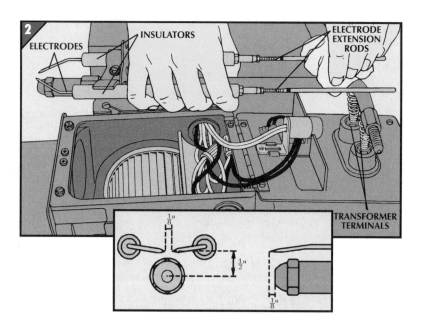

3. Removing the nozzle.

◆ With one wrench holding the hexagonal adapter at the end of the nozzle oil line, unscrew the nozzle with another. Take care not to twist the oil line or alter the positions of the electrodes.

◆ Examine the tip of the nozzle (inset); the stamped specifications show the firing rate in gallons of oil per hour, or gph (1.75 in this case), and the angle of spray (60 degrees). Letters usually identify the type of spray pattern.

◆ If the nozzle has a firing rate of 1.50 gph or less, replace it with an identical nozzle. If the nozzle has a higher rate, you can clean and reuse it (Step 4).

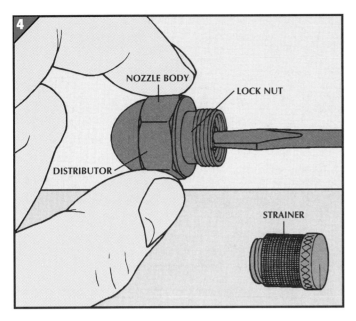

4. Disassembling the nozzle.

◆ With your fingers, unscrew the strainer from the back of the nozzle. Then unscrew the lock nut holding the distributor inside the nozzle tip *(left)*. Slide the lock nut and distributor out of the nozzle body.

◆ Soak all nozzle parts in solvent for a few minutes, then scrub gently with a small toothbrush. Clean distributor slots with a piece of stiff paper, and the nozzle orifice with compressed air or a clean bristle. Flush all the parts with hot water, shake them, and air-dry them on a clean surface.

◆ Reassemble on a clean surface, making sure your hands and tools are clean. Screw the nozzle onto the adapter finger tight, then snug it a quarter-turn with the wrenches.

 CAUTION *Never use a pin or wire to clean the nozzle orifice; scratches might alter the spray pattern.*

5. Opening the oil line.

(Skip this step if your storage tank is below the pump on your oil burner.)

◆ Loosen the cap screw on the unused intake port of the underside of the pump cover *(left)*.

◆ Place the pan filled with cat litter or sand under the oil pump and open the supply valve. When oil begins to flow from the intake port, let it run into the pan for about 15 seconds before tightening the cap screw.

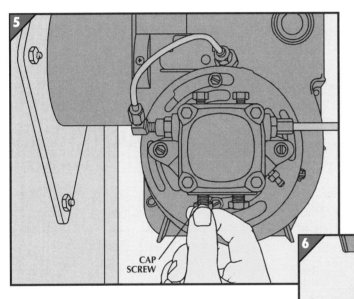

6. Priming the pump.

◆ Loosen the pump oil line at the pump to feed the unattached end into a bucket. (For safety, temporarily swing the transformer down or, on an old-style burner, screw on the rear plate.) Set the house thermostat to a high temperature and restore power at the service panel.

◆ Hold the bucket and have a helper throw the master switch. Oil will gush from the line with great force. Let the pump run for about 10 seconds, then have your helper turn off power at the master switch and the service panel.

◆ Lift the transformer (or remove the rear plate). Guided by the marks made in Step 1, install the firing assembly in the air tube, centering the nozzle oil line in the tube. Connect the pump and nozzle oil lines by tightening the lock nut and flare nut with your fingers—plus a quarter-turn with a wrench.

◆ Screw the transformer down (on an old-style burner, reconnect the electrodes and replace the rear plate). Restore power at the service panel.

◆ To expel any air that may remain in the oil line, partially open the observation port in the fire door and turn on the burner at the master switch. Run the burner for 10 seconds and shut it off. Repeat five times, or until the burner shuts down smoothly and instantaneously.

MAKING AN OIL BURNER AIRTIGHT

FLUE JOINT

FIRE DOOR

COVER PLATE

MOUNTING FLANGE

1. Locating leaks.

◆ Examine the flue and replace any section that is badly rusted and perforated with small holes.
◆ Check for leaks at the seams by firing up the burner and moving a lighted candle along each seam. The flame will deflect inward at leaks. Use this method to inspect the combustion-chamber cover plate, the burner mounting flange, the fire door, and the flue joints *(red)*.

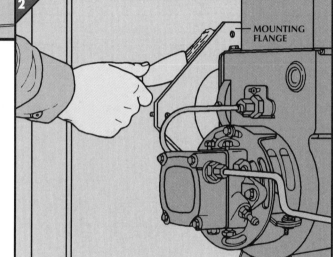

MOUNTING FLANGE

2. Sealing a leak.

◆ Turn off the burner and allow the furnace to cool. Clean the surfaces around the leak with a wire brush. Use a putty knife to fill gaps with refractory furnace cement.
◆ To seal a leak around the burner mounting flange *(right)*, loosen the bolts around the edge and pull the flange back a fraction of an inch. Scrape away old gasket material under the flange and apply a thin layer of cement around the edges. Retighten the bolts.

RELINING THE COMBUSTION CHAMBER

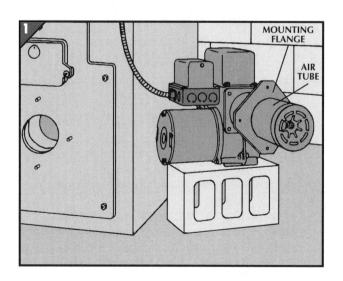

MOUNTING FLANGE

AIR TUBE

1. Removing the burner.

◆ Shut down the burner at the master switch and service panel, then close the oil-supply valve. Mark the air tube so that you can insert it the same distance into the combustion chamber when you reinstall the burner.
◆ Unscrew the bolts on the mounting flange and pull the burner away from the combustion chamber. If you cannot do so without bending the oil-supply line, disconnect the line at the oil-burner pump.
◆ As you pull the burner from the air-tube port, make sure that any gasket material encircling the air tube does not fall off and break. Set the burner down on its own pedestal or support it on a cinder block.

2. Measuring the combustion chamber.

◆ Inspect the chamber by looking through the air-tube port or fire door and by reaching inside and feeling the walls and floor with your hand.
◆ Measure the depth of the chamber with a tape measure or yardstick *(right)*.
◆ Calculate chamber width by measuring the width of the furnace and subtracting twice the thickness of the combustion-chamber walls, measured at the air-tube port.
◆ Take your measurements to a heating supplier and buy a liner to fit.

⚠ **CAUTION** *In old oil burners, the combustion liners and the patching material used around joints (opposite) may contain asbestos. Before disturbing any suspect material, test it (page 276).*

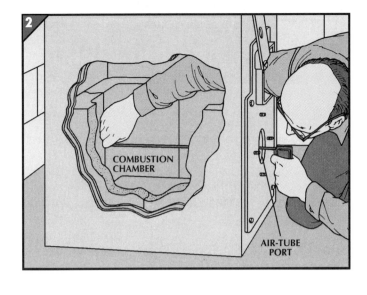

COMBUSTION CHAMBER

AIR-TUBE PORT

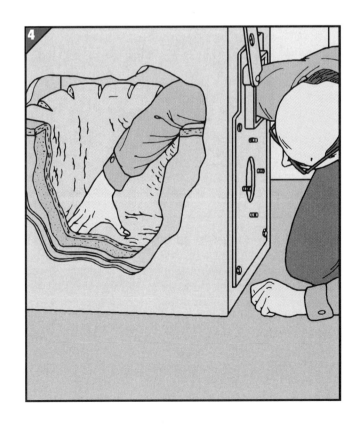

LINER

AIR-TUBE HOLE

3. Preparing the liner.

◆ Remove the damp liner from its plastic bag and spread it open.
◆ Measure the height of the combustion chamber and mark it on the liner. Use scissors to cut from the liner edge to the line to make flaps 4 inches wide.

◆ If the liner does not have a hole for the air tube, measure from the top of the combustion chamber to the top of the air-tube port. Then, the same distance below the flaps, cut out a circle slightly smaller than the diameter of the air tube.

4. Lining the chamber.

◆ Roll up the liner and push it into the combustion chamber through the air-tube port. Reach through the fire door and the air-tube port and unroll the liner; align the air-tube hole with the air-tube port.
◆ Working back to front, mold the liner against the walls and floor of the chamber. Pat the liner smooth and fold any flaps at the top of the liner over the top edge of the chamber.
◆ If the liner tears, press the torn edges back together. You can also patch torn sections with scraps from the air-tube hole.
◆ Partially dry the liner with a light bulb of at least 100 watts until it has the

consistency of stale bread. Then trim the air-tube opening in the liner with a sharp knife so that the edge is flush with the air-tube port.
◆ Push the air tube into the port up to the mark made in Step 1. Screw the mounting flange to the furnace. Reconnect the oil line, if you disconnected it earlier, and prime the pump *(page 271, Step 6)*. In all cases, open the oil valve and restore power to the burner.
◆ Turn on the burner at the master switch, let it run for 3 minutes, and shut it off for 3 minutes. You may see a little smoke and detect an unfamiliar odor; both are normal. Repeat this procedure twice to set the liner.

Maintaining a Furnace Blower

The blower—or fan—that distributes the air in a typical forced-air system is spun by a motor attached to the fan shaft. Such a unit seldom needs repairs, and any problems that do occur are generally easy to correct.

Poor Airflow: If the blower fails to deliver enough warm or cool air, dust and lint may be clogging the system. Check the filter to see if it needs to be cleaned or replaced. At the same time, pull the blower from the unit *(opposite, top)*, brush any dirt from the fins of the blower wheel, then vacuum it out.

Proper airflow also depends on blower speed. To strengthen or moderate the flow on older units, adjust the speed *(below)*. Before changing the blower speed on mid- and high-efficiency systems—which came into use in the late 1980s— read the information on checking the temperature rise *(page 260)*.

Noise: Vibration noises often can be quieted simply by tightening the screws holding the blower housing and the motor. A squealing or grating noise may be due to dry bearings in the blower: Although newer fans

have permanently lubricated and sealed bearings, some older models require oiling before the heating season starts, and again at the end of the season if the blower also serves a central air conditioner.

Replacing the Motor: If a blower motor burns out, replace it with one of the same size *(opposite, bottom)*.

⚠️ **CAUTION** *Before you begin any job that involves touching the unit's wires, turn off the master switch, and also shut off the circuit breaker or remove the fuse.*

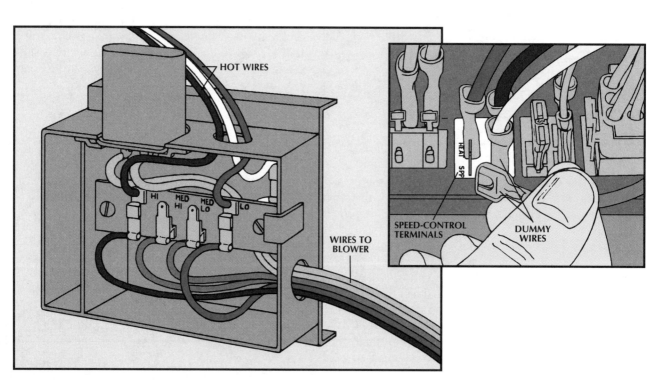

Adjusting a multispeed motor.
An older unit may have a blower-mounted junction box *(above)* housing the blower-speed terminals. More modern units may have a set of plastic modular plugs *(inset)* mounted on the blower. In both cases the blower speed is adjusted by changing the positions of the hot wires. A hot red wire connects to the low or medium-low terminal to run the blower when the furnace is in

operation. A hot black wire connects to the high or medium-high terminal to supply power during air conditioning. The unit also may have blue or yellow "dummy" wires that carry no electrical power *(inset)* on unused terminals. To change the blower speed proceed as follows:

◆ Remove the access panels from the unit—and from the junction box on older models.

◆ To increase or decrease blower speed for the heating system, unplug the red hot wire and attach it to the adjacent terminal.
◆ To increase or decrease blower speed for the air conditioner, unplug the black hot wire and attach it to the adjacent terminal.
◆ If the panel has dummy wires, exchange the position of one with that of the red or black wire *(inset)*.

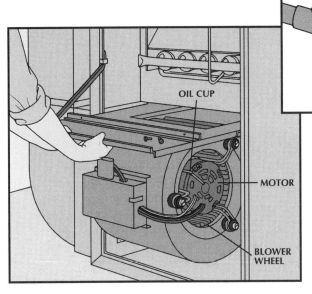

OIL CUP

MOTOR

BLOWER WHEEL

Oiling the bearings.

◆ Remove the access panels from both the blower and furnace compartments. If the control panel is in the way, remove the screws or nuts holding it in place, and move the panel aside.

◆ Loosen the screws or nuts securing the metal blower shelf to the unit.

◆ Slide the blower partway forward by pulling the shelf. If the electrical wires are too taut to permit the blower to slide easily, unclip the wires from the side of the furnace or detach them at the blower-speed terminals (opposite, bottom).

◆ Look for oil cups (inset) or plastic plugs at the visible end of the blower motor; if there are none, lubrication is not needed.

◆ Otherwise, lift the lids of the cups or pull the plugs and drip six to eight drops of 10- to 20-weight nondetergent electric-motor oil into each.

◆ Slide the blower back into place, replace the screws or nuts, and put back the access panels.

TRICKS OF THE TRADE

Oiling from a Distance

The oil ports on some motors are deep in the blower and hard to reach. To get lubrication to an inaccessible oil port, insert a thin wire into the port, hold the wire in a vertical position, and drip oil slowly onto the wire so that it runs into the hole.

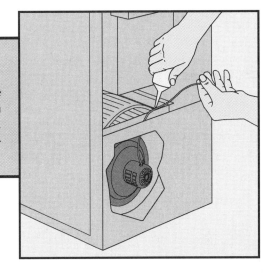

Replacing the motor.

◆ Unplug the blower wires from the blower-speed terminals (opposite, bottom).

◆ Slide the blower and attached shelf onto the floor.

◆ Loosen the bolt that connects the end of the motor shaft to the blower wheel.

◆ Remove the bolt assemblies that are holding the motor mounting bracket to the blower housing; ease the motor out of the blower.

◆ Remove the nut and washer at the ends of the mounting bracket's braceletlike ring (inset).

◆ Slip the bracket off the motor and attach it to the new motor in approximately the same position as it was on the old one.

◆ Slide the motor into the blower, reattach the mounting bracket, and tighten the bolt against the flat spot on the motor shaft.

◆ Rotate the blower wheel by hand; if the wheel rubs the housing, loosen the bolt and shift the wheel sideways until it is able to rotate freely.

◆ Slide the blower back in place.

◆ Tighten the screws or nuts, reconnect the wires, and replace the access panel.

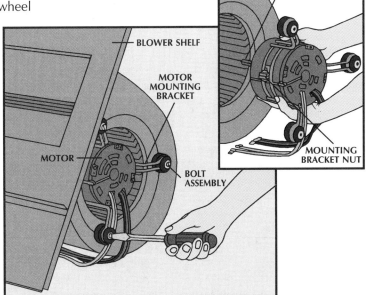

BLOWER SHELF

MOTOR MOUNTING BRACKET

MOTOR

BOLT ASSEMBLY

MOTOR SHAFT

MOUNTING BRACKET NUT

Hot-Water Heat: Easy to Maintain

A forced hot-water heating system is built for reliability, and regular servicing should keep it running smoothly for years. If problems do arise, the system may have to be drained to make repairs, as explained below. Draining may also be necessary if you want to add valves to improve the system *(page 279)*.

Components of a hot-water system rarely fail, but when breakdown occurs, it usually involves the pump motor, the coupler holding the motor to the pump shaft, or the pump seal. Remove the burned-out or broken part *(pages 277-278)*, and take it to a heating-supply dealer for an identical replacement.

Maintenance Basics: Once a year, before starting the boiler, bleed the convectors to rid the system of air *(page 253)*. If your circulator pump is not self-lubricating *(box, page 278)*, put a few drops of No. 20 nondetergent electric-motor oil in the oil cups at both ends of the motor and on the top of the bearing assembly between the motor and pump body.

Checking Water Pressure: During the heating season, periodically examine the combination gauge on the side or front of the boiler. Depending on the size of your house, the pressure can safely range from as little as 3 pounds per square inch when the water cools and contracts, to about 30 pounds when it heats and expands. The expansion tank *(page 279)* provides a cushion of air for the expanding and contracting water. A conventional tank has a top layer of air in direct contact with a layer of water, while a diaphragm tank keeps the air layer at the bottom, separated from the water by a rubber membrane.

If the movable "pressure" pointer on the gauge drops below the stationary "altitude" pointer, increase the pressure in the system by adding water to a conventional tank, or recharging the air in a diaphragm tank. If the movable pointer passes 30 pounds, there is too much pressure. Call for service if you have a diaphragm tank. Recharge a conventional tank with air *(page 279)*.

⚠ **CAUTION** *Old boilers may have asbestos insulation in the liner or around the pipes. To test, mist a small area with a solution of 1 teaspoon of low-sudsing detergent per quart of water, then remove a small sample and take it to a local lab certified by the National Institute of Standards and Technology. If the test is positive, hire a plumber or other professional licensed to handle asbestos.*

 TOOLS

Hex wrench
Open-end wrench
Box or socket
  wrench
Tire gauge
Bicycle pump
Hacksaw or tube
  cutter
Propane torch
Flameproof pad

 MATERIALS

No. 20 nondeter-
  gent electric-
  motor oil
Garden hose
Wood block
Bucket
Solder
Flux
Three nipples
Shutoff valve
Union

🪖 **SAFETY TIPS**

When soldering, wear gloves and eye protection.

Draining and refilling the system.

◆ Turn off the power to the boiler at the master switch and the service panel.

◆ When the combination gauge indicates the water in the system is lukewarm, close the water-supply shutoff valve. Attach one end of a garden hose to the boiler drain cock, and run the other end of the hose to a floor drain.

◆ Open the boiler drain cock and the bleed valves of all the convectors on the upper floors of the house and let the water drain.

◆ Refill the system by closing the convector bleed valves and the boiler drain cock and opening the water-supply valve. If there is a pressure-regulating valve on the line, the flow will stop automatically when the system is full. Otherwise, fill until the combination gauge's movable pointer corresponds to the position of the stationary pointer.

◆ Bleed all of the heating units on the upper floor. If you do not have a pressure regulator, have someone bleed each unit while you watch the gauge.

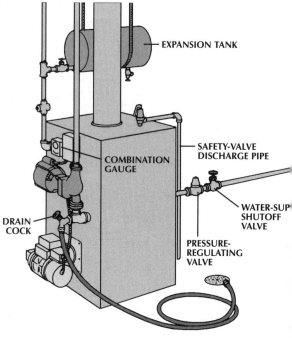

EXPANSION TANK

SAFETY-VALVE DISCHARGE PIPE

COMBINATION GAUGE

WATER-SUP SHUTOFF VALVE

DRAIN COCK

PRESSURE-REGULATING VALVE

Troubleshooting Guide

PROBLEM	REMEDY
No heat.	Replace fuse or reset circuit breaker. Bleed air from convectors *(page 253)*. Replace coupler *(page 278)*. Replace circulator pump motor *(below)*.
No heat, motor housing hot, burning odor.	Replace motor *(below)*.
Heat uneven throughout house.	Bleed air from convectors *(page 253)*. Replace coupler *(page 278)*. Replace circulator pump motor *(below)*.
Not enough heat, convector is lukewarm.	Vacuum and straighten convector fins *(page 253)*. Bleed air from convectors *(page 253)*. Replace circulator pump motor *(below)*.
Circulator motor noisy.	Lubricate circulator pump and motor.
Circulator motor sounds like a chain being dragged through system.	Replace coupler *(page 278)*.
Water spills from safety-valve discharge pipe.	Recharge conventional expansion tank *(page 279)*. Replace diaphragm-type expansion tank.
Circulator pump leaks.	Replace seal *(page 278)*.

REPLACING PUMP PARTS

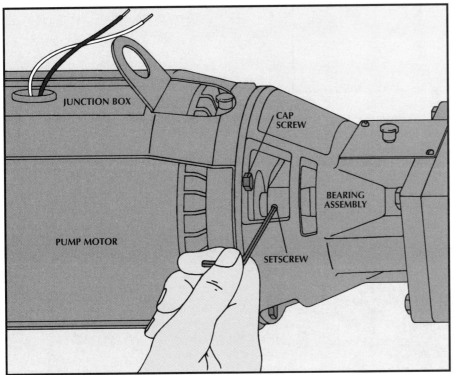

Installing a new motor.
◆ Turn off the power to the boiler at the master switch and service panel.
◆ Remove the junction box cover from the pump motor, and disconnect the wires.
◆ With a hex wrench, remove the setscrew holding the coupler to the motor shaft.
◆ Grip the motor in one hand, and using an open-end wrench, loosen the cap screws that hold the motor to the bearing assembly.
◆ Back the motor out, leaving the coupler attached to the pump shaft.
◆ Fit the free end of the coupler onto the shaft of the new motor.
◆ Holding the new motor against the bearing assembly, reinsert the cap screws and secure the coupler setscrew.
◆ Reconnect the junction box wires and replace the junction box cover.

Changing the coupler.

◆ Remove the motor *(page 277)*.

◆ With a hex wrench, loosen the setscrew that is holding the coupler to the pump shaft, and slide off the coupler.

◆ Secure one end of the new coupler to the pump shaft with the setscrew.

◆ Replace the motor and attach the other end of the coupler to the motor shaft.

COUPLER

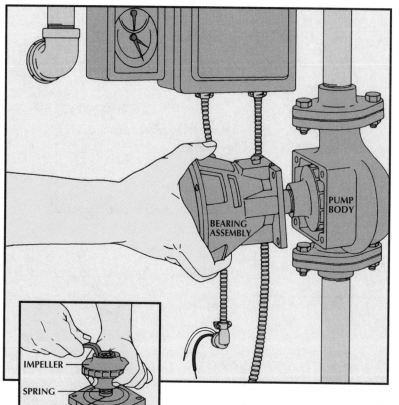

PUMP BODY

BEARING ASSEMBLY

IMPELLER

SPRING

SEAL

Replacing the pump seal.

◆ Drain the system *(page 276)*. Alternatively, turn off the power to the boiler at the master switch and service panel, then cut off the water to the pump by shutting the valves above and below it.

◆ Remove the motor and the coupler *(page 277 and above)*.

◆ Undo the cap screws holding the bearing assembly to the pump body, and pull the assembly out.

◆ With the bearing assembly standing on a wood block for support *(inset)*, turn a box or socket wrench clockwise to loosen the nut holding the impeller to the pump shaft.

◆ Slide off the impeller and spring, and save them.

◆ Pull off the brass seal. Slide a new one onto the shaft, and press it tight.

◆ Attach the old spring and impeller with the nut and washer, and reassemble the pump.

◆ Refill the system, or open the valves at the pump. Restore the power.

A LOW-MAINTENANCE PUMP

Many modern circulator pumps are self-lubricating (that is, the motor and bearings require no oil), and they also may have fewer parts than older models, reducing the chances of a breakdown. Some, like the pump at left, also offer a choice of speeds, allowing you to adjust the rate at which hot water circulates. By altering the pump's speed to closely match your system's needs, you can reduce water noise in the pipes and at the same time save energy.

SERVICING THE EXPANSION TANK

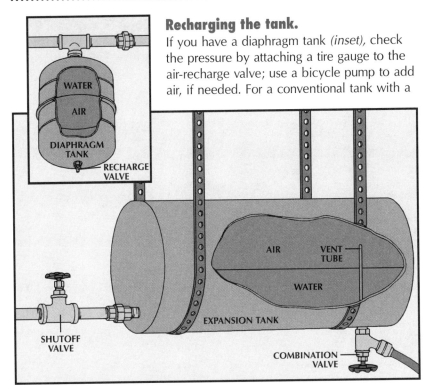

Recharging the tank.
If you have a diaphragm tank *(inset)*, check the pressure by attaching a tire gauge to the air-recharge valve; use a bicycle pump to add air, if needed. For a conventional tank with a shutoff valve and a combination valve, turn off power to the boiler at the master switch and service panel, close the shutoff valve on the line between the tank and boiler, run a hose from the combination valve to a nearby drain, open the valve, and empty the tank. For a conventional tank that lacks a combination valve, open the plug or drain cock at the tank's base and let the water empty into buckets. For one lacking a shutoff valve, drain and refill the entire system *(page 276)*.

You can add a shutoff valve as described below. You can also add a combination valve:
◆ Turn off the power to the boiler at the master switch and service panel, empty the tank, and close the shutoff valve.
◆ Cut the vent tube of the valve to two-thirds the height of the expansion tank.
◆ Remove the plug or drain cock from the tank's base, and screw the combination valve into the opening.

ADDING A SHUTOFF VALVE

A fitting of copper.
◆ Drain the system *(page 276)*.
◆ Working on the line between the expansion tank and the boiler, use a tube cutter or hacksaw to cut out a section 1 inch shorter than the length of the shutoff valve.

◆ Unscrew the bonnet from the valve body with a wrench and lift out the disk assembly; otherwise the soldering heat may warp the disk or post.
◆ Solder the valve to the pipe and, once it has cooled, replace the disk assembly.

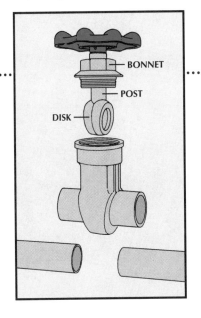

A threaded steel fitting.
◆ Drain the system *(page 276)*.
◆ Cut the line near the inlet of the expansion tank, and unscrew the pieces of pipe from their fittings at both ends of the section.
◆ Attach a 2-inch nipple—a short pipe with threads at both ends—to a shutoff valve.
◆ Screw an assembled union to the other end of the nipple, undo the ring nut, and lift off the free union nut.
◆ Attach a 6-inch nipple to the expansion tank. Add the valve assembly by slipping the ring nut over the nipple and attaching the remaining union nut.
◆ Slide the ring nut over the union nuts and tighten it *(right)*.
◆ Measure from the free end of the shutoff valve to the closest fitting, and buy a nipple to fit the gap. If it is not a standard length, have a metal shop cut and thread a pipe.
◆ Refill the system *(page 276)*.

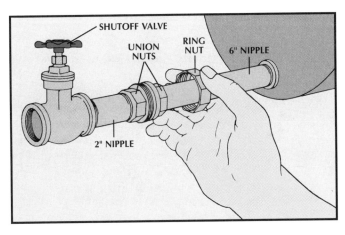

Maintaining Window Air Conditioners

With proper maintenance, the average window air conditioner will serve you well for many years. Once a year, clean the grille and the drain system. Gently vacuum both the evaporator and condenser coils (located at the front and back of the unit, respectively). At the same time, check the coil fins; vibration or extreme temperature change may have bent them out of shape. Most important, clean or replace your air filter at least once a month.

Except for changing the air filter, all of these maintenance chores require first removing the unit from the window. Since it is heavy, have someone help you.

⚠️ **CAUTION** *Avoid handling the coils or refrigerant lines; these carry high-pressure refrigerant and should be serviced only by a professional.*

TOOLS

Nutdriver or socket wrench
Screwdriver
Multiheaded fin comb

SAFETY TIPS

Protect your hands with heavy work gloves when cleaning the coil fins.

CLEANING THE AIR FILTER

FRONT PANEL

1. Removing the front panel.
If you are just changing the air filter, unplug the air conditioner but leave it in the window. To take off the front panel, remove any screws, then pull the panel straight off. If the panel is secured by clips, grip its sides and snap it off *(left).*

AIR FILTER

2. Removing the air filter.
On some models, the filter is located in front of the evaporator coils or on the back of the front panel; unfasten the retaining clips holding the filter in place and remove it *(right).* On other models, the filter is mounted in front of the blower and below the evaporator coils; unfasten the filter from its clips and pull it out.

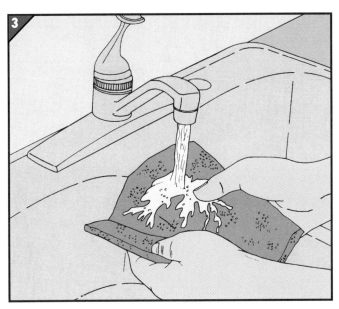

3. Washing the filter.

Each month during the cooling season, vacuum surface dirt from the filter, then wash it in a detergent-and-water solution, rinse it with fresh water, and wring it dry. If the filter is not washable or is torn, replace it with an identical filter.

4. Cleaning the front panel.

Use a moist cloth or stiff-bristled brush to wipe accumulated dust off both sides of the grille and the louvers of the front panel. Wash the panel in a detergent-and-water solution to remove greasy dirt, then rinse it in clear water and dry it. Reinstall the front panel and plug in the air conditioner.

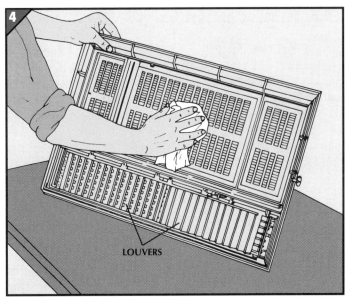

LOUVERS

ACCESSING INTERNAL COMPONENTS

CHASSIS

Freeing a large unit.

Most larger, heavier air conditioners, such as the one at left, have a slide-out chassis that fits into a cabinet bolted permanently to the window frame. Place a sturdy table next to the window, under the air conditioner, and work with a helper to remove the unit. Keeping your back straight and your knees bent to avoid muscle strain, slide the chassis out of the window onto the table.

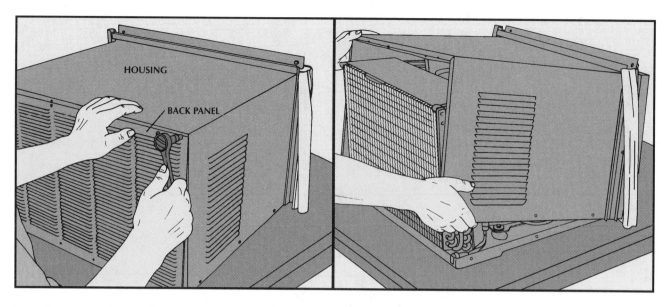

Opening a smaller unit.
Many small air conditioners have sliding panels at the sides, and the unit may be supported by a bracket outside the window. Have a helper support the unit while you carefully open the window.

Then collapse the side panels and ease the unit from the window. With a nutdriver, remove the sheet-metal screws securing the back panel to the chassis; if they are rusted, apply several drops of penetrating oil and use a sock-

et wrench to free them *(above, left)*. Next, remove the screws from the top and sides of the housing and, on some models, at the front. Grasp the bottom edges of the housing and pull it off *(above, right)*.

CARING FOR THE COILS AND DRAIN SYSTEM

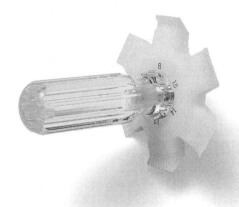

Cleaning and straightening the coil fins.
Vacuum the coil fins periodically with an upholstery-brush attachment. Use a multiheaded fin comb *(photograph)* to dislodge any debris stuck between the fins. Determine which head of the comb corresponds to the spacing of your unit's fins; the teeth on the head should fit easily between the fins. The comb can also be used to straighten bent coil fins. Gently insert the teeth into an undamaged section above the area to be straightened. Pull the fin comb down, sliding it through the damaged area *(above, right)*. Never straighten fins with a knife or screwdriver; they could damage the coils.

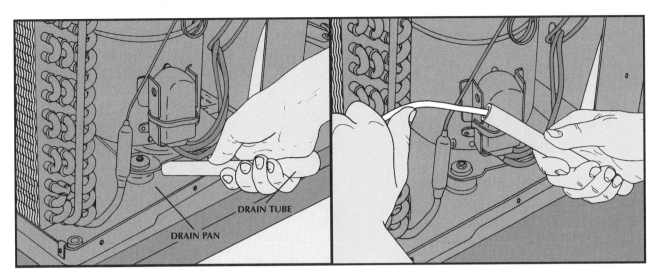

DRAIN TUBE

DRAIN PAN

Clearing the drain tube.

If your model has an evaporator drain pan and a condenser drain pan, locate the rubber or plastic drain tube connecting them. Pull the tube out from under the compressor base *(above, left)* and run a heavy wire through the tube to dislodge obstructions *(above, right)*. To prevent algae formation, flush the tube with a solution of 1 tablespoon of chlorine bleach in $\frac{1}{2}$ cup of water. If the air conditioner does not have a drain tube, use a cloth to wipe the drain channels molded into the drain pan.

Unclogging the drain hole.

Locate the drain hole leading out of the chassis. If the hole is blocked, use a screwdriver or heavy wire to clear the hole *(below)*.

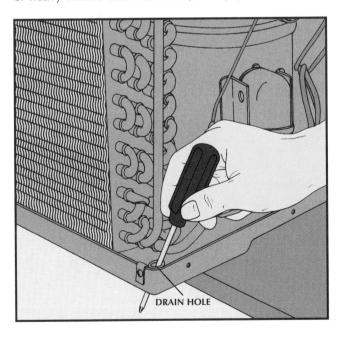

DRAIN HOLE

Cleaning the drain pans.

To prevent algae formation in the drain pans, place a bucket under the drain hole to catch overflow, and flush each pan with a solution of 1 cup of chlorine bleach and 1 cup of water. Rinse the pans with clear water.

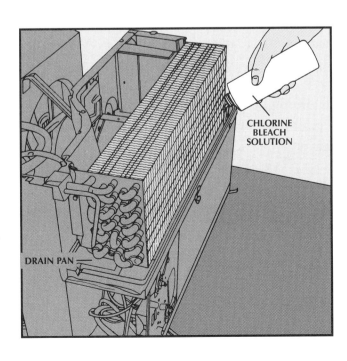

CHLORINE BLEACH SOLUTION

DRAIN PAN

CHAPTER 9

INSULATING AND WEATHERPROOFING

Your closest ally in keeping a home warm in winter and cool in summer is adequate insulation. This chapter shows how to evaluate your needs and match insulation with the areas of the house where it will do the most good—in the attic, in the exterior walls, and in the basement or crawl space.

Weatherproofing a home is a matter of establishing priorities. It's best to focus your efforts where they will be most beneficial and save you the most money. The first areas to address are leaky doors and windows. For most homes, this means finding and filling small openings all over the house. A few dollars spent applying weather stripping and sealing gaps will be repaid many times over.

Water seepage can cause serious problems in a home. These problems can range from peeling paint and a damp basement to rotted framing. In many cases you can prevent this damage by plugging cracks in basement walls and, as shown on pages 324 and 325, maintaining your home's gutters and downspouts so they can properly channel water away from the foundation.

Exterior doors can be a ▶ significant source of heat loss in many homes. Weatherproof thresholds and bottom sweeps are among the simplest products to install for sealing the bottom of a door.

Latex concrete-patching compound represents an easy remedy for cracks in basement walls.
▼

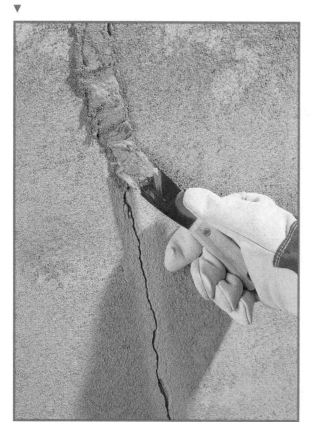

Simple to apply, weather stripping is a permanent solution for sealing gaps around doors and windows. Plugging such openings throughout a house can appreciably cut heating and air-conditioning costs.
▼

▲

The most important part of the house to insulate is the attic; not only does heat escape through it in winter, but heat builds up there in summer. Fiberglass batts or blankets are the most practical insulation materials for the attic.

◄ Available in handy roll-up tubes, caulk is indispensable for closing gaps and sealing cracks around the outside of windows. Depending on the type of product, caulk can remain effective for up to 20 years.

Key Areas for Potential Heat Loss

Houses come in a wide variety of shapes and sizes, but most homes incorporate some of the elements in the illustration at right. The diagram shows the spaces that typically require insulation; finished walls have been removed for clarity.

Use the drawing as a guide, and make a list of the areas in your home that need insulation. The principle is simple: Insulate any surface separating living spaces from unheated areas.

Insulation prevents heat from escaping from your house in winter, but it also keeps the house cooler in summer. A well-insulated attic, for example, shields living areas from the heat of the sun. When bolstered by the weatherproofing measures described on pages 296 to 305, and by the addition of awnings over the windows, insulation will make the interior of a house noticeably cooler than the outside temperature in summer—even without air-conditioning.

Attics and Ceilings: Because the attic is potentially the greatest source of heat exchange in a house, deal with it first. For an unfinished attic, you need only insulate the floor; finished attics call for a bit more work—both the walls and ceiling should be insulated. Cathedral ceilings are difficult to access and don't offer much space for insulation. For such a ceiling, it's best to have a professional do the job.

Walls: All exterior walls should be insulated, including any wall of a split-level home that rises above an adjacent roof. It's simplest to install insulation in a wall during its construction, but even if a wall is finished, there are a number of ways to insulate it without removing the wall covering. Methods include blowing insulation into the walls from outside, overlaying rigid foam panels, adding insulated backing to new siding, and spraying in foam insulation.

Cellars and Crawl Spaces: If your house has an unheated cellar or crawl space, the floor directly above it—as well as pipes and ducts running through it—should be insulated. For a heated cellar, crawl space, or finished basement, the best approach is to insulate the walls.

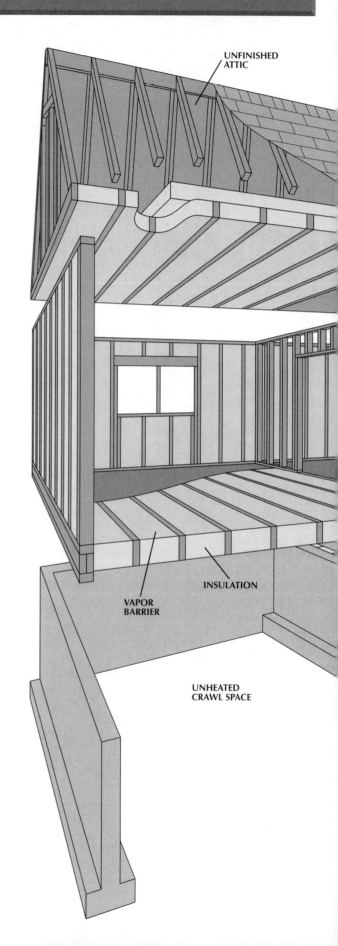

UNFINISHED
ATTIC

INSULATION

VAPOR
BARRIER

UNHEATED
CRAWL SPACE

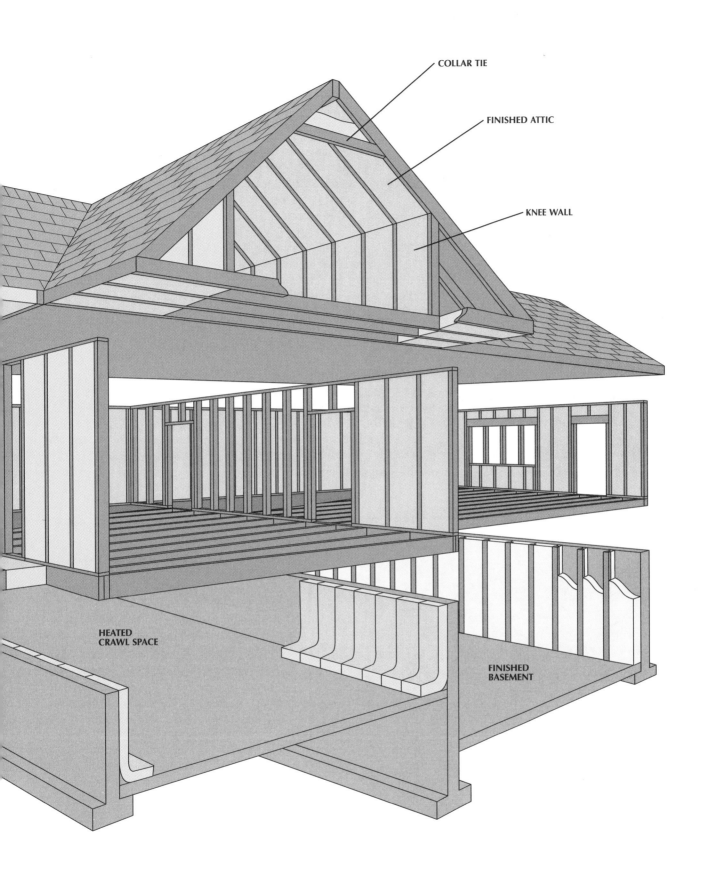

COLLAR TIE

FINISHED ATTIC

KNEE WALL

HEATED
CRAWL SPACE

FINISHED
BASEMENT

Checking for Adequate Insulation

Before you can estimate your insulation needs, you must determine what kind and how much the house already has. The most common types are listed on page 294.

A good place to begin an insulation audit is an unfinished area such as the attic, basement, crawl space, or garage. Insulation here will be visible between joists, beams, and studs; the thickness of the material can be measured with a ruler.

Looking behind Walls: Insulation inside finished walls can often be checked through existing openings such as light switches and receptacles *(below)*. When a wall has no such apertures, remove the louvers of forced-air ducts and examine the edge of the duct; or, pry off a section of baseboard and drill a small peephole through the exposed wall.

If the insulation has a vapor barrier —a lining of kraft paper, plastic, or aluminum foil to keep moisture from condensing on interior walls—patch any holes you make in it with duct tape, and plastic sheeting if necessary, before resealing the wall.

Evaluating Your Needs: Plan on replacing insulation that has been damaged by moisture, as well as any flammable materials like sawdust or rags used as insulation.

Once you know the type of insulation you have and how thick it is, estimate its approximate R-value—or insulating capacity—by multiplying the thickness in inches by the R-value per inch in the chart on page 294. Then refer to the map *(page 292)* and chart *(page 293)* to determine the optimum R-values for different parts of the house in your region.

 TOOLS

Tape measure	Handsaw
Screwdriver	Electric drill
Pry bars	

 **MATERIALS**

Wire
Masking tape
Plastic sheeting
Dowel ($\frac{1}{2}$")

 SAFETY TIPS

Wear a dust mask, a long-sleeved shirt, and gloves when handling fiberglass insulation.

Checking wall insulation at an outlet.

◆ Shut off power to the outlet at the service panel.
◆ Remove the outlet's cover plate and look into the gap between the electrical box and the plaster or wallboard, lighting the opening with a flashlight. If there is a vapor barrier just inside the opening, you probably have blanket or batt-type insulation. Otherwise, the insulation is likely loose fill or foamed-in-place. Identify the type of loose fill by inserting a hooked length of stiff wire into the gap and pulling out a sample *(left)*.

For the loose-fill type, check whether it has settled in the wall, leaving gaps near the ceiling. Place the palm of your hand against the wall every 3 feet, starting at the baseboard and working toward the ceiling. When the temperature outside is cold and you feel the wall become noticeably cooler as your hand climbs the wall, the fill has settled; during hot weather, the wall will feel warmer. When either is the case, refill the cavity.

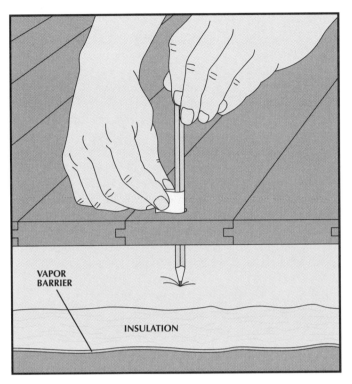

VAPOR
BARRIER

INSULATION

Measuring the insulation under a floor.

If your attic flooring consists of straightedged boards nailed down, pull up a board with a pair of pry bars and inspect the insulation.

◆ Where the floorboards are tongue-and-groove, drill a $\frac{1}{2}$-inch hole through a board between two joists.

◆ Insert a sharpened pencil into the hole and when you feel resistance as the pencil contacts the insulation, wrap a strip of tape around the pencil at floor level (left).

◆ Push the pencil through the insulation so the point reaches the vapor barrier and wrap another tape strip around the pencil.

◆ Measure the distance between the strips to determine the thickness of the insulation.

◆ To identify the insulating material, remove a piece with a hooked wire.

◆ Plug the hole in the floorboard by gluing in a dowel.

TESTING INSULATION WITH INFRARED SCANNING

A visual inspection is one way to assess a home's insulation, but a more precise technique called infrared scanning can pinpoint areas where heat is escaping.

Readings are usually taken when there is a 25°F to 30°F difference between inside and outside temperatures. The various temperature levels appear on an infrared image as colors: warm colors such as red and brown indicate greater heat loss than cool colors like green and blue. The image at left, for example, shows that heat is escaping from the wall above the two windows.

After you've identified areas of your house that need more insulation, you can check which ones are losing the most heat and attend to them first. Or, if you have contractors install the insulation, you can take a reading afterward to assess the work. To find this service in the Yellow Pages, look under "Infrared Inspection Services" or "Thermography—Inspection Services."

Deciding How Much to Add

There is no simple formula for determining the precise amount of insulation you need. Variations in climate, fuel costs, and the efficiency of a heating system all figure in the equation. Even the type and site of a house can make a difference. A one-story house requires more insulation than a two-story one with the same floor space because its roof is larger. The same is true of a house that isn't sheltered—it tends to be chilled by winds.

Climate Zones: The map below, used to establish minimum R-values for insulation in different regions, divides the United States into eight climate zones. A number of different factors are used to define the zones, but the most important is the "degree-day"—the difference between the average temperature of a single day and 65°F. On a day with an average temperature of 42°F, for example, the degree-day reading is 23 (or 65 less 42). When totaled for an entire year, degree days range from less than 2,500 in the South to more than 10,000 in parts of Alaska. The insulation requirement rises with the total. Another factor is the lowest temperature that can be expected during the winter. This ranges from 40°F in Florida to -50°F in parts of Alaska.

Insulating to Improve Cooling: Insulation needs are influenced by how hot it gets in your area. Cooling hours—the total number of hours in a year above 78°F, when air conditioners are usually in operation—can top 1,500 in some regions. As in winter, these temperature extremes call for insulation—in this case, to minimize air-conditioning costs. For example, a house in Miami, situated in a warm climate, needs more insulation than one in San Francisco, whose climate is temperate.

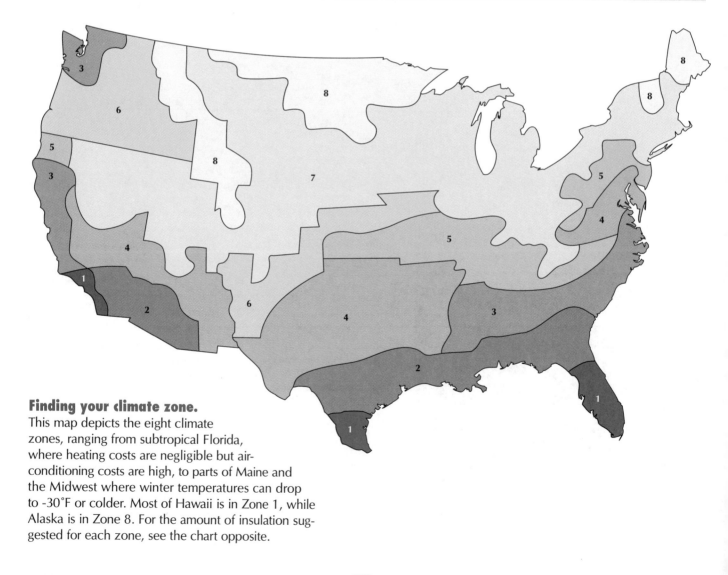

Finding your climate zone.
This map depicts the eight climate zones, ranging from subtropical Florida, where heating costs are negligible but air-conditioning costs are high, to parts of Maine and the Midwest where winter temperatures can drop to -30°F or colder. Most of Hawaii is in Zone 1, while Alaska is in Zone 8. For the amount of insulation suggested for each zone, see the chart opposite.

FIND THE R-VALUES OF YOUR ZONE

Zone	Ceilings directly below roof or unheated attic		Exterior walls	Floors above unheated basement or crawl spaces	Walls of heated crawl spaces
	Fossil fuel	Electric heat			
1	R-19	R-30	R-11	R-11	R-11
2	R-30	R-30	R-11	R-11	R-19
3	R-30	R-38	R-11	R-19	R-19
4	R-30	R-38	R-11	R-19	R-19
5	R-38	R-38	R-11	R-19	R-19
6	R-38	R-38	R-11	R-19	R-19
7	R-38	R-49	R-11	R-19	R-19
8	R-49	R-49	R-11	R-19	R-19

Insulation R-value standards.
This chart lists minimum acceptable standards for insulation. Since a large part of the cost of insulating is labor, exceeding the standards does not appreciably increase costs.

As you plan your insulation strategy, keep in mind that houses with electric-resistance heating systems require about 25 percent more insulation in the attic. In addition, most houses have walls built with $3\frac{1}{2}$-inch studs, so the amount of insulation you can add is limited unless you want to install rigid panels on the exterior of the house. Insulating floors over an unheated basement beyond the thickness of the joists is usually not worth the extra effort. Similarly, insulating heated crawl spaces beyond R-19 is not cost effective.

Choosing the Right Materials

The type of insulation you choose will depend on your climate, your budget, and the part of the house you are insulating. The first consideration is maximizing the R-value most economically. Other factors include ease of installation, and fire and moisture resistance.

All types of insulation, whether in the form of batts or blankets, loose fill, or foam, work by trapping air in millions of tiny pockets. Since air is a very poor conductor, it resists the flow of heat.

Batts or Blankets: Fiberglass is reasonably priced, fire resistant, and nonabsorbent. Rock wool, which is spun from molten limestone, has similar characteristics.

A batt of either material is about 99 percent air and 1 percent spun fiber and phenolic binder.

Loose Fill: Cellulose insulation, derived from newspaper and wood wastes, is usually applied as loose fill. It has a higher R-value than fiberglass or rock wool, but must be treated with fire retardants, which can lose their effectiveness over time. Loose fill may also be made of vermiculite (a form of mica) or perlite (volcanic ash). To prevent loose fill from settling in walls, apply it to the density recommended by the manufacturer.

Foam: One type of foam insulation, polystyrene, comes in rigid boards

or sheets and is widely used to insulate masonry walls and basements. Another, called foamed-in-place, consists of a plastic foam that flows around obstructions to fill a space completely, then hardens.

Stopping Condensation: By blocking heat flow, insulation solves one problem, but creates another—condensation. When temperature differences between inside and outside wall surfaces increase, and vapor passes through the insulation, moisture condenses on the colder wall. This reduces the effectiveness of fibrous insulation, and the damage to paint and wood can be significant. The solution is a vapor barrier (*opposite*).

TYPES OF INSULATION

Material	Approximate R-value per inch of thickness	Common Forms	Advantages	Disadvantages
Fiberglass	3.1-3.7 (blankets, batts) 2.9-3.7 (loose fill)	Blankets, batts, loose fill	Inexpensive, fire resistant	Particles irritate skin and lungs during installation
Rock wool	3.1-3.7 (blankets, batts) 2.9-3.7 (loose fill)	Blankets, batts, loose fill	Inexpensive, fire resistant	Particles irritate skin and lungs during installation
Cellulose	3.1-3.7	Loose fill	Easy to blow in; nonirritating	Absorbs moisture; fire retardants can corrode metal; may settle
Vermiculite and perlite	2.1-2.3 (vermiculite) 2.7 (perlite)	Loose fill	Fire resistant; easily poured into wall cavities	Low R-value; may settle; expensive in some regions
Polystyrene	4.4-5.0 (extruded type); 3.8-5.0 (expanded type)	Rigid boards	Extruded type is moisture resistant	Flammable; gives off toxic fumes when burning. Expanded type not moisture resistant
Polyurethane	5.8-6.2	Foamed-in-place	Expands to fill small cracks; moisture resistant	Requires professional installation; gives off toxic fumes when burning

A FORM FOR EVERY PURPOSE

Insulation comes in many forms, but the four shown here are the most common. Rigid boards of extruded polystyrene *(top)*, due to their high resistance to moisture, are especially good for insulating basements. However, they are flammable and must be covered with at least $\frac{1}{2}$ inch of gypsum wallboard for fire protection. Fiberglass batts *(second from top)*—available in thicknesses of $3\frac{1}{2}$ to 7 inches and 8-foot lengths—are designed to fit between 16- or 24-inch stud and joist spacings. For an uninsulated space, buy the type that has a vapor barrier already attached, with flanges for stapling the batt to the framing; buy plain batts to lay over existing insulation for extra R-value. Available in rolls, blankets *(third from top)* are ideal for covering a large space quickly. Like batts, they are available with or without a vapor barrier. Loose fill *(bottom)*, which requires a separate vapor barrier, is easy to spread over open, flat spaces like attic floors; or to blow inside finished walls through access holes.

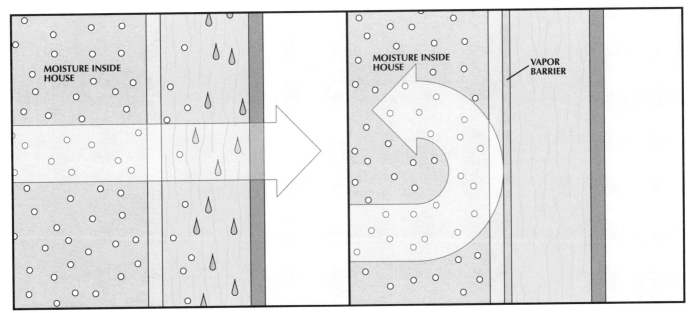

MOISTURE INSIDE HOUSE

MOISTURE INSIDE HOUSE

VAPOR BARRIER

How a vapor barrier works.

In winter, warm humid air passes through insulation without a vapor barrier and condenses when it meets the cold of an exterior wall *(above, left)*. Adding a vapor barrier of kraft paper, heavy polyethylene sheeting, aluminum foil, or waterproof paint prevents moisture from passing beyond the interior surface of the insulation *(above, right)*. Since it never contacts the cold, it cannot condense.

The rule of thumb is to install the vapor barrier on the side of the insulation that is warmer in winter. An exception is the humid Southeast, where the barrier should face the outside. In areas where the average January temperature is 35°F or higher and the number of days the house is cooled greatly exceeds the number of days it is heated, the vapor barrier should be omitted.

Blocking Drafts around Windows

Gaps around doors and windows are the main causes of air leakage in most homes. Sealing these gaps with weather stripping can reduce heating and air-conditioning costs by as much as 30 percent.

Preparing Windows: Before applying stripping, make sure the windows work properly. Try scraping or sanding paint or dirt off the sashes and their channels.

A Range of Solutions: One of the simplest ways to block window drafts in winter is with an inexpensive window insulator kit *(pages 300-301)*. A plastic membrane is hung over the window and secured with double-faced tape. It can then be shrunk, forming a nearly invisible seal.

More permanent and versatile products include metal, plastic, rubber, and vinyl weather stripping *(below)*. For double-hung and sliding windows, spring-metal or vinyl flanges work well. Invisible when the window is shut, these products are secured along only one edge; the other edge springs out to block leaks. Tubular gaskets seal better than spring strips, but are not as durable. Adhesive-backed foam tapes are a good choice for casement windows.

 TOOLS

Tape measure
Hammer
Nail set
Utility knife
Screwdriver
Tin snips
Blow-dryer

 **MATERIALS**

Tubular gaskets
Adhesive-backed
  foam stripping
Spring strips
Window insulator kit

 SAFETY TIPS

Protect your eyes with goggles when driving nails.

WEATHER STRIPPING FOR WINDOWS

With the vast array of products available, there is probably one for every need. It's a good idea to spend some time browsing the offerings at your hardware store. Here is a sample of some of the most popular types. Most packages contain enough material to cover at least one window, and include nails or screws. Weather stripping with adhesive backing is popular because it is much easier to attach than the type requiring fasteners.

VINYL AND ALUMINUM TUBULAR GASKET

NEOPRENE FOAM RUBBER TAPE

RIBBED FOAM-RUBBER TAPE

METAL SPRING STRIP

VINYL V-STRIP

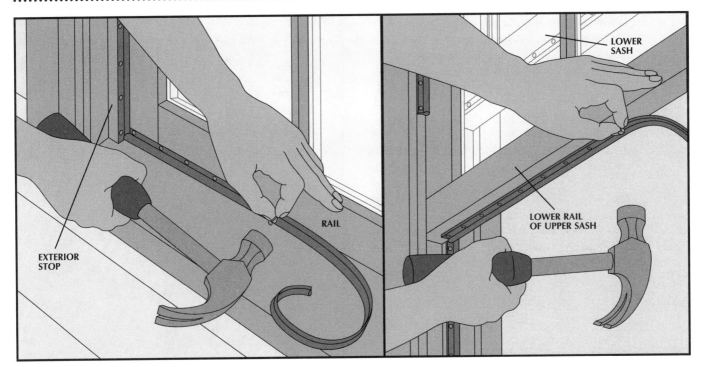

Nailing on tubular gaskets.

◆ Close the sashes. From outside the house, measure and cut lengths of tubular gaskets to fit the top, bottom, and sides of the upper sash; and the bottom and sides of the lower sash.

◆ Nail gaskets to the exterior stops, stretching the strip slightly so the tube-shaped part of the strip is tight and straight against the sash.

◆ Nail a strip along the bottom edge of the lower sash rail *(above, left)* and the top edge of the upper sash rail so the gaskets press tightly against the frame when the window is shut.

◆ Raise the lower sash out of the way and pull down the upper sash, then secure a strip to the underside of the upper sash's bottom rail flush with the inside edge *(above, right)*. This strip will seal the gap between the upper and lower sashes when the window is shut.

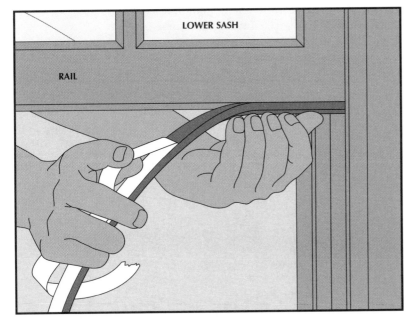

Applying adhesive-backed strips.

Adhesive-backed foam stripping works best on friction-free surfaces such as the underside of the bottom rail of lower sashes.

◆ Wipe the window frame clean.

◆ Slowly pull the protective backing off the strip as you press the adhesive against the surface *(left)*.

1. Measuring the strips.

On double-hung windows, spring strips are installed in the side channels of the upper and lower sashes, on the top and bottom rails of the upper sash, and on the bottom rail of the lower sash. The metal type is shown on this page; vinyl V-strips are installed similarly, but with self-adhesive backing.

◆ For the four side-channel strips, close the upper sash, raise the lower sash, and measure from the bottom of the channel to a point 2 inches above the bottom rail of the upper sash (right). Cut the strips to length with tin snips.

◆ For the sash strips, measure the bottom rail of the lower sash from channel to channel and cut three strips to length.

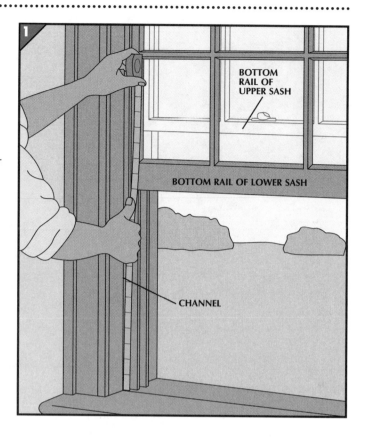

BOTTOM RAIL OF UPPER SASH

BOTTOM RAIL OF LOWER SASH

CHANNEL

NAILING FLANGE

2. Fitting the side-channel strips.

◆ Open the lower sash as high as it will go and clean loose paint or dirt from the channels.

◆ With its nailing flange against the inside edge of the channel, slip the end of a lower-sash strip into the gap between the sash and channel (left) and slide it up until its bottom end is flush with the bottom of the channel.

◆ Repeat for the opposite lower-sash channel.

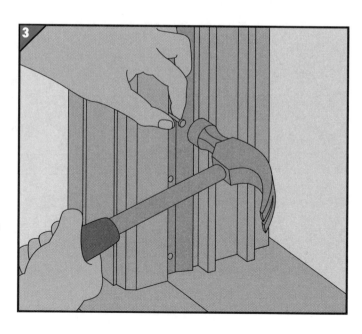

3. Securing the side-channel strips.

◆ Nail each strip to the channel up to the bottom rail of the lower sash (right).

◆ Drop the lower sash and fasten the part of the strips that extend 2 inches above the bottom rail of the upper sash.

◆ Lower the upper sash and install the upper-sash strips in the channels by slipping them into position from the top.

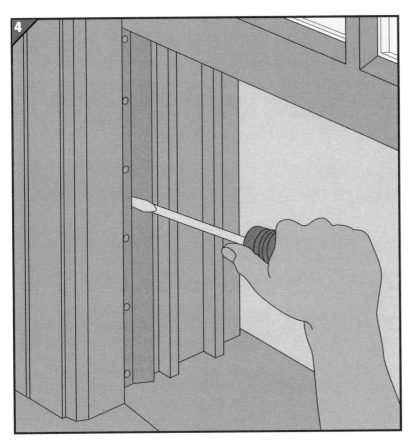

4. Tightening the seal.

With moderate pressure, run a wide-blade screwdriver down the crease in each strip a few times *(left)*, until the strip presses firmly against the sash. This will increase the spring action of the strips, providing a better seal.

TOP RAIL OF
UPPER SASH

BOTTOM RAIL
OF LOWER SASH

5. Fastening top and bottom strips.

◆ Nail a strip to the top of the upper sash's top rail, positioning the nailing flange along the inside face of the window *(above, left)*. Hammer gently to avoid cracking the glass.

◆ Fasten a strip to the underside of the bottom sash's lower rail *(above, right)*.

◆ Tighten the seal on both strips as shown in Step 4.

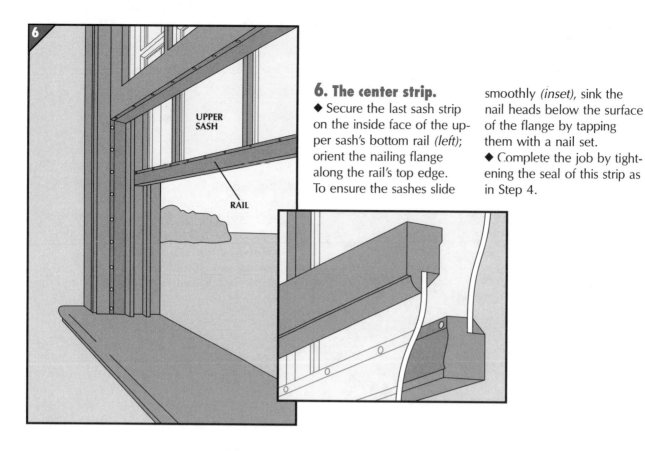

6. The center strip.

◆ Secure the last sash strip on the inside face of the upper sash's bottom rail *(left)*; orient the nailing flange along the rail's top edge. To ensure the sashes slide smoothly *(inset)*, sink the nail heads below the surface of the flange by tapping them with a nail set.

◆ Complete the job by tightening the seal of this strip as in Step 4.

COVERING A WINDOW WITH AN INSULATOR KIT

1. Applying the tape.

Insulator kits usually come with a roll of double-sided tape and enough plastic film to cover a large double-hung window.

◆ Clean the window frame of all dust, dirt, and loose paint. Make sure the frame is dry.

◆ Apply a length of tape along each side of the frame.

◆ Trim the ends so there is no gap or overlap.

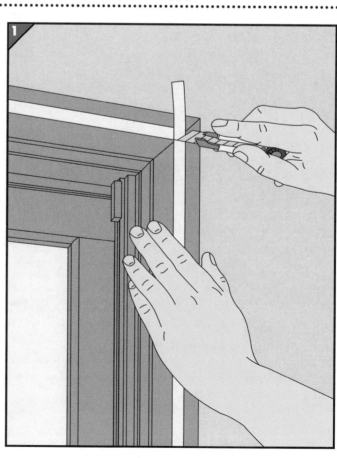

2. Hanging the plastic film.

◆ Measure the distance between the outside edges of the tape strips and add 2 inches to each side. Lay out the plastic film on a flat surface and cut it to size.

◆ Position the film over the opening, pressing it very lightly on the tape. Reposition the film as needed, then press it firmly in place *(left)*.

3. Tightening the film.

Remove all the wrinkles from the film with a blow-dryer set to maximum heat. With the nozzle $\frac{1}{4}$ inch from the film, pass the dryer over the plastic *(right)*. To avoid melting the plastic, keep the dryer in constant motion, and do not let it touch the film.

4. Trimming the film.

With a utility knife, cut the film flush with the outside edges of the tape *(left)*.

To remove the film at the end of winter, pull the plastic off the tape, then slowly peel the tape off the window frame.

Weather-Stripping Doors

Doors cannot be closed as tightly as windows, so they are more difficult to seal. But a variety of products—weather stripping, thresholds, and sweeps—keep air from leaking through.

Straightening a Door: Weather stripping can't do its job properly on a binding door. Before applying any product, adjust the hinges and sand or plane the door edges until the door opens and closes smoothly with a narrow, uniform gap between edges and jamb.

A door may bind because loose hinge screws make it sag. If the screws don't hold, replace them with longer ones. Or, drill out the screw hole, glue in a length of dowel, and bore a new clearance

hole for the screw. If this does not solve the problem, plane the binding door edge.

Blocking Door Drafts: Door sweeps and weatherproof thresholds seal the bottom of swinging doors *(pages 304-305)*, while garage doors require a special type of weather stripping to provide a tight seal against uneven concrete floors *(page 305)*.

Simple to apply, self-adhesive V-strips are commonly used to weather-strip doors. These doubled-over strips of vinyl fit between door edges and jambs, filling gaps. V-strips are not as sturdy as door-stop stripping, which can be more tricky to apply. Installation of both products is described opposite.

 TOOLS

Hammer
Screwdriver
Pry bar
Utility knife

Tin snips
Hacksaw
Backsaw
Wood chisel
   and mallet

 **MATERIALS**

2 x 4
V-strip weather
   stripping
Door sweep

Door-stop weather
   stripping
Weatherproof
   threshold
Garage door
   weather stripping

 SAFETY TIPS

Always wear safety gloggles when driving nails.

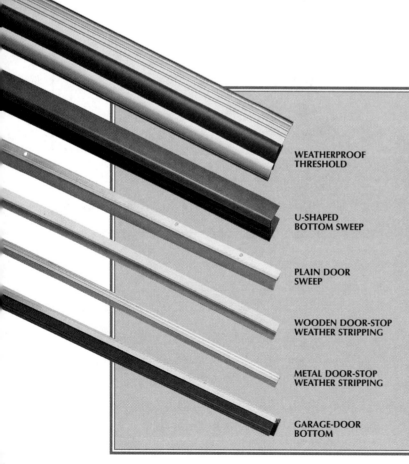

WEATHERPROOF THRESHOLD

U-SHAPED BOTTOM SWEEP

PLAIN DOOR SWEEP

WOODEN DOOR-STOP WEATHER STRIPPING

METAL DOOR-STOP WEATHER STRIPPING

GARAGE-DOOR BOTTOM

AN ARRAY OF PRODUCTS

Weatherproof thresholds seal the bottom of doors best, but the easiest product to install is a sweep fastened under or against the bottom edge of a door.

Weather stripping attaches to the jambs at the sides and top—usually to the door-stop molding—so its flexible edges press against the door face when it is closed. You can choose from a variety of shapes depending on the shape and size of gap you need to seal. Widely used products include wood, metal, and plastic door-stop strips edged with plastic tubing or foam, and closed-cell adhesive-backed foam tapes.

Unless the product is self-adhesive, fasteners are generally included in the package. Some products may come with specific installation instructions.

SEALING DOOR OPENINGS

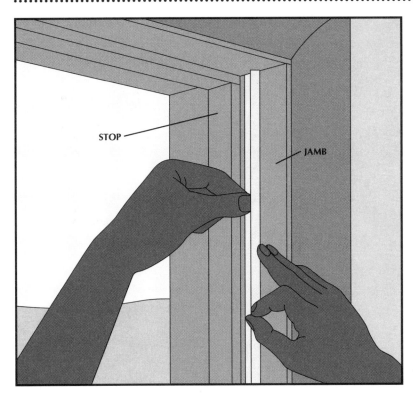

Installing V-stripping.
◆ With a utility knife or tin snips, cut strips for both sides and the top of the door, trimming the pieces as necessary to accommodate the hinges and lock.
◆ Remove the backing paper and position a strip along the jamb with the point of the V facing the door and the other edge about $\frac{1}{8}$ inch from the stop.
◆ Press the strip in place *(left)*.

Attaching door-stop stripping.
◆ With tin snips, cut strips the same length as the stops at the top and sides of the door.
◆ With the door closed, position the top piece against the top stop, lightly pressing the flexible edge against the door.
◆ With a helper holding the stripping in place, slide a piece of paper between the door and the flexible edge—it should barely slide. Adjust the position of the strip as necessary, then nail it to the jamb.
◆ Position the strips along the sides of the door *(right)*, then nail them in place.

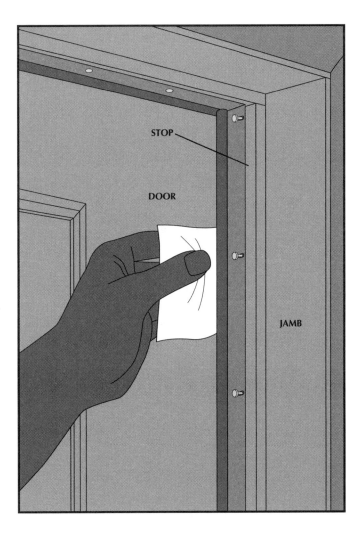

ADDING A DOOR SWEEP

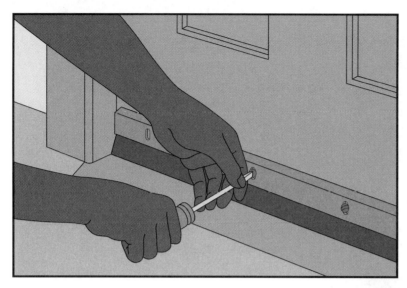

Attaching a standard door sweep.
◆ Working outside with the door closed, measure the width of the door and cut the sweep to length with tin snips.
◆ Position the sweep so it fits snugly against the threshold when the door is shut while allowing the door to operate smoothly.
◆ Screw the sweep to the door *(left)*. The oblong screw holes allow you to adjust the sweep up or down as needed.

Fastening a bottom sweep.
◆ With tin snips, cut the sweep to the width of the door.
◆ Open the door and slip the sweep on the bottom of the door *(right)*. If necessary, adjust the width of the sweep to the door thickness by squeezing the sides together.
◆ Close the door, let the sweep drop onto the threshold, and drive the screws partway into their slots.
◆ Adjust the height of the sweep so it is snug, but not so tight that the door binds. Tighten the screws.

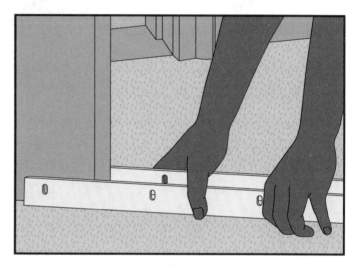

INSTALLING A WEATHERPROOF THRESHOLD

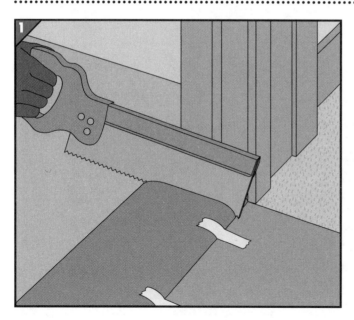

1. Removing the existing threshold.
◆ Cover the floor around the door with pieces of cardboard secured by masking tape.
◆ Try to remove the threshold with a pry bar. If it does not lift up easily, cut through each end with a backsaw *(left)* and pry up the center piece; chip out the rest of the threshold with a chisel and mallet.
◆ Clean the sill.

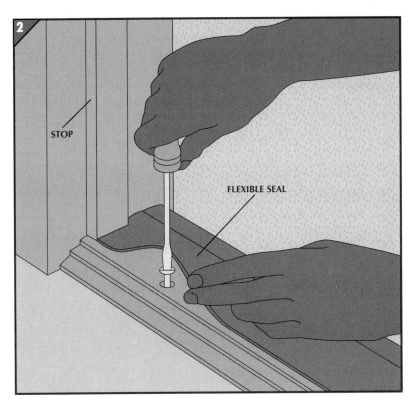

STOP

FLEXIBLE SEAL

2. Fitting the threshold.

◆ With a hacksaw, cut the new threshold to fit snugly between the side jamb. If necessary, trim the door stop with a backsaw or chisel to accommodate the threshold.
◆ Position the threshold so that the flap side of the flexible seal faces away from the door.
◆ Lift up the plastic flap and screw the threshold in place *(left)*.

On some thresholds, the screw holes are exposed. Once the piece is attached, slide the flexible insert into place over the screws.

STRIPS FOR A GARAGE DOOR

Sealing a wood overhead door.

◆ Before installing weather stripping, paint the bottom of the door to protect it against moisture.
◆ Cut the weather stripping to the width of the door with tin snips, a utility knife, or a hacksaw.
◆ Pull the door partway down so the bottom is at a convenient height and brace it on a 2-by-4.
◆ Position the stripping against the door bottom with the flap facing the outside, then nail it in place.

If you have an automatic garage door opener, you may need to recalibrate it to account for the increased door height.

FLAP

Plugging Up the Cracks and Gaps

Because the materials that go into building a house expand and contract at different rates as temperatures change, cracks and gaps are bound to appear at the junction of two different materials. Breaches around windows and doors, and around pipes and wires that pass through walls, can be equivalent to a 2-foot-square vent opening.

Locating Air Leaks: Professionals test a house's air-tightness with a device called a blower door. After shutting all the windows and every door but one, they mount a fan in the open door. As the fan reduces pressure in the house, they locate leaks with smoke sticks. Any draft that stirs smoke is investigated.

You can subject your house to a similar test by opening a door on the leeward side of the house on a windy day. Burn an incense stick to generate the smoke.

Choosing a Sealant: Dozens of sealant materials are available to close gaps. The characteristics of the most common products are provided in the chart below. Others, such as glazing compound for window panes and special caulk for chimney and ducts, may be required for special applications. Keep in mind that shrinkage is sometimes an advantage, since a caulk that shrinks will become less visible.

Whichever sealant you choose, read the label instructions to ensure it is the best one for the job. Follow the product's safety precautions. Always work in a well-ventilated area when applying toxic materials.

 TOOLS

Caulking gun
Utility knife

 **MATERIALS**

Caulk

A SEALANT FOR EVERY PURPOSE

Sealant	Special Uses	Durability	Adhesion	Shrinkage
Polybutene Rope Caulk	Temporary sealing	1-2 years	Fair	Moderate
Butyl Rubber Caulk	Metal to masonry	7-10 years	Excellent	Moderate
Polyurethane Caulk	All purposes	20 years	Excellent	Very low
Acrylic Latex Caulk	Indoors and protected areas	2-10 years	Excellent, except to metal	Moderate
Latex Caulk	All purposes	5-15 years	Excellent	Low
Silicone Caulk	All purposes	20 or more years	Excellent	Very low
Silicone/Latex Caulk	All purposes	10-20 years	Excellent	Moderate
Insulating Foam	Large gaps	10 or more years	Excellent	Very low
Foam Backer Rod	Large gaps	10 or more years	None	Very low

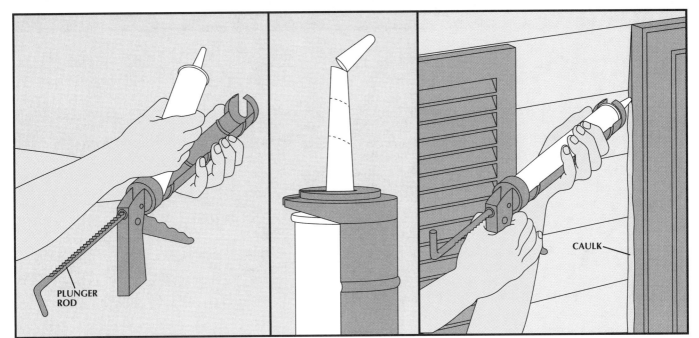

Applying caulk with a gun.

◆ Load a caulking gun by first rotating the plunger rod so its teeth face up, then fully retracting it. Insert the caulk cartridge *(above, left)*, rotate the plunger rod so the teeth face down, and pull on the trigger.

◆ With a utility knife, nip off the tapered nozzle tip at a 45-degree angle, cutting an opening for a thin, medium, or heavy bead *(above, center)*. Push a nail through the tip to puncture the seal at the base of the nozzle.

◆ With the gun at a 45-degree angle to the surface, slide it upward and squeeze the trigger with steady pressure *(above, right)*, producing a smooth, even bead. Where several passes are necessary, release the trigger at the end of each pass and continue to move the gun as you slowly squeeze the trigger to begin the next pass.

◆ To stop the flow of caulk, rotate the plunger rod so its teeth point upward, then pull the rod back 1 or 2 inches.

Surface-Drying Time	Curing Time	Cleaner	Primer	Paint
Remains moist and pliant	N/A	None needed	None needed	Should not be painted
24 hours	7 days	Naphtha; paint thinner	None needed	Can be painted
24 hours	7 days	Toluene	Neoprene primer required	Can be painted
$\frac{1}{4}$-$\frac{1}{2}$ hour	3 days	Water	Needed on porous surfaces	Can be painted
$\frac{1}{4}$-$\frac{1}{2}$ hour	5 days	Naphtha; paint thinner	Rarely needed	Can be painted
1 hour	2-5 days	Naphtha; paint thinner	Check label instructions	Check label instructions
1 hour	1-5 days	Water	Rarely needed	Can be painted
$\frac{1}{2}$ hour	4 hours	Acetone	None needed	Required outdoors; not needed indoors
N/A	N/A	N/A	None	Cover with all-purpose caulk; paint, if desired

Plugging Leaks in a Damp Basement

Water can enter basements by several paths. On a rainy day, it may seep through the walls or stream in through cracks and holes in the foundation. But dampness is not always caused by water coming in from outside; basements are generally cooler than the rooms upstairs, so moisture may condense on the walls. Some simple fixes are shown on the following pages, but if your problem is one of the few caused by an underground source that cannot be corrected, you may need to install a sump pump.

Solutions for Damp Walls: Conduct the test below to determine the source of the dampness. If condensation is the cause, try a dehumidifier. Minor seepage through walls can often be cured by attention to gutters and downspouts *(pages 324-325)*, or by diverting water away from the foundation. When gutters and grading are in good shape and walls are still slightly damp, the solution may be to coat them with waterproof cement paint.

Sealing Wall Cracks: The location, orientation, and movement of a crack are all clues to its severity *(opposite)*, and will help you determine whether to fix the crack *(pages 310-311)* or consult a structural engineer. Even dry cracks should be investigated—they could indicate a weakened foundation. If you will have to dig deeper than 2 feet to repair an underground crack, you may want to have a professional repair it.

 TOOLS

Tape measure	Putty knife
Paintbrush	Cold chisel
Heat gun	Ball-peen hammer
Stiff fiber brush	Mason's hawk
	Pointing trowel
	Caulking gun

 **MATERIALS**

Polyethylene sheeting	Bonding agent
Duct tape	Foam backer rod
Latex concrete-patching	Flexible masonry sealant
compound	Hydraulic cement

 SAFETY TIPS

Wear gloves and a long-sleeved shirt when working with concrete patching materials. Protect your eyes with goggles when chipping out loose concrete.

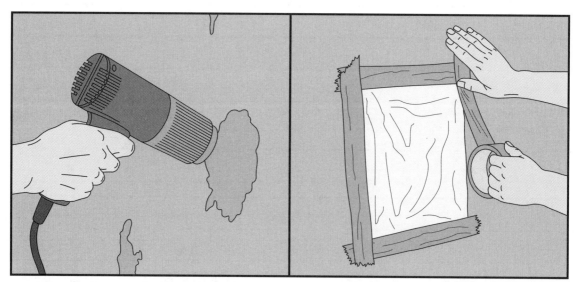

Testing for the source of dampness.
◆ Dry a 12-inch-square section of the damp wall with a heat gun or blow-dryer *(above, left)*.
◆ Cut a slightly smaller square piece of polyethylene sheeting or aluminum foil and fasten it to the wall with duct tape *(above, right)*, sealing all edges to keep out air.

◆ Leave the piece of sheeting or foil in place for 24 hours, then check it for moisture. If the exposed side is wet, then condensation is the problem. If the side against the wall is wet, the problem is seepage. If it is damp on both sides, you likely have both problems.

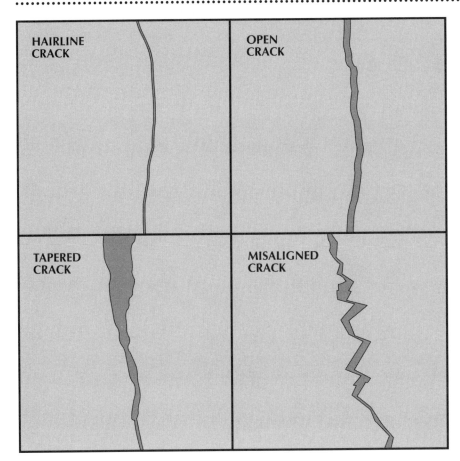

HAIRLINE CRACK

OPEN CRACK

TAPERED CRACK

MISALIGNED CRACK

Evaluating foundation wall cracks.

A crack in a foundation wall can point to a serious structural problem, and should be evaluated carefully. A crack is evidence of movement, usually from settlement or expansion and contraction as a result of temperature fluctuations. Four basic types are shown at left. A hairline crack or an open crack is usually not serious if it is vertical and its edges are aligned and no more than $\frac{1}{8}$ inch apart *(upper left and right)*. However, a crack can be serious if it is horizontal or its edges are tapered, misaligned, or farther apart than $\frac{1}{8}$ inch *(lower left and right)*. Such cracks warrant an inspection by a building professional or structural engineer. If you determine that the crack is not serious, monitor it to find out whether it is stationary or moving *(below)*, then seal the crack using one of the techniques on the following pages.

Monitoring a crack.

◆ If the crack is leaking water, stop the leak with a plug made from hydraulic cement and water.
◆ With a felt-tip pen, mark the crack. Start with a length mark at each end and, across the crack, draw an alignment line a few inches long with width marks at each end *(right)*.
◆ Measure and record the distance between the width and length marks, then monitor the crack for six months.
◆ Consult a building professional if the crack widens by more than $\frac{1}{8}$ inch, lengthens by more than $\frac{1}{4}$ inch, or the alignment line shifts. If the crack is stable, repair it as shown on pages 310 and 311; when it has widened or lengthened only slightly, fill the gap with a length of foam backer rod, then fill to the wall surface with an elastic sealant formulated for masonry.

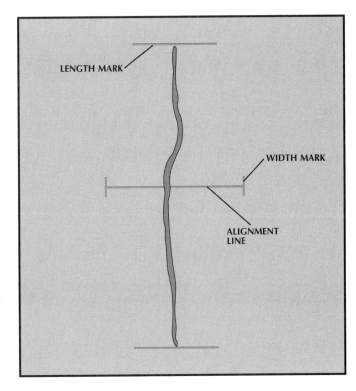

LENGTH MARK

WIDTH MARK

ALIGNMENT LINE

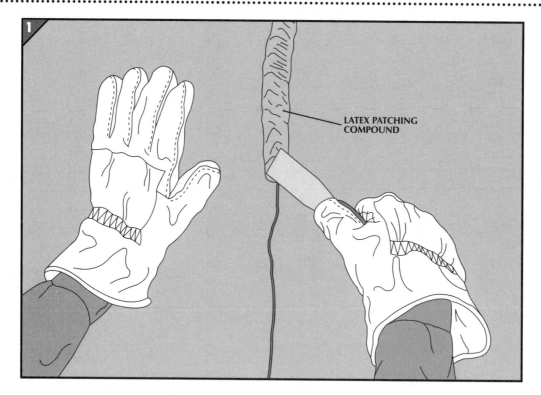

LATEX PATCHING COMPOUND

1. Applying compound.
◆ Clean the crack with a stiff fiber brush.
◆ Prepare enough latex concrete-patching compound and brush on a bonding agent if recommended by the manufacturer.

◆ Starting at the top of the crack, spread compound into the crack with a putty knife *(above)*.
◆ With the tip of the knife, press the compound into the crack, overfilling it slightly.

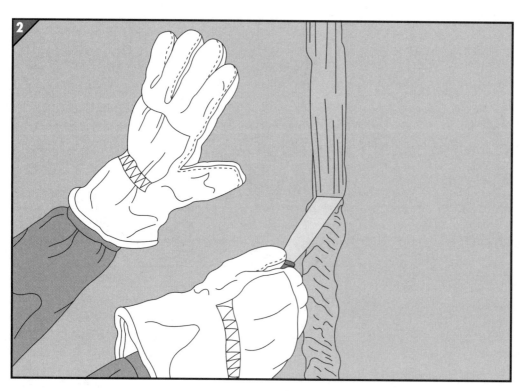

2. Smoothing the patch.
◆ Once the crack is full, draw the putty knife along the compound to smooth it flush against the wall.
◆ Tape polyethylene sheeting over the patch and let it cure for the length of time specified by the manufacturer.

MENDING AN OPEN BREAK

1. Preparing the crack.
◆ Chip any loose concrete from the crack with a cold chisel and a ball-peen hammer *(left)*.
◆ With the chisel and hammer, enlarge the crack to at least $\frac{1}{4}$ inch wide and $\frac{1}{2}$ inch deep. Try to undercut the opening *(inset, left)*; if you can't, cut the sides straight *(inset, right)*. Avoid cutting a V-shaped opening. If you reach a steel reinforcing bar—or rebar—chisel out about 1 inch of concrete behind it.
◆ Clean out the crack with a stiff fiber brush.

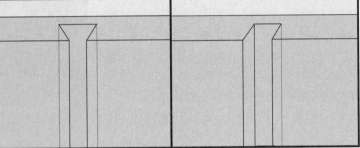

2. Applying patching compound.
◆ Prepare a latex concrete-patching compound following the manufacturer's directions. If necessary, dampen the crack with water or brush on a bonding agent.
◆ Place the patching compound on a mason's hawk. Then, holding the hawk against the wall at the bottom of the crack, pack the compound firmly into it with a pointing trowel *(right)*. Gradually move the hawk up the wall, overfilling the crack slightly. Add enough compound to fill the cavity behind any rebar.

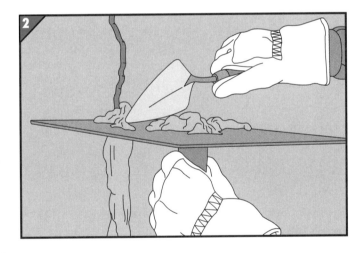

3. Finishing the patch.
◆ Starting at the top of the patch, draw the edge of the trowel along it, scraping off the excess compound onto the mason's hawk *(left)*.
◆ Draw the back of the trowel along the patch to smooth it, working from top to bottom in an arc.
◆ Tape polyethylene sheeting over the patch and let it cure.

10 CHAPTER

ROOFS AND EXTERIORS

Over the lifetime of a house, the roof and siding must hold up against wind, rain, sun, and temperature extremes. In addition to protecting your house from the elements, roofing and siding defines its personality. To help you maintain your home's integrity, appearance, and character, this chapter shows how to repair a wide range of roofing materials, from gutters and downspouts, metal flashing, and asphalt shingles to flat roofing, roof tiles, and slate. These pages also provide easy fixes for siding, such as clapboard, vinyl and aluminum, shingles and shakes, and stucco.

Whether your task is simple or complex, the job will be easier if you understand how your house is put together. This chapter explains the basic structure of several types of houses, from the exterior to the skeleton underneath. It also shows you various ways to do the job safely, using ladders, rooftop platforms, and a roofer's seat.

After years of service, even the sturdiest deck, porch, or patio may need a measure of restoration. Screens are damaged with surprising ease. Wooden structures eventually deteriorate even if built of rot-resistant lumber, and concrete may crack, admitting water that can crumble a patio. Timely repairs can prevent irreparable damage and assure continued durability of valued outdoor amenities.

Asphalt shingles are inexpensive and relatively easy to maintain. Holes and cracks can often be remedied with roofing cement. Curling shingles can be cemented back down, and badly damaged ones can be replaced. But be sure to take precautions anytime you climb to the roof. ►

◄ *For durability and ease of repair and maintenance, clapboard siding is hard to equal. Small problems and minor damage can usually be cured by replacing individual boards.*

Over time, porches can succumb to damage as a result of rot and insects, which can weaken wood structures. In most cases, damaged parts—floorboards, posts, and columns—are easy to repair or replace. Buy pressure-treated lumber to prevent rot. ►

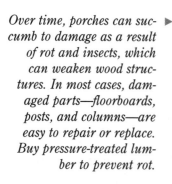

▲
*Routine maintenance can pre-
vent trouble with a wood deck.
For a painted structure,
scrape any blisters or cracks
and repaint. Treat an un-
painted deck with a wood
preservative once a year.*

◄ *Gutters and downspouts should be inspected for
blockage and misalignment once a year. Immedi-
ate inspection is called for if water does not flow
well from downspout exits. Leaf guards and strain-
ers can help prevent gutters from clogging, but they
need to be cleaned two or three times a year.*

Understanding Your Roof and Walls

The exterior of a house is a web of interlocking parts, each with a name. To discuss your plans with an architect or building inspector or to order materials, it is a good idea to learn some of the language of the trade.

The Structure of Roofs: Most roof shapes are variations on two types: the gable roof and the hip roof. These shapes, as well as some other common ones, are illustrated below. Dormers—roofed projections designed to house windows—are also described by their roof style: gable, hip, or shed.

The peak of a roof where two slopes meet is the ridge; the lower edges are eaves; and, on a gable roof, the sloping edges are the rakes. At their eaves, most roofs project beyond the building wall to car-ry rain away from sidings and foundations. The projection, called the overhang or cornice, usually consists of a fascia board nailed to the rafter ends and a soffit board that forms the underside of the overhang. Many gable roofs also overhang at the rakes: The underside is a soffit; the outer face is called a rake board or rake fascia.

Roof Vents: Vent openings are named according to their locations: Ridge vents provide a continuous opening along the ridge line, gable vents are mounted high in an end wall, and roof vents are set into the slope of the roof. Chimneys may be set into the roof slope or built into a gable wall; a stack vent—a pipe that releases gases from the plumbing system—usually rises from one of the main slopes near the ridge.

Handling Water Runoff: The joints around projections—and the valleys where roof slopes meet and where a roof meets a wall—must be waterproofed with thin metal called flashing. Rain gutters usually hang from the fascia, metal drip edges line the eaves, and rakes direct runoff away from the fascia.

Siding: The structure of siding is relatively simple. The gap between the siding and the soffit is finished with a frieze board, and the lower edge of the siding extends below the top of the foundation wall. Siding edges are covered by corner boards at outside corners and butted against corner strips or moldings at inside corners. Metal drip caps over door and window frames protect the brickmolds (or exterior casings) from water damage.

THE SHAPE OF YOUR ROOF

A flat roof has no slope at all; a shed, or lean-to, roof has only one slope. The gable roof, sloping on two sides, is named for the triangular wall section, or gable, formed by the slopes at each end wall. A hip roof has slopes and eaves on all four sides; the slopes intersect at raised corners, or hips. A mansard roof features a gently sloped, almost flat top and a steeped lower section of roof. A gambrel roof is a gable roof with two slopes on each side of the ridge.

Different roof styles are often combined in a single building. A gable-roofed home may have an extension covered by a flat roof or an enclosed patio with a shed roof.

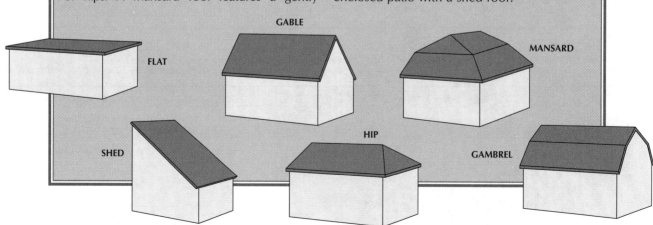

FLAT · SHED · GABLE · HIP · MANSARD · GAMBREL

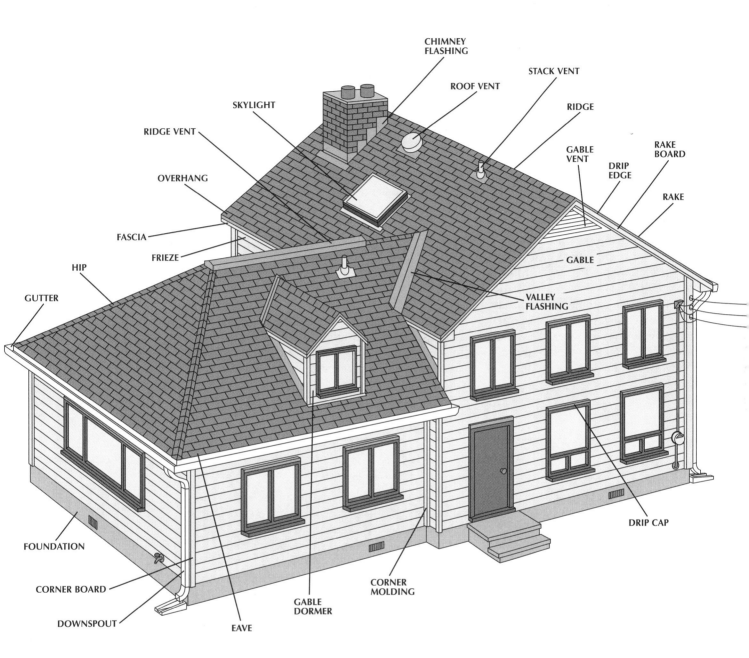

CHIMNEY FLASHING

ROOF VENT

STACK VENT

SKYLIGHT

RIDGE

RIDGE VENT

GABLE VENT

RAKE BOARD

DRIP EDGE

OVERHANG

RAKE

FASCIA

FRIEZE

GABLE

HIP

VALLEY FLASHING

GUTTER

DRIP CAP

FOUNDATION

CORNER BOARD

CORNER MOLDING

DOWNSPOUT

GABLE DORMER

EAVE

Anatomy of an unlikely exterior.
This improbable house is a composite
of styles and features, illustrating the
basic structure of roofs and walls
discussed opposite. The right half
of the house has a gable roof while
the left half has a hip roof with
a gable dormer, all covered with
asphalt shingles.

The walls are covered with horizontal
boards referred to as clapboard siding.

Types of Frames

Before you embark on repairing your roofing or siding, it helps to be familiar with the framing—the skeleton of the house. The type of framing depends on whether the house is wood-framed or masonry.

Framing: A wood frame *(opposite)* consists entirely of lengths of wood, named for their location and function. Normally, studs frame the walls, joists support the ceilings and floors, and rafters or trusses —prefabricated triangular roof framing assemblies—hold up the roof. These framing members are generally installed with the edge facing outward or upward; this edge provides a nailing surface for the layers that form the walls and roof.

With a masonry house *(page 320)*, the walls are solid brick, stone, or concrete blocks; the roof is framed of wood.

A Base for Siding: On a wood-frame house, the walls are usually sheathed with plywood or oriented strand board (OSB) panels. Building paper is stapled to the sheathing as a barrier against moisture and air, and the siding *(page 336)* is nailed through the sheathing to the studs.

The spacing of the studs determines the nailing pattern of sheathing and siding. In most wood-frame houses, studs are either 16 or 24 inches apart, but the spacing may vary between the studs used to frame doors and windows, or between a stud and a corner post.

To fasten siding to a masonry house or to a wood-frame house covered with stucco or brick veneer, you must first attach vertical wood supports called furring strips on the outside walls. These are spaced 16 or 24 inches apart.

A Base for Roofing: Newer roofs are usually sheathed with plywood or OSB panels; older roofs may be decked with boards. All three materials are nailed to the rafters (or trusses) and covered with roofing felt; flashing is then installed at chimneys, vents, dormers, skylights, and valleys *(page 329)*. The roof covering *(page 326)* is fastened to the sheathing.

PLYWOOD RATINGS

When buying plywood or OSB sheathing, select only performance-rated panels and check the grade stamp to ensure the panels are rated for your application. A typical stamp is shown here. The APA is the grading authority. "32/16" is the maximum rafter (32 inches) or floor joist (16 inches) spacing for which the panel is rated. "   " indicates the panel thickness. "SIZED FOR SPACING" means the panel may be slightly less than 4-by-8 feet to allow for a $\frac{1}{8}$-inch gap at panel ends and edges. "EXPOSURE 1" means the panel can be exposed outdoors temporarily until the siding or roofing is in place; other outdoor-use ratings are "EXTERIOR" (can be exposed indefinitely) and "EXPOSURE 2" (should not be left exposed but can withstand some moisture). The bottom line of the stamp lists industry standards. A panel graded as shown would be appropriate for sheathing a roof with rafters or trusses up to 32 inches apart. For walls with studs spaced up to 24 inches apart, $\frac{3}{8}$-inch panels rated for 24-inch rafter spacing would be adequate.

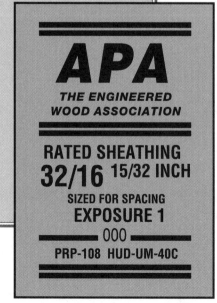

APA
THE ENGINEERED
WOOD ASSOCIATION

RATED SHEATHING
32/16 15/32 INCH
SIZED FOR SPACING
EXPOSURE 1
000
PRP-108 HUD-UM-40C

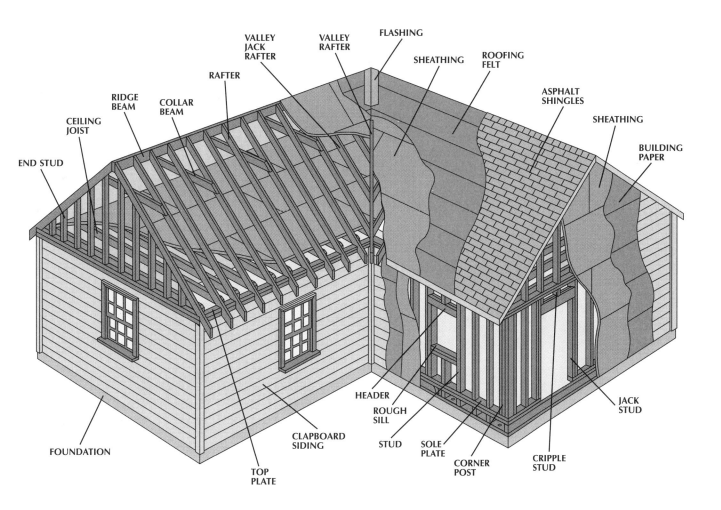

VALLEY JACK RAFTER
VALLEY RAFTER
FLASHING
SHEATHING
ROOFING FELT
RAFTER
RIDGE BEAM
COLLAR BEAM
ASPHALT SHINGLES
SHEATHING
CEILING JOIST
BUILDING PAPER
END STUD
HEADER
ROUGH SILL
JACK STUD
FOUNDATION
STUD
SOLE PLATE
CLAPBOARD SIDING
CRIPPLE STUD
CORNER POST
TOP PLATE

A wood-frame house.

Beneath the clapboard siding and asphalt shingle roof of the typical frame house shown above, vertical wall studs and sloping rafters or trusses make up the main structural members. The studs rest on a horizontal 2-by-4 called a sole plate; a horizontal top plate consisting of doubled 2-by-4s runs across the top of the wall studs.

In the gable roof on this house, the lower ends of the rafters rest on the top plate; the upper ends are attached to a ridge beam. Horizontal ceiling joists, nailed to the rafters, also rest

on the top plate. Collar beams are fastened to some of the rafters to add rigidity to the structure.

Special framing is needed wherever walls are interrupted by windows or doors and wherever roof slopes or walls intersect. In the walls, windows and doors are framed with headers above, rough sills below, and with jack and cripple studs at the sides. Corner posts made of three studs nailed together link adjoining walls, and each gable wall is framed with end studs installed between the top plate and

the end rafters. In the roof, a valley is framed with a valley rafter, which runs from the ridge boards to the top plate. The valley rafter is supported on each side by shorter valley jack rafters.

To create a solid surface for the final coverings, both the walls and roof are sheathed with plywood or OSB sheets; roofing felt on roofs and building paper on walls shield the sheathing against moisture. The valley and other critical joints are protected with metal flashing and the roofing and siding are nailed over the sheathing.

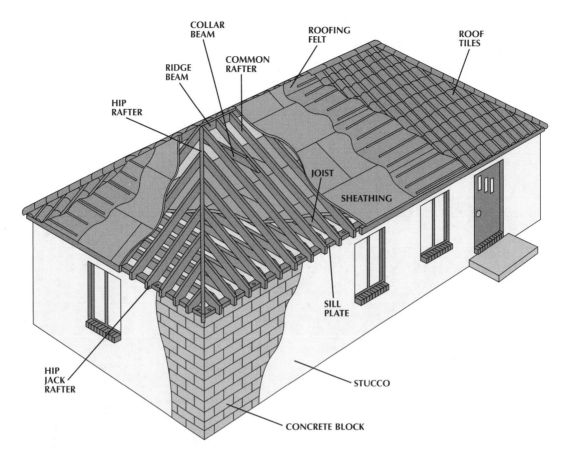

COLLAR BEAM

ROOFING FELT

ROOF TILES

RIDGE BEAM

COMMON RAFTER

HIP RAFTER

JOIST

SHEATHING

SILL PLATE

HIP JACK RAFTER

STUCCO

CONCRETE BLOCK

A masonry house.

The house shown above is built of concrete blocks and features a hip roof. To anchor the roof framing to the walls, a wood sill plate is bolted to the top row, or course, of concrete blocks. Hip rafters extend from the sill plate at the corners to the horizontal ridge beam; these rafters are supported by hip jack rafters fastened to the sill plate.

The ceiling and the main part of the roof are framed with joists, common rafters, and collar beams as for a gable roof *(page 319)*.

Plywood sheathing is nailed to the rafters and covered with roofing felt and tiles. On the walls, cement mortar creates the stucco exterior: a thick base coat, applied directly to the blocks; and a finish coat, spread over the base.

Inspecting Your Roof and Walls

Inspect your roof and siding each spring and fall for signs of damage. Follow these basic steps:

✔ In the attic, probe all rafters and joists with a screwdriver to check for rot. Rotted rafters should be reinforced *(page 328)* or replaced. Rotted trusses must be repaired by a professional. Also look for visible leaks and, with the lights off, look for cracks of daylight. Signs of moisture that don't seem to originate from leaks may indicate a ventilation problem. Check roof vents for damage or blockage.

✔ On the roof, look for missing, cracked, or curled shingles. Dark patches on asphalt shingles mean the surface granules may have worn away. A few missing or damaged shingles can be replaced.

✔ Clear valleys of all debris. Check flashing for small holes or rust spots from corroded nails. These areas can be patched *(page 329)*. Also check that the top of chimney flashing is still embedded in the mortar joint and properly caulked *(page 329)*.

✔ Check flat roofs for blisters. On a roof with built-up or roll roofing, repair the blister *(page 333)*. For modified bitumen roofing, you'll have to call in a professional.

✔ Check siding for damaged areas and repair individual boards or panels. Inspect eaves for signs of decay. Also check for peeling or bubbling paint. This may indicate a problem with the house insulation or its vapor barrier.

✔ Inspect trim around doors and windows. Refasten any loose trim and make sure all joints are properly caulked.

✔ Check for large expanses of deteriorated roofing, flashing, or siding—this may indicate that the entire roof needs to be redone, or that the house requires residing.

Safety in High Places

Most of the equipment required for working at heights is available at rental agencies. You may need some basic tools for assembly.

Ladders: Tall stepladders can reach up to 12 feet. Above this height, you'll need an extension ladder. Single ladders, similar to a section of extension ladder, are also available. Whichever type you use, choose a Type I or IA. New models are marked with this classification. They can be made of aluminum, wood, or fiberglass; all follow the same rating system. If you have doubts about the strength of a ladder you own, it is wise to rent one that you can rely on.

Scaffolds: For large jobs, a scaffold at least 8 feet long can save the time spent in moving ladders. Elaborate metal scaffolds are expensive to rent but worth considering for a job involving several helpers.

Working on the Roof: The equipment you'll need depends on the slope of your roof *(page 326)*. For roofs whose slope is 4 inches of rise (or less) for every foot of run, you can move around carefully without special equipment. For roofs with a slope of 4-in-12 to 6-in-12, install roof brackets with scaffold-grade planks *(page 323)* all the way along the eaves unless you

have a scaffold right below the edge of the roof. For additional security, add roof brackets below the work area. You may also want a ladder with ladder hooks *(page 323)* for moving up and down the slope. Jobs on roofs with slopes more than 6-in-12 should be left to a professional.

Above all, rely on your own sense of security. If you don't feel comfortable on a gently sloping roof, take the precautions usually reserved for working on a steep roof or leave the job to a professional. Or, consider buying a safety harness. However, unless this equipment is anchored and assembled properly, it can fail. Make sure to get detailed written instructions with the equipment. Never use an improvised or homemade harness.

Hauling Materials: One of the most dangerous tasks is lifting materials up to the roof. If possible, have your supplier load the materials onto the roof for you. Otherwise, use the ladder as a ramp to haul the materials up, or consider renting a hoist.

⚠ **CAUTION** *To avoid skidding on the roof, never work on a rainy or windy day. Keep the surface free of loose nails, tools, and debris.*

Ladder Safety

✔ Always lean an extension ladder against the wall so the distance between the foot of the ladder and the wall is one-quarter the distance the ladder extends up the wall.

✔ Make sure the ladder is level and properly secured *(page 322)*

✔ Don't prop a ladder against a window or door.

✔ Keep ladders away from overhead electric wires.

✔ Extend an extension ladder at least 3 feet above the roof edge.

✔ Make sure the spreaders on a stepladder are pushed all the way down to the locked position. (Never use a stepladder folded up.)

✔ As you climb a ladder, have someone steady it, and hold the rungs with both hands; don't carry anything in your hands.

✔ Don't stand above the third-highest rung of an extension ladder or the second-highest step of a stepladder.

✔ Don't overreach to either side of the ladder and never step from one ladder to another.

 SAFETY TIPS

Wear goggles when hammering. For roof work, put on rubber-soled shoes.

A TOOL BELT FOR SAFETY

Nails and tools left on the roof are a serious hazard. Stepping on a loose object can cause you to lose your footing, and a dropped tool can be a danger to people working below the roof. To keep track of nails and tools, always wear a tool belt. Doing so also leaves your hands free for climbing the ladder.

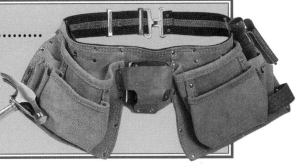

ANCHORING AN EXTENSION LADDER

SAFETY SHOE

Stabilizing the bottom of the ladder.
Make sure your ladder is equipped with safety shoes; tilt them to grip the surface. To check the stability of the ladder, stand on the bottom rung. If the ladder is unstable, place a board under the shoes, digging out the earth to level the board. If you're placing the ladder on an uneven surface, use leg levelers *(photograph)*.

To prevent the ladder from slipping on a slick surface, tie the siderails to a stake between the ladder and the wall with good-quality nylon rope and a slip-proof knot *(left)*. On pavement, tie the ladder to a screw eye anchored to the house wall.

Stabilizing the top of the ladder.
If you will be getting on and off the roof often, anchor the top of the ladder.

Where the ladder rests against a gutter, first place a 2-by-4 in the gutter to keep it from being crushed by the ladder. Fasten a screw eye in the fascia in line with each ladder siderail and tie the siderails to the screw eyes with good-quality nylon rope and a slip-proof knot.

To rest the ladder against the wall of the house, attach a ladder stabilizer *(photograph)* to keep it from slipping sideways.

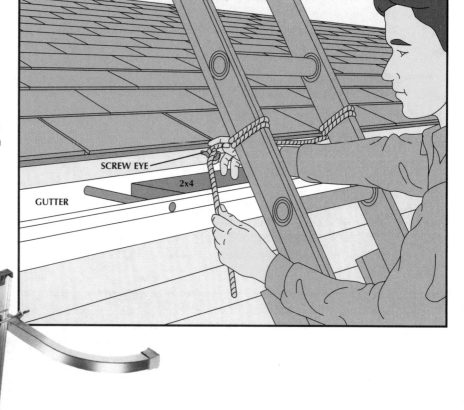

SCREW EYE

2x4

GUTTER

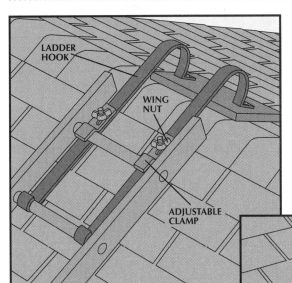

Fixing a ladder to the roof.

Fitted with a pair of ladder hooks, a single ladder can provide a toehold for working on the roof. Ladder hooks with wheels enable you to roll the ladder up the slope before hooking it in place.

Screw a wood block to the hooks to spread the weight and prevent damage to the roofing. Attach the hooks to the top two rungs of the ladder by tightening the wing nuts on the adjustable clamps, then hook the assembly over the ridge (left).

Setting up a rooftop platform.

A pair of roof brackets supporting a plank provides a level surface on asphalt shingles or sheathing. Each bracket consists of a steel strap with mounting slots or holes at one end; attached to the strap is a shelf, braced by an upright, which supports a 2-by-10 scaffold-grade plank. Adjustable brackets (right) can accommodate any roof pitch and feature a lock to keep the upright from slipping.

To install a bracket, bend back a shingle tab and slide the strap under the shingle. Insert a $2\frac{1}{2}$-inch roofing nail in a bracket mounting slot (or hole), and drive it through the shingle. Install the second bracket no more than 6 feet from the first. To remove a bracket, tap it toward the ridge and slip it off the nail; lift the shingle tab and pound the nail flush.

TRICKS OF THE TRADE

Making a Roofer's Seat

The roofer's seat shown here features a base with protruding nail tips that keep it from slipping. From a 1-by-12, cut a seat 18 inches long. Multiply 18 inches by the fraction that expresses the pitch of your roof (page 326) and cut a 1-by-12 support to that length. Nail one end of the seat to one end of the support, forming a right angle. Cut a 1-by-12 base to span the distance between the free ends of the seat and support. Cut four strips from 1-by-3s $11\frac{1}{2}$ inches long. Hammer three 1-inch roofing nails through each strip and fasten the strips to the base with wood glue. Nail the base to the seat and support. You can bevel the bottom edges of the support and seat, if desired.

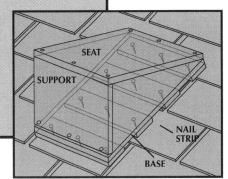

GUTTER MAINTENANCE

Unclogging a downspout.
First try removing debris from a clogged downspout by hand or by flushing it with a garden hose. If these methods don't work, use a plumber's trap-and-drain auger.
◆ Feed the end of the auger's coil into the downspout as far as possible, then lock the handle.
◆ Slowly turn the handle clockwise (right). When the handle moves easily, feed in more coil and repeat.
◆ Once the downspout is clear of debris, flush it with water.

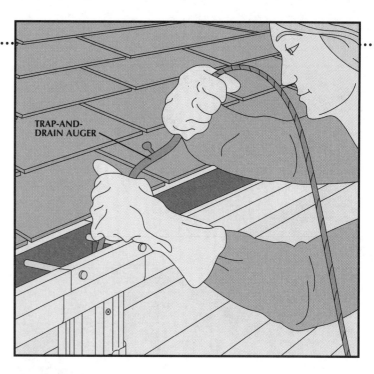

Adding a leaf strainer.
◆ Adjust the strainer to fit the drop outlet snugly by squeezing or expanding the tines.
◆ Fit it into the drop outlet (left).

Fitting a leaf guard.
◆ Cut the guard to length; use a utility knife on plastic, tin snips on metal.
◆ Fold the material across its width into a cylindrical shape and fit it between the edge of the roof and the inside lip of the gutter (right).

Some types of leaf guard are secured to the outside of the gutter with clips (photograph).

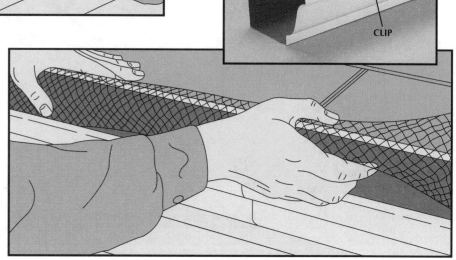

1. Checking for misalignment.

To determine whether a gutter is bent out of alignment, hose water onto the roof, directing the spray from side to side *(above)*. Watch the flow of water in the gutter; if the gutter is misaligned, water will pool in the low spots.

2. Realigning the gutter.

◆ On a gutter fastened by spikes and ferrules, twist the spikes free with locking-grip pliers *(right)*; remove the ferrules.

◆ Reposition the gutter to raise the low spots and fasten the spikes and ferrules. If more support is necessary, drive additional spikes and ferrules into adjacent rafter ends.

For a fascia bracket or wraparound hanger, remove the hanger to align the gutter, then reposition the hanger. Replace a badly bent hanger.

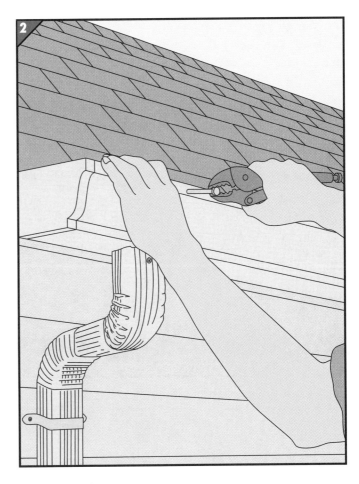

Choosing the Right Roofing

The materials for roofing—like those for siding—differ in appearance, cost, durability, and ease of installation. But an added factor—the roof slope—limits the choice of materials suitable for a particular roof.

Gentle and Steep Slopes: The more level the pitch of the roof, the slower the runoff of water; and a slow runoff calls for an especially waterproof covering. A flat surface is usually covered with modified bitumen roofing or a built-up roof. Because of the special skills and tools involved, these materials are best installed by a professional; however, they can be repaired fairly easily *(page 333)*. A gentle slope can be covered with roll roofing; but a roof that rises more than 3 inches per foot is considered to be steep, and is suited for a wider range of materials such as asphalt shingles, slate, tile, or wood shingles and shakes. The chart opposite will help you determine what kind of roof is best for your job.

Estimating and Ordering: Most roofing materials are sold in units called squares, each capable of covering 100 square feet of roof (the only exception is roll roofing, which comes in rolls of varying lengths and weights). To estimate the amount of roofing material you need, determine the area of the roof surface, add 5 to 10 percent to allow for double layers of covering along ridges, eaves, and hips, and round the total up to the next highest square (the next 100 square feet).

Roofing Cement: For most jobs, plastic roofing cement is the product of choice. It is available in cartridges—to be applied with a caulking gun—and in cans or buckets—to be spread on with a putty knife. To install roll roofing, you will need a thinner, brushable product, referred to as lap cement.

> ⚠️ **CAUTION** *Old roof shingles and roofing felt may contain asbestos. You cannot tell by looking, however, and must have the material tested by a lab certified by the National Institute of Standards and Technology.*
> *To remove a small sample for testing—and the rest of the materials if they test positive for asbestos—follow the guidelines on page 83.*

GETTING READY

Measuring roof slope.
The slope, or pitch, of a roof equals the roof rise in inches for every 12 inches of horizontal run.
◆ Set up an extension ladder to reach the eaves *(pages 321-322)*; then mark a reference line on a board 12 inches from its end.
◆ With a level on the board and the end of the board butted against the roof, hold the board level.
◆ Measure the distance between the roof and the reference line on the board *(left)*. The resulting figure is the number of inches per foot that the roof slopes. If it is more than 6 inches per foot—6 in 12—consider having the work done by a professional.

A GUIDE TO ROOFING MATERIALS

Type	Cost	Durability (years)	Minimum slope	Advantages	Limitations
Asphalt shingles	Inexpensive	15-20	4 in 12	Easy installation; available in a variety of weights and colors; requires little maintenance; easy to repair	Only fiberglass type fire resistant; organic mat type—made of wood or rag fiber—not fire resistant
Roll roofing	Inexpensive	5-7	1 in 12	Easy installation and repair	Poor fire resistance for some types; drab appearance
Built-up or modified bitumin	Moderate	10-20	$\frac{1}{4}$ in 12	More waterproof than any other roofing material	Poor fire resistance for some types; must be installed professionally; leaks difficult to locate
Wood shingles and shakes	Moderate to expensive	15-30	3 in 12 for shingles; 4 in 12 for shakes	Attractive rustic appearance; natural insulator	Highly flammable unless specially treated; shingles must be laid over open planks or spaced battens
Slate	Expensive	50-100	4 in 12	Attractive traditional appearance; fire resistant	Heavy; brittle; requires sturdy roof support; tricky installation that may require special tools; needs regular replacement of damaged pieces; difficult to repair
Tile	Moderate (concrete) to expensive (clay)	50-100	4 in 12	Attractive traditional appearance; fire resistant	Heavy; brittle; requires sturdy roof support; time-consuming installation; availability of replacement pieces unreliable; difficult to repair

Comparing materials.

In this chart, "Cost" refers to the relative cost of materials alone—not the cost of labor. In most cases, the cost of professional installation is higher for roofing materials like slate, tile, and wood shingles and shakes than for asphalt shingles or roll roofing. The minimum slope is the pitch at which a specific material begins to provide adequate protection against water. All the materials listed can be applied to surfaces steeper than the minimum, but as slopes increase such considerations as appearance and durability become more important.

"Durability" provides a rough measure of the length of time a roof will last with proper maintenance in a temperate climate.

Remedies for Damaged Rafters

Before reroofing, it is a good idea to check for rafter damage. Wet spots that are not rotted can be allowed to dry thoroughly and then treated with wood preservative. But any signs of rot, insect damage, or cracks or bows in rafters call for remedial action. Probe for rot with an awl, which penetrates damaged wood easily.

Damaged and Sagging Rafters:
A rafter damaged near the middle can be reinforced with sisters *(below)*. If the damage is near the ridge beam, the top ends of the sisters must be mitered; the sisters are then nailed to the old rafter below the damage and to the ridge beam above it. For damage near the eaves, cut the bottom ends of the sisters to fit against the top plate of the wall. With extensive damage, sisters must extend from the ridge to the top plate. Such full-length sisters are tricky to cut and fit. But if the sheathing is to be taken off, the old rafter can be removed and used as a template to prepare and install its replacement.

You can correct a sagging rafter as described below without removing the sheathing. However, extensive sags should be repaired by a professional.

⚠️ **CAUTION** *Trusses must be repaired by a professional. Never cut any part of a truss roof.*

TOOLS
Tape measure
Hammer
Awl
Handsaw or circular saw

MATERIALS
2x4s, rafter boards
Shims
Common nails ($2\frac{1}{2}$", $3\frac{1}{2}$")

SAFETY TIPS
Wear goggles when nailing, and a hard hat when working in an unfinished attic.

SISTER RAFTER

Reinforcing a rafter.
◆ Cut two sister rafters—boards the same width as the damaged rafter and long enough to extend 2 feet on each side of the damage.
◆ While a helper holds one sister in place, fasten it with $3\frac{1}{2}$-inch common nails *(above)*; space the nails at 6-inch intervals along both edges of the rafters.
◆ Nail the twin sister to the other side of the old rafter the same way, hammering it onto the protruding nail points.

Correcting a sag.
◆ Hold a block of wood against the sheathing next to the bowed rafter, and strike the block with a hammer to lift the sheathing slightly *(above)*. Continue, forcing the sheathing up until it is level.
◆ If necessary, slip shims between the rafter and the sheathing to hold the sheathing straight.
◆ With $3\frac{1}{2}$-inch common nails, fasten 2-by-4s to each side of the bowed rafter to bridge the sag and hold the sheathing flat.
◆ Drive two locator nails through the sheathing alongside the rafter, climb onto the roof, and nail the sheathing to the 2-by-4s with $2\frac{1}{2}$-inch nails at 6-inch intervals.

⚠️ **CAUTION**
The above procedure will cause leaks; follow it only when you are about to reroof.

Waterproofing with Metal

Roofs are most vulnerable to leaks where their slopes are broken by chimneys, dormers, vent pipes and valleys; these breaks are covered by a continuous watertight material called flashing. The most common flashing materials are aluminum and galvanized steel, but for slate, tile, and wood roofs, copper is often used. Make sure the nails you buy are of the same material as the flashing. Installation methods for flashing may vary slightly depending on the material that has been used on the roof; consult a roofing supplier.

Repairs: Holes in flashing can be patched temporarily with roofing cement covered with fiberglass reinforcing mesh and more cement; after curing for a couple of days, a reflective aluminum coating is brushed over the patch. Flashing that pulls away from a chimney can also be repaired *(below)*.

Replacing Flashing: Badly deteriorated flashing can be replaced by removing the shingles covering it, sliding in a new piece, and replacing the shingles. However, once flashing begins to fail, it is often time to reroof —remove old flashing and replace it as you install the new roofing. Cut flashing with tin snips.

Closed and Open Valleys: Valleys for asphalt shingles can be open or closed. In a closed valley, the shingles on the two adjoining slopes overlap, so no flashing is required at the seam. Open valleys require metal flashing, as the shingles of each slope do not overlap. Shake, shingle, tile, and slate roofs, which typically have open valleys, require special flashing to help contain water in the valley. This flashing has flanges—called slater's edges—and a W-shaped ridge in the center.

Chimney Flashing: Two layers of flashing are usually required where a roof meets a vertical surface. The first layer—called base flashing—is fastened to the roof and extends along the vertical surface; it is partly covered by a layer of counterflashing fastened to the vertical surface. This arrangement maintains a watertight joint even if the roof or chimney shifts. Existing counterflashing in good shape can be left in place; just bend it up temporarily until you are ready to bend it back in place.

 TOOLS

Screwdriver
Wire brush
Caulking gun

 **MATERIALS**

Flashing metal
Exterior caulk
Lead wedges

 SAFETY TIPS

Flashing has sharp edges—protect you hands with heavy work gloves when handling it. Put on goggles when hammering.

REATTACHING FLASHING TO MASONRY

Securing flashing at mortar joints.
◆ Pull the flashing away from the joint to free its flanged edge.
◆ Clean out the mortar joint with a wire brush and a flat-tipped screwdriver.
◆ Push the flanged edge of the flashing back into the joint.
◆ Insert small lead wedges—available at hardware stores—between the flashing and the brick, driving in two wedges per step in the flashing.
◆ Fill the joint with exterior caulk *(right)*.

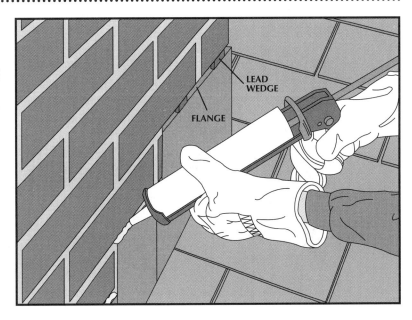

LEAD WEDGE

FLANGE

Asphalt Shingles

Inexpensive and relatively easy to install, asphalt shingles are made of organic felt or fiberglass, impregnated with asphalt and coated with fine gravel. The most common form is a strip 3 feet long and 1 foot wide divided by cutouts into three 1-by-1 foot tabs. The strips usually have a line of adhesive above the cutouts; the heat of the sun on the roof softens the adhesive and seals the shingles together.

Easy Repairs: Small holes or cracks in shingles can be sealed by troweling on plastic roofing cement; curling or buckling pieces can be cemented back in place. Individual shingles that are badly damaged can be replaced without much fuss *(opposite)*.

Buying Materials: Shingles are available in various weights; heavier types generally last longer, but fiberglass shingles—though relatively light—are as durable as heavier felt ones. Colors can vary from one production run to another, so buy all your shingles at the same time and in packages with the same lot number. If you live in a hot, humid climate, buy those that are treated to prevent algae and fungus growth. Store bundles where they will stay dry and cool.

Installing Shingles: When attaching shingles in cold weather—or if your area has high winds—the factory-applied adhesive may not be enough to hold the pieces flat; add a 1-inch dab of plastic roofing cement under each flap as you work.

When your old roofing is not made of asphalt shingles or if adding another layer will result in more layers than codes allow, you must tear off the old roofing materials and repair the roof decking, if necessary.

If you decide to apply new shingles over an existing layer, first remove hip and ridge shingles, cement any buckled pieces, and replace those that are deteriorated or missing. Install new valley flashing unless you will be shingling closed valleys, then sweep the roof clean. On an asphalt-shingled roof with course lines 5 inches apart, you can butt new shingles up against the bottoms of the old.

TOOLS

Hammer
Pry bar
Putty knife

MATERIALS

Roofing nails
($1\frac{1}{4}$", $1\frac{1}{2}$")
Plastic roofing
cement

SAFETY TIPS

Whenever nailing, protect your eyes with goggles.

ARCHITECTURAL SHINGLES

Also known as laminated shingles, architectural shingles are thicker than the standard three-tab type. A sculptured surface—and sometimes the color of the granulated coating—are used to simulate shadows, creating the illusion of three dimensions. Architectural shingles can be designed to imitate other materials such as wood shingles or slate.

NAILING METHODS

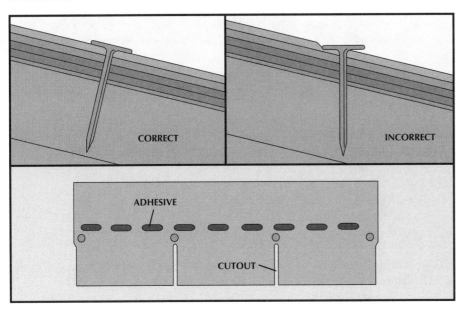

CORRECT

INCORRECT

ADHESIVE

CUTOUT

Positioning the nails.
Drive roofing nails so the heads sit flush on the shingle *(far left)*—driving the nails at an angle *(near left)* will break the surface of the shingle. When applying a new layer of shingles over an old one, use $1\frac{1}{2}$-inch nails; over a bare deck, $1\frac{1}{4}$-inch nails are suitable.

In each shingle, drive four nails below the line of adhesive as shown at bottom: one nail above each cutout and one nail 1 inch from each end. If any nail does not penetrate solid wood, drive another beside it.

REPLACING A SHINGLE

1. Removing the damaged piece.
◆ If the shingle is stuck to the one below it, work a putty knife under it to free it.
◆ Slip a pry bar under the damaged shingle and raise the nail heads *(right)*. Pull the exposed heads with the pry bar. If you must make the repair in cold weather, work carefully to avoid cracking shingles.
◆ Slip the pry bar under the shingle and remove its nails the same way.
◆ Slide out the damaged shingle.

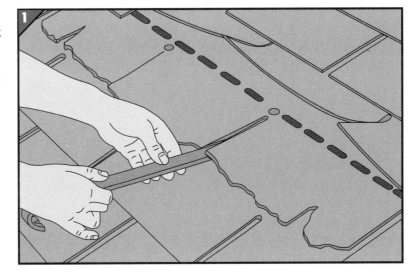

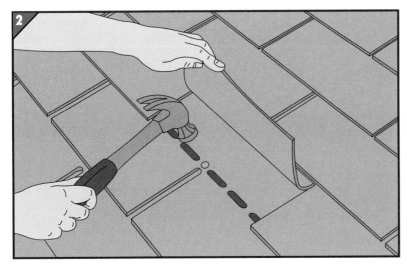

2. Fastening the new shingle.
◆ Slide the piece into position, aligning it with those on each side of the opening.
◆ Holding the upper shingle out of the way, nail the shingle to the roof *(left)*.
◆ Nail the upper shingle in place, locating the nails beside the old holes; then seal the holes with plastic roofing cement.
◆ Apply roofing cement under the bottom edges of the new shingle and the one above.

Repairs for Flat Roofs

The materials that most often cover flat or nearly flat roofs are built-up roofing (commonly known as tar-and-gravel) and modified bitumen roofing.

Built-up Roofing: Consisting of alternating layers of felt and asphalt, built-up roofing is best installed by a professional—the job calls for specialized equipment and the use of hot asphalt. But you can fix isolated blisters—spots where expanding water vapor has been trapped under or in the membrane—by following the technique shown opposite. Do not, however, attempt to repair a roof covered with numerous blisters; instead, consult a roofer.

Leaks in a built-up roof are not always easy to track down. If they occur at points where the membrane ends or is interrupted—at the roof edge or around chimneys and vent pipes—stop them by repairing the flashing *(page 329)*. Leaks within the membrane are more difficult to pinpoint; have the job analyzed by a professional.

Modified Bitumen Roofing: Made of asphalt sheets with plastic or rubber, this type of roofing is applied with a torch, hot asphalt, or cold asphalt.

Repairing blisters in modified bitumin is quite straightforward: Cut out the damaged section, coat the area with asphalt primer, and cement down a patch.

 TOOLS

Utility knife
Mason's
  trowel
Push broom

 **MATERIALS**

Plastic roofing
  cement
Roofing felt

 SAFETY TIPS

Always protect your eyes with goggles when nailing. Wear gloves when handling metal flashing and, although roofing cement is not caustic, gloves keep your hands clean when applying it.

Anatomy of a built-up roof.

Athough built-up roofing can be made with various combinations of asphalt, roofing felt, roofing cement, and roll roofing, the basic three-ply arrangement shown at right is perhaps the most common. A layer of 43-pound "base sheet" is laid over the roof decking and covered with hot liquid asphalt. Courses of roofing felt then alternate with layers of asphalt. On most roofs, a layer of gravel is embedded in the top layer of asphalt, but the roof can be finished with asphalt alone or with roll roofing.

Special flashing pieces are installed to protect vulnerable spots. Vent pipes, for example, are enclosed in close-fitting flashing assemblies. At roof edges, additional layers of roofing are brought to the top of a short wall around the perimeter called a parapet and cap flashing covers the edge of the roofing and the top of the wall.

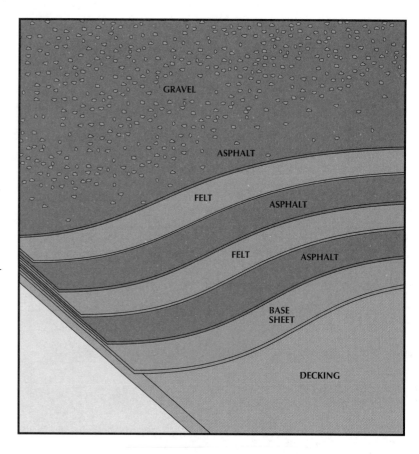

DEALING WITH BLISTERS

1. Removing the gravel.

Gravel clings to a hot roof; in warm weather, remove gravel early in the morning. With a stiff push broom or a heavy-bladed roofer's tool called a spud bar *(photograph)*, scrape the gravel from the blister and a 12-inch ring around it *(right)*.

2. Cementing the patch.

◆ Cut an X through the blister with a utility knife, fold back the resulting flaps of roofing, and let dry for an hour.

◆ Trowel plastic roofing cement on the exposed area *(above)*, working cement under the flaps. Smooth the flaps into the cement.

◆ Cut two patches of roofing felt, one 3 inches and the other 6 inches larger than the X cut earlier. Trowel cement on the area and embed the smaller patch in it. Cover the patch with cement and apply the second patch.

◆ Coat the topmost patch with cement and cover it with gravel.

Repairs to Tile and Slate Roofing

REPLACING A DAMAGED TILE

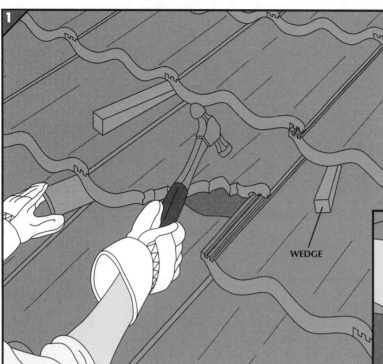

WEDGE

1. Removing the tile.
◆ With wooden wedges, prop up any tiles in the course above that overlap the damaged one.
◆ Prop up the tile with a wooden wedge and break it up with a ball-peen hammer *(left)*. Pull the pieces free.
◆ With a pry bar, extract any nails from the batten to which the tile was fastened *(inset)*.

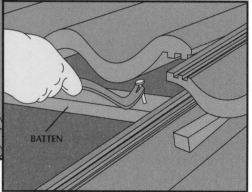

BATTEN

2. Fitting the new tile.
◆ Slide the replacement tile into position *(left)*, hooking it over the batten and interlocking it with the tiles on each side of the opening.
◆ With a putty knife, apply plastic roofing cement to the surface that will be covered by the tile above.
◆ Pull out the wedges and reseat the tiles above and adjacent to the new tile.

TOOLS

Tape measure	Mallet
Slate ripper or mini-hacksaw	Hammer
	Ball-peen hammer
	Pry bar
	Putty knife

MATERIALS

Slate hooks
Plastic roofing cement

SAFETY TIPS

Protect your eyes with goggles when cutting or breaking tile or slate, and when hammering. Wear gloves to protect your hands from the sharp edges of tiles, slates, and sheet metal.

1. Removing the slate.
To cut the nails holding the slate, slide the blade of a slate ripper under the slate and around the nail *(above)*. Pull sharply on the handle. If necessary, strike the handle with a mallet. Or, use a mini-hacksaw to cut the nail. Take the slate you removed to a roofing supplier and buy a matching replacement. Determine the length of the replacement slate by measuring a slate at a rake; or, measure the exposed length of a slate, then multiply by 2 and add 3 inches.

2. Fastening the new slate.
◆ Trim the replacement to width.
◆ Since you can't nail the slate to the roof, drive the pointed end of a slate hook—designed to keep the slate from sliding down—between two slates in the course below the gap *(right)*, aligning the hooked end with the bottom of the slates adjoining the gap.
◆ Slide the replacement under the slates of the course above and lower it to seat the bottom end on the hook.

SLATE HOOK

Choosing Siding

Beyond the obvious considerations of cost and appearance, your choice of siding should take into account the challenges of installing a specific material, the kind of maintenance it will require, and any special characteristics, such as fire resistance. The illustrations below and the chart opposite will help you to compare several widely available siding materials.

A Range of Materials: Clapboard, stucco, and wood shingles and shakes are traditional materials that have remained popular for centuries. Vinyl and aluminum siding, more recent developments, are usually shaped and finished to resemble clapboard, and are suitable for both new and old houses. They are relatively inexpensive, easy to install, and almost maintenance free.

Storage: After your siding is delivered, you should keep it sheltered until it is ready to be installed. Rain can cause wood siding to warp; aluminum siding is easily dented or scratched; and vinyl can become brittle in cold weather. To protect siding from the elements, keep it in a basement or garage, ideally off the ground so that air can circulate around it.

Common siding materials.

Six popular types of siding are shown at right. Long boards of solid wood or hardboard nailed across walls can be installed in a variety of patterns. Clapboard, the most common, consists of lapped boards tapered toward one edge. Most boards can be painted; some can be left unfinished. Wood shingles and shakes—commonly made of cedar—are similar, but shingles are milled to a uniform size while shakes are thicker and irregularly shaped. Both can be stained or painted, or in the case of cedar, simply left unfinished for a weathered look. Large panels of plywood or hardboard are available unfinished for painting or staining, or in finishes that resemble other materials.

Vinyl and aluminum generally resemble clapboard when installed, but come from the factory precolored. Both materials can be painted.

Stucco is made from a wet mortar that is spread over a wall in layers. Its surface can be finished in a variety of ways to achieve different textures. Stucco may be left uncolored but, more often, it is either precolored or painted after installation. Stucco is difficult for a do-it-yourselfer to apply.

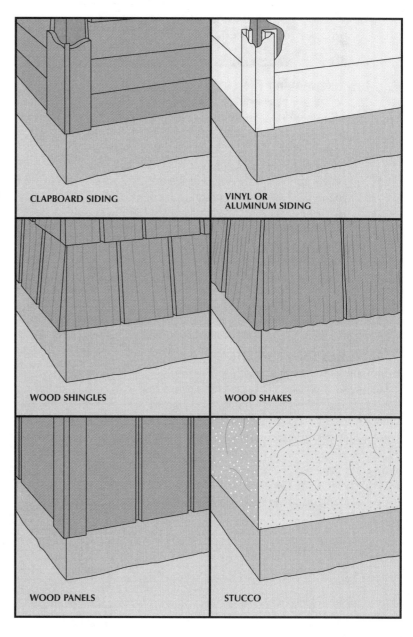

CLAPBOARD SIDING

VINYL OR ALUMINUM SIDING

WOOD SHINGLES

WOOD SHAKES

WOOD PANELS

STUCCO

A GUIDE TO SIDING

Type	Cost	Maintenance	Advantages	Limitations
Wood panels	Inexpensive (unfinished plywood) to moderate (finished hardboard)	Regular painting or staining	Quick installation; goes over most existing siding; available in a wide variety of styles	Poor fire resistance; installation usually requires two workers, and can be especially difficult at the borders of windows, doors, and rake
Clapboard	Moderate	Regular painting or staining	Goes over most existing siding	Poor fire resistance; installation usually requires two workers; some types of boards are subject to rot
Vinyl	Inexpensive to moderate	None	Easy installation; goes over most existing siding; can be repainted	May melt near intense heat; brittle in very cold weather; narrow range of colors; subject to fading
Aluminum	Inexpensive to moderate	None	Easy installation; goes over most existing siding; fire resistant; available in wide variety of colors; can be repainted	Scratches and dents easily; subject to fading; may clatter in wind if not insulated
Wood shingles or shakes	Expensive	Replacement of missing or damaged pieces; regular painting or staining for some woods	Goes over most existing siding; single pieces easily replaced; some woods can be left unfinished for rustic look	Flammable; installation slow and often difficult around doors and windows
Stucco	Moderate	Occasional patching and repair of cracks	Fire resistant; surface can be molded or decorated; can be colored or painted	Long and difficult installation requiring special skills and caustic materials; cracks or crumbles if incorrectly applied

Comparing materials.

In the chart above, "Cost" refers to the relative cost of each material as compared with the others; it does not reflect the labor involved in a professional installation. In general, labor costs are considerably higher for the traditional materials—clapboard, wood shingles and shakes, and stucco—than for the newer types of siding, most of which are relatively easy to put up.

The column headed "Maintenance" indicates what must be done to keep a siding structurally sound and weatherproof. With reasonable care, all the materials listed will last as long as the houses they cover. Aluminum and vinyl, though sound, may look weathered after several years; they can then be replaced or repainted. Occasional cleaning will keep them looking good longer.

The last two columns summarize the general advantages and limitations of each material. For a homeowner, the most important considerations are ease of installation and the ability to cover existing siding.

Siding Repairs

TOOLS
Compass saw
Pry bar
Backsaw
Mini-hacksaw
Zip tool
Hammer

MATERIALS
Galvanized box
nails (2", 2½", 3")

SAFETY TIPS

Wear goggles when nailing.

REPAIRING CLAPBOARD SIDING

Replacing a damaged board.

◆ To remove a short section of clapboard, tap wedges under the board to raise it. Tape scrap wood pads along the edges of the board in line with your cutting mark to protect the boards above and below.

◆ With a backsaw, cut through the board between the wedges *(right)*. Move the wedges to the other side of the damage and repeat the cut on this side. Insert the wedges under the board directly above and finish cutting through the board with a compass saw.

◆ Pull out the damaged section, removing any nails you find. Use a mini-hacksaw to cut hidden nails.

◆ Install a replacement section.

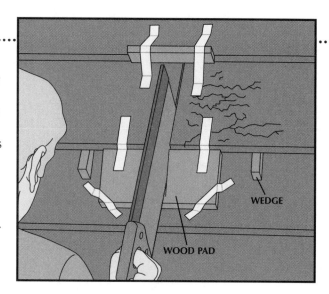

WEDGE

WOOD PAD

REPLACING DAMAGED VINYL OR ALUMINUM SIDING

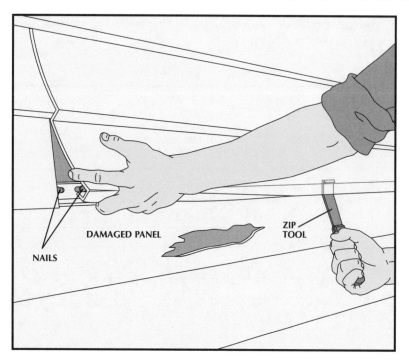

DAMAGED PANEL

ZIP TOOL

NAILS

Unlocking a vinyl siding panel.

◆ Reach under the panel directly above the damaged one with a zip tool available from siding dealers. Hook the tool onto the locking strip at the top of the damaged panel *(left)*. Pulling down firmly while sliding the tool sideways, unlock the upper panel.

◆ Prop up the upper panel and remove the nails that secure the damaged panel.

◆ Nail the replacement panel to the wall, then relock it above with the zip tool.

REPLACING A SHINGLE OR SHAKE

1. Removing the damaged piece.

With a wood chisel and hammer, split the shingle or shake into strips along the grain *(above)*. Pull out all the strips of the damaged piece. Pull any protruding nails that secured the piece, using a mini-hacksaw to cut hidden nails.

TOOLS

Tape measure
Hammer
Nail set
Mallet

Wood chisel
Electric drill
    or push drill
Shingler's hatchet
Mini-hacksaw

MATERIALS

Double-dipped, aluminum,
    or stainless steel shingle nails
    ($1\frac{1}{4}$" or $1\frac{3}{4}$")

SAFETY TIPS

Always protect your eyes with goggles when hammering.

2. Fastening the replacement piece.

◆ With a shingler's hatchet, cut the replacement shingle or shake $\frac{1}{4}$ inch narrower than the gap in the siding.
◆ Slide the piece into position so its bottom extends about $\frac{1}{4}$ inch below the bottom ends of the adjacent pieces.
◆ Drill two pilot holes into the replacement piece $\frac{3}{4}$ inch from each edge along the bottom of the row above. Angle the holes upward.
◆ Drive a nail into each hole and set the heads with a nail set *(above)*.

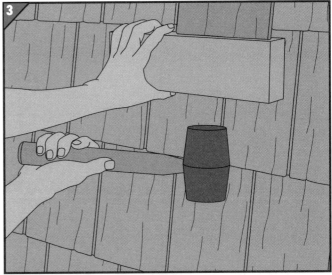

3. Tapping the piece into place.

With a mallet and a wood block, tap the replacement shingle or shake upward so its bottom end is flush with those of the adjacent pieces. Because the nails were driven at an angle, they will straighten out as the shingle or shake is tapped upward.

Mending Damaged Stucco

TOOLS
Hammer
Ball-peen hammer
Cold chisel
Putty knife
Tin snips
Stiff fiber brush
Mason's trowel
Scarifier
Wood float or
  metal trowel

MATERIALS
Self-furring masonry
  nails and plugs
Galvanized
  metal lath
Stucco patching
  compound

SAFETY TIPS

*Stucco compound contains lime,
which can irritate the skin and burn
eyes. Wear goggles, gloves, and a
long-sleeved shirt while mixing or
applying stucco compound and when
chipping or brushing out old stucco.
Wash all work clothing before wearing it again.*

PATCHING A LARGE HOLE

1. Removing the damaged stucco.
With a ball-peen hammer and a cold chisel,
chip out the damaged stucco, exposing the
metal lath *(right)*. Undercut the edges of the
hole *(inset)*. Clean out loose particles with a stiff
fiber brush. If the lath is in good shape, leave it
in place and patch the stucco *(Step 3)*. If the
lath is broken or rusted, add new lath *(Step 2)*.

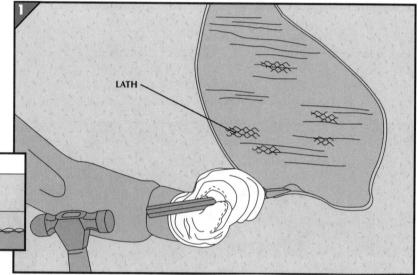

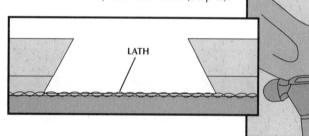

2. Adding new lath.
Cut out the damaged section of lath with tin snips, being
careful not to tear the building paper behind it. Cut replacement lath 2 to 4 inches larger than the piece removed. Fasten the lath in position with self-furring nails:
Hold a nail plug against the wall, position the lath on top
of it, and drive the nail through the plug into the wall
(left). Repeat every 4 to 6 inches along the lath's edge.
The plugs will hold the lath
away from the wall.

As an alternative to conventional
lath, add self-furring lath *(photograph)*. The dimples in its surface
hold the lath away from the wall,
enabling it to be installed with
standard nails.

3. Troweling on the first coat.
◆ Soak the damaged area with clean water.
◆ With a mason's trowel, fill the hole with patching compound to within $\frac{1}{2}$ inch of the surface level *(right)*. Scrape off the excess with the edge of the trowel and smooth the patch with the back of the trowel.

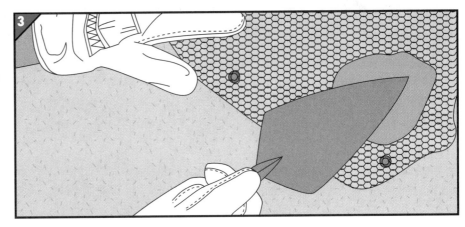

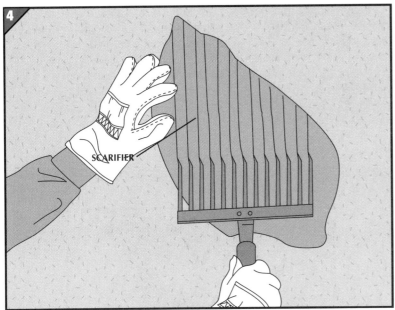

4. Applying successive coats.
◆ Lightly scratch the surface of the first coat with a scarifier *(left)*, and allow the patch to cure for two days, misting it periodically to keep it damp.
◆ Apply a second coat of compound to within $\frac{1}{8}$ inch of the surface level and let it cure for another two days.
◆ Apply a finish coat flush with the surrounding surface. Texture the patch *(Step 5)*, if desired, as soon as the final coat begins to set.

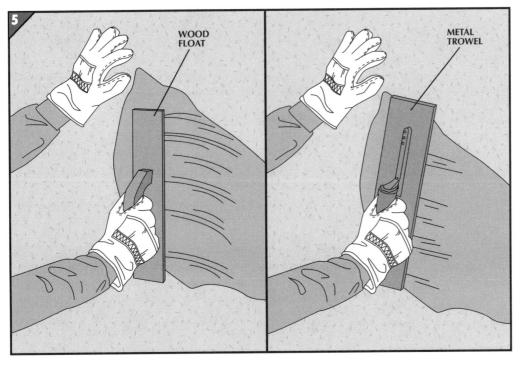

5. Texturing the patch.
A wood float produces a coarse, sandpaper-like texture. Working from the center of the patch to the edges, drag the float across the surface of the patch in broad arcing motions *(far left)*. For a smooth texture, sweep a metal trowel across the surface *(near left)*, applying even pressure and keeping the leading edge lifted slightly to avoid digging into the compound. You can also match special textures. Allow the patch to cure for four days, misting it periodically with a fine spray of water, then paint it.

Repairing Screens

Although they are tough and durable, screens are often accidentally torn or punctured. Holes up to a few inches across can be patched with the technique shown below, but repairing greater damage—or deterioration from age—requires a new panel of mesh.

Types of Mesh: Replacement screening comes in a variety of widths and mesh sizes in lengths up to 100 feet. Standard widths are 24, 36, 48, 60, and 72 inches. The most common mesh size is 16 by 18. Having 16 horizontal filaments per inch and 18 per inch vertically, this mesh is fine enough to keep out most flies and mosquitoes.

Among screening materials, fiberglass and aluminum are the most popular. Aluminum is the more durable choice, but fiberglass is less expensive, is available in more colors, and comes in a densely woven variety called solar screening. This type of mesh blocks up to two-thirds of the sun's rays, making it a good choice for southern and western exposures.

Wood Frames or Aluminum: To replace screening on a wood frame, you'll need shears to cut the mesh, a stiff putty knife to pry molding off the frame, and a staple gun loaded with $\frac{3}{8}$-inch copper-coated staples. If the frame is rotten or broken, build a new one *(page 344)*. To do so you will need a miter box and backsaw to cut the frame pieces, as well as corner clamps to hold the pieces for nailing. To install mesh in an aluminum frame, buy several feet of vinyl cord called screen spline and a tool called a screen-spline roller.

Covering a hole.

◆ Cut a piece of matching screening about twice as large as the opening.

◆ For aluminum screening, fold opposite sides of the patch to 90-degree angles, about $\frac{1}{2}$ inch from the edges, as shown at right. Then detach wires to make a fringe *(inset)*.

◆ Pass the wires through the screen mesh around the hole and fold them against the screen to hold the patch in place.

◆ For fiberglass screening, sew the patch around the edges with nylon monofilament thread.

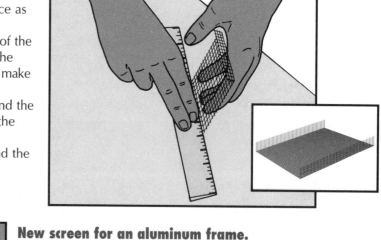

New screen for an aluminum frame.

◆ Remove damaged screening by pulling the flexible vinyl spline out of the channel around the edge, and cut a new piece of screening that overlaps the spline channel by 1 inch on each side.

◆ If you are using aluminum screening, crease it into the channel with a screen-spline roller. *(Skip this step with fiberglass screening.)*

◆ Position a length of new spline over the screening at one end of the frame, and roll the spline and screening into the channel. Trim away excess spline at the corners.

◆ Repeat this procedure at the opposite end and then along the sides, pulling the screen tight as you work. When finished, trim the screen along the outer edge of the spline.

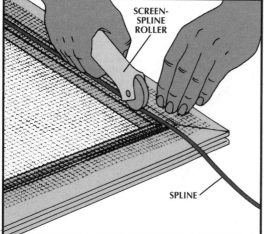

SCREEN-SPLINE ROLLER

SPLINE

Rescreening a wood frame.

◆ Pry off the molding that covers the screen edges and remove the old screening.

◆ Clamp the middle of the frame to boards laid across sawhorses or other supports and push narrow shims under each corner so that the frame is slightly bowed *(right)*.

◆ Unroll the screening over the frame, overlapping the ends of the frame by at least 1 inch. Starting at one corner, staple the screening to one end of the frame at 2-inch intervals, $\frac{1}{2}$ inch

from the inside edge of the frame.

◆ Pull the screening to remove wrinkles and staple it across the other end. Next, remove the shims and staple the screen to the sides, corner to corner,

then use a utility knife to trim the edges about $\frac{1}{2}$ inch from the staples.

◆ If the molding is sound, reinstall it; otherwise, cut new molding *(page 344, Step 1)*.

WIRE CLAMP

Support for a sagging door.

To stop a screen door from scraping a porch floor or patio as it opens and closes, true the door with a wire-and-turnbuckle stay.

◆ Open a 3-inch turnbuckle to its full extension, and attach a 4-foot length of woven wire to each of its eyes with a wire clamp *(inset)*.

◆ Drive $\frac{1}{2}$-inch screw eyes into the corners of the door as shown above and clamp the free ends of the turnbuckle wires to them. Trim excess wire.

◆ Using pliers if needed, tighten the turnbuckle to restore the door to a rectangular shape.

ASSEMBLING A FRAME FOR A SCREEN

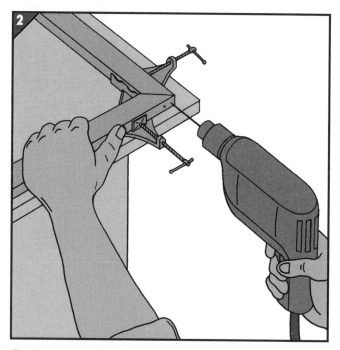

1. Mitering the frame corners.
Using a backsaw and miter box, cut each end of four 1-by-2s at a 45° angle as shown above. Make the long edge of each piece $\frac{1}{4}$ inch shorter than the corresponding edge of the opening for the screen.

2. Joining the pieces.
◆ Secure two adjacent sides of the frame in a corner clamp, then remove one of the sides and apply glue to the end. Reposition it in the clamp.
◆ Drill two $\frac{1}{16}$-inch pilot holes into the corner *(above)* and drive a 2-inch finishing nail into each. Repeat this procedure to join the other three corners.
◆ Staple screening to the frame *(page 343)*.

3. Adding the molding.
Cover the staples with $1\frac{3}{8}$-by-$\frac{1}{4}$-inch lattice strips, mitered to match the frame pieces. Align the outer edges of the lattice strips with the outer edges of the frame, and fasten them with $\frac{3}{4}$-inch brads driven near each edge at 6-inch intervals.

Extending the Life of Wood Structures

The major causes of damage to porches and decks are rot and insects. Spongy, discolored wood indicates rot; piles of wood fibers or detached wings signal insect activity. If insects are present, exterminate them before trying any repairs.

Widespread damage may require replacing the entire structure, but in most cases, the affected parts can simply be repaired or replaced. With the exception of porch flooring, which is usually protected by weather-resistant paint, make all repairs with pressure-treated lumber to prevent rot and galvanized nails and hardware to prevent rust.

Using a Jack: Before replacing a post or a column, support the structure above with a screw-operated, telescoping jack. Use a bell jack—a strong, bell-shaped screw jack about 1 foot tall—under a low deck or porch. Before using either type, grease the threads so the jack will operate smoothly.

Periodic Checks: After the repair has been completed, a little routine maintenance can prevent further trouble. If the porch or deck is painted, scrape clean and repaint any blisters or cracked areas as soon as they appear. If the structure is not painted, treat it once a year with a wood preservative. And regular inspections for rot and insect damage will catch any problems before they become severe.

⚠️ **CAUTION** *Do not use a hydraulic jack; the weight of a porch or deck may gradually compress the jack.*

SAFETY TIPS *Protect your eyes when hammering nails and when using a circular saw. Wearing earplugs reduces the noise of this tool to a safe level. Wearing a dust mask is advisable when sawing pressure-treated lumber, which contains arsenic compounds as preservatives. And be sure to wash your hands thoroughly after handling pressure-treated wood. Finally, wear a hard hat when handling heavy objects overhead.*

PATCHING A TONGUE-AND-GROOVE FLOOR

DAMAGED AREA

1. Chiseling floorboards.
With a 1-inch wood chisel, chip deep grooves across each damaged floorboard on both sides of the damage.
◆ Center the chisel on a joist, with the tool's beveled edge facing the damage. Drive the chisel straight down to cut deep across the board.
◆ Reverse the chisel, move it about ½ inch closer to the damaged area, then drive it toward the first cut, chipping out a groove.
◆ Repeat for each damaged board, staggering the grooves so that adjacent boards are not cut over the same joist.

2. Removing the boards.
◆ With a circular saw set to the thickness of the floorboards, make two parallel cuts down the middle of every damaged board that is longer than damaged boards next to it. Start and stop the saw just short of the chiseled ends, and complete the cuts with a wood chisel.
◆ Use a pry bar to remove first the middle strip, then the tongued side, and finally the grooved side of each board. The remaining boards can be pried out without sawing.

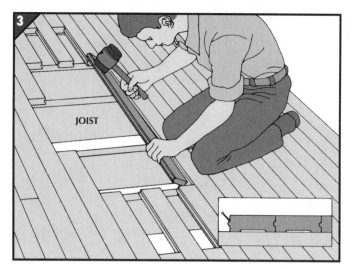

3. Inserting new boards.

◆ Where no floorboard blocks the way, tap a replacement into position with a rubber mallet, fitting the grooved edge over the tongue of the undamaged board next to it.

◆ Drive a $2\frac{1}{2}$-inch finishing nail through the corner of its tongue into the joists below *(inset)*.

◆ Fit as many boards as possible this way. For any pieces that cannot be wedged into place, use the alternative method described in Step 4.

4. Installing the final boards.

◆ Where a neighboring floorboard hinders fitting a replacement, chisel off the lower lip of the new board's grooved edge. Place its tongue in the groove of the adjacent board, and drop its trimmed edge into place *(inset),* tapping it gently with a rubber mallet to seat it.

◆ Nail the board at each joist with two $2\frac{1}{2}$-inch finishing nails, set at an angle to minimize shifting of the board. Countersink the nails and fill the holes with wood putty.

STRENGTHENING JOISTS

Reinforcing a joist.

To strengthen a weak joist, fit a new joist alongside the existing one, as shown above.

◆ Cut a joist having the same dimensions as the original, then bevel one of its edges to ease installation *(inset)*.

◆ With a helper, rotate the new joist into position atop the beam supporting the deck and fasten it to the ledger board and ribbon board with 7-inch galvanized angle plates held by $1\frac{1}{2}$-inch nails.

◆ Nail the two joists together with $3\frac{1}{2}$-inch nails, staggered top and bottom at 12-inch intervals.

◆ Finally, nail the floorboards to the top edge of the new joist.

Cure for a Rickety Deck

A simple diagonal brace adds rigidity to a wobbly deck. With a helper, temporarily tack a 1-by-8 board diagonally across the underside of the deck so that when trimmed to fit it can be nailed to the end joists on both sides of the deck. Mark the top of the board along the end joists, then take the board down and cut along the two lines. Nail the board to the underside of each joist with three $2\frac{1}{2}$-inch galvanized nails.

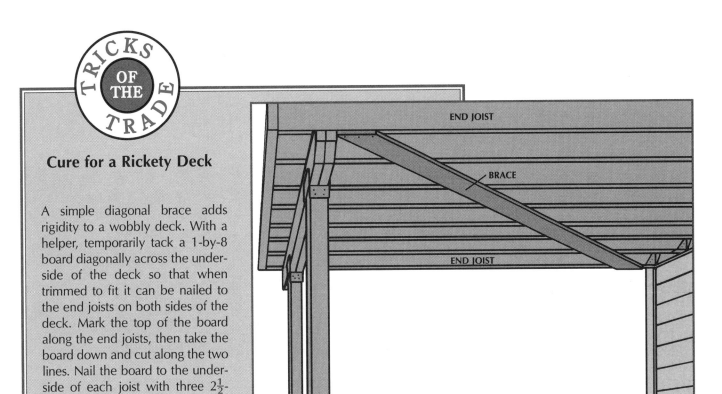

END JOIST

BRACE

END JOIST

REMOVING PORCH POSTS AND COLUMNS

1. Jacking a porch roof.

◆ Set the jack on a 2-by-12 board and line it up between the roof header and the floor joist nearest the damaged column.

◆ Extend the jack's telescoping tubes so that the top is about 2 inches from the roof header. Lock the tube in place with the steel pins provided.

◆ While a helper holds the jack plumb and steadies a second board atop the jack, extend the jack by turning the screw handle. When the jack is snug against the boards, give the handle a quarter turn—enough for the jack to support the roof without lifting it.

2. Disassembling the support.

◆ To remove a porch post or solid column *(above),* use a handsaw to cut through the post in two places about 1 foot apart. Knock out the middle section with a mallet, and work the top and bottom sections loose. Install a new post using the hardware from the old post.

◆ To remove a hollow column *(above, right),* make two vertical cuts, opposite each other, down the length of the shaft with a circular saw. Then make a horizontal cut around the middle. Pull the two upper sections apart and re-move them, staying clear of the capital in case it falls—it may not be nailed to the header.

◆ If the capital is attached to the head-er, detach it with a pry bar; to free the capital from the post, cut it in two. Remove the two lower shaft sections and the base.

◆ Check the post inside to see if it is damaged, and replace it if necessary. Cover the post with a new shaft, capi-tal, and base.

SALVAGING A DECK SUPPORT

Reusing a ground-level footing.

◆ First, support the deck with a jack set near the damaged post, then cut off the post flush with the top of the footing. Chisel the bottom of the post from the footing.

◆ Fill the resulting cavity with new concrete. Then use a plumb bob to es-tablish the postion of a J bolt, directly under the beam. Push the J bolt into the concrete *(inset).*

◆ When the concrete has cured for 24 to 48 hours, attach a post anchor to the bolt.

◆ Cut a new post to fit between the beam and the post anchor. Nail it to the post anchor and to the beam, us-ing the original hardware if possible.

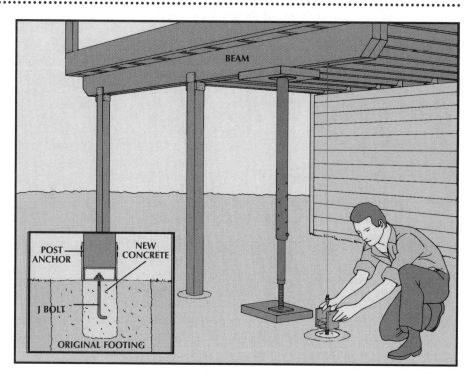

NEW CONCRETE

OLD CONCRETE

Building up a buried footing.

◆ To prepare the new footing, support the frame with a jack, dig down to expose the top of the old footing, and cut off the post as close as possible to the footing. Fill the hole with concrete, covering the remnants of the old post by at least 8 inches.

◆ Measure and cut a new post long enough to sink about 1 inch into the new footing, and set it into the concrete.

◆ Hold the post plumb while a helper fastens it at the top. Brace the bottom of the post with scrap lumber to hold it plumb *(insct)*. Allow the concrete to set at least 24 hours before removing the jack.

Splicing a weak post.

When only the upper or lower part of a porch or deck post is rotten, you can splice in a new section instead of replacing the whole post.

◆ Support the deck on a jack and saw through the post just outside the damaged area. Measure and cut a replacement section long enough to sink into a new footing if one is needed *(above)*.

◆ Cut an L-shaped notch, half the thickness of the post and 6 inches long, in the end of the undamaged section, and a matching notch in one end of the replacement section. Clamp the notched sections together and drill three $\frac{3}{8}$-inch holes through the joint, staggering their positions. Counterbore the holes for nuts and

washers, then secure the joint with $\frac{3}{8}$-inch carriage bolts.

◆ Attach the other end of the replacement section to the deck or footing.

Making Repairs in Concrete

Holes, pockmarks, and cracks in concrete can usually be filled with patching mortar. The procedure to use depends on the size of the flaw. Cracks and holes less than 1 inch deep can be brushed clean and filled with tough latex or epoxy patching mortar. Epoxy compounds are slightly stronger and more water-resistant than latex ones.

Major Repairs: Larger flaws must be dressed with a cold chisel before patching. Epoxy and latex mortars may be too expensive for filling big cracks and holes. Moreover, they are unsuitable for mending concrete steps *(opposite bottom)*. Instead, use bonding adhesive and prepackaged patching mortar—a dry mix of sand and cement to which you add water.

A Test for Failed Concrete: Such repairs may not suffice if the concrete around a flaw crumbles when chiseled, a possible sign of wide- spread deterioration. To test for overall soundness, drop a tire iron in several places. A sharp ringing noise indicates firm concrete; a dull thud signals crumbling beneath the surface. Concrete that fails this test is best broken up and rebuilt.

SAFETY TIP

As shown here, wear goggles and gloves when chiseling concrete.

PATCHING A LARGE HOLE OR CRACK

1. Preparing the damaged area.
Chip out the concrete in the damaged area with a cold chisel and a maul to a depth of about $1\frac{1}{2}$ inches. Under- cut the edge slightly so that the bot- tom of the cavity is wider than the top *(inset)*. Clear away the debris, then wet the area with a hose. Blot up ex- cess water with a sponge.

2. Adding the adhesive and mortar.
◆ Brush bonding adhesive evenly around the cavity, and wipe up any spills around the edge of the hole with a rag.
◆ Wait for the adhesive to become tacky—usually from 30 minutes to two hours, depending on the brand— then prepare the sand-and- cement patching mortar ac- cording to the manufac- turer's instructions. Trowel the mixture into the hole be- fore the bonding adhesive can harden.

3. Smoothing the patch.

Level the surface of the mortar by drawing a wood float back and forth across it several times. Remove excess mortar around the edges of the patch with a trowel; then, before the patch hardens, wipe the edge joint smooth with burlap or a rag. Cover the patch with a towel or a piece of burlap. Keep the cloth moist for a week to be sure that the patch cures completely.

REBUILDING A CRUMBLING STEP CORNER

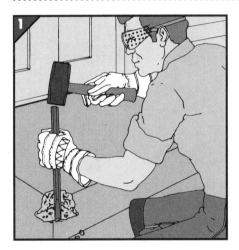

1. Preparing the corner.

◆ Chisel away the damaged corner until you reach solid concrete on all sides, then flatten the bottom of the cavity and undercut the sides slightly. Clear the cavity of debris.

◆ Cut form boards to enclose the corner and contain the mortar. Brace the boards in position, even with the top of the step, and nail their ends together at the corner (right).

◆ Coat the inside of the form boards with motor oil, and paint the cavity with bonding adhesive.

2. Filling in the corner.

◆ After the adhesive has had a chance to become tacky, trowel in sand-and-cement patching mortar and tamp it down to fill the entire hole. As the patch begins to harden, level the surface with a wood float and remove any excess mortar with a trowel.

◆ Cover with burlap and keep the burlap damp for a week.

11 CHAPTER

HOME SAFETY AND SECURITY

A safe and secure home requires protection against fire and accidents as well as against burglary. Yet for many homeowners, break-ins remain the principal concern, largely because many residences are poorly equipped to bar intrusion. The improvements on the following pages—well-placed yard lights and sturdy locks on doors and windows—can provide all the protection most homes need, simply and economically.

Electric alarms that detect intruders, fire, and other dangers were once found only in businesses and the homes of the wealthy. Today, any homeowner can attain a high level of security by installing inexpensive, stand-alone sensors.

Building and electrical codes make new houses relatively fireproof. Yet no home possesses all the features to fully eliminate the chance of fire and slow its spread. Taking the steps in this chapter, such as installing smoke detectors and fire extinguishers, can fill fire-safety gaps that codes don't often address.

Home is second only to the automobile as a dangerous place to be. Cuts, poisonings, and other household accidents kill thousands of Americans and injure millions each year. Yet homeowners can prevent most mishaps by taking common-sense measures. Modest effort makes life easier for family members and keeps toddlers safe.

Most small fires in a home—flames in an oven or burning furniture upholstery—can be doused safely with a fire extinguisher. Your odds of putting out a fire increase substantially if you hang extinguishers in several locations in the house, and you know how to use the devices.

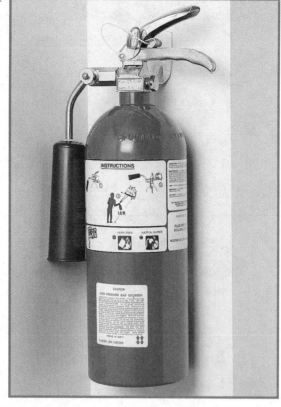

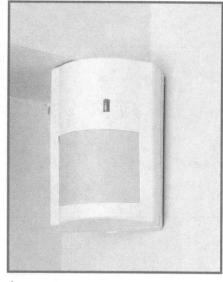

Interior sensors are an effective line of defense against burglary. Designed to detect the presence of an intruder who manages to get into the house, these stand-alone devices are simple to install.

Cabinets that contain medicines, poisonous products, and tools are potentially dangerous, especially for children. A variety of child-proofing locks and latches are available for keeping cabinet doors safely shut.

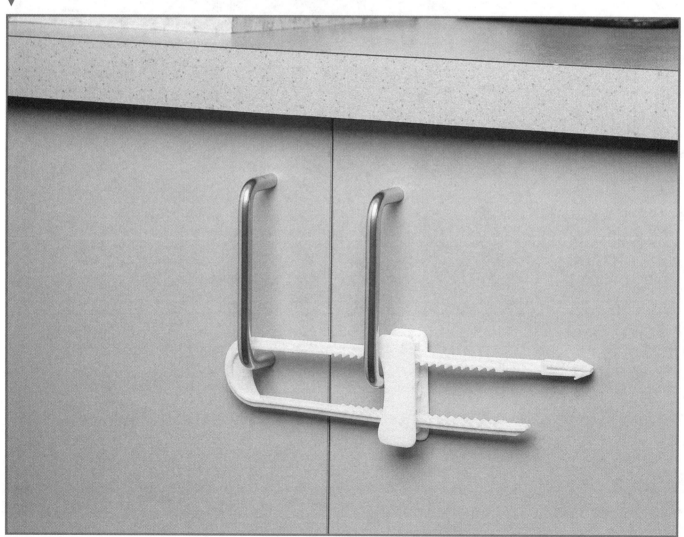

Gaining entry into a house ▶
through a door or window
is a simple matter for many
burglars. To guard against
such attacks, install a lock
on all doors and windows
accessible from the outside.

◀ *A locking door alarm can*
bolster the deterrent value
of a sturdy lock in protect-
ing a house against break-
ins. Easy to install, most
of these devices are de-
signed to sound a piercing
alarm whenever the door
is opened.

Exterior Lighting

A few well-placed outdoor lights can be highly effective in deterring night prowlers. Just one mercury-vapor lamp mounted on either a utility fixture or a rewired lamppost will illuminate the entire side of a house; incandescent floodlights and low-voltage lights will take care of any remaining dark spots in the yard. Both low-voltage lights and mercury-vapor fixtures for lampposts are sold in kit form, simplifying assembly.

Tapping Power: The handiest power source for new outdoor lights is an existing exterior fixture or receptacle. Otherwise, tap an outlet or junction box in the basement or attic *(page 359)*, making certain that it is part of a 120-volt circuit, not 240 volts.

Nearly any outlet that has two cables entering it contains a suitable power source—a hot supply wire uninterrupted by a switch. A junction box, however, may have only switch-controlled wires. To check, cut off all power at the service panel *(pages 182-183)*, then unscrew the wire cap from a connection in the junction box that has at least one black wire. Use a voltage tester to be sure power is off: Hold one probe against the bare wires and the other against a bare copper ground wire. The tester light should not glow. Hold the probes in the same position while a helper restores power; if the light now glows, the wire is hot and can serve as a power source.

Protective Armor: Conduit—the electrician's term for pipe—is a feature of virtually any 120-volt outdoor circuit. It must always be used to protect wires aboveground and is often used underground as well. Rigid conduit *(opposite and page 358)* is popular because the required burial depth is only 6 inches.

 TOOLS

Voltage tester
Hacksaw
Metal file
Pipe wrenches (10")
Conduit bender

Adjustable wrench (12") or open-end wrench (1⅛")
Electric drill with masonry and spade bits and an extender
Cold chisel

Ball-peen hammer
Star drill
Putty knife
Multipurpose electrician's pliers
Edging tool

 **MATERIALS**

Cable connector
Wire caps
Box extenders
Metal conduit
Conduit fittings
Conduit straps

Weatherproof caulking
Mortar
Green insulated wire
Splice caps and insulators

 **SAFETY TIPS** *Wear goggles to protect your eyes when hammering a cold chisel or star drill against concrete or masonry.*

A security lighting system.

Although specific requirements can vary widely, the principles of the security light system illustrated at right can be applied to almost any house. In this situation, a mercury-vapor lamppost fixture illuminates the door, the windows on both sides of the entrance, and most of the front yard. The shadow cast over the garage door and driveway by the retaining wall is eliminated by an incandescent floodlight aimed down from above. Light from a single mercury-vapor utility fixture bathes both the right side and the back of the house. A streetlight suffices for the left side.

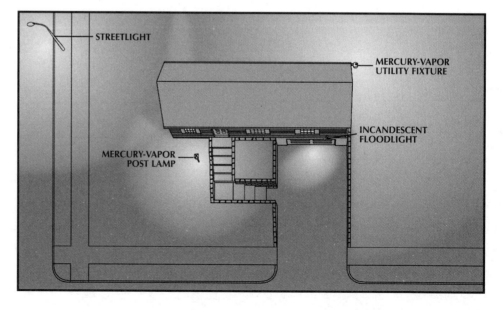

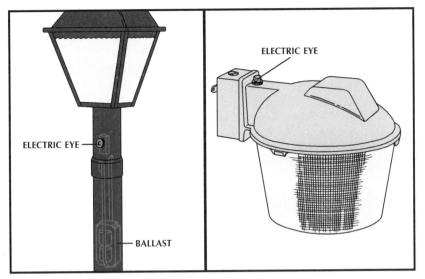

Yard-brightening lamps.

The lamppost fixture at far left has been adapted for mercury-vapor security lighting with two additions: a ballast hanging inside the post and a section of tubing that houses an electric-eye switch. The lamp illuminates a circle about 30 feet in diameter. The 175-watt mercury-vapor utility fixture at near left has a built-in ballast and electric eye. When mounted high above the ground, it lights a circle about 80 feet wide.

Sensor-controlled floodlights.

The motion sensor mounted beneath the fixture at near right and the wand-type electric eye on top of the fixture at far right switch on incandescent spotlights automatically. Both lights can be aimed to shine where needed most. They cast narrow cones of light with a base diameter roughly equal to the height of the fixture above the ground.

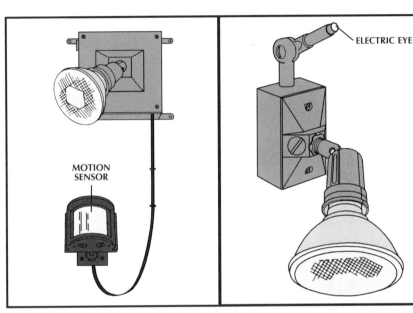

WORKING WITH CONDUIT

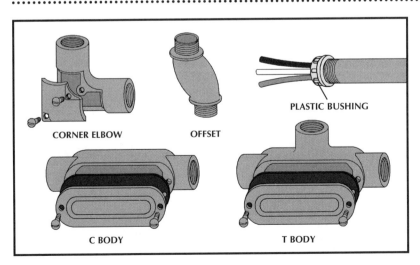

An array of fittings.

At left are the most common fittings for rigid, or heavy-wall, metal conduit. Elbows, for turning corners, have curved access plates that must be weatherproofed with caulking cord. Offsets help jog conduit past small obstacles. Screw-on plastic bushings keep insulation from chafing against conduit edges. The continuous-feed, or C, body provides access to wires in conduit with many turns, while a T body branches a circuit. Both fittings come with weatherproof gaskets.

Buried rigid conduit must be laid at least 6 inches below the surface. If you bury an elbow, C body, or T body, you must mark its location permanently with a fixture or a short stake.

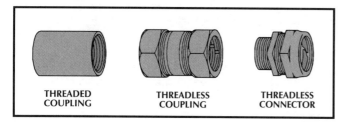

THREADED COUPLING   THREADLESS COUPLING   THREADLESS CONNECTOR

Couplings and connectors.

Couplings join two lengths of conduit, and connectors usually serve to fasten conduit to various pieces of hardware. Some used with heavy-wall conduit are shown at left. Threaded couplings, tightened with a pair of 10-inch pipe wrenches, join uncut conduit ends. Threadless couplings join pieces of cut conduit that no longer have threaded ends. After inserting conduit into the coupling, use a 12-inch-long adjustable wrench or a $1\frac{1}{8}$-inch open-end wrench to tighten the nut until the conduit is secure. Threadless connectors join cut conduit to an outlet box, a threaded coupling, or a conduit fitting. Because threadless couplings and connectors are tightened by turning nuts rather than an entire section of conduit, they are also used to join large, unwieldy conduit assemblies.

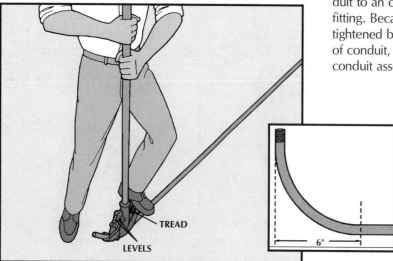

TREAD

LEVELS

6"

Bending metal conduit.

◆ Cut conduit to measure with a hacksaw and deburr the edges with a metal file.

◆ Pencil a mark on the conduit where the bend is to begin.

◆ Insert the conduit into the bender and align the mark with the arrow on the side of the tool.

◆ Step on the rocker tread and pull on the handle *(above)*. To get proper leverage, you may need to brace the opposite end of the conduit against a wall.

◆ Some benders are equipped with 45- and 90-degree levels to indicate when the conduit is bent to the desired angle. Otherwise, use the following rules: For a 45-degree bend, pull the handle until it is vertical; for a 90-degree bend, continue pulling until the handle is halfway to the ground. Either way, the bend will be about 6 inches across *(inset)*.

For an S bend, begin as described above. To make the next part of the curve, turn the bender over so that its handle rests on the ground. Position the conduit in the bender and bend it downward by hand, using a helper if necessary.

RUNNING A CABLE FOR AN OUTSIDE LIGHT

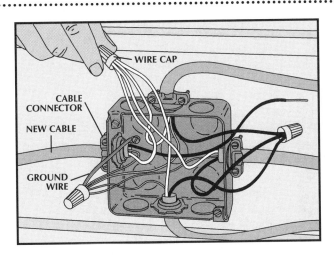

WIRE CAP

CABLE
CONNECTOR

NEW CABLE

GROUND
WIRE

Tapping power.

◆ Turn off power at the service panel.
◆ Remove a circular knockout from the box and install a cable connector in the knockout hole.
◆ Thread a new cable into the box and tighten the connector clamp onto the cable.

◆ Using wire caps large enough to accommodate the extra wire, make the connections—black wire to black, white to white, and the bare copper ground wire to the bare or green wires. Replace the box cover.
◆ Run the new cable to the planned location of the outdoor fixture.

TAPPING AN EXISTING FIXTURE

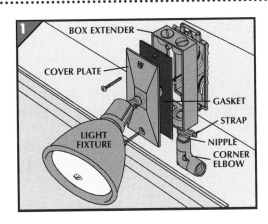

BOX EXTENDER

COVER PLATE

GASKET

STRAP

LIGHT
FIXTURE

NIPPLE

CORNER
ELBOW

1. Modifying the outlet box.

A fitting called a box extender provides the room needed to make wiring connections and attach conduit.
◆ Turn off the power. Remove the light fixture (or receptacle) from the box. Undo the electrical connections.
◆ Screw one end of a short piece of conduit called a nipple into an elbow and the other end into a conduit hole in the box extender. Temporarily screw the fixture, gasket, cover plate, and extender to the outlet box.
◆ Clamp the nipple to the wall with a conduit strap and caulk any gap between the box extender and the house.
◆ Later, remove the fixture to fish cable into the extender and to make the necessary wire connections, then screw the fixture permanently in place.

2. Assembling conduit along the house.

◆ Run conduit from the elbow at the box extender to the bottom course of siding. Strap the conduit to the wall.
◆ With a conduit bender *(opposite),* shape a conduit section to curve around the bottom of the siding and rest on the floor of the trench. Check the fit of this piece after making each bend.
◆ With a threadless coupling, link the contoured section to the conduit strapped to the house.

RECESSING A LIGHT IN A STAIRWAY WALL

Securing the fixture.
◆ With a cold chisel, chip out a brick and the surrounding mortar.
◆ Bore a $\frac{7}{8}$-inch hole through the wall and into the conduit trench with a star drill.
◆ Assemble the fixture as necessary. In the back, screw a nipple long enough to extend into the trench *(left)*. Push the fixture into the recess.
◆ If there is space around the front of the fixture, hammer in wood shims at the top and bottom. Pack mortar around the fixture and the nipple where it protrudes from the back of the wall.
◆ After the mortar dries, screw an outdoor box to the protruding nipple and thread the fixture leads through the nipple and into the box.
◆ Install a light bulb and mount the fixture cover plate.

LOW-VOLTAGE LIGHTING

1. Installing the transformer.
◆ Mount the wall bracket supplied with the transformer at least 12 inches above the ground on a wall or post, and within 6 feet of a receptacle; then push the transformer onto the bracket.
◆ Place the fixtures and string the low-voltage cable from the transformer, leaving enough slack to follow walkways and flower beds. Leave 12 inches of additional slack at each fixture.

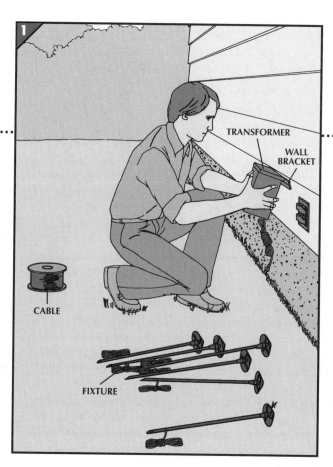

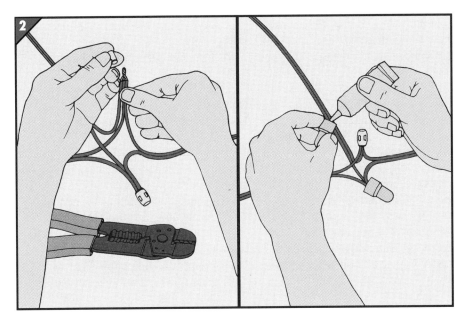

2. Using splice caps.

◆ For a fixture with wire leads, cut the cable at the locations you have chosen, strip $\frac{3}{8}$ inch of insulation from each cable and fixture wire, and twist each fixture wire to the wires from each end of the cut cable. Crimp a splice cap over each three-wire connection with multipurpose electrician's pliers *(far left)*.

◆ Partially fill an insulator with silicone caulking compound and slip it over the splice cap *(near left)*, making sure that the cap is embedded in the compound.

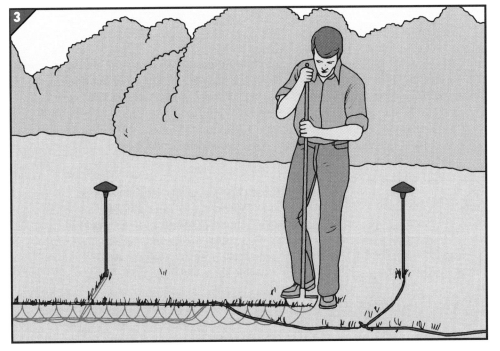

3. Hiding the cable underground.

◆ Push an edging tool into the ground with one foot, rocking it back and forth to exert a downward and sideward pressure. Overlapping strokes will cut a narrow slit.

◆ Tuck the cable into the slit and step along the top to press the turf back together.

Doorway security begins with a metal door or a solid-core wood door. Hollow-core and paneled wood doors are both too weak to offer much protection. A metal door made of steel no thinner than 16 gauge is adequate. In wood doors, a core of laminated 2-by-4s is stronger than a particle board core.

Windows in an exterior door reduce security, as does a mail slot within reach of the latch. To see who is outside, install a viewer (below). Steel rods slipped into the edge of a wood door (opposite) help thwart attempts to saw out locks and latches.

A Strong Frame: If your door jambs are made of steel—check them with a magnet—you need do nothing to strengthen them. With wood jambs, however, even the sturdiest door may be installed in ways that make a break-in easy.

To check the door mounting, begin by removing a hinge screw. Replace short screws with 3-inch No. 10 wood screws that extend into the stud behind the jamb.

Unless adequately reinforced at hinges, deadbolts, and latches, many wood jambs can be levered away from the door far enough to free the bolt or latch. To determine whether your doorway has this weakness, remove the interior casing and inspect the spaces immediately outside the jambs. Add plywood filler and shims as necessary (pages 364-365).

Look into the deadbolt hole in the jamb. If you see wood at the bottom, replace the metal frame, or strike, with a heavy-duty strike box (pages 363-364) to encase the bolt in metal.

Putting On a Better Lock: Improving the security of a lock may be as simple as changing the key, but frequently a new lock is the answer. A deadbolt lock (pages 366-367) or a rim lock (page 368) can be added without having to change the hardware that is already there.

Window Security: Most windows pose little deterrent to intruders. One way to secure the common double-hung window is to install a lock (page 369). Relying on a metal shaft that pierces both sashes and holds them tightly together, such locks are relatively pry resistant.

 TOOLS

Electric drill
Bell-hanger drill bit
  (12")
Drill guide

Chisel
Pry bar
Carpenter's nippers
Mallet
Hammer
Hacksaw

 **MATERIALS**

Steel rods ($\frac{1}{4}$" diameter, $7\frac{1}{4}$" long)
Wood screws (3"
  No. 10)
Scrap plywood

Shims
Common nails
  (2" and 4")
Finishing nails ($1\frac{1}{2}$"
  and 2")
Sheet-metal screws
  ($1\frac{1}{2}$" No. 12)

 SAFETY TIPS

Goggles protect your eyes from metal filings when you are hammering nails and drilling overhead.

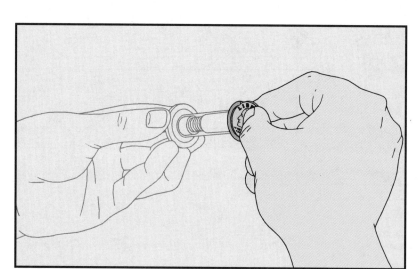

Installing a wide-angle viewer.

To see who is outside without having to open the door, install a viewer. Models with a 180-degree field of view, sometimes called fisheye viewers, make it impossible for a person to duck out of sight.

◆ At eye level in the center of the door, drill a hole as wide as the viewer shank, usually $\frac{1}{2}$ inch.
◆ Insert the two halves of the viewer and screw them together by hand if the interior section is knurled, or with a coin if it is slotted (left).

SAWPROOFING A DOOR

Steel bars for the lock area.

To shield the lock in a solid-core wood door, bore holes into the lock-side edge and insert steel rods.

◆ With a 12-inch-long, $\frac{1}{4}$-inch bell-hanger bit and drilling no closer than 1 inch to the bolt or latch plates, bore five holes above the locks and five holes below them. Space the holes 2 inches apart, and use a drill guide to keep them at a 90-degree angle to the door edge. To make all holes an equal depth, wrap tape $8\frac{1}{2}$ inches from the tip of the bit.

◆ In cases where the door has a deadbolt, drill as many holes as possible between the deadbolt and the main lock.

◆ Into each hole, tap a $7\frac{1}{2}$-inch length of unthreaded $\frac{1}{4}$-inch steel rod, then seal the holes with wood filler.

A DEADBOLT STRIKE BOX

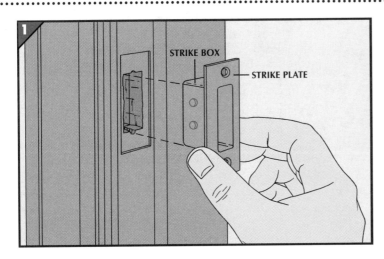

1. Recessing the strike.

◆ Unscrew the old strike plate and enlarge the opening in the jamb with a chisel to accommodate the new strike box.

◆ Set the box in the jamb periodically as you work to check its position; the bolt of the lock must slide into the box without binding. If necessary, enlarge the opening for a good fit.

◆ Hold the box in the jamb and trace around the strike plate with a pencil.

◆ Chisel a recess, or mortise, within the outline so that the strike plate lies flush with the surface of the wood.

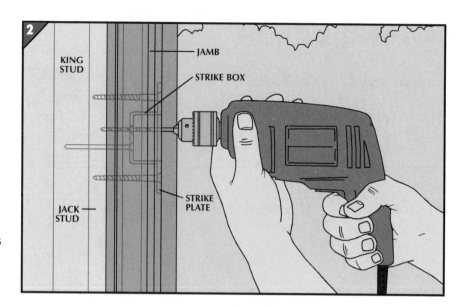

2. Fastening the strike.

With the strike in the jamb, use the screw holes in the strike plate and strike box as guides to bore into the studs beyond the jamb. Drill the holes to fit 3-inch No. 10 wood screws.

STIFFENING A FRAME

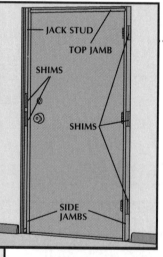

1. Removing the side casing.

A securely braced doorjamb requires, at each of the points indicated in the inset, 4- by 6-inch fillers of $\frac{1}{4}$-inch plywood and two pieces of door shim.

◆ Remove the strikes from the doorjamb.

◆ Working from the bottom up, remove both side casings with a pry bar, using a thin scrap of wood behind the bar to protect the wall *(left)*. Extract nails left in the wall or casings with carpenter's nippers, pulling casing nails through the back of the boards.

◆ Check the space between the jambs and the jack studs. If you find no shims at the locations indicated *(inset)*, proceed to Step 2; if you do, go to Step 3.

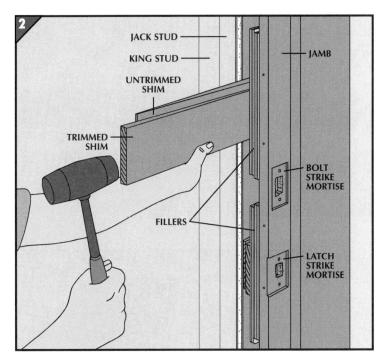

2. Adding shims.

◆ Insert plywood filler behind the jamb, leaving space for the thick end of an untrimmed shim.

◆ Push the shim into the gap between filler and stud, then tap a shim with 3 inches trimmed from its thin end into the opening, thin end first, until the shims are snug. Score and snap off shim ends.

◆ Install one shim assembly behind each hinge; at the deadbolt strike, use two fillers separated by a gap for the box of a high-security strike *(pages 363-364)*.

◆ To secure the fillers, replace short hinge screws with 3-inch No. 10 wood screws and drive pairs of identical screws above and below each strike plate.

3. Reinstalling the casing.

◆ Nail the side casings to the jambs and the jack studs, from top to bottom, using 2-inch finishing nails in the studs and $1\frac{1}{2}$-inch finishing nails in the jambs, reusing old nail holes where feasible.

◆ Secure the side casings to the top casing with one 2-inch nail driven horizontally and another driven vertically into each mitered joint *(right)*.

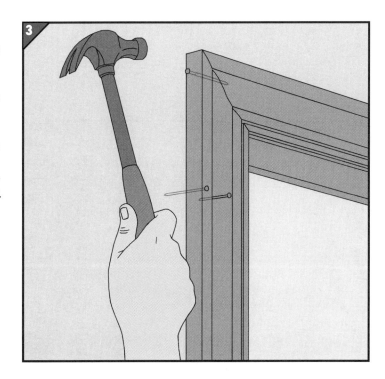

ADDING A DEADBOLT

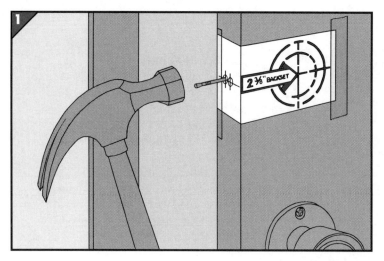

1. Marking the holes.
◆ Tape the paper template that came with the lock to the edge and face of the door about 6 inches above the knob.

◆ Mark each screw hole by driving a finishing nail $\frac{1}{4}$ inch through the marks on the paper template, making sure the nail remains perpendicular to the surface. To allow for variations in door thickness, some templates are marked with alternate locations for drilling the edge holes; be sure to use the mark specified for the size of your door.

2. Boring the cylinder hole.
With the door closed, or firmly wedged open, use a hole saw to bore a cylinder hole the size that is specified by the manufacturer. To avoid splintering the thin veneer of the door face as the teeth of the saw exit, stop drilling as soon as the small center bit of the saw breaks through the opposite side and complete the hole from that side of the door.

3. Drilling the bolt hole.
Wedge the door open. To make sure that the bit stays on course as you drill into the narrow edge of the door, enlist a helper. While you watch from above to keep the bit from straying right or left, have the helper check that it remains horizontal.

Alternatively, use a drill guide to ensure that holes are drilled perfectly.

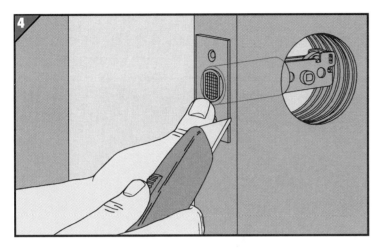

4. Seating the bolt assembly.

◆ Insert the bolt assembly into the bolt hole, then scribe the outline of the faceplate with a utility knife. The line left by a sharp knife is thinner and more precise than a pencil line.

◆ Chisel a mortise in the marked area for the faceplate, carving only as deep as the plate is thick.

◆ Fasten the assembly with screws.

5. Installing the lock.

◆ For a deadbolt with thumb turn *(left),* assemble the cylinder, drive bar, and the reinforcing plate and ring as directed by the manufacturer.

◆ Fit the assembly into the cylinder hole from outside the door, inserting the drive bar through the drive bar hole in the bolt assembly.

◆ Screw the rear reinforcing plate, if any, to the cylinder hole from inside the door, then set the thumb turn against the door, fitting the drive bar into the hole in the thumb turn.

◆ Insert mounting bolts through the thumb turn, the reinforcing plate, and the bolt assembly and screw them into the back of the cylinder. For a double-cylinder lock, fit the drive bars of both cylinders into the drive bar hole.

◆ Test the deadbolt with both the key and the thumb turn. If the bolt will not move in or out, remove the drive bar from the cylinder, rotate the bar 180 degrees, and reassemble the lock.

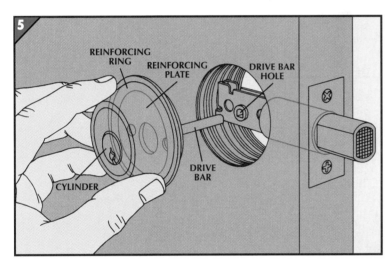

REINFORCING RING
REINFORCING PLATE
DRIVE BAR HOLE
CYLINDER
DRIVE BAR

6. Marking for the strike box.

◆ Coat the end of the bolt with lipstick or a grease pencil, close the door, and turn the bolt against the jamb, leaving a mark on it.

◆ At the mark, bore a hole for the strike box in the jamb, drilling with the same bit used for the bolt hole in the door. If you hit a finishing nail, chisel around it until you can pull it out with pliers.

THE RIGHT WAY TO ATTACH A RIM LOCK

1. Mounting the lock.
◆ Bore a hole for the cylinder about 6 inches above the doorknob.
◆ Insert the cylinder from the outside, screw the rear reinforcing plate to it, and set the lock case against the door so that the drive bar fits into the thumb turn slot of the case. If necessary, shorten the drive bar by snapping it at one of the grooves with pliers.
◆ Bore holes for the attachment bolts, using the lock case to locate the holes.
◆ Bolt on the lock case, placing lock washers and nuts on the interior side of the door.

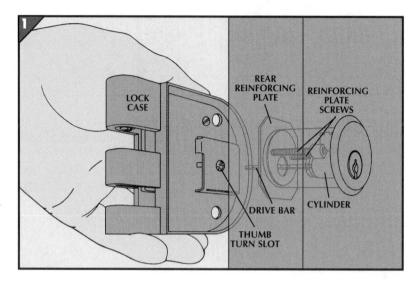

2. Mortising for the strike.
When you are chiseling the mortises for the strike, pare away small amounts of wood and periodically test the mortise depth until the lock bolts slip easily into the rings. If you cut too deeply, shim behind the strike with cardboard.
◆ With the door closed, score lines in those places where the top and bottom of the lock case meet

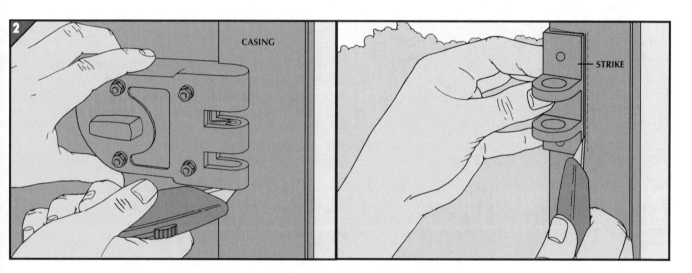

the door casing *(above, left)*.
◆ With the door open, hold the strike between these marks and score a vertical line along the outer edge of the strike *(above, right)*.
◆ To allow for the part of the strike that wraps around the jamb, mark a second vertical line farther out on the door casing by a distance equal to the thickness of the strike *(dashed line)*.

◆ Tap a chisel, bevel side in, along the outermost marks to cut straight into the casing; then, holding the chisel bevel side down, pare out the wood within the marked area.
◆ Mark the jamb mortise by holding the strike in the casing mortise. Score around it, and chisel out a recess in the jamb as you did in the casing.

Locking a window with a nail.

◆ Drill a $\frac{3}{16}$-inch hole through the top rail of the bottom sash and at least $\frac{1}{2}$ inch into the bottom rail of the top sash. Angle the hole slightly downward so that the nail cannot fall out if the window is rattled.

◆ Trim the head from a 3-inch common nail with wire cutters so that the nail is just out of reach when slipped into the hole.

◆ Keep a magnet near the window to retrieve the nail and unlock the window.

Fitting a rod lock.

◆ Holding the body of the lock against the top rail of the bottom sash, locate a rod hole that misses the glass in both sashes. Mark holes for the rod and mounting screws with an awl.

◆ Drill holes for the mounting screws, then tape a $\frac{1}{4}$-inch bit for a hole about $2\frac{3}{8}$ inches deep and drill the hole for the rod.

◆ Screw the lock body to the sash.

◆ To allow ventilation, open the bottom sash no more than 4 inches, insert the rod in the lock to mark the top sash for a second rod hole, and drill a $\frac{1}{4}$-inch hole about $\frac{1}{2}$ inch deep.

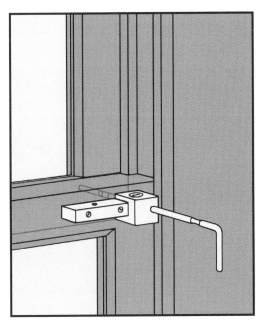

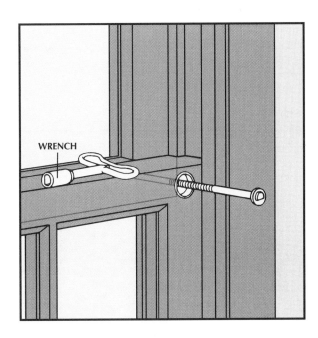

A lag bolt lock.

◆ Drill a $\frac{1}{4}$-inch hole through the top rail of the bottom sash and about halfway into the bottom rail of the top sash. Position the hole about $\frac{1}{2}$ inch from both the window frame and the top of the bottom sash to miss the glass.

◆ Enlarge the first $\frac{1}{4}$ inch of the hole with a $\frac{5}{8}$-inch bit for the metal shield at the head of the lag bolt.

◆ Slip the shield onto the bolt and screw it in place with the wrench provided by the manufacturer.

Self-Contained Warning Systems

A stranger approaches your home while you are away, slips to the side of the house, and starts to raise an unlocked window. A piercing alarm sounds, and the would-be intruder hurries away.

Protecting your home against intrusion need not require an elaborately wired system monitored by a security firm. Just as smoke detectors can give warning of a fire *(opposite)*, screw-on alarms are adequate in low-crime areas.

The models shown here can be bought at hardware and electronic-equipment stores. Make sure to put in fresh batteries when you install them; then periodically test the de-vices, and replace the batteries at least once a year.

Choosing the Right Unit: The most common intrusion alarm is a battery-operated protector that buzzes loudly when the door or window is opened *(below)*.

A door-chain alarm *(bottom)* can be set to sound only while you are inside the house. It makes enough noise to alert you and to frighten off most potential intruders, but one who stays long enough to see where the noise is coming from can silence the alarm simply by flicking the ON/OFF switch.

More difficult to silence is the model opposite, which is set with a removable key. Although it is more costly, it also comes with a special disarming switch that lets you turn the protector on, then come and go without tripping the alarm.

A Canine Guardian: Many home-owners rely on a family dog to alert them in case of fire or burglars—and some security consultants con-sider a dog the best protection of all. Follow the advice of a veterinari-an to find a puppy suitable for both protection and family life.

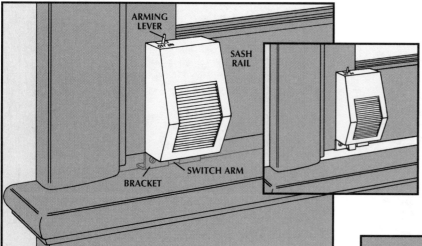

A window buzzer.
◆ With the window open, push the prongs on the unit's bracket up into the bottom rail of the lower window sash, then stick the bracket in place, using its adhesive backing strip.
◆ Close the window and set the arm-ing lever to ON *(left)*. The pressure of the window sill retracts a spring-loaded switch arm. If an intruder raises the window *(inset)*, the switch arm is released and the alarm sounds.

A door-chain alarm.
◆ Mount the battery-powered alarm unit at the edge of the door about 18 inches above the doorknob.
◆ Set the chain knob at the center of the alarm slot, then position the chain bracket on the doorframe so that there is about $\frac{1}{2}$ inch of slack in the chain when the door is closed. Mount the bracket.
◆ Turn the unit on *(right)*. When the door is opened, the chain pulls its knob to the side of the alarm slot. The knob then presses two electrical contacts together so that the alarm is activated and the buzzer sounds.

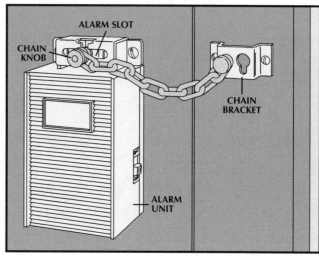

A locking door alarm.

Alarms vary, but the one shown at right is typical.

◆ Mount the alarm unit 18 inches above the doorknob and about $\frac{1}{8}$ inch from the edge of the door.

◆ Position the magnetic sensor at the edge of the doorframe, $\frac{1}{4}$ inch below the top of the unit. The alarm sounds when contact is broken between the magnetic sensor in the alarm unit and the one on the doorframe.

◆ Turn on the alarm with the key and confirm that the indicator light is on.

◆ When everyone is in for the night, set the disarming switch to IN. The buzzer will sound if the door opens.

◆ To leave the house, move the switch to OUT. This gives an occupant 30 seconds to walk out the door and close it; if the door stays open longer, the buzzer will sound. Similarly, you can unlock and reenter the house without sounding an alarm, provided you do not leave the door open more than 30 seconds.

◆ While the alarm is on, use the cutoff button when you answer the door to keep the buzzer silent.

◆ Whenever the buzzer sounds, it will continue to do so until turned off with the key.

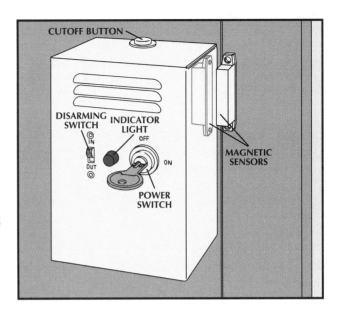

Locating a smoke detector in a room.

Wherever possible, place a smoke detector at the center of the ceiling. If this location is not practical, observe the following guidelines to avoid dead-air spaces in which the smoke from a fire is unlikely to circulate and a detector will be ineffective:

In most rooms, install a ceiling-mounted detector at least 4 inches from a wall; place a wall-mounted unit no less than 4 inches from the ceiling. In rooms with cathedral or A-frame ceilings, position the smoke detector about 12 inches below the peak of the ceiling. On a beamed ceiling, install the detector on the bottom of a beam, not in the space between beams.

Testing and Maintaining Detectors

Test smoke detectors once a month. Push the test button on a photoelectric model, and test ionization detectors with special aerosol sprays designed for this purpose. If the alarm fails to sound, try a fresh battery. If it still fails, replace the entire detector.

An occasional cleaning prevents dust buildups that can cause a detector to malfunction or to sound false alarms. The upholstery nozzle of a vacuum cleaner is ideal for removing dust or cobwebs. An air blower such as the one at right, available at camera stores, blows dust out of crevices.

Portable Extinguishers for Small Fires

Nearly everyone has had an unsettling experience with a minor household fire or the threat of one. Fires in their early stages, however, are often contained in a small space and may be extinguished if attended to quickly.

Quick Solutions: Flames in an oven many times can be put out by closing the door and turning off the heat. A grease fire in a pan can usually be extinguished by sliding a metal cover over the pan and turning off the heat. On an electric stove, move the pan to a cold burner. Do not use water or try to carry a pan of flaming grease outside.

As with grease fires, never use water on an electrical fire. Often you can stop it before it gets well started by pulling the plug or turning off electricity at the service panel.

Water is the best choice, however, on fires in mattresses or cushions. Douse the flames with a pan of water, and when the fire is out, carry the item outdoors and soak it thoroughly.

If your clothes catch fire, roll on the ground or floor to smother the flames—never run. When someone else's clothes are aflame, force the victim down and roll the person over and over. Use a rug, blanket, or coat to help put out the flames. When the fire is out, call an ambulance.

Extinguishers: With a few exceptions, all of these small fires can be put out more safely with fire extinguishers. Do not use an extinguisher on burning grease or burning clothes, however. And if the room is filled with smoke or the fire is fed by plastics or foam rubber—which often produces poisonous fumes—do not attempt to extinguish the fire. In all other cases, if a fire breaks out, alert others to leave the house and to call the fire department, then use an extinguisher *(opposite, bottom)*. If the fire continues to burn after the extinguisher is empty, leave the room, close the door, and wait outside for the firefighters.

Hang fire extinguishers in several locations from hooks screwed to wall studs, and always in the kitchen, garage, and basement. Mount them in plain view near doorways, no more than 5 feet above the floor and as far as possible from spots where a fire is likely to start, such as a stove.

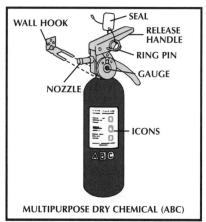

MULTIPURPOSE DRY CHEMICAL (ABC)

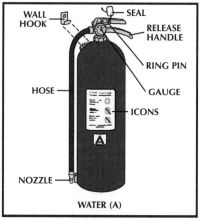

WATER (A)

CARBON DIOXIDE (BC)

An arsenal of extinguishers.

Household fires fall into three basic categories: A Class A fire is fed by a solid fuel such as paper or wood; a Class B fire involves a burning liquid such as gasoline or grease; and a Class C fire is one in a live electrical circuit.

Extinguishers—whether containing dry chemicals, water, or carbon dioxide—are labeled with icons representing the classes of fire for which they are intended *(above).* Each extinguisher has a ring pin or other safety device that immobilizes the release handle to prevent an accidental discharge. A seal, which is easily broken when the ring pin is removed, indicates whether the extinguisher has been used. Check the gauge once a month to see that the canister is fully charged.

THE RIGHT TYPE FOR EVERY BLAZE

Type of extinguisher	Class of fire	Capacity (lbs.)	Range of stream (ft.)	Discharge time (sec.)	Advantages	Limitations
Multipurpose dry chemical	ABC	1–5 2½–9 9–17 17–30	5–12 5–12 5–20 5–20	8–10 8–15 10–25 10–25	Can be used on all classes of fires; lightweight; inexpensive.	May not completely extinguish a deep-seated upholstery fire; leaves residue; dry chemical vapor may hamper visibility.
Pressured water	A	30	30–40	60	Longer discharge time; greater range.	Must be protected from freezing; initial discharge may create more smoke, hampering visibility.
Carbon dioxide	BC	2½–5 10–15 20	3–8 3–8 3–8	8–30 8–30 10–30	Leaves no residue.	Dissipates in wind; carbon dioxide "snow" may burn skin; eliminates oxygen around immediate area.

Selecting an extinguisher.

Use the chart above to select fire extinguishers for your home. For complete protection, you will need more than one type. An extinguisher used against a class of fire for which it is not clearly labeled can actually increase the intensity of the fire.

Multipurpose dry-chemical models, though lighter and less expensive than other kinds, leave behind a powder that is difficult to clean up and that does not work as well against Class A fires as water does. A water extinguisher, though limited to Class A fires, lets you fight a fire longer and at a safer distance than do other types. Carbon dioxide extinguishers, more costly than dry-chemical or water models, leave no residue.

Buy only those approved by Underwriters Laboratories and at least the size of the smallest units in the chart. Larger units expel their contents at a faster rate to put out a fire quicker, and will put out a larger fire than the smaller units.

ATTACKING THE FLAMES SAFELY

Targeting the fire.
◆ Pull the ring pin from the extinguisher to free the release handle.
◆ At 6 to 8 feet from the fire and with your back to the nearest exit, hold the extinguisher upright and point the nozzle at the base of the flames.
◆ Squeeze the handle and play the stream on the fire, sweeping slowly from side to side, until the fire is out.
◆ Watch the area to make sure the fire does not rekindle, and be prepared to spray again.

Childproofing Storage Areas

Safeguarding medicines, poisonous products, and dangerous utensils and tools is a necessity in a house with children. You can keep these items secure by installing a few inexpensive latches and locks on doors and cabinets.

Safety Latches: A variety of products for childproofing kitchen appliances are available at home-improvement centers, but with very young children, a simple homemade latch will keep the door of a refrigerator or other appliance closed *(opposite, bottom)*. A cabinet door can be kept safely shut with a concealed latch. The model opposite will foil youngsters but open at the touch of an adult's finger.

Locks: A storage area sometimes may need a true lock to guard its contents. For sliding doors, a showcase lock *(below)*—the kind used in jewelry stores—is easy to install; it simply clamps into place. Swinging doors can be fitted with a hasp *(opposite, middle)* and a locking cam that are screwed to the outside of the doors.

 TOOLS

Screwdriver
Tape measure

 **MATERIALS**

Showcase lock
Cabinet latch
Hasp lock

Fabric fastening
  tape
Double-sided foam
  adhesive tape

Attaching a showcase lock.
◆ With the doors open, slip the hook of the serrated lock bar around the edge of the inner door.
◆ Close the doors and slide the lock barrel over the bar until the barrel is flush with the edge of the outside door. The lock cannot be removed, nor the doors opened, until you unlock the barrel with a key.

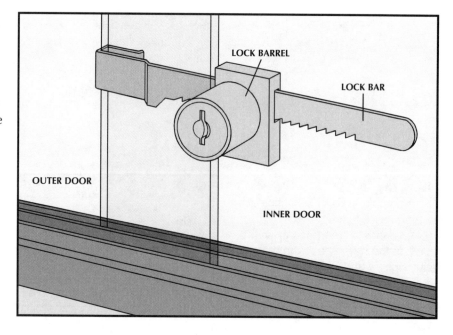

LOCK BARREL

LOCK BAR

OUTER DOOR

INNER DOOR

Childproofing a cabinet.

◆ Screw the catch inside the cabinet top no more than 1 inch from the front edge.

◆ Set the end of the latch shaft in the catch, swing the door onto the base of the shaft, and mark where the base meets the inside of the door.

◆ Fasten the base of the shaft to the door with screws. When the door is closed, the shaft will engage the catch *(inset);* to release it, open the door just wide enough to slip a finger over the shaft and push it down.

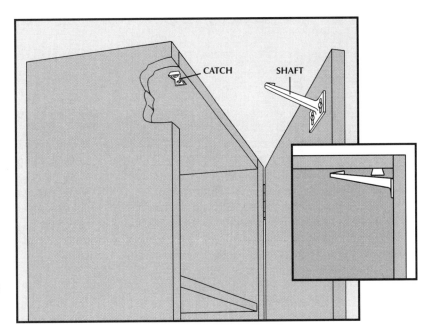

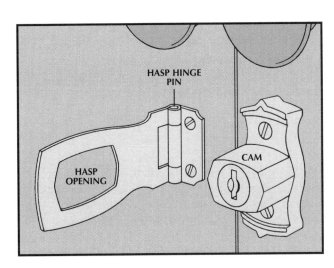

Installing a hasp lock.

◆ Measure the distance between the centers of the hasp hinge pin and the hasp opening, and mark the face of one cabinet door at a point that is one-half this distance from the edge of the door.

◆ Set the hasp against the door with its hinge pin centered over the mark.

◆ Mark the screw holes and attach the hasp to the door.

◆ Set the lock against the adjoining door and fold the hasp over the cam.

◆ Remove the hasp and mark the positions of the lock's screw holes, then fasten the lock to the door. To secure the hasp to the lock, turn the cam 90 degrees; open it with the key.

Securing an Appliance Door

A simple latch for an appliance door can be made from strips of fastening tape (commonly known by its trade name, Velcro) fixed to the door at a height beyond the reach of your child. With double-sided foam adhesive tape, fasten short strips of Velcro on the door and on the side of the appliance. Lay the fastening strip over them to keep the door secured.

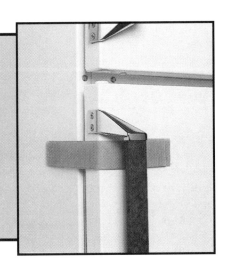

Appendix: Finding the Right Specialist

There are few improvements that a homeowner cannot accomplish with patience and careful planning. Although a professional generally can work faster, homeowners possess the greatest incentive to do a job well: They have to live with the results.

Nonetheless, few homeowners have the time, the inclination, or the tools to tackle every job, and some tasks should be left to a professional for the sake of safety—changing an electric meter, for instance, or connecting natural-gas piping. In these situations, turning to a specialist makes sense.

Before you do, consult the directory below. It lists the most common building trades and services, describes what these professionals do, and offers tips on what to look for in a contract with them.

Evaluating Subcontractors: Successful subcontracting depends on careful planning and thorough research. In considering potential subcontractors, first see that they are reliable. Find out how long they have been in business. If they are new to the trade, try to determine their current credit rating. Check for any complaints with a local consumer-protection agency or ask suppliers whether they pay bills promptly. A bankrupt subcontractor can mean heavy losses for you.

Equally important are quality of work and the ability to finish it on time. Ask previous clients for references and, if possible, inspect the workmanship of past jobs. In many cases you can get sound referrals in your neighborhood, as it is a sign of good performance when a builder can rely on word of mouth to make a business prosper.

Whenever possible, secure more than one bid, but make sure you are comparing apples with apples. To do this, you may need to provide each bidder with a written list of materials and a description of the scope of work, as well as with copies of any sketches or plans.

Defining the Work: Once you have settled on a subcontractor, draw up a contract. Include your drawings and spell out—in writing—exactly what work is to be done, specifying the quantities, brand names, grades, and model numbers for any materials. Include a timetable for work and payments and stipulate that the workers clean up after the job. Finally, make certain that your subcontractor carries general liability insurance and provides workers' compensation for everyone employed on the project.

 ## Architect

Traditional contracts with architects give them full responsibility for projects and pay them a percentage of the total cost, but for renovation projects you may be able to find someone who will work at an hourly rate. On this basis, the architect can serve largely in an advisory capacity, helping you decide what to do, providing you with drawings, and recommending other specialists. But make sure that the architect's tastes and ideas are compatible with your own.

 ## Bricklayer

These specialists will repoint mortar joints, clean brickwork, repair stucco, and perform the heavier jobs involved in building or rebuilding masonry walls, fireplaces, and chimneys. Contact bricklayers early, because they may be hard to find during times when the weather is good.

 ## Carpenter

The versatility of carpenters makes their skills essential for any renovation work. Some specialize in rough carpentry: framing new walls and floors, reinforcing old, and building forms for concrete. Others do finish carpentry: laying wood floors, hanging doors, and installing cabinets and decorative trim. Experienced carpenters are often competent at both. Carpenters can often recommend other specialists and give scheduling advice. Most will use the materials you supply, but many get discounts at lumberyards and are willing to pass on the savings.

 ## Cement Mason

Check with these concrete or paving contractors when you want a professional to pour cement or to repair a driveway or sidewalk. You may have to make several calls; many companies are reluctant to do small jobs or give estimates.

 ## Contractor

Generally, you will save time and money dealing directly with subcontractors. But if you have a large number of complicated or interrelated jobs, a coordinator may be essential. General contractors will digest the plans, assemble a team of specialists, schedule their work, and see that it is executed properly. Some, particularly those who operate small companies, will allow you to do portions of the work yourself to save money. If you take on an intermediate part of a long job, plan to conform to the contractor's schedule.

 ## Drywall Installer

Any careful amateur can fasten small pieces of drywall to studs, but large sheets are unwieldy, and unless you have a helper, subcontracting may be the best way to guarantee a neat job. Many general carpenters will also do this work.

376

Electrician

Whenever you call in an electrician, you can reasonably expect the job to be done to professional standards. In most areas an electrician must pass a licensing examination, and electrical work must be inspected after the rough wiring is in and again after the job is completed. Most electricians will take small jobs or completely rewire a house.

 ## Excavating Contractor

This subcontractor has the heavy equipment to do grading, trenching, or backfilling around a house, or even to excavate a basement or swimming pool. Many excavating contractors may be reluctant to take a small grading job, so checking with paving and landscape contractors may prove worthwhile. The latter prefer jobs in which they can sell you some trees, plants, or sod, but they are equipped to do grading around houses.

 ## Exterminator

Most exterminators will contract for a single job or for ongoing services with a renewable guarantee. The market is competitive; shop for the best price.

 ## Floor Layer

Professional floor layers work with carpeting, linoleum, and tile floor coverings and may specialize in one of these. Usually floor layers supply materials and labor; check the quality and price of materials as well as workmanship. This service is sometimes available through department stores.

 ## Floor Sander and Refinisher

This specialty is also performed by some floor layers and carpenters. Be sure to hire someone who does such work frequently, and always postpone floor refinishing until all other messy interior jobs have been finished.

 ## Glazier

You can easily replace small panes of glass yourself, but contract with a glaz-ier to cut, fit, and install insulating glass or plate-glass windows, mirrors, and glass doors. Glaziers will generally provide both materials and labor.

 ## Heating and Cooling Contractor

Most heating and cooling companies feature a specific brand of furnace or air conditioner, so first determine the most appropriate appliance for your needs. Generally, the contractor provides all the equipment and oversees a crew of specialists—sheet-metal workers for air ducts, licensed plumbers or electricians for final connections. For repair jobs, ascertain the minimum charge for a service call as well as the hourly rates.

 ## Insulation Worker

Insulation materials come in a variety of forms—rolls, sheets, pellets, blocks, and pastes—and some contractors specialize in only one or two. In many areas the home-insulation business has become very competitive. Get several bids and familiarize yourself with the type, insulating value, and fire rating of the material each contractor is promoting.

 ## Ornamental-Iron Worker

Listings for ornamental-iron workers are usually mixed with those for heavy industry under "Iron Works." These specialists can fabricate and install, or repair, metal balconies, gates, fences, stairways, window grilles, and the like.

 ## Painter and Paperhanger

Some professionals do both, but painting and paperhanging are often considered separate trades. Most of the cost of either goes for labor, so shop for the best rate you can get for quality work. A recommendation from your neighbors is often the best bet—whether you are looking to hire a small subcontractor or a large firm that may be better equipped for exterior projects requiring extension ladders and scaffolding.

 ## Plasterer and Lather

Because most interior-wall finishing is now done with gypsum wallboard, locating a plasterer for interior walls, exterior stucco, or ornamental moldings may call for some detective work on your part. Ask local carpenters, general contractors, or the managers of old apartment buildings to make recommendations. Call a plasterer as far in advance as possible.

 ## Plumber

Like electrical work, plumbing work is regulated by code and licensing requirements. The plumber assembles and maintains any piping that carries water, steam, or gas, and installs and connects such household appliances as water heaters or dishwashers.

 ## Roofer

Roofers resurface or repair the outer layer of a roof to ensure that it is watertight. Some will work on the underlying structure, while others employ carpenters to replace sheathing or rafters. Select a recommended roofer specializing in your type of surface—asphalt, slate, tile, wood shingles, tin. Insist on a guarantee for a new roof; try to get one for any repair work as well. Many roofers repair gutters and will waterproof walls and basements. Some department stores contract for roofing and gutter work.

 ## Septic Tank Servicer

These specialists pump out and clean septic tanks. They frequently offer sewer- and drain-cleaning services as well. Septic tank servicing is available in most areas, for a single job or as a continuing service.

 ## Stonemason

A stonemason works with stone as a structural material in walls and chimneys and as a decorative surface for floors, patios, and stairs. You may have to make several calls to find a stonemason willing to do a small repair job.

INDEX

INDEX

124; fisheye viewers, 362; lead safety, 116, 130; locking alarms, 355; painting, 94; planing doors, 122, 123; repairing warped doors, 122; replacing sliding door rollers, 122; rim locks, 368; security measures, 362-368; straightening jambs, 122, 124-125

Doors, weatherproofing, 284-286; garage doors, 305; installing sweeps, 304; installing thresholds, 304-305; sealing, 303; types of weather stripping, 302

Door screens. *See* Screens

Dormers, 316, 317

Drains: augers, 64, 65; drain cleaners, 64; drain flushers, 64

Drip caps, 316, 317

E

Eaves, 316, 317

Electrical systems: amperage, 180, 181; blown fuses, 182; cable types, 188; circuit-breaker service panels, 182, 183; connecting wires with crimping barrels, 191; connecting wires with wire caps, 188, 190; CSA markings, 211; discharging a capacitor, 27; electric meters, 181; evaluating wiring, 180, 181; exposing wires in cables, 188; fuse-protected service panels, 180, 183; fuses, 183-185; identifying the feed wire, 187; multitesters, 21; polarized plugs and receptacles, 196, 208, 209; removing cable sheathing, 189; safety, 182, 359; service panels, 180, 182-183; stripping

insulation, 189; terminal types, 191; testing circuits, 186-187; testing electric-range terminal blocks, 30, 31; testing switches for power, 187; tools, 178-179; tripped circuit breakers, 182; UL markings, 211. *See also* GFCIs; Lighting; Receptacles; Switches

Electric heating systems: recommended R-values, 293; thermostats, 254, 256

Electric ranges, 30; adjusting oven temperature, 34-35; calibrating oven thermostats, 34; capillary tubes, 30, 35; electronic control-board malfunctions, 34; safety, 30; testing bake elements, 34-35; testing control switches, 33; testing oven temperature, 30; testing receptacles, 32-33; testing surface elements, 32; testing temperature sensors, 34; testing the oven thermostat, 35; testing the terminal block, 30, 31; testing voltage, 30; Troubleshooting Guide, 31

End-of-the-run light-receptacle installations, 213

End-of-the-run receptacles, 212

Exposure ratings, for sheathing, 318

F

Fans, ceiling, 214-215

Fascia, 316, 317

Faucet-handle pullers, 57

Faucets, 56; repairing single-lever ball faucets, 62-63; repairing single-lever cartridge faucets,

60; repairing single-lever ceramic disk faucets, 61; repairing stem faucets, 56-59

Ferrules, 184

Fiberglass insulation, 294, 295

Fin combs, 282

Finishing, wood floors, 150-153

Fire extinguishers, 354

Fireplaces: air vents, 225; designs, 220-223; firebox dampers, 224; gas fireplace inserts, 245; installing a fireplace insert, 243-245; installing a glass door, 225; installing a smoke guard, 226; installing a top-sealing damper, 229-230; repairing firebrick mortar joints, 227. *See also* Chimneys

Fisheye viewers, 362

Fish tape, 179

Flashing, 316, 317; repairing or replacing, 329

Flat roofs, 316, 332; repairing blisters, 333

Floors: doubling joists, 144-145; inspecting floor framework, 142; jacking, 142, 143; recommended R-values, 293; repairing sagging floors, 142-143; replacing framework posts, 147-149; replacing joists, 144, 145-146; styles, 132-135

Floors, ceramic tile: repairing, 158-159

Floors, resilient, 154; asbestos safety, 156; patching sheet flooring, 157; removing stains, 155; repairing blisters, 155; replacing tiles, 156; securing loose tiles, 154

Floors, wood, 136; anchoring loose floorboards, 137; eliminating squeaks, 136, 137-138; installing steel

bridging between joists, 138; refinishing, 150-153; repairing surface defects, 136; replacing floorboards, 136, 139-141; sanding, 150-152; sealing, 150, 152-153; sealing cracks, 136; testing for insects, 142; testing for rot, 142

Flue brushes, 239, 240

Flues. *See* Chimneys

Fluorescent fixtures, 202-203

Foam backer rod, 306-307

Foam insulation, 294

Forced-air systems: balancing, 250-251; changing blower speed, 274; correcting airflow, 274; oiling the blower motor, 275; reducing noise, 274; replacing the blower motor, 275

Foundations, repairing cracks in, 286, 308-311

Framing, house: masonry, 320; wood, 318-319

Frieze boards, 316, 317

Furnace blowers, 274-275

Furnaces. *See* Forced-air systems; Gas furnaces; Oil burners

Fuse pullers, 27, 179, 185

Fuses: blown fuses, 182; fuse-protected service panels, 180, 183; microwave oven fuses, 26, 27; replacing cartridge fuses, 185; types, 183-184

G

Gable roofs, 316, 317

Gable vents, 316, 317

Gambrel roofs, 316

Garage door bottoms, 302, 305

Garbage disposers, 25

Gas fireplaces, 245

Gas furnaces, 248, 258; adjusting the burner flame, 265; adjusting the pilot flame, 263; measuring temperature rise, 260; operation

INDEX

INDEX

INDEX

INDEX

TIME LIFE BOOKS

Time-Life Books is a division of
TIME LIFE INC.

TIME-LIFE CUSTOM PUBLISHING

VICE PRESIDENT and PUBLISHER: Terry Newell

Vice President of Sales and Marketing: Neil Levin

Project Manager: Jennifer Michelle Lee

Director of Special Sales: Liz Ziehl

Managing Editor: Donia Ann Steele

Director of Design: Christopher M. Register

Production Manager: Carolyn Clark

Quality Assurance Manager: James D. King

Produced by ST. REMY MULTIMEDIA

President/Chief Executive Officer: Fernand Lecoq

President/Chief Operating Officer: Pierre Leveille

Vice President, Finance: Natalie Watanabe

Managing Editor: Carolyn Jackson

Managing Art Director: Diane Denoncourt

Production Manager: Michelle Turbide

Marketing Manager: Christopher Jackson

Staff for this Book:

Senior Editor: Marc Cassini

Art Director: Normand Boudreault

Writer: Adam Van Sertima

Photo Research: Jennifer Meltzer

System Coordinator: Eric Beaulieu

Scanner Operators: Martin Francoeur, Sara Grynspan

Indexer: Linda Cournoyer

First printing. Printed in U.S.A.

Time-Life is a trademark of Time Warner Inc. U.S.A.

ISBN 0-7370-0001-5

The Library of Congress has cataloged the trade version
of this title as follows:
THE BIG BOOK OF EASY HOME FIX-UPS
/by the editors of Time-Life Books.
   p. cm.
   Includes index.
   ISBN 0-7835-4914-8
   1. Dwellings—Maintenance and repair—Amateurs' manuals.
I. Time-Life Books.
TH4817.3.B53   1997   97-5711
643'.7 — dc21   CIP

Books produced by Time-Life Custom Publishing are available
at special bulk discount for promotional and premium use.
Custom adaptations can also be created to meet
your specific marketing goals.
Call 1-800-323-5255.

Photography Credits:

6, 7 Whirlpool Home Appliances
8 (upper) Riviera Cabinets
8 (lower left) Frigidaire Company
8 (lower right) Whirlpool Home Appliances
9 (upper) Whirlpool Home Appliances
9 (lower) Frigidaire Company
50, 51 Gary Russ/Image Bank
52 (upper) Crandall & Crandall
52 (lower) Riviera Cabinets
53 (upper) Kohler Co.
53 (lower left) Riviera Cabinets
53 (lower right) Robert Chartier
76, 77 Benjamin Moore & Co.
78 (upper) Benjamin Moore & Co.
78 (lower) Sunworthy Wallcoverings
79 (upper) Benjamin Moore & Co.
79 (lower left) Sunworthy Wallcoverings
79 (lower right) Andersen Windows, Inc.
112, 113 Andersen Windows, Inc.
114 (upper) Andersen Windows, Inc.
114 (lower left) Jack McConnell, McConnell & McNamara
114 (lower right) Stanley Door Systems
115 (upper) Kolbe & Kolbe Millwork
115 (lower) Rodrigo Guttiérez
132, 133 Crossville Porcelain Stone/USA
134 (upper) Harris-Tarkett, Inc.
134 (lower) NAFCO
135 (upper left) DOMCO
135 (upper right) Mountain Lumber
135 (lower) Crossville Porcelain Stone/USA
174, 175 Marvin Windows & Doors
176 (upper) Marvin Windows & Doors
176 (lower) Norman McGrath
177 (upper) Robert Chartier
177 (lower left & right) Crandall & Crandall
220, 221 Wolf Steel Ltd.
222 (upper) Crandall & Crandall
222 (lower) Marvin Windows & Doors
223 (upper & lower left) Crandall & Crandall
223 (lower right) Country Stoves Inc.
246, 247 Michael Mahovlich
248 (upper) The Reggio Register Co.
248 (lower) Gaz Métropolitain
249 (upper left) Whirlpool Home Appliances
249 (upper right) Christian Lévesque
249 (lower) Robert Chartier
284, 285 Pemko Manufacturing Co.
286 Pemko Manufacturing Co.
287 (upper) Robert Chartier
287 (lower) DAP Inc.
312, 313 Marvin Windows & Doors
314 (upper right) ©Tamko Roofing Products, Inc.
314 (upper left & lower) Crandall & Crandall
315 (upper) Crandall & Crandall
315 (lower) Amerimax Home Products Inc.
352, 353 Nightscaping by Loran Inc.
354 (upper left) Robert Chartier
354 (upper right) Christian Lévesque
354 (lower) Robert Chartier
355 (upper & lower) Christian Lévesque